CW01460277

Sanjeev P. Sahni · Tithi Bhatn
Editors

Spirituality and Management

From Models to Applications

Springer

Editors
Sanjeev P. Sahni
Jindal Institute of Behavioural Sciences
O. P. Jindal Global University
Sonipat, Haryana, India

Tithi Bhatnagar
Jindal Institute of Behavioural Sciences
O. P. Jindal Global University
Sonipat, Haryana, India

Pankaj Gupta
O. P. Jindal Global University
Sonipat, Haryana, India

ISBN 978-981-19-1027-2 ISBN 978-981-19-1025-8 (eBook)
https://doi.org/10.1007/978-981-19-1025-8

© Jindal Institute of Behavioral Sciences 2022
This work is subject to copyright. All rights are solely and exclusively licensed by the Publisher, whether the whole or part of the material is concerned, specifically the rights of translation, reprinting, reuse of illustrations, recitation, broadcasting, reproduction on microfilms or in any other physical way, and transmission or information storage and retrieval, electronic adaptation, computer software, or by similar or dissimilar methodology now known or hereafter developed.
The use of general descriptive names, registered names, trademarks, service marks, etc. in this publication does not imply, even in the absence of a specific statement, that such names are exempt from the relevant protective laws and regulations and therefore free for general use.
The publisher, the authors, and the editors are safe to assume that the advice and information in this book are believed to be true and accurate at the date of publication. Neither the publisher nor the authors or the editors give a warranty, expressed or implied, with respect to the material contained herein or for any errors or omissions that may have been made. The publisher remains neutral with regard to jurisdictional claims in published maps and institutional affiliations.

This Springer imprint is published by the registered company Springer Nature Singapore Pte Ltd.
The registered company address is: 152 Beach Road, #21-01/04 Gateway East, Singapore 189721, Singapore

Spirituality and Management

Preface

The human society has undergone a rapid transformation at a very fast pace. The uncertainties of our times, highly volatile environment, and digitization of lives and businesses give rise to their own set of perplexities. Technological advancements are inevitable, but so then should be the wisdom that tells us where to draw the line. Scientists have been exploring and experimenting on how to ensure the right and the most appropriate way of dealing with environmental ambiguities. A sustainable business model can be possible only if its foundation is rooted in following business ethics. Anything that lacks value will not be a long-term prospect. With the rapid changes being experienced in the different walks of life, particularly the workplaces, individuals experience extreme stress and lack quality-of-life. Interestingly, human life is not just hedonic in nature but is more eudaimonic. It is also about the search for meaning, purpose, inter-connectedness, and growth. This is where spirituality helps management retain its essence for long-term sustainable goals.

The essence of spirituality is achieved through the development of an all-encompassing self that transcends limitations of everyday reality, brings together individual and common human identity with the broader understanding of our thinking patterns and conflicts for the better coordination of global well-being. This transformed and extended self is quintessential for overcoming challenges and applies wisdom to optimize technological advancements and their applications.

This book attempts at clarifying the conceptual foundations for a viable crossover of spirituality and management and to discuss models that can be applied in daily working life. It covers a variety of interrelated subjects addressing the possibilities for integrating spirituality and management. Chapters 1–3 are introductory in nature discussing the concept of spirituality and the Indian worldview; Chaps. 4–9 discuss the different models and frameworks on spirituality; Chaps. 10 and 11 provide the link to understanding the relation between spirituality and management; Chaps. 12–15 discuss how the concept of spirituality can be applied to the discipline of management and talk about workplace spirituality and related aspects; and Chaps. 16–18 discuss the concept of spiritual leadership and its effectiveness.

We hope that the readers will enjoy reading this book and that it will contribute toward their intellectual pursuits as it attempts to provide an authentic, research-based, and contemporary perspective on spirituality and management and ancient wisdom connected with contemporary management, and day-to-day life. This book is an attempt toward profound insights on creating a life you love and live powerfully, purposefully with peace, effectiveness, and bliss—it equips one with the knowledge and tools to help focus on the holistic development of people and organizations.

Sonipat, India

Sanjeev P. Sahni, Ph.D.
Tithi Bhatnagar, Ph.D.
Pankaj Gupta, Ph.D.

Acknowledgements

Arise! Awake! Stop not until the Goal is reached.
—Swami Vivekanand

This book is an attempt to bring to the fore aspects of spirituality embedded in the language and methods of science to enable the understanding and significance of such concepts and how they can lead individuals and organizations toward exploring meaning and purpose in what they do. This book is a cumulative effort of many, and we, as the editors, would take the opportunity to extend our heartfelt appreciation for them.

We wish to accord our humble and sincere thanks to our esteemed founding Chancellor of O. P. Jindal Global University, Mr. Naveen Jindal, for his philanthropic endeavor of establishing this university. It is because of his vision and encouragement in creation of a congenial environment that promotes intellectual pursuits and rigorous academic endeavors, this book has been possible. We wish to extend a special note of thanks to our founding Vice Chancellor, Prof. C. Rajkumar, for his incessant support and encouragement for all JIBS endeavors.

We would like to duly acknowledge the efforts of our JIBS staff, Mr. Gerard Thomas, Mr. Sunil Kumar M. V., and Mr. Deepak Kaushik, for their unending support at different stages, which goes even beyond office hours. A very special thanks to Ms. Tanni Choudhury, Lecturer, at Jindal Institute of Behavioural Sciences for her unparalleled and dedicated efforts in assisting with the book at all stages.

We wish to place on record our sincere thanks and appreciation to all our contributing authors. Their intellectual acumen has shaped the book to what it is in its current form. We wish to express our deep appreciation for our reviewers and gratitude to our publishing editors at Springer Nature Singapore, especially Ms. Satvinder Kaur, for the forever support and patient presence.

Sanjeev P. Sahni
Tithi Bhatnagar
Pankaj Gupta

We wish to extend our special and profound thanks to Ms. Shilpa Mehta for her benevolent, efficient, and opulent language acumen. We sincerely appreciate her efforts as regards this book.

Contents

Editors and Contributors

About the Editors

Sanjeev P. Sahni is Professor of Eminence and Principal Director of the Jindal Institute of Behavioural Sciences (JIBS), Director for Center for Victimology and Psychological Sciences, Member of the Governing Body, and Advisor to the Vice Chancellor at O. P. Jindal Global University. He holds a Ph.D. degree in Psychology and possesses an extensive and rich experience of 32 years in Academia, Industry and Government Sector. His work spans in the areas of organizational behavior, criminal psychology, cognitive and neuropsychology, forensic psychology and policing and law enforcement. He has trained over more than 32000 professionals in over 50 countries. He has served and contributed 14 years as Scientist in the Ministry of Human Resource Development and Sports Authority of India. He has also served as Head of Human Resources at the Jindal Group. He has worked as Research Scientist at several universities like University of Houston, Texas; University of Illinois, Chicago, to name a few. He has published more than 41 research articles in international and national indexed journals, and about 22 chapters. With 17 books to his credit, some of the recent ones are *Internet Infidelity* (Springer), *Digital Piracy in the Digital Era* (Springer), *Crime And Criminal Law Perspectives On Global Migration* (Har-Anand), *Refugee Jurisprudence And Criminal Justice* (Har-Anand), *Conflict: The Police and The People* (Lexis Nexis) and *Global Perspectives*

of Victimology and Criminology (Bloomsbury). e-mail: drspsahni@jgu.edu.in

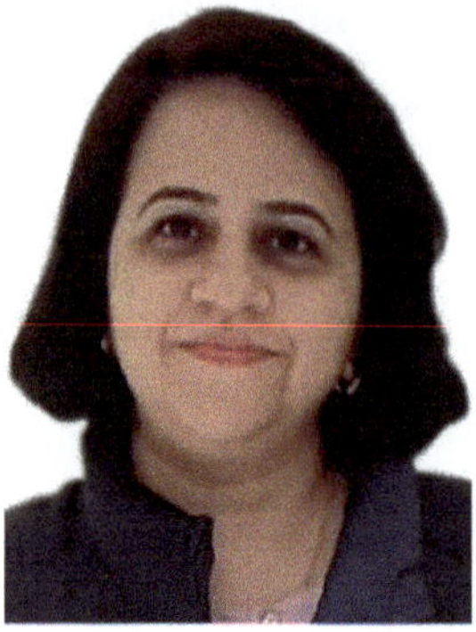

Tithi Bhatnagar is currently working as an Associate Professor and Deputy Director, Centre for Leadership and Change (CLC). She is responsible for Professional and Teachers Training and Capacity Building Programs conducted at the Jindal Institute of Behavioural Sciences, O. P. Jindal Global University. She has trained around 9000+ teachers, students, Government Officials, and executives on topics like Understanding Stress, Stress Management, Performance Enhancement, Subjective Well-Being, Multiple Intelligence, Work Life Balance, Effective Decision Making, Training Evaluation, and Motivation at Workplace. She is a Psychologist by training and a Wellbeing and Happiness researcher and teacher by profession. Her doctoral research was in the area of Subjective Well-Being (SWB) from the Indian Institute of Technology, Bombay. Her professional experience is a mix of industry, freelance consulting, academics, training, and advisory roles. She teaches Research Methods and has been a resource person for various Faculty Development Programs. Her research interests include Subjective Well-Being, Positive Psychology, Quality of Life, Happiness, Psychometrics, and Leadership. She is a Certified Positive Psychology Coach and is a member of the American Psychological Association (APA), the International Society of Quality-of-Life Studies (ISQOLS), and the Academic Council of United Nations (ACUNS). e-mail: tbhatnagar@jgu.edu.in

Pankaj Gupta is currently Professor and Executive Director-Centre for Ethics, Spirituality and Meditation at O. P. Jindal Global University, India. He is a Global Academic Leader with successful professional experience of over 25 years—as a professor, researcher, and institution builder Earlier, he has served in several senior positions in top organizations such as President IIHMR University, Director Symbiosis Bangalore, Professor at IMT/IIM Kozhikode, University of Washington, S. P. Jain (Dubai and Singapore) among others. He teaches courses and does research in the areas of Finance, Cost Management, Mindful Leadership, Mental and Spiritual Health, Self-Awareness, and Ethics, etc. Dr. Gupta is a Ph.D., Fulbright Fellow, CMA, GCPCL (Harvard), Fellow of ICAI, and an alumnus of Lucknow University and IIM Ahmedabad. e-mail: pgupta@jgu.edu.in

Contributors

Wolfgang Amann *(Corresponding Author)* is Professor of strategy and leadership at HEC Paris, based on the Qatar campus. He directs degree, certificate, open enrollment, and custom programs in the Middle East. He graduated from the University of St. Gallen in Switzerland with a doctorate in international strategy and also a doctorate in educational psychology based on a new learning tool for leaders in executive education. He is a graduate of key faculty development programs, such as Harvard University's Institute for Management and Leadership in Education, besides many others. Next to designing and delivering executive education seminars worldwide for more than 20 years, he advises senior leaders and serves on a number of boards. He published 50+ books for executives and compiled more than 100 case studies for his executive education seminars. He received a number of research, teaching, and impact awards along with honorary professorships. Most notably, his course on strategy has repeatedly won the most prestigious global CEMS teaching award for best course in top business schools. e-mail: amann.wolfgang@gmail.com

Dharm P. S. Bhawuk *(Corresponding Author)* is Professor of Management and Culture and Community Psychology, University of Hawai'i, Manoa, USA. He has published more than 100 papers and book chapters and made over 250 presentations internationally. He is Founding Fellow of International Academy of Intercultural Research (IAIR), Fellow of Indian Academy of Management (INDAM), Foreign Fellow of National Academy of Psychology (NAoP), India, and was H. Smith Richardson, Jr. Visiting Fellow, Center for Creative Leadership, Greensboro, North Carolina (2009–2010), and recipients of many awards. e-mail: bhawuk@hawaii.edu

Anthony Cullen ***(Corresponding Author)*** is Senior Lecturer in Law at the School of Law, Middlesex University, London. He currently teaches public law and international human rights law and supervises the research of Ph.D. students in the field of international criminal law. He is also Visiting Professor at the University of Bordeaux, France, External Examiner at Dublin City University, Ireland, and Senior Fellow of the UK Higher Education Academy. His research interests include the areas of international humanitarian law, international human rights law, the use of contemplative methods in teaching, the decolonization of higher education, and student well-being. e-mail: A.T.Cullen@mdx.ac.uk

Kamini Desai ***(Corresponding Author)*** Ph.D., is Founder and Director of I AM Education, author of Yoga Nidra The Art of Transformational Sleep, Life Lessons Love Lessons, and Developer of the I AM Yoga Nidra app. For the past 30 years, she has created a unique body of teachings combining ancient Yogic wisdom with science and psychology. Considered an expert in Yoga Nidra, Yoga therapy, and artful living, her practical and accessible teaching style has been welcomed worldwide. Her corporate clients have included Bahamas Princess Resorts, Kellogg's, Keds, Sony, and Mars Confectionary among others. In 2013, she was awarded the title "Yogeshwari" in recognition for her keen ability to bring ancient illumination to the genuine challenges of the human experience. e-mail: kamini@iameducation.org

Koenraad Elst (Leuven 1959) ***(Corresponding Author)*** distinguished himself early on as eager to learn and to dissent. After a few hippie years, he studied at the KU Leuven, obtaining MA degrees in Sinology, Indology, and Philosophy. After a research stay at Banaras Hindu University, he did original fieldwork for a doctorate on Hindu nationalism, which he obtained magna cum laude in 1998. As an independent researcher, he earned laurels and ostracism with his findings on controversial topics like Islam, multiculturalism, and the secular state, besides others. He also published on the interface of religion and politics, correlative cosmologies, the dark side of Buddhism, the reinvention of Hinduism, and many more. Regarding religion, he combines human sympathy with substantive skepticism. e-mail: koenraad.elst@gmail.com

Tatjana Kochetkova ***(Corresponding Author)*** is Associate Professor at the Global Law Faculty at O. P. Jindal Global University. She studied Philosophy in Kiev, Ukraine (MA in 1995, cum laude), and Social Sciences at the Institute for Social Studies in the Hague, the Netherlands (MA in 1998). In 2001, she obtained her Ph.D. at the Radboud University of Nijmegen (the Netherlands) with a thesis in which she reconstructed Vladimir Solovyov's philosophical anthropology. Her research focuses on the domains of philosophical anthropology, environmental philosophy, ecospirituality, and philosophy of culture and technology. She has published three monographs and dozens of academic articles and book contributions. She has taught at the University of Twente and Fontys University for Applied Science in the Netherlands and conducted research at Louis Bolk Institute for Biosciences. e-mail: tatjana@jgu.edu.in

Umesh Mukhi ***(Corresponding Author)*** belongs to Faculty of Management Department at FGV EAESP, São Paulo School of Business Administration. He completed his bachelors in Electronics and Telecommunication Engineering from University of Mumbai, India. He then moved to France where he obtained his Master's in Management at Audencia Business School and his Doctorate in Management from University of Nantes. His teaching and research interests encompass topics such as role of business schools, organizational behavior, sustainability, spirituality, and cross-cultural leadership development. He has been Visiting Researcher at United Nations Principles of Responsible Management Education, New York. He has also delivered training sessions for business schools, public and social sector organizations in Europe, Asia, and Latin America. He is also a recipient for Tesla Silver Coin Award in 2014 for youth empowerment and holds the title of Honorary Cross-Cultural Ambassador of UNESCO Club, Sorbonne University, Paris, for his educational and inter-cultural contribution. e-mail: umesh.mukhi@fgv.br

Rekha Navneet ***(Corresponding Author)*** is Associate Professor in the Department of Philosophy, Gargi College (University of Delhi). She has a teaching experience of over 26 years. She has earned her Ph.D. degree from University of Delhi in 2004. She has been teaching undergraduate students at Gargi College over the last two decades and has also taught students pursuing Master's courses in Philosophy at the Department of Philosophy, University of Delhi. She has a number of publications to her credit across journals such as the Indian Philosophical Quarterly (IPQ), Journal of Indian Council of Philosophical Research (JICPR), and other peer-reviewed journals. Her academic interests include platonic studies, applied ethics, aesthetics, and Indian spiritual philosophical tradition. e-mail: rekha.navneet65@gmail.com

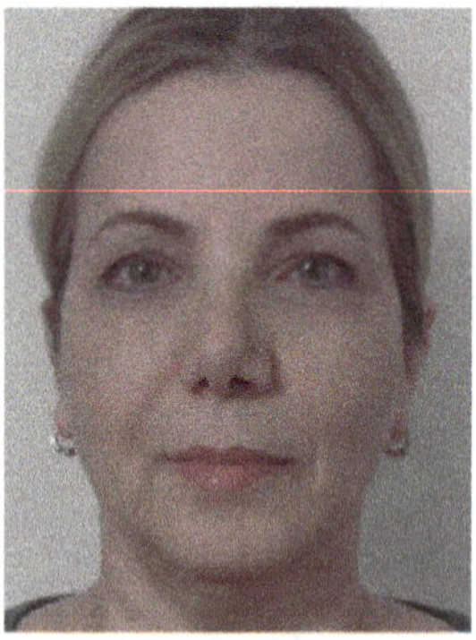

Fara Nejad is a graduate from Athabasca University, Canada, with a BA in General Studies, minoring in Education. She also obtained a TESOL certificate from the University of New South Wales, Sydney, Australia. She is also a graduate from Seneca College, Canada, in the Computer Programming diploma program with honors. e-mail: fanifj@yahoo.ca

Harry G. Nejad ***(Corresponding Author)*** Ph.D., MACP (Master's of Arts in Counselling Psychology), BA (Liberal Studies) and BA (Arts and Sciences) is a Quantitative Research Analyst and Investigator, and an adjunct professor at Yorkville University in Canada. He is Educational/Psychological Researcher and Educator with experience in large-scale nationally representative research projects and collaborations with internationally renowned researchers in Australia, Canada, the UK, and the USA. He has been extensively involved with teaching and academic administrative offices at several universities of repute. Dr. Nejad primarily specialises in Behavioural Sciences, Counselling Psychology, REBT Counselling, Research

Methods, Academic as well as non-Academic Adaptability, Learning, Motivation, Positive Psychology, Values, Personal Bests, Developmental Psychology, Professional Ethics in Counselling Psychology, and Educational Psychology. He is a certified Personality Dimensions® Facilitator and Trainer. He is also the Marketing Director and Strategic Planning Management Officer at Recency e.K. Financial and General Trading in Germany and holds the same position with the GMD-Holding since 2007. e-mail: harrygn@yahoo.ca

Ashish Pandey is Associate Professor with Shailesh J. Mehta School of Management (SJMSOM) in Indian Institute of Technology (IIT) Bombay in Mumbai. His research areas are spirituality in management, yoga and positive psychology, and business and society interface. His research work was awarded by MSR division of Academy of Management, Indian Academy of Management, Fowler Centre in Case Western Reserve University, Doctoral Consortiums at IISc Bangalore, IIM Indore, and IRMA. He has more than 30 research papers in reputed academic journals like Journal of Management, Journal of Business Ethics, Personnel Review, and so forth. He regularly engages with corporate and institutions for leadership and organization development work based on the integration of contemporary management knowledge and ancient Indian wisdom and practices. e-mail: ashish.pandey@iitb.ac.in

Sangeeta Pandit ***(Corresponding Author)*** was partner in a Chartered Accountancy firm of repute and now diversified to teaching and training. She is head of Department of Finance at the premier B-school—Sydenham Management—SIMSREE. She is also invited to conduct workshops at other B-schools of repute and for programs of the Institute of Chartered Accountants of India. She is a popular corporate trainer. She has many publications to her credit. She has authored books relating to accounting and taxation. She is an independent director in listed companies, mentor to entrepreneurs, and life coach. She works for the cause of cancer and for financial inclusion. e-mail: sangeeta@pdkunte.com; sangeetapandit@simsree.net

Kamlesh Patel ***(Corresponding Author)*** known to many as Daaji, is the Heartfulness Guide in a tradition of Yoga meditation that is over 100 years old, and he oversees 14,000 certified Heartfulness trainers, thousands of volunteers, and millions of practitioners in over 130 countries. He is bringing the essence of Yogic spiritual practices to the modern world in a scientific way, to help people regulate their minds, manage their emotions, and elevate their consciousness to the highest possible level. He is an innovator and researcher, equally at home in the fields of spirituality and science, blending the two into transcendental research on the evolution of consciousness, and expanding our understanding of the purpose of human existence to a new level. e-mail: kamlesh@srcm.org

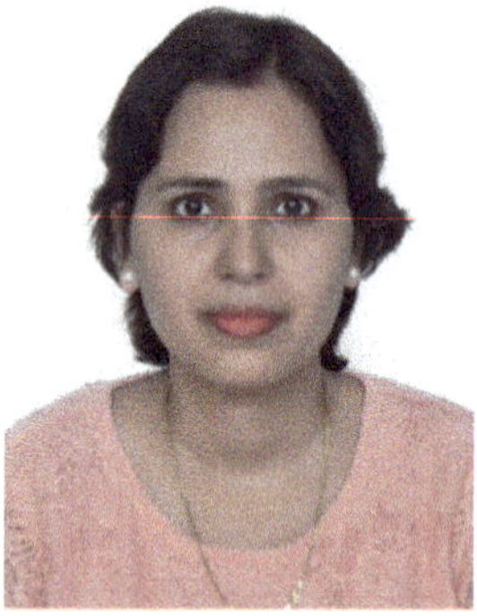

Sadhna Sargam ***(Corresponding Author)*** is Research Scholar with Shailesh J. Mehta School of Management, Indian Institute of Technology (IIT) Bombay in Mumbai. e-mail: prasadhna@gmail.com

Jeevan Deep Sehgal ***(Corresponding Author)*** is Assistant Professor of Management Practice at O. P. Jindal Global University. He has over 18 years of corporate experience in various organizations. During his tenure in corporations, he has accumulated an extensive exposure in consulting, strategic, and operational HR. His expertise areas are compensation and benefits, HR technology, HR analytics, diversity and inclusion, competency management, employee engagement, and employee experience. At O. P. Jindal Global University, he has been teaching courses on organizational development, psychology of entrepreneurship, compensation and benefits, and management consulting fundamentals with focus on HR. He has also trained over 200 people in areas of HR analytics, HR consultancy, and HR audit. He completed his executive program from

XLRI Jamshedpur and certification in People Analytics by University of Pennsylvania. He is currently pursuing his Ph.D. from Jindal Institute of Behavioural Sciences at O. P. Jindal Global University. e-mail: jdsehgal@jgu.edu.in

Subhash Sharma ***(Corresponding Author)*** is currently Director at Indus Business Academy, Bangalore. He holds Post Graduate Diploma in Management (PGDM) from Indian Institute of Management (IIM) Ahmedabad and Ph.D. from the University of Southern California (USC), Los Angeles, USA. He is author of well-known books such as Management in New Age: Western Windows Eastern Doors, New Mantras in Corporate Corridors, and New Earth Sastra. He has made significant contributions to institution building as founding member of Women's Institute for Studies in Development Oriented Management (WISDOM) at Banasthali University, Rajasthan; founding Director, Indian Institute of Plantation Management, Bangalore; and founding member Indus Business Academy (IBA), Bangalore. He is also a recipient of excellence, achievement, and leadership awards. He was awarded title of "Academic Rishi" by PES University, Bangalore, and Life Time Achievement Award by Association of Indian Management Scholars (AIMS) International, Houston. e-mail: prof.subhash.sharma789@gmail.com

John E. Simms ***(Corresponding Author)*** Ph.D., Ed.D, CMA, CSCA, is Associate Professor of Accounting at the University of St. Thomas in Houston, Texas, USA. His professional history began in broadcast television and then the automotive industry. He began a consulting firm in 1993, specializing in cost analysis, strategy development, and the alignment of resource usage with organizational mission. e-mail: simmsj@stthom.edu

Paridhi Singh is qualifying to be a solicitor in England and Wales and is currently pursuing a training contract at Baker McKenzie LLP. She has three Master of Law degrees including specialism in international law from the University of Cambridge. She completed her undergraduate law studies at Jindal Global Law School, India. Before securing her training contract, she worked in management consultancy (Accenture UK), human rights (UNDP), and education sectors, across 12 countries. She was a ILA scholar for the ILA 79th Biennial International Law Conference in Kyoto, Japan. Her research interests include law and spirituality, business and human rights, and public international law. e-mail: parisingh.ra@gmail.com

H. W. Sneller ***(Corresponding Author)*** has been teaching continental philosophy and ethics at Leiden University and the Technical University of Eindhoven (the Netherlands). Currently, he is an independent scholar teaching at various institutions and universities such as the Jungian Institute, Mandeville Academy, besides others. As Vice President of the global think tank and network organization APGC, he is responsible for strategic planning and policy making for the network as a whole. He is active on various boards, both nationally and internationally. His current research focuses on exceptional states of consciousness in relation to philosophy. He recently published Perspectives on Synchronicity, Inspiration, and the Soul (Cambridge Scholars 2021). e-mail: h.w.sneller@gmail.com

Shiv K. Tripathi ***(Corresponding Author)*** is Vice Chancellor at Atmiya University, Rajkot. He also leads Humanistic Management Network India Chapter. He has more than 24 years of experience in teaching, research, and higher education management while working in different roles as Dean, Director, Professor, Vice Chancellor, and Advisor with different institutions and organizations nationally as well as internationally. He has supervised 12 students for the award for Ph.D. and has also served in doctoral jury/committee in India, Tanzania, and France. He has published more than 75 articles, book chapters, and case studies including six books. He has delivered invited presentations and talks in number of international events. He is member in United

Nations Principles for Responsible Management Education (PRME) "Anti-Corruption" and "Poverty Eradication" Working Groups. He is Fellow and Board member of One Planet Education Network (OPEN), UK. He earned his graduation in Electrical and Electronics Engineering followed by MBA, and Doctorate in General Management. e-mail: shivktripathi@hotmail.com

Ernst von Kimakowitz is founding Director of the Humanistic Management Center, an independent think tank, learning institution, and advisory firm, focused on business ethics and sustainability. He also cofounded and leads the Humanistic Management Network, a global network of scholars, policy makers, and management practitioners working toward enhancing the body of knowledge and implementing humanistic management principles. He holds a research position at the University of Lucerne where he is focusing on dignity at work, or in other words, if and how respect for our dignity is engrained in organizational behavior and what impact it makes. He has been Visiting Faculty at universities in Colombia, Germany, India, and Japan and holds various editorial, reviewer, and board positions. e-mail: ernst.von.kimakowitz@humanisticmanagement.org; ernst.vonkimakowitz@unilu.ch

Chapter 1
Enlightened Management: Reflections on Spirituality and its Significance for the Future of Work

Anthony Cullen and Paridhi Singh

Abstract This chapter explores the import of spirituality for the theory and practice of management. The first part focuses on how spirituality is defined, providing context for the discussion of its significance in the world of work. The second part addresses workplace spirituality, its evolution and importance to the future of work. In doing so, it considers the impact of technological disruptions, issues of employee well-being, and changes resulting from the COVID-19 pandemic. The third part highlights the role of spirituality in this context and the potential for a shift in praxis as a means of facilitating a more holistic approach to the development of people and organizations.

Keywords Spirituality · Management · Law · Transcendence · Religion · Meaning

Introduction

This chapter explores the import of spirituality for the theory and practice of management. The chapter begins by first exploring how spirituality is defined. It then considers its significance in the fields of law, business, and management in light of the evolving nature of professional and legal services and challenges arising from the COVID-19 pandemic. Highlighting the role of spirituality in employee well-being, the potential for a shift in praxis is discussed as a means of facilitating a more holistic approach to the development of people and organizations.

A. Cullen (✉)
Middlesex University, London, UK
e-mail: A.T.Cullen@mdx.ac.uk

P. Singh
Hughes Hall, University of Cambridge, Cambridge, UK

© Jindal Institute of Behavioral Sciences 2022

S. P. Sahni et al. (eds.), *Spirituality and Management*,
https://doi.org/10.1007/978-981-19-1025-8_1

Defining Spirituality

As noted by Raysa Geaquinto Rocha and Paulo Gonçalves Pinheiro, spirituality appears in "management studies from three main perspectives: individual spirituality, spirituality in the workplace, and organizational spirituality" (2020, p. 1). This section explores how spirituality is defined from the perspective of the individual. Informed by the concept of spirituality developed here, Sect. "Workplace Spirituality" addresses spirituality in the workplace. For the purposes of section, Sect. "Defining Spirituality" particular attention will be given to the role of connectedness, transcendence, and meaning in life in defining what spirituality consists of (Weathers et al., 2016). Before doing so, it is important to distinguish the concept of spirituality from that of religion.

Distinguishing "spirituality" from "religion"

There is an increasingly well-recognized distinction between the concepts of spirituality and religion. Paul Heelas and Linda Woodhead state that "in recent years the emergence of something called "spirituality" has-increasingly-demanded attention. Survey after survey shows that increasing numbers of people now prefer to call themselves "spiritual" rather than "religious"" (Heelas and Woodhead, 2005: p. 1). Spirituality is often distinguished from religion as being much broader in scope. Johnathan Rowson states

> While the terms 'spirituality' and 'religion' were previously undifferentiated, modern conceptions tend to see them as either polar opposites, or as one (spirituality) being a core function of the other (religion). The observed shift has paralleled an increased public and academic interest in spirituality. The number of citations in the psychological research literature with the word "religion" in the title doubled between 1970 and 2005, while the number of citations with the word "spirituality" in the title experienced a 40-fold increase over the same time period (Rowson, 2014, pp. 18–19)

Commenting on popular interest in spirituality in contrast to religion, the philosopher Paul O'Grady states that

> It is obvious that 'spirituality' is a word very much in vogue at the start of the twenty-first century. Bookshops stock numerous volumes with the word 'spiritual' somewhere in the title. Radio and TV programmes are devoted to the topic and interviewers are not afraid to ask celebrities about their spiritual views (and they are not averse to responding) … People who otherwise would have nothing to do with religion are happy to subscribe to some notion of spirituality (O'Grady, 2004, p. 5).

O'Grady refers to the "gradual collapse of faith in institutional religion" in the West, resulting in a strong emphasis on "the distinction between religion and spirituality" (O'Grady, 2004, pp. 11–12). However, as noted by Holly Nelson-Becker, "Religion and spirituality have many meanings" (Nelson-Becker, 2003: p. 86). She observed that "Some are personal, such as forming a relationship with a transcendent power. Others are social, such as giving or receiving support in the context of a religious fellowship. Just as there are different types of intelligence and learning styles, individuals respond differently to components of religion and spirituality" (Nelson-Becker, 2003: p. 86). Reporting on the meaning attributed to religion and spirituality by African American and European American Elders, Nelson-Becker stated that "Religion was described primarily as beliefs, while spirituality was primarily identified as a feeling in the heart" (Nelson-Becker, 2003: p. 86).

Reviewing both the theoretical and empirical literature pertaining to spirituality, Elizabeth Weathers, Geraldine McCarthy, and Alice Coffey identified connectedness, transcendence, and meaning in life as three defining attributes of the concept. The following definition was posited on the basis of these attributes: "Spirituality is a way of being in the world in which a person feels a sense of connectedness to self, others, and/or a higher power or nature; a sense of meaning in life; and transcendence beyond self, everyday living, and suffering" (Weathers et al., 2016: p. 93). The sections which follow explore these attributes as a way of unfolding the concept of spirituality.

Connectedness

The attribute of connectedness to self, others, and/or a higher power or nature is often mentioned as a characteristic of spirituality (e.g., Buck, 2006: p. 290; Nelson-Becker, 2003: p. 98; Rowson, 2014: p. 48). The sense of relatedness in the attribute has an implicit ethical dimension. In *Secular Spirituality*, Harald Walach states

> There is no single spiritual tradition that would not also impart some ethical norms of conduct and behavior, remarkably similar across traditions. This implication of ethics in spirituality is less an external than an internal one. One who has had a spiritual experience knows that he must not do certain things, not because they are forbidden in a general sense and by a higher authority, but because he is damaging himself. A spiritual experience often contains the element of interconnectedness (Walach, 2014: p. 25).

Connectedness (or interconnectedness) in individual spirituality conveys "a sense of belonging" in contrast to "a common background feeling of loneliness or alienation" in "normal experience" (Rowson, 2014: p. 48). According to Weathers et al., "[c]onnectedness, as defined in the literature, is said to include a sense of relatedness to oneself, to others, to nature or the world, and to a Higher Power, God, or Supreme Being" (Weathers et al., 2016: p. 83). This sense of relatedness is often referred to in conjunction with the attribute of transcendence discussed below.

Transcendence

The attribute of transcendence is closely related to that of connectedness. Weathers et al. (2016) define transcendence as follows:

> Self-transcendence has been defined as the ability to see beyond the boundaries of the self, the environment, and present limitations. Every person is said to have the capacity to self-transcend and transcend suffering. Thus, transcendence emerged in this analysis as a capacity to change one's outlook on a given situation and on life overall (Weathers et al., 2016: p. 91).

Transcendence addresses that which goes beyond the conditioning of an individual in terms of education, culture, or other more limiting aspects of human experience. Alexandrea Withers, Kimberly Zuniga, and Sharon Van refer to the "transcendence of religion" as "vital in understanding spirituality" (Withers et al., 2017: p. 234). The attribute of transcendence is thus associated with attainment of a higher, more liberating perspective. In doing so, it provides context for an individual's understanding of the meaning and purpose of life. The section which follows explores this attribute of spirituality.

Meaning and Purpose

Spirituality is often frequently cited as a point of reference for meaning and purpose in the life of an individual. The psychologist David Elkins refers to "[t]he need for meaning and purpose" as "one of the strongest human drives" (Elkins et al., 1988, p. 13). He comments that

> The actual ground and content of this meaning vary from person to person, but the common factor is that each person has filled the "existential vacuum" with an authentic sense that life has meaning and purpose (Elkins et al., 1988, p. 11).

The psychiatrist and concentration camp survivor Viktor Frankl refers to the "will to meaning" as the most fundamental of all human motivations (Frankl, 1963: p. 172). He states that the main concern of an individual "consists in fulfilling a meaning, rather than in the mere gratification and satisfaction of drives and instincts, or in merely reconciling the conflicting claims of id, ego and superego, or in the mere adaptation and adjustment to society and environment" (Frankl, 1963: p. 182). Frankl emphasizes that "knowledge that there is a meaning in one's life" may serve as the very basis of a person's survival (Frankl, 1963: p. 182). Drawing on his experience in Nazi concentration camps, he quotes Friedrich Nietzsche: "He who has a why to live for can bear almost any how" (Frankl, 1963: p. 182).

Jonathan Rowson states that the "Spiritual is more about meaning than "happiness"" (Rowson, 2014: p. 11). In this context—one relating to the conceptualization of spirituality—the attribute of meaning is understood in terms that are existential in nature. As a consequence, the concept necessarily engages the subjectivity of the human condition. Indeed, the decline of religion and the growth of interest in spirituality have been credited to the "subjective turn" of modern culture (Heelas and Woodhead, 2005). Citing Charles Taylor's *Ethics of Authenticity*, Heelas and Woodhead explain the rise in interest in spirituality in terms of the "subjectivities of each individual" as follows:

> The subjectivities of each individual become a, if not the, unique source of significance, meaning and authority. Here 'the good life' consists in living one's life in full awareness of

> one's states of being; in enriching one's experiences; in finding ways of handling negative emotions; in becoming sensitive enough to find out where and how the quality of one's life - alone or in relation - may be improved. The goal is not to defer to higher authority, but to have the courage to become one's own authority. Not to follow established paths, but to forge one's own inner-directed, as subjective, life. Not to become what others want one to be, but to 'become who I truly am'. Not to rely on the knowledge and wisdom of others ('To the other be true'), but to live out the Delphic 'know thyself' and the Shakespearian 'To thine own self be true' (Heelas and Woodhead, 2005: pp. 3–4).

The attribution of meaning and purpose in individual spirituality is naturally reflected in the attribution of meaning and purpose in workplace spirituality. As noted by Raysa Geaquinto Rocha and Paulo Gonçalves Pinheiro, "Individual spirituality is also a component of workplace spirituality because interactions of spirituality within the organisation occur in the workplace as the members search for meaning in their work" (Rocha & Pinheiro, 2020: p. 8). The section that follows explores this further in light of the evolving nature of professional and legal services and changes arising from the COVID-19 pandemic.

Law, Business, and Management

Workplace Spirituality

Peter Case and Jonathan Gosling comment on the rise academic interest in workplace spirituality:

> Academic interest in the subject is following the corporate trend for workshops, seminars, culture change and corporate transformation programmes that, in many instances, are increasingly aimed at harnessing not only the mind and body of employees but also their spiritual essence or soul. Major companies, such as, Apple, Ford, GlaxoSmithKline, McDonalds, Nike, Shell Oil and the World Bank are embracing this recent drive to secure competitive advantage through what might be understood from a critical standpoint as the appropriation of employee spirituality for primarily economic ends (Case & Gosling, 2010: p. 2).

A critique of this transactional approach has been made in the context of the legal professional services industry. This industry is notorious for high rates of burnout, stress, depression, anxiety, and other mental health issues driven by a high-pressure and competitive environment (Muça, 2019). Rebecca Michalak reports that "Lawyers suffer from significantly lower levels of psychological and psychosomatic health … than other professionals" (Michalak, 2015: p. 21), and it is estimated that lawyers suffer depression at a rate that is 3.6 times greater than other professions (Port, 2018).

Ronald Purser posits that many organisations including law firms are using workplace spiritual practices to relieve the stress of employees (Purser, 2019a). Such interventions often come at the expense of introducing meaningful long-term changes addressing the causes of stress and anxiety, which are commonplace in the modern workplace.

McMindfulness: How Mindfulness Became the New Capitalist Spirituality, Purser argues that mindfulness interventions may in fact be counterproductive to the long-term health of employees. This is because the burden of maintaining employee well-being shifts almost exclusively to the employee. The expectation being that the employee should be able to cope with the difficulty of their circumstances through the adoption of spiritual practices. It is evident that this compounds the problem: The employee's environment continues to negatively impact on their well-being/mental health, *and* additionally, the employee has to cope with the situation on their own through whatever means is available to them. Meanwhile, the employer has a lesser imperative to change the prevailing *status quo* or investigate the organizational policies and ways of working damaging employee wellness.

Such a transactional approach, whether deliberate or unintended, highlights the limitations of several prevalent organizational attitudes toward workplace spirituality. To expect employees to weather silently, a steady erosion of their overall health, and to use workplace spirituality as a means not to introduce meaningful changes, negates the good of such interventions. The key question which emerges then is as follows: *How should organizations or executive leadership understand the value of workplace spirituality?* A shift away from a transactional view of workplace spirituality is needed. The reasons why are discussed below.

The Future of Work

The Industrial Revolution marks one of the most disruptive periods in modern history. The sudden shift from an agrarian and handicraft economy to large-scale machine-led manufacturing industries led to job losses as demand for craftspeople fell. Many artisans—such as handloom weavers—could not compete with the economies of scale and low costs offered by the industrial giants of the nineteenth and twentieth centuries (Hobsbawm, 1962, p. 37). In the twenty-first century, the Fourth Industrial Revolution led by the convergence of emerging technologies such as artificial intelligence (AI), robotics, and quantum computing, has catalyzed a new wave of disruption. As noted by Morgan Frank and others, "[w]hile technology generally increases productivity, AI may diminish some of today's valuable employment opportunities" (Frank et al., 2019: p. 6531).

The disruptive potential of AI is evident from its use in a variety of different contexts. According to Noam Brown, Research Scientist at Facebook AI Research, it is now possible to create "an AI algorithm that can bluff better than any human" (Hernandez, 2019). Together with Tuomas Sandholm (his PhD Supervisor at Carnegie Mellon University), Brown created two AI systems—Libratus and Pluribus—both of which succeeded in defeating top poker professionals (Brown & Sandholm, 2019). Poker is a game that "involves hidden information, deception, and bluffing" (Brown, 2020: p. 16). The fact the AI has been utilized in this way—to build "the most effective non-human bluffer to date" (Hernandez, 2019)—conveys something of the potential that exists for its application in other contexts. On the potential impact of AI on the future of work, Didem Özkiziltan and Anke Hassel state that

> [E]xperts warn us that AI-driven technologies are also poised to perpetuate and exacerbate prevailing socio-economic problems, including but not limited to inequalities, discrimination, human rights violations, and undermining of democratic values. Projected into the world of work, these issues take the form of - among many others - replacement of human labour by machines, workers' relegation to mundane tasks, aggravation of disparities in wages and working conditions, invasion of workers' privacy, erosion of workers' traditional power resources, and intensification of power asymmetries between capital and labour. Taken from this perspective, the AI-driven future of work, as reflected by the scholarly work, is likely to perpetuate and aggravate work-related inequalities and discrimination, diminishing further the prospects of decent work, fair remuneration and adequate social protection for all (Özkiziltan & Hassel, 2021: p. 63).

Similar concerns about the impact of technologies such as artificial intelligence were raised by the Global Commission on the Future of Work:

> Technological advances – artificial intelligence, automation and robotics – will create new jobs, but those who lose their jobs in this transition may be the least equipped to seize the new job opportunities. The skills of today will not match the jobs of tomorrow and newly acquired skills may quickly become obsolete (Commission on the Future of Work, 2019: p. 18).

The implications for the future of the services industry are profound. In 2019, Deloitte Australia published a report on the future of work, referring to skills as "the job currency of the future" (Rumbens et al., 2019: p. 19). The report—"The path to prosperity: Why the future of work is human"—categorized skills into three types: "skills requiring our hands, skills requiring our heads and skills requiring our hearts" (Rumbens et al., 2019: p. 19). The last of the three types mentioned—"heart skills"—is of particular interest here. The significance of such skills to the future of work is explained as follows:

> The nature of work is changing. Today's jobs are increasingly likely to require you to use your head rather than your hands, a trend that has been playing out for some time.
>
> There is another factor at play. Regardless if jobs rely on brains or brawn, it's the less routine jobs that are harder to automate, and that is where employment has been growing.
>
> …
>
> And while today's jobs require us to use our heads, rather than our hands, this binary classification is hiding something important – the work of the heart. These are the skills that are embedded in both the work of the hands and the work of the head.
>
> What do we mean by work of the heart? It is the interpersonal and creative roles that will be hardest of all to mechanise (Rumbens et al., 2019: p. ii).

Interpersonal and creative work requires the exercise of skills that are distinctly human in nature. Such skills cannot be automated. Decisions requiring ethics, empathy, or emotional intelligence fall outside the scope of that which can be determined by way of artificial intelligence. As noted by Kai-Fu Lee, "[w]ith all of the advances in machine learning, the truth remains that we are still nowhere near creating AI machines that feel any emotions at all" (Lee, 2021: p. 263).

It is difficult to conceive interpersonal and creative work without the exercise of "heart skills" such as empathy or ethics. Such skills are central to the efficacious practice of management. In this context, it is instructive to refer to the "work of the heart" as an area which should be prioritized in future:

> The shift from work of the hands (manual labour) to work of the head (cognitive tasks) will continue. But the next stage will be a move towards work of the heart. Humans are still better at being human. Interacting with others, being creative, understanding and reacting to emotions. These are all inherently human skills and focusing on these will bring the greatest benefits in the long run (Rumbens et al., 2019: p. 19).

The shift "from hands to heads to hearts" captures succinctly the past, present, and future of work (Rumbens et al., 2019: p. ii). However, it is noteworthy that "despite this demand suggesting that we should be most focused on the skills required for work of the heart, followed by head and then hands, in fact we have the most acute shortages in the areas of most demand" (Rumbens et al., 2019: p. 21). The emphasis placed on the "work of the heart" corresponds well with the human-centric focus of workplace spirituality. The values associated with spirituality—including an individual's sense of meaning and purpose—are the basis for the exercise of the "heart skills". Such values inform not only how work's creative or interpersonal dimension is approached, but also the underlying intention in other areas of work as ethnicity, religion, sex, economic comments:

> Spiritual intention arises from the deepest part of the human being, the heart, and it affects and embraces all dimensions. It is metarational and therefore not mental, although it is connected with the mind. Spiritual intention determines the purity or simplicity of heart, that is, the intensity of love, the level of communion with others, and the degree of self-giving in any human action. This spiritual intention can be present in all human actions, not only in strictly spiritual ones, due to its metadimensional nature... Teaching, painting, cooking and driving are not strictly spiritual actions, but the spiritual element can inspire and be present in all these activities (Domingo, 2019: pp. 337–338).

The spiritual element is one that necessitates a holistic approach to management, understanding employee well-being as an intrinsic good. Mindful of changes arising from the use of new technologies, the implications for the theory and practice of management are discussed further in Sect. "From Models to Application: Implications for the Practice of Management". Before doing so, the section that follows discusses the impact of the COVID-19 global pandemic on prioritization of employee well-being and need for a fundamental reassessment of the employer–employee relationship.

The Impact of the COVID-19 Pandemic

The changes wrought by the COVID-19 pandemic will no doubt exert a lasting influence on the *modus operandi* of employers and employees. While global employment losses have been unprecedented (International Labour Organization, 2021: p. 1), the shift to "working from home" has resulted in a rise in mental health problems among those employed in the professional services. Stephen Koss, Partner in Ernst & Young's People Advisory Services, comments that

> [T]hose now working remotely face the mental stress of isolation and the physical challenges of new workspaces – kitchen tables, bedrooms and garages – that are far from fit for purpose. Staff may also be juggling business commitments with increased childcare and home-schooling responsibilities – and worries about older, immunocompromised or absent friends and family members (Koss, 2020).

Writing for the Financial Times, Kate Beioley reported in March 2021 that "[j]unior lawyers and consultants are warning they are suffering burnout after working longer hours in isolation during the pandemic, sparking fears of an exodus from the biggest global law and advisory firms" (Beioley, 2021). The changes experienced as a result of the pandemic—such as increased workload and longer hours—raise significant issues for the relationship between employer and employee, including of the responsibility of the former for the well-being of the latter.

A report issued by Accenture in September 2020, authored by Ellyn Shook (Accenture's Chief Leadership and HR Officer) and David Rodriguez (Global Chief HR Officer for Marriott), provides insight into how workers' perception of the relationship between employer and employee has changed as a result of the pandemic. The study found that 78% "of workers strongly believe their employer is responsible for helping them become net better off" (Shook & Rodriguez, 2020: p. 14). Becoming "net better off" was defined in terms of the following six dimensions: relational, financial, purposeful, physical, employable, and emotional and mental (Shook & Rodriguez, 2020: p. 8). The percentage referring to the responsibility of employer to help workers to become "net better off" grew sharply during the pandemic in comparison with the position before the pandemic (Shook & Rodriguez, 2020: p. 14). Further, this understanding was also shared by 50% of the executive leaders surveyed by Accenture, a significant rise from before the pandemic.

Nevertheless, the figures reveal a disconnect between what employers and employees think about what truly matters. According to David Rodriguez, "the pandemic has accelerated what was already in motion: a questioning of relationship between employer & employee" (Debevoise, 2020). Indeed, questions concerning responsibility for employee well-being have been brought into sharp focus by the pandemic. As noted by Stephen Koss, "the current crisis has hit organizations very differently. But the single common factor for everyone is that life is infinitely more stressful" (Koss, 2020). Encouraging employees to "take ownership and accountability for their own well-being" (Koss, 2020) without addressing workload issues is questionable. Reporting on a global survey conducted by the Financial Times on work and mental health, Emma Jacobs and Lucy Warwick-Ching stated that

> The overwhelming sentiment was that all the supportive messages and apps were ultimately meaningless if they did not address workloads. Many reported increased hours due to job losses, furlough and illnesses, while also struggling to keep businesses afloat. Research by Stanford University found that more than a third of Americans who were working from

> home last August spent the time they would have used on their commute doing extra work (Jacobs & Warwick-Ching, 2021).

The issues highlighted by the pandemic call for a reorientation of the relationship between employer and employee. The *status quo* is arguably unsustainable. While it is common for employee well-being to be treated as a means to particular organizational ends, the authors posit here that an alternative approach is needed. The section that follows explores such an alternative approach, highlighting the significance of spirituality for the reorientation required.

From Models to Application: Implications for the Practice of Management

The integration of spirituality into the workplace raises a number of issues for the theory and practice of management. One of the most significant for the professional and legal services concerns recognition of the intrinsic worth of employee well-being. Understood in terms incorporating spirituality, a holistic approach to employee well-being places a categorical imperative on managers to address a diverse range of concerns. The sections that follow explore these in more detail.

Ethics

In *Secular Spirituality: The Next Step Towards Enlightenment*, Harald Walach states that: "Ethical behavior is a natural result of spiritual experience, and from a certain point onwards it is also a precondition for further spiritual growth" (Walach, 2014, 2017: p. 26). In the same way that the spiritual life of an individual is supported by ethics, ethics in decision making is also supported by values of a spiritual nature. On account of this, there is an onus on managers to be proactive in addressing concerns of an ethical nature at all levels. Unethical practices undermine not only the individual spirituality of employees but also the integrity of the organization as a whole. In this context, it is important to be mindful of the relationship between workplace spirituality and ethical well-being. George Gotsis and Zoi Kortezi state that "Spiritual values … are not only expected to enhance ethical well-being, but also to affect issues of organisational justice, both in terms of distributive equity and of the intention to behave fairly" (Gotsis & Kortezi, 2008: p. 593).

Evidence of the ethical impact of workplace spirituality is provided in a number of studies (e.g., Geigle, 2012; Göçen & Özğan, 2018; McGhee & Grant, 2017). As noted by Davide Geigle,

> Many of the empirical studies demonstrate a positive effect of [workplace spirituality] on job commitment, satisfaction, and performance. In addition, the empirical research on workplace spirituality has demonstrated results in altruism and conscientiousness, self-career

> management, reduced inter-role conflict, reduced frustration, organization based self-esteem, involvement, retention, and ethical behavior. (Geigle, 2012: p. 14)

Exploring the transcendent influence of spirituality on ethical action in organizations, Peter McGhee and Patricia Grant studied claims concerning spiritual individuals being more ethical and therefore "of significant value to the long-term viability of organizations and ultimately society" (McGhee & Grant, 2017: p. 160). The study, conducted in a New Zealand business context, found that

> participants' spirituality was manifested through an awareness of others that guided and enabled them to act in authentically ethical ways that transcended organizational conditions. When participants reported doing this, they felt increased well-being; when they were unable to enact their spirituality, they suffered a variety of negative feelings (McGhee & Grant, 2017: p. 160).

This finding was explained in terms of personal authenticity as follows:

> As part of their spiritual (and thus moral) identity, participants had a consciousness that, in part at least, was directed toward the welfare of others. This spiritual other-orientation provides direction via principles (e.g. do unto others) and values (e.g. fairness, compassion, and selflessness) to act ethically. Participants were motivated to operate this way in order to be authentic to their spirituality. When individuals were spiritually authentic, they reported an enhanced sense of well-being. In instances where they were not authentic, they reported diminished welfare (McGhee & Grant, 2017: p. 171).

Mindful of the intrinsic value of employee well-being, the instrumentalization of workplace spirituality should be guarded against at all levels of an organization. As noted by George Gotsis and Zoi Kortezi, "spiritual values should not be reduced to mere instrumentalities principally and exclusively at the service of exogenous, desirable organisational ends" (Gotsis & Kortezi, 2008: p. 595). Such an approach negates the authenticity required for spirituality to flourish in the workplace in a sustainable way. The section that follows explores the importance of developing an inclusive, open culture supportive of workplace spirituality.

Culture

In supporting the spiritual life of employees, a space must exist for consideration of matters pertaining to personal development, employee well-being, and work–life balance. Policies should be in place to address such considerations, mindful of how they affect employees on a day-to-day basis. To cultivate an environment supportive of workplace spirituality, it is important to look beyond policy to the actual culture of an organization.

The culture of an organization is defined not only by values espoused by its leadership, but also by basic assumptions that are "taken for granted," "invisible," or "preconscious" (Schein, 1984: p. 4). Bearing in mind the diversity of approaches to the "spiritual," it is difficult to overemphasize the importance of taking an inclusive approach to workplace spirituality. Fahri Karakas states that

> [W]orkplaces of today are more diverse and multicultural than ever before. Therefore, it has become crucial to acknowledge diversity in the workplace and absolutely respect individual differences ... Promoting "one right path" or favoring a specific spiritual or religious framework will not work in these diverse work environments. A culture of respect for diversity of beliefs and faiths should be cultivated in the workplace by enforcing codes of conduct as well as instilling values of tolerance and compassion (Karakas, 2010: p. 31).

The instilling of values such as tolerance and compassion has the potential to transform the culture of an organization. Peter McGhee and Patricia Grant refer to the fact that "highly spiritual people are ethical at work" and that "they enact their spirituality in ways that improve the overall ethicality of the organization by transforming its "dominant schema"" (McGhee & Grant, 2017: p. 173). They describe the transformative potential of workplace spirituality on the culture of an organization in the following way:

> The effects of consistent spiritual enactment may be a gradual transformation of norms and expectations toward an organizational culture with higher moral values such as altruism, integrity and community. Such a process ultimately produces beneficial effects for an organization. Consequently, organizations should implement tactics that enhance and encourage an authentic spirituality. For example, cultures that provide opportunities and resources to "speak openly and express inner feelings and values, regardless of fear, alienation or exclusion" in a manner that includes constructive feedback may encourage actions in the workplace that positively reinforce spirituality. Some authors also note that less bureaucratic and more self-managed, autonomous, and democratic structures could also contribute to this process (McGhee & Grant, 2017: p. 173).

In changing the culture of an organization, it is important to bear in mind that "spirituality is not something to be accomplished in the next week or quarter, but rather is a task that extends over the entire course of a person's—and organization's—life" (Mitroff & Denton, 1999: p. 176). While the process is one which must support the developmental needs and ethical well-being of employees, for it to be holistic it should be conceived in terms that are broader than this. The process of organizational culture change must also take into consideration the overarching impact of the organization on society, including that which affects future generations. The section that follows explores the significance of this for workplace spirituality.

The Common Good of Humanity

The realization of the universal, non-sectarian, and inclusive values associated with spirituality would have far-reaching impact on any organization. Moreover, a natural and foreseeable consequence of such values and their authentic expression would be the expansion of concern beyond that of the organization itself. Judith Neal reasons that "[i]f personal spirituality is a process of expanding one's consciousness and focus beyond one's own ego, then perhaps organizational spirituality is a process of expanding the organization's collective consciousness beyond just the culture and mission of the company to a focus on the greater collective good" (Neal, 2018: p. 25).

The dissolution of distinctions between persons—including those relating to nationality, ethnicity, religion, sex, economic or social status—provides a basis for the integration of such persons within an organization. The same logic is applicable outside the organization. For integration to occur at any level of human society—including regional, national, and international—certain distinctions must be accorded irrelevance. Spirituality in this context serves as a unifying principle, facilitating a "heart-centred" approach to the integration of humanity (Patel et al., 2018: p. 181).

According to Judge Antônio Augusto Cançado Trindade, "[u]niversal human rights find support in the spirituality of all cultures and religions and are rooted in the human spirit itself; as such, they are not the expression of a given culture (Western or any other), but rather of the *universal juridical conscience* itself" (Trindade, 2014: p. 207). Mindful that the progress of humanity is "often characterised in terms of the realisation of universally shared values (including the abolition of slavery, the prohibition of torture, the proscription of apartheid, etc.)," it is arguable that "greater attention should be given to the spiritual basis for progressive realization of such values" (Cullen, 2017: p. 304).

The challenge is one that concerns the spiritual life not only of individuals and organizations but that of humanity as a whole. Many of the challenges faced by organizations cannot be addressed without attention at a global level. These include the spread of infectious diseases such as COVID-19, the extreme weather attributable to climate change, the pollution of the high seas, and global poverty. Accordingly, "the choice confronting humanity at this critical point in history is not *whether* organizations should become more spiritual but rather *how* they can. If organizations are to survive, let alone prosper, then frankly we see no alternative to their becoming spiritual" (Mitroff & Denton, 1999: pp. 168–169).

Conclusion

Spirituality, it has been posited, is to be approached in terms that are universal, inclusive, and non-sectarian in nature. Understood in such terms, spirituality is to be taken as a good that is intrinsically beneficial to individuals, organizations, and humanity as a whole. As an intrinsic good, it is not to be treated as a means to end but as an end in itself. As noted by Mitroff and Denton, "Spirituality is not a final state. It is an ongoing process—a process that leads to itself. Above all, spirituality is not a simpleminded how-to list or checklist. It is a perpetual process of becoming, a continual unfolding of the human spirit" (Mitroff & Denton, 1999: p. 185).

References

Ashmos, D. P., & Duchon, D. (2000). Spirituality at work: A conceptualization and measure. *Journal of Management Inquiry, 9*(2), 134–145.

Beioley, K. (2021, March 22). Professional services face losing junior staff to burnout. *Financial Times*. Retrieved from https://www.ft.com/content/f037991e-4481-4641-8186-0862f1f07c97.
Brown, N. (2020). *Equilibrium finding for large adversarial imperfect-information games*. Carnegie Mellon University.
Brown, N., & Sandholm, T. (2019). Superhuman AI for multiplayer poker. *Science, 365*(6456), 885–890.
Brown, V. (2021, April 4). FT readers respond: burnout during the Covid pandemic. *Financial Times*. Retrieved from https://www.ft.com/content/19feae61-01dc-4248-b98c-90aa34fccfb4.
Buck, H. G. (2006). Spirituality: Concept analysis and model development. *Holistic Nursing Practice, 20*(6), 288–292.
Burk, D. (2017, August 11). Five ways to make your work spiritual practice. *Bright Way Zen*. Retrieved from https://brightwayzen.org/work-practice/.
Case, P., & Gosling, J. (2010). The spiritual organization: Critical reflections on the instrumentality of workplace spirituality. *Journal of Management, Spirituality and Religion, 7*(4), 257–282.
Cullen, A. (2017). Spirituality and law: Reflections on the universality of humanitarian concern. *Science and Spirituality in Literature*, 303–305.
Cullen, J. G. (2017). Educating business students about sustainability: A bibliometric review of current trends and research needs. *Journal of Business Ethics, 145*(2), 429–439.
Debevoise, N. D. (2020, October 8). Accenture research shows employees care about much more than money—Here's what they need to build your business. *Forbes*. Retrieved from https://www.forbes.com/sites/nelldebevoise/2020/10/08/your-employees-dont-care-about-money--heres-what-they-need-to-build-your-business/?sh=17bec1481645.
Domingo, R. (2019). Why spirituality matters for law: An explanation. *Oxford Journal of Law and Religion, 8*(2), 326–349.
Elkins, D. N, James Hedstrom, L., Hughes, L. L., Andrew Leaf, J., & Saunders, C. (1988). Toward a humanistic-phenomenological spirituality: Definition, description, and measurement. *Journal of humanistic Psychology, 28*(4), 5–18.
Ernst, E., Merola, R., & Samaan, D. (2019). Economics of artificial intelligence: Implications for the future of work. *IZA Journal of Labor Policy, 9*(1), 1–35.
Frank, M. R., Autor, D., Bessen, J. E., Brynjolfsson, E., Cebrian, M., Deming, D. J., … Moro, E. (2019). Toward understanding the impact of artificial intelligence on labor. *Proceedings of the National Academy of Sciences, 116*(14), 6531–6539.
Frankl, V. (1963). *Man's search for meaning*. Pocket Books.
Geigle, D. (2012). Workplace spirituality empirical research: A literature review. *Business and Management Review, 2*(10), 14–27.
Global Commission on the Future of Work. (2019). Work for a brighter future. *International Labour Organization*. Retrieved from https://www.ilo.org/wcmsp5/groups/public/---dgreports/---cabinet/documents/publication/wcms_662410.pdf.
Göçen, A., & Özğan, H. (2018). Spirituality and ethics: A literature review. *Gaziantep Üniversitesi Sosyal Bilimler Dergisi, 17*, 58–65.
Gotsis, G., & Kortezi, Z. (2008). Philosophical foundations of workplace spirituality: A critical approach. *Journal of Business Ethics, 78*(4), 575–600.
Heaton, D. P, Schmidt-Wilk, J., & Travis, F. (2004) Constructs, methods, and measures for researching spirituality in organizations. *Journal of Organizational Change Management*.
ILO. (2019). Work for a brighter future—Global commission on the future of work. *International Labour Organization*. Retrieved from https://www.ilo.org/wcmsp5/groups/public/---dgreports/---cabinet/documents/publication/wcms_662410.pdf.
ILO. (2021, January 25). COVID-19 and the world of work (7th edn). *International Labour Organization*. Retrieved from https://www.ilo.org/global/topics/coronavirus/impacts-and-responses/WCMS_767028/lang--en/index.htm.
Jacobs, E., & Warwick-Ching, L. (2021, February 8). Feeling the strain: Stress and anxiety weigh on world's workers. *Financial Times*. Retrieved from https://www.ft.com/content/02d39d97-23ed-45ff-b982-7335770ae512.

James, W. (1928). *The varieties of religious experience: A study in human nature*. Longmans, Green and Co.

Jena, L. K. (2021). Does workplace spirituality lead to raising employee performance? The role of citizenship behavior and emotional intelligence. *International Journal of Organizational Analysis*.

Karakas, F. (2010). Spirituality and performance in organizations: A literature review. *Journal of Business Ethics, 94*(1), 89–106.

King, J. E, & Crowther, M. R. (2004). The measurement of religiosity and spirituality: Examples and issues from psychology. *Journal of Organizational Change Management*.

Koss, S. (2020, May 20). How leaders can protect employee wellbeing during COVID-19. *EY Global*. Retrieved from https://www.ey.com/en_gl/workforce/how-leaders-can-protect-employee-wellbeing-during-covid-19.

Lee, K.-F. (2021). A human blueprint for AI coexistence. In J. Von Braun, M. Archer, G. Reichberg, & M. S. Sorondo (Eds.), *Robotics, AI, and humanity: Science, ethics, and policy* (pp. 261–269). Springer.

McBrien, B. (2006). A concept analysis of spirituality. *British Journal of Nursing, 15*(1), 42–45.

McGhee, P., & Grant, P. (2017). The transcendent influence of spirituality on ethical action in organizations. *Journal of Management, Spirituality & Religion, 14*(2), 160–178.

Mitroff, I., & Denton, E. (1999). *A spiritual audit of corporate America: A hard look at spirituality, religion, and values in the workplace*. Wiley.

Muça, D. (2019, November 28). Elevated incidence of mental illness in the legal profession. *McGill Journal of Law and Health Blog*. Retrieved from https://mjlh.mcgill.ca/2019/11/28/elevated-incidence-of-mental-illness-in-the-legal-profession/.

Neal, J. (2018) Overview of workplace spirituality research. In *The Palgrave handbook of workplace spirituality and fulfillment* (1st edn., pp. 3–57). Palgrave Macmillan.

Nelson-Becker, H. B. (2003). Practical philosophies: Interpretations of religion and spirituality by African American and European American elders. *Journal of Religious Gerontology, 14*(2–3), 85–99.

O'Grady, P. (2004). The concept of spirituality. In M. Cogan (Eds.), *An introduction to Christian spirituality*. Priory Institute.

Oswick, C. (2009). Burgeoning workplace spirituality? A textual analysis of momentum and directions. *Journal of Management, Spirituality and Religion, 6*(1), 15–25.

Özkiziltan, D., & Hassel, A. (2021, March 3). Artificial intelligence at work: An overview of the literature. In *Governing Work in the Digital Age Project Working Paper Series 2021–01*. Retrieved from https://papers.ssrn.com/sol3/papers.cfm?abstract_id=3796746.

Patel, K. D., Pollock, J., Soni, V., & Doty, J. R. (2018). *The heartfulness way: Heart-based meditations for spiritual transformation*. New Harbinger Publications.

Port, D. R. (2018, May 11). Lawyers weigh in: Why is there a depression epidemic in the profession? *ABA Journal: Your Voice*. Retrieved from https://www.abajournal.com/voice/article/lawyers_weigh_in_why_is_there_a_depression_epidemic_in_the_profession.

Principe, W. (1983). Toward defining spirituality. *Studies in Religion/sciences Religieuses, 12*(2), 127–141.

Purser, R. (2019). *McMindfulness: How mindfulness became the new capitalist spirituality*. Watkins Media.

Purser, R. (2019, June 14). The mindfulness conspiracy. *The Guardian, 14*. Retrieved from https://www.theguardian.com/lifeandstyle/2019/jun/14/the-mindfulness-conspiracy-capitalist-spirituality.

Rathee, R., & Rajain, P. (2020). Workplace spirituality: A comparative study of various models. *Jindal Journal of Business Research, 9*(1), 27–40.

Ribeiro, M., Caldeira, S., Nunes, E., & Vieira, M. (2020). A commentary on spiritual leadership and workplace spirituality in nursing management. *Journal of Nursing Management*.

Rocha, R. G., & Pinheiro, P. G. (2020). Organizational spirituality: Concept and perspectives. *Journal of Business Ethics*, 1–12.

Rowson, J. (2014). *Spiritualise. Revitalising spirituality to address 21st century challenges*. RSA.
Rumbens, D., Richardson, C., Lee, C., Mizrahi, J., & Roche, C. (2019). *The path to prosperity: Why the future of work is human*. Deloitte.
Saad, M., & de Medeiros, R. (2021). Spirituality and healthcare—Common grounds for the secular and religious worlds and its clinical implications. *Religions, 12*(1), 22.
Schein, E. H. (1984). Coming to a new awareness of organizational culture. *Sloan Management Review, 25*(2), 3–16.
Schneiders, S. M. (1989). Spirituality in the academy. *Theological Studies, 50*(4), 676–697.
Sheldrake, P. (2012). *Spirituality: A very short introduction* (Vol. 336). Oxford University Press.
Shook, E., & Rodriguez, D. (2020, September 23). Care to do better: Building trust to leave your people and your business net better off. *Accenture*. Retrieved from https://www.accenture.com/us-en/insights/future-workforce/employee-potential-talent-management-strategy.
Taylor, C. (1992). *The ethics of authenticity*. Harvard University Press.
Trindade, A. A. C. (2014). *Judge Antônio A. Cançado Trindade. The construction of a humanized international law: A collection of individual opinions (1991–2013)*. Brill.
Walach, H. (2014). *Secular spirituality: The next step towards enlightenment*. Springer International Publishing.
Weathers, E., McCarthy, G., & Coffey, A. (2016). Concept analysis of spirituality: An evolutionary approach. *Nursing Forum, 51*(2), 79–96.
Weber, M. (1930) *The protestant ethic and the spirit of capitalism*. Translated by Talcott Parsons. George Allen & Unwin Ltd.
Withers, A., Zuniga, K., & Van Sell, S. (2017). Spirituality: Concept analysis. *International Journal of Nursing & Clinical Practices, 4*(1).
Woodhead, L., & Heelas, P. (2005). *The spiritual revolution: Why religion is giving way to spirituality*. JSTOR.

Chapter 2
From Contradiction to Oneness: an Indian Spiritual Worldview for Dealing with Paradoxes

Sadhna Sargam and Ashish Pandey

Abstract The study on paradox in the field of management and organization studies has grown rapidly over the last two to three decades. Paradox is understood as contradictory yet interrelated opposites that exist simultaneously and persist over time. For example, organizations have to meet the profit objectives as well as the socially valuable goals, collaborate and compete for technological advancement with the peers in industry, and promote the consumption at the same time need to be conscious of preserving the natural environment. Paradox perspective is used in various fields such as managing hybrid organizations, working through multiple institutional logics, promoting innovation, facilitating managerial cognition, and for developing practice theory. Interestingly, Indian wisdom embraces the paradoxical notion of life and reality since the fundamental notions of this tradition were laid down in prehistoric times. Indian wisdom is replete with many paradoxes such as simultaneously achieving the four broad aims of life that seem to be at stark contrast with each other—Dharma, Artha, Kama, and Mokhsa. This chapter is aimed at exploring the Indian Vedantic wisdom tradition to view paradoxes with ontological and epistemological perspective and attempt to decipher the insights relevant for organization and management scholarship.

Keywords Paradox · Culture · Vedanta · Buddhism · Yoga · Oneness

Introduction

The study on paradox is gaining much popularity in leadership and management literature owing to the surge of globalization which has put organizations at the forefront to deal with multiple stakeholders and their conflicting demands to survive the intense competition. Literature defines paradoxes as "contradiction that persist over time and

S. Sargam (✉) · A. Pandey
Shailesh J. Mehta School of Management, Indian Institute of Technology, Bombay, India
e-mail: prasadhna@gmail.com

A. Pandey
e-mail: ashish.pandey@iitb.ac.in

© Jindal Institute of Behavioral Sciences 2022

S. P. Sahni et al. (eds.), *Spirituality and Management*,
https://doi.org/10.1007/978-981-19-1025-8_2

defy resolution whereas dilemmas as contradiction that involves tradeoffs that can be resolved by weighting alternatives and choosing one option" (Smith, 2014: 1615). Paradox can be understood as a dilemma occurring in a specific context, whereas their persistence over time defines it as paradox. Paradoxes or dilemma may surface taking different nature such as strategic, moral, and general. Strategic paradox crops up when organization and its stakeholders demand leaders and managers to select a course of action out of two or more equally compelling courses (such as exploration or exploitation) for the competitive survival and growth of the organization. Moral dilemma and paradox surface when decision-makers have to choose between two courses of action, each having its own legitimacy and side of truth, for example, emphasizing on profit or social value creation; supporting well-being of organization or well-being of people in any particular situation, and many other such contradictions. Such equivocal nature of contradiction becomes a source of stress and anxiety under the context of plurality, change, and scarcity (Schad et al., 2016).

Need for Indigenous Research

Looking at such day-to-day mutually exclusive challenges that employees and managers face, literature offers valuable insights predominantly from the Western context. Although offering a glimpse of the role that different cultural contexts play in dealing with paradox, scholars limit their research to a few limited, the findings of which may not be applicable to the other cultures. To this end, Ven et al. (Ven et al., 2018) assert that errors occur when a phenomenon is studied in a particular context and the knowledge thus generated is extrapolated to represent a generic concept. A stronger argument for this assertion comes from Bhawuk (2008) who says that although surge in travel and technology has reduced the world to a global village, yet people across the globe behave differently in the same context. He further asserts that the same means of technology and travel can be used by people from different cultures to fulfill different purposes consistent with their long-held traditional values and belief systems.

Although a few, there have been attempts to show the contrasting difference between the cognition and behaviors of Chinese in particular and East Asians in general compared to Westerns in dealing with contradiction and dilemma. These differences in contradiction that have been fostered and transmitted through their religion and philosophy are termed as Naïve dialecticism (Spencer-Rodgers et al., 2012). Influenced by Taoism, Confucianism, and Buddhism, naïve dialecticism shapes the holistic thinking of East Asians and is governed by three principles: the principle of contradiction, the principle of change, and the principle of holism (Yama & Zakaria, 2019). The principle of contradiction asserts reality as complex not precise; the principle of change asserts nothing as static, and therefore reality itself is in flux of time; and lastly the principle of holism asserts all phenomena in the world as interconnected.

While the contemporary theory of cultures such as collectivism, context-sensitivity, power distance, and other such underscore the similarity in the way of organizing of Easterners compared to the Western people; these theories have been proposed from an etic approach to find out the broad categories of similarities in the countries with the same geography (Triandis, 1995). When taking an emic approach, much differentiation in the pattern of behavior surfaces (Sinha & Kumar, 2004); owing to the difference in their lay belief or folk wisdom originating from their religious and philosophical foundations (Bhawuk, 2008). A much-fitted example is seen during the recent crisis of COVID-19, wherein although situated in the same geography of Asia, different prominent countries such as China, India, and others in the region respond differently. When the most resourced countries in the world are internally grappling, how India, the second most populated country with relatively scarce resource, is managing to fight this crisis and extending a helping hand to the other nations is an excellent example of responding to paradox. India's approach of solidarity and generosity in combating this crisis by helping poor and developing nations with Covid vaccine supply under the "Covid Maitri" program is much applauded at the world stage.[1] This gesture is a reflection of its long-held folk wisdom of Vedanta which says, "Vasudhaiva Kutumbakam", which means "the entire earth is one family". The Indian worldview is influenced by the different spiritual philosophies which emphasizes "Unity, Oneness, and Wholeness in perception". Therefore, although there exists some similarity between the pattern of individual behavior, socializing, and decision making among different countries in Asia as already theoretically propounded by cultural scientists, there still exists some differences in their ontological values and belief system. This warrants a need to look into the Indian philosophies and wisdom tradition that can be helpful in developing a fresh perspective and identifying the ways of dealing with paradoxes of organizational and personal lives. Also, this study may offer deeper insights toward broadening the eastern perspective on "paradox management" from the Indian spiritual perspective, because of its prominence in the geography and growing importance at the world stage.

Paradox Management: The Salience of Worldview

While underscoring the importance of managing paradoxes, research asserts the root cause as individual's desire for consistency in their cognition which gets erupted while confronting paradoxes. Inconsistency in cognition causes psychological discomfort, stress, and aversion; and therefore as a natural tendency, people tend to avoid them (Schad et al., 2016). Supporting this, the theory of behavioral complexity suggests that the inconsistent, complex, or paradoxical psyche of the individual are at ease with dealing paradoxes or dilemmas present in the environment

---

[1] https://www.thehindu.com/news/international/african-caribbean-nations-support-india-at-wto-on-covid-19-vaccine-supplies/article33988670.ece.

(Denison et al., 1995). Studies on Indian culture and behavior unanimously support the contradictory value orientation and behavioral pattern that Indians display as a consequence of paradoxical psyche (Sinha & Kanungo, 1997). This is the reason, Indians in particular and Easterners in general have been found to be comfortable in dealing with contradictory nature of paradoxes, ambiguity, and uncertainty (Yama & Zakaria, 2019).

Paradoxes have been referred to as "double-edged sword" (Miron-Spektor et al., 2018; 4); a bitch to manage the contradiction (Smith, 2014: 1592); which tears the mind apart (Schad et al., 2016; 8). Pervading in organization at different levels of hierarchy and organizational unit, these contradictions challenge the thought process of leaders. This generates stress, frustration, anxiety, and many other defensive responses and therefore, must be coped with. Consistent with this, the literature on coping asserts that an encounter between the individual and environment may generate stress and require coping only if individual has any stake in the encounter (Lazarus & Folkman, 1984). The same problem or situation which may be perceived as threat or challenge to the well-being of someone may not be perceived same for other set of people. The answer to it lies in the individual goals, values, and belief system that shape their paradoxical mindset and cultural worldviews; which shape the collective values, assumptions and norms of socialization, and problem solving of people of a particular geographical area (Hofstede, 2011). While talking about the salience of worldview, Pandey et al. (2020) asserts that worldview works as a framework of meaning-making that informs our understanding of reality and it includes beliefs and assumption that may not be provable but provides ontological and epistemological foundations for other belief systems. Individual from the cultural worldview wherein paradox, dilemmas, and dualities are seen as inevitable and interdependent element of reality usually find themselves at ease without feeling any stress or anxiety while confronting these contradictions.

In his detailed work on culture and its products, Kroeber (1969) highlights uniqueness of Indian culture in the form of spirituality which dates back to over 2500 years. Since "geniuses come from the field what is most valued in a culture", Kroeber asserts that highest innovations in India come from the field of spirituality. Ronald (1988) supports it by asserting that spirituality is built into the Indian psyche and has been found to be the most internalized value in this culture (294). Since Indian psyche is spiritual as well as paradoxical, it can be inferred that the spirituality that is drawn from the old age wisdom traditions unique to Indian culture shapes the holistic mindset of its people to look at paradox as an integral part of life. Although a few literatures do talk about the role of culture in managing paradoxes, less scholarship talks about spirituality as an ontological worldview to address the unaddressed questions of management of paradoxes. While talking in detail about the contemporary influences and traditional wisdom that shape the complex psychology of Indians, Sinha and Kanungo (1997) refer to a vast empirical study supporting their viewpoint. For example, paternalistic leadership, the most prevalent and effective leadership style in the Indian culture, is higher on task orientation as well as consideration. Individuals display collectivist behavior to realize their individualistic goals and individualistic behavior to realize their collectivistic goals and a mix of these intentions and behavior as per the need of the situation. Indians have been found to be comfortable with ambiguity and uncertainty yet strive to avoid it via their conscious effort of taking a long-term perspective.

Indian culture has a long-documented history of over 4000 years (Sinha, 2014); and research suggests that "the older the culture, the more people are attached to their way of life or cultural worldview of looking at a problem and solving it" (Bhawuk, 2008; p. 308). Further, the worldview of individuals is influenced by the wisdom traditions, classical texts, history, and contemporary influences. While talking about the failure of the developmental projects in a certain part of the world due to the research starting with theoretical positions grounded in Western cultures and then extrapolating the knowledge to the rest of the world, Bhawuk (2010) emphasizes the role of folk wisdom and classical texts in enriching the indigenous psychology. This approach may offer more nuanced insight to look at the phenomena from a different ontological perspective and offer natural solutions to the difficult problems. Thus, knowledge so created by looking at paradox from Indian spiritual worldview may offer a vast managerial implication and help in building and bridging literature on paradox.

With the imperatives mentioned above to understand paradoxes from ontological perspective of Indian wisdom tradition, let us discuss about the conception of paradox, dilemma, and duality from two schools of thought: Vedanta and Buddhism. The section further discusses about how these school of thoughts further influences the overarching values and belief system that stresses the concept of "Oneness" in the emotion, cognition, and behavior of Indians.

Insights from Philosophy of Vedanta for Dealing with Paradox

How contradictions are the conception of mind that needs to be trained and cultivated to see them as interdependent aspects where the notion of one polar opposite is incomplete without the existence of other, drives from the different schools of thoughts of Indian philosophy. These schools of thought range from Buddhism, Jainism, Vedanta, and many others, but at the core of their philosophy, it is one's own mind. The Vedanta philosophy says "Aham Bhrahamasmi" or the supreme resides in me. Contrary to the other cultural thoughts where the supreme is separate from ordinary people, Indian wisdom tradition believes that the good, the bad, and the evil all emanate from me, my mind (an ordinary person). It is the mind that has to be controlled, trained, and cultivated to realize the deepest spiritual meaning in the ordinary chores of life. Looking from an etic approach, the four broad aims of Hinduism seem in stark contrast with each other. These aims are Dharma, Artha, Kaam, and Moksha (Pandey & Navare, 2018). Dharma is defined as righteousness or virtue; Artha refers to the achievement of social needs including material gains, social status; Kama is defined as the fulfillment of physiological and sensual needs; and Moksha as liberation from worldly bondage and union with the ultimate reality. Now the question arises "how can someone who is pursuing the material world and fulfilling sexual desires stick to dharma and achieve self-realization, since the goals seem contradictory, mutually exclusive, and defy logical and linear thinking of cause and effect?". According to the Vedantic philosophy, when every endeavor of the human being is underpinned by dharma or virtuousness, it leads to the well-being of self and others around us and the opposite of this leads to the suffering of all (Pandey et al., 2020). The virtue of Dharma talks about the mindfulness, morality and ethics in one's worldly affairs. An appropriate example to understand this notion can be drawn from any organization in today's world. When an individual or any entity gets lured for extra profit, it compromises the well-being of all the stakeholders which causes their suffering and further recursively leads to the suffering of individual/entity either due to the withdrawal of the stakeholders from the relationship or their extinction as a consequence of improper attention given. Sanlu Group Co. is a befitting example of the extinction (bankruptcy) of an organization which lured for profit by contaminating the baby milk powder with melamine a chemical (Maak et al., 2016). With the sheer intention to increase the profit of the company, the leaders of the company risked the health and life of three lakhs babies, out of which four died and fifty-four thousand required medical treatment. The scandal surfaced in 2008 and led to the customers and other stakeholder activism which further resulted in company's bankruptcy.[2] This example is an illustration of the leader's decision to prioritize economic value at the cost of social value (Dharma) which led to the suffering of self and all associated with the self.

A further question arises "how one ensures that their actions are consistently virtuous or underpinned by Dharma?". The answer to this can be found in the philosophy of NisKam Karma or Karma Yoga, which says that one should look at the paradoxical situation (or work) with the purpose of solving it without considering the end result or outcome. When no attachment is associated with the outcomes such as loss, reward, promotion, the mind is anchored in the process of solving the problem; the result has to be the right decision. This is quite similar to what Aristotle (1934) asserts as practical rationality, where the aim of any problem resolution or decision making is to ensure how people associated with the operations or decision making grows as a human being (Melé, 2010). Here the difference between the philosophy of Karma Yoga and Aristotle lies in the frame of mind. The former stresses an individual to detach oneself from self-serving goals, biasness, agentic behavior, or desire of a particular outcome, which will automatically lead to the overall well-being. The latter reminds individual to put a conscious effort into the process with a notion to achieve the well-being of all. When individuals work with a goal in mind (achievement of well-being of all), it may be prone to biasness. Now the question still persists as to "how one can perform an action without being concerned about the outcome?". The answer lies in constant self-reflection, contemplation, and cultivation of mind (Chinmayananda, 2018). For ages, Indian soil has been a breeding ground for contemplative and meditative practices which is continuously under the scrutiny of the Western method of examination (Hagelin et al., 1998; Kabat-Zinn,

[2] http://www.china.org.cn/china/news/2009-02/12/content_17268441.htm.

2003; Travis et al., 2009; Wallace & Shapiro, 2014). Constant learning and introspection of the practicality of those learning, transcendental, and mindfulness mediations are some of the ways which help in the cultivation of the mind. A cultivated mind thus becomes Sthitha Pragya, which is constantly detached from the outcome of one's action or decision making and perceives objects or phenomena with a mind in a constant state of calm, neither rejoicing over success nor lamenting over failure (Bhawuk, 2008). Looking at the contradictory nature of phenomena with SamDrishti or with constant perception, one doesn't get threatened by the challenges of the situation rather perceives the whole phenomena as incomplete or shallow, if looked at through tunnel vision. This warrants the perceiver to look at it from both the ends to appreciate and justify the contradiction and its co-occurrence as a requisite to amplify the beauty of phenomena. Looking at problem with such a perception allows individual to find a solution in tandem with the time, place, and the ecology in which it has occurred. According to the literature, even though the decision is "either/or", there is a logic or justification to it rather than having a feeling of frustration, guilt, or other emotion; which generally is the case reported in the literature while solving the paradox (Smith, 2014).

Ishavasya Upanishad, one of the most revered Hindu scripture, beautifully translated by Swami Chinmayananda emphasizes the beauty of wholeness in perception. The gist of this Upanishad is how this wholeness reaches the eternal truth hidden in the outer world full of conflicting truths, the plurality of thoughts, ideas, and opinions. The lessons of this scripture may provide a direction to the struggle of today's scholars in the field of paradox to reach the reality (Schad et al., 2016). One of the verses of the Upanishad beautifully captures the agitation that the present world feels while confronting perplexing phenomena and thus with this agitated mind loses sight of the truth. The verse is as follows:

"Om Poornamadah Poornamidam Poornnaat-Poornam-udachyate
Poo-rnnasya Poornamadaya Poornam-eva-avashissyate ||
Om Shaantih Shaantih Shaantih ||".

It says, Om (the divine within all of us) that is whole, this is whole; from the whole the whole becomes manifest. From the whole when the whole is negated, what remains is again a whole (p-70). If this verse is to be understood from the Western perceptual lens, then it would sound like a paradox as to when a whole which is reduced from a whole, still remains a whole rather than becoming a zero. This is consistent with the conclusion drawn by the scholars following Western rule-based or linear thinking in which Westerners are comfortable with "if p" then "q" (Yama & Zakaria, 2019) or "if X" then "not X" (Bhawuk, 2011). Contrary to this, the verse asks individuals to discover or reach what is unseen by transcending the equipment of mind and intellect and to purify the perception which is the key to finding the eternal truth. A purified perception is requisite to penetrate through the delusion of plurality, perceived contradiction, and inconsistency which seems whole and borrows its reality from the truth which is eternal and whole in itself. Thus, a mind and intellect with ability to discriminate find the plurality of worldview and contradiction getting subsumed in the pervading truth which is eternal and whole in itself (p-71). This suggests the oneness of the reality wherein different pluralities draw their identity from the truth itself. The latter submerges into the truth or reality, if contemplated properly. Therefore, great seers (rsi) of old revered as the scientists of life emphasizes more on the experiencer to contemplate on the experiencing rather than the experienced; which is contrary to what is generally done by today's scientists who explore the truth from the object or experienced itself. This suggests the role of a calm, composed, and constant mind in reaching to the reality of achieving "One and Whole" in itself.

Vedanta emphasizes that the subject or experiencer of the outer world is torn apart due to the desires and demands of different personalities working within individuals continuously. The physical personality has a different desire than the mental personality, which again has a different desire from an intellectual personality. The spiritual personality may not be satisfied with the satiation of the desires of the rest of the personality. Therefore, when all these personalities get subsumed within one and work in tandem as a whole, only then the ultimate desire of achieving a peaceful mind and a heart full of joy is bestowed upon all the different personalities working within. Such a subject has a greater ability to discriminate and penetrate through the superimposition of different layers of plurality. Supporting which philosophy of Jnana Yoga asks people to unleash the potential of vision to create knowledge that is free from all falsification (Pandey & Navare, 2018).

Another perspective, the root of which is embedded in Vedanta, known as philosophy of integral humanism (Upadhyaya, 1965) looks at contradiction as unnecessary objectification of mind. This philosophy refers to the human being as a microcosmos who hold its existence by borrowing elements from the macrocosmos ranging from the earth, water, fire, air, and sky (panchtatva). Since self is made up of everything that exists in the environment, it cannot be separated from it. So, the same soul or "Atman" resides in all the animate and inanimate objects including humans. This shapes the holistic worldview of individuals wherein they consider everything around them as a part of their self and inseparable whether it is nature, other people, community, society, or planet. Therefore, every endeavor of the individual strives toward living in harmony with the environment and to adapt themselves with the flux of time and place or surrounding to legitimate its existence. Since the individual retains the same soul as members of the society and planet, therefore there is no conflict in their interest, they are interdependent and are mutually complementary. This consciousness of "Oneness or Ekatma" is termed as philosophy of integral humanism (Upadhyaya, 1965) or the theory of Oneness, which guides the emotion, cognition, and behavior of Indians in all pursuits of their life. In support of this, Sinha and Kanungo (1997) believe that Indians generally tend to have an external or secondary locus of control to change themselves with the ever-changing flux of time and to adapt to the environment (95). Contrary to this, the predominant approach in the west holds a Cartesian worldview where they consider themselves separate from the outer world or nature (Bhawuk, 2011). Their context-free thinking allows them to develop a belief that they can control, predict, or change the environment for the desired outcome (Rotter, 1966). This is well reflected in their cognition, emotion, and agentic behavior. They consider their surroundings as quite stable, predictable, which can be mastered with a positivist paradigm, and by measuring every variable of interest by quantifying it.

Literature reports the suffering that leaders and managers go through in their sustained endeavor to control and predict the situation which changes seamlessly with the time. These can be explained by the theory of coping, which originates from ego psychology (Folkman & Moskowitz, 2000; 647). When the ego or the "I" within the self encounters the multiple conflicting truth and the inherent contradictions and ambiguity, the characteristics of such a situation challenges their positivist worldview and threatens their well-being. Pressurized by the organizational demand to make effective decisions (to legitimize and justify the power and positions they hold), the consequence or the outcome of which is not instantly visible induces a feeling of helplessness. This feeling of helplessness to fix the situation or improvise it immediately if a wrong decision has been taken often causes frustration, agitation, and other such sufferings (Smith, 2014). Probably, these behavioral changes caught the attention of the scholars and a surge in the study on paradox, dilemma, and contradictions. With respect to this, the philosophy of Vedanta offers much relief to humankind. It suggests that the "mastery over the situations of life, without mastery of mind (perception), would be a vain dream" (Chinmayananda, 2018; 44). As mentioned earlier, mastery of mind can be learned through the art of constant introspection, contemplation, and meditation. A trained mind frees itself from all the follies vicariously generated through identification with mind, body, and intellect and diminishes the concept of ego or self. The thoughts which are generated now are least agitating and leads one to a maximum state of happiness and harmony. With the mind so calm, composed, and detached, one gets the ability to reason well the dilemmas or paradoxes of life (Ardelt, 2003).

As mentioned earlier, the philosophy of integral humanism asserts that when the person considers himself/herself an integral and inseparable part of the universe, it guides his/her moral to offer Yogakshem or pious offering. He/she feels an obligation to her/his existence from the environment. Vedanta further elucidates that any Yogakshem or offering has to be given from the wealth created through the right means or ethical ways. This has an important lesson for any organization and its leader in today's world. It offers an outlook to consider oneself (as microsystems) or as a part of the larger universe, which is a macrosystem. So there is no conflict in interest, and every interest is mutually complementary (Upadhyaya, 1965; 13). The endeavor thus taken with a perception of "Oneness" while performing one's obligation toward every stakeholder eliminates the perception of contradiction and induces a feeling that every interest served leads to self-sustenance. This has been beautifully exemplified by Cappelli et al. (2010) in their inductive research "The India way: Lessons for The U.S.". In this research with the primary interview data of 105 Indian leaders and secondary data on US leaders, they explain the process through which Indian organizations ensure sustainability while emphasizing the overarching values of "obligation toward community" (p-21). They further give example of Tata Group Companies, and how their value of integrity in business operations and compassion toward employees, supply chain partners, community and society at large eliminate business constraints and ensures self-sustainability of organization. Two-thirds of its profit goes to the charitable foundation, which then finds its way back to the society. Purpose-driven stakeholders in turn contribute toward the profit making directly (such as employees and other government bodies by facilitating a faster operation of providing clearances, licenses) and indirectly by showering their love and affection toward the company.

Insights from Philosophy of Buddhism for Dealing with Paradox

In organizations, scholars assert paradox as a situation of tug of war that pulls employees or leaders in different directions internally and externally. It occurs due to multiple commitments to different strategic goals, legitimacy challenges of stakeholders, and other structural inertia. This tug of war teases the mind apart due to the incompetency of rational linear logic to provide a solution which further obscures the situation and enhances ambiguity and uncertainty (Jay, 2013). In support of this, Sternberg (1998) observes that solving a paradox or dilemma requires wisdom or wise reasoning. Now the question persists that a mind which gets chaotic and unstable at the very conception of the paradoxical situation, as to how will it reason out well? In her introductory lessons on mindfulness, monk Nyanaponika Thera (1962) talks in great detail about the emphasis of Buddhist philosophy on requisite and the process of cultivation of the mind. The philosophy of Buddhism emphasizes that any object of analysis has to be cleansed first from the defilements, falsifying impurities, wrong associations, prejudices, and wishful thinking. The attitude of bare and receptive attention on the object of perception without any mental commentary on it frees the object from all the above-mentioned impurities and allows it to speak for oneself. Prolonged attentional qualities of mindfulness allow individual to focus on phenomena or problem for a prolonged period rather than announcing a rash verdict. It results in allowing the object to offer more newer insight which would not have been possible earlier due to the chaotic or biased mind. Mindfulness allows greater clarity of the central object and its association with others in the network or environment while first attending to each one separately and later attending to its interconnectedness. This association is free from any bias and provides a sound background to arrive at any judgment or decision making.

Although Buddhism talks about right mindfulness to reduce the suffering of the human being in the form of stress, depression, frustration, and other similar emotions. It also insists that the role of human heartedness is equally important. A sound mind is a reliable object for sound reasoning. But a heart devoid of compassion, possessive toward self-goals, extremely materialistic will ultimately lead to suffering in the form of body killing invention and mind killing distraction toward the end. Therefore, one must consider an element of human connect, social well-being, compassion which all converge into spirituality while deciding the goals of life or making any decision. When the mind is trained to reason well and the heart is trained to find the cosmic connectedness, any paradox, dilemma or duality ceases to exist. This philosophy of

Buddhism is termed as the middle path to avoid the extreme of any goal for humanity to sustain, thrive, and flourish for long.

Empirical studies on the different form of Buddhist meditation practices ranging from Vipassana, Mindfulness-Based Stress Reduction (MBSR), Mindfulness-Based Cognitive Therapy (MBCT) to others consistently support the result that higher mindfulness level increases one's ability of decentering or reperceiving (Shapiro et al., 2006). Decentering or reperceiving is defined as a meta-mechanism that allows individual to disidentify from the contents of consciousness (Pearson et al., 2015) and grants greater ability and agency to attend to the ongoing thoughts and emotions with greater objectivity and clarity without being judgmental or evaluative of it (Good et al., 2016). Extensive laboratory research on insight meditation (Vipassana meditation) or with other forms of Buddhist meditation finds this mechanism as a strong reason for the people to overcome formed or afflictive association, prejudices or biasness in their thinking or reasoning process (Emavardhana & Tori, 1997; Wallace & Shapiro, 2014). Meditation ranging from few to thousands of hours increases the attentional quality of individual (stability, control, and efficiency) which helps to cast wider attention to the object at hand and its environment for a longer time without any distraction, and effectively switch attention from inappropriate stimuli to the relevant one (Good et al., 2016). This allows the problem to speak for oneself for a longer time and offer more relevant cues rather than solving it with a preconceived notion and prior experience of encountering a similar situation. Extensive research in organization and among the clinical patients in the experiment and the control group supports the evidence that mindfulness increases the working memory which increases one's cognitive ability to hold a storehouse of information, differentiate, and finally, integrate it to conceive the holistic perspective on the problem at hand (Good et al., 2016; Teasdale et al., 2002). Consistent with this, when the situations are novel, difficult to be resolved by customary interpretation and habitual problem solving strategies, mindfulness training improves the ability to resolve it by increasing fluid intelligence (Ostafin & Kassman, 2012); which is required in leadership decision making. Therefore, the person with the perception thus purified (through decentering) and having a cognitive ability to understand the object and its complex relationship with the environment in a detailed way is now prepared to resolve any complexity and paradoxical situation at hand.

Theory of behavioral complexity (Denison et al., 1995) asserts that individual must have cognitive complexity as the necessary condition and behavioral complexity as sufficient condition to deal with any paradox existing in his environment. Consistent with this empirical research on mindfulness unanimously support the notion that mindfulness increases one's behavioral flexibility (complexity) through various mechanisms (Shapiro et al. 2006). Whereas in his research, Baron et al. (2018) experimentally prove the notion that mindfulness increases one's behavioral complexity (repertoire) to respond to the complex environment and conflicting demands.

Mindfulness works as a savior even when the situations seem out of control or the outcome of the decision taken results in odd or induces suffering such as stress and anxiety (and depression) by reducing the defense mechanism and increasing the greater acceptance and tolerance of it (Teasdale et al., 2002). This change in perspective brought by decentering increases one's ability to look at the previously stressful event with greater distance without identifying with it. Mindfulness training increases the heart quality such as compassion for self and others and reduces egocentric bias. This is an important mechanism to arrive at moral reasoning (Pandey et al., 2018); and therefore retain the ability to address much of the paradoxical dilemma at workplace such as social value vs economic value, layoff vs organizational survival, authoritative vs participative leadership style. The introduction of mindfulness practices to the Western world in the late 1970s offered much relief to their stressed and depressed population (Teasdale et al., 2002), and looking at its beneficial outcome, it caught the attention of some of the best employers of the world later on. Now the experimental research on mindfulness at workplace in management research is growing exponentially. It offers a vast literature on the mechanism through which it facilitates individual, interpersonal, and organizational functioning.

Discussion

Rapid globalization has resulted in intense competition, and leaders and managers often find themselves torn apart in choosing one right solution from the multiple strategies in constant conflict. These strategic paradoxes defy resolution and create a vicious cycle resurfacing demand for others if opted either-or solution (Smith, 2014, 1594). Looking at these challenges, research draws scholar's attention to delve deeper into these phenomena to offer more insight to manage these contradictions. From conducting interviews of Western leaders to synthesizing literature that is predominantly influenced by Western theory may offer little insight to understand these phenomena holistically. The reason behind this is attributed to their Cartesian worldview, internal locus of control to master the situation, linear thinking process and temperament to quantify every variable of interest. Contrary to this, the philosophy of integral humanism or the theory of "Oneness (or Ekatma)" propounded in Vedanta acts as a guiding force to identify complexity, dilemma, and paradox as inevitable, interdependent, and complementary in nature. Since the ordinary man may lose the sight of Oneness (dues to his/her agitated and chaotic mind) which is at the heart of resolving all the paradoxes, the more cultivated the mind is, the brighter will be the beams of consciousness to underneath the superimpositions of plurality in perception. With the mind so cultivated, the plurality and conflict in the perception get subsumed to unearth the real truth which is non-dual and pervades the world. With the awareness of Oneness or *Ekatma* or existence of one soul in all the human being and environment, a noble value of obligation toward each and every animate and inanimate object in the environment gets ensued. This consciousness of obligation toward each members of society and planet is a reason why most of the Indian organizations have been found to chasing social responsibility as the purpose of their organization (Cappelli et al., 2010).

Patanjali Ayurveda Limited is a living example of how the obligation toward the well-being of all ensued through the sense of oneness enabled its leaders to seize the market opportunity which seemed paradoxical at surface. By reinvigorating and reenergizing the deeply held Vedantic spiritual values in people and offering product and services that resonates with the cultural values and belief system of Indians, Patanjali has become a threat to the top most player of FMCG sector in India (Gnanakumar, 2020). This company innovated products in the existing segments of market where there is fierce competition. Offering products which are Ayurvedic and medicinal in nature at reasonable price and resonate with long-held wisdom tradition of India seemed to be conflicting in nature, and this is the reason the innovative products of this company disrupted the existing market and forced the world leaders re-evaluate their strategy.[3] Adopting innovation in sync with the long-held traditions of the customer ensured the short-term (exploitation) as well as long-term sustainability of Patanjali. The source of wealth creation is purely underpinned by Dharma/noble values of increasing the well-being of people; and the major part of its wealth goes back to the society through philanthropic activities (Ann Alexander et al., 2020).

Supporting the philosophy of Vedanta which put much emphasis on the cultivation of mind, the philosophy of Buddhism asserts that the one-side development of mind has led the world to man killing innovation and the mind killing the distraction. Therefore, spirituality ensures the overall development of mind by granting it the ability to avoid the extremes and follow the middle path on the safe foundation of human heartedness. This suggests a requisite to look at the phenomena of paradox, dilemma, and dualities from a spiritual paradigm. Materialistic paradigm may not grant a mind which is so discernible to unravel the ultimate reality within the conflicting yet legitimate truth.

Conclusion

We have discussed in great detail how the spiritual worldview of Indians shapes their collective values and belief systems to respond to the situation in a consistently complex way. Their ability to understand and reconcile the conflicting truth hidden behind contradiction and paradox is underpinned by the notion of "Oneness". With this notion of Ekatma/Oneness, they strive to attain the unattainable, the four broad aims of life (Dharma, Artha, Kama, and Moksha). No goal or situation in the humanity and mankind would be as conflicting and perplexing as achieving these four broad aims simultaneously which most of the Indians strive for. Probably, these constitute one of the reasons behind their paradoxical behavior. Therefore, the Indian spiritual worldview holds the capacity to illuminate the mind of today's leaders/ managers and steer their path toward reconciling what they term as paradox.

Organizations and their leaders must offer the avenues to their managers and employees for constant learning (while dealing with different situations) with introspection along with the contemplative practices to attain a mind which is free from

---

[3] https://m.economictimes.com/industry/cons-products/fmcg/patanjali-eats-into-colgate-hul-share-in-oral-care-space/articleshow/69258136.cms.

distraction, chaos, and defilements generated by his/her day-to-day engagement in worldly affairs. Training in mindfulness and transcendental mediations proves to be effective in offering a calm and composed mind which retains discriminative ability to reach the ultimate reality of Oneness/Ekatma in every conflicting interest. Organizations must offer employees time and platform for their spiritual regeneration and upliftment which induces noble values to realize the cosmic connectedness and offers easy solutions to the difficult problems. With mind having such a discriminative ability and heart full of compassion, most of the paradoxes are resolved by attaining a dynamic harmony among the different element of interest.

References

Ann Alexander, A., Jha, S., & Pandey, A. (2020). Understanding how hybrid organisations tackle social challenges: An institutional logics approach. *South Asian Journal of Business Studies, 9*(2), 193–213. https://doi.org/10.1108/SAJBS-02-2019-0031

Ardelt, M. (2003). Article research on aging ardelt/empirical assessment empirical assessment of a three-dimensional wisdom scale *25*(3). https://doi.org/10.1177/0164027503251764

Baron, L., Rouleau, V., Grégoire, S., & Baron, C. (2018). Mindfulness and leadership flexibility. *Journal of Management Development, 37*(2), 165–177. https://doi.org/10.1108/JMD-06-2017-0213

Bhawuk, D. P. S. (2011). Spirituality and Indian psychology: lessons from the Bhagavad-Gita. *Spirituality and Indian Psychology* https://doi.org/10.1007/978-1-4419-8110-3

Bhawuk, D. P. S. (2008). Globalization and indigenous cultures: Homogenization or differentiation? *International Journal of Intercultural Relations, 32*(4), 305–317. https://doi.org/10.1016/j.ijintrel.2008.06.002

Bhawuk, D. P. S. (2010). Methodology for building psychological models from scriptures: Contributions of Indian psychology to indigenous and universal psychologies. *Psychology and Developing Societies, 22*(1), 49–93. https://doi.org/10.1177/097133360902200103

Cappelli, P., Singh, H., Singh, J., & Useem, M. (2010). The India way: Lessons for the U.S. *Academy of Management Perspectives, 24*(2). https://doi.org/10.5465/AMP.2010.51827771

Chinmayananda, S. (2018). Isavasya Upanisad/God in and as everything. *Central Chinmaya Mission Trust*, ISBN: 978-81-7597-663-4.

Denison, D. R., Hooijberg, R., & Quinn, R. E. (1995). Paradox and performance: Toward a theory of behavioral complexity in managerial leadership. *Organization Science, 6*(5), 524–540. https://doi.org/10.1287/orsc.6.5.524

Emavardhana, T., & Tori, C. D. (1997). Changes in self-concept, ego defense mechanisms, and religiosity following seven-day Vipassana meditation retreats. *Journal for the Scientific Study of Religion, 36*(2), 194. https://doi.org/10.2307/1387552

Folkman, S., & Moskowitz, J. T. (2000). Positive affect and the other side of coping *55*(6), 647–654.https://doi.org/10.1037//0003-066X.55.6.647

Gnanakumar, B. (2020). Reinforcement of brands of faith with the paradox of cultural divergence in Indian perspective. *European Business Review, 32*(3), 513–530. https://doi.org/10.1108/EBR-03-2019-0049

Good, D. J., Lyddy, C. J., Glomb, T. M., Bono, J. E., Brown, K. W., Duffy, M. K., Baer, R. A., Brewer, J. A., & Lazar, S. W. (2016). Contemplating mindfulness at work: An integrative review. *Journal of Management, 42*(1), 114–142. https://doi.org/10.1177/0149206315617003

Hagelin, J. S., Rainforth, M. V, Orme-johnson, D. W., Cavanaugh, K. L., Alexander, C. N., Shatkin, S. F., Davies, J. L., Hughes, A. O., & Ross, E. (1998). Effects of group practice of the transcendental meditation program on preventing violent crime in washington , D.C .: Results of the

national demonstration project, June–July 1993 The United States has higher violent crime rates than all western Euro, pp. 153–201.
Hofstede, G. (2011). Dimensionalizing cultures: The hofstede model in context. *Online Readings in Psychology and Culture, 2*(1), 1–26. https://doi.org/10.9707/2307-0919.1014
Jay, J. (2013). Navigating paradox as a mechanism of change and innovation in hybrid organizations. *Academy of Management Journal, 56*(1), 137–159
Kabat-Zinn, J. (2003). Mindfulness-based interventions in context: Past, present, and future. In *Clinical Psychology: Science and Practice* (Vol. 10, Issue 2, pp. 144–156). https://doi.org/10.1093/clipsy/bpg016
Kroeber, A. L. (1969). Configurations of culture growth. Univ of California Press.
Lazarus, R.S., & Folkman, S. (1984). Stress appraisal and coping. In *感染症誌* (Vol. 91).
Maak, T., Pless, N. M., & Voegtlin, C. (2016). Business statesman or shareholder advocate? CEO responsible leadership styles and the micro-foundations of political CSR. *Journal of Management Studies, 53*(3), 463–493. https://doi.org/10.1111/joms.12195
Melé, D. (2010). Practical wisdom in managerial decision making. *Journal of Management Development, 29*(7), 637–645. https://doi.org/10.1108/02621711011059068
Miron-Spektor, E., Ingram, A., Keller, J., Smith, W. K., & Lewis, M. W. (2018). Microfoundations of organizational paradox: The problem is how we think about the problem. *Academy of Management Journal, 61*(1), 26–45. https://doi.org/10.5465/amj.2016.0594
Nyanaponika, T. (1962). The heart of Buddhist meditation. In *San Francsico: Weiser*.
Ostafin, B. D., & Kassman, K. T. (2012). Stepping out of history: Mindfulness improves insight problem solving. *Consciousness and Cognition, 21*(2), 1031–1036. https://doi.org/10.1016/j.concog.2012.02.014
Pandey, A., Chandwani, R., & Navare, A. (2018). How can mindfulness enhance moral reasoning? An examination using business school students. *Business Ethics, 27*(1), 56–71. https://doi.org/10.1111/beer.12171
Pandey, A., & Navare, A. V. (2018). Paths of Yoga: Perspective for workplace spirituality. *The Palgrave Handbook of Workplace Spirituality and Fulfillment, 1–2*, 101–126. https://doi.org/10.1007/978-3-319-62163-0_4
Pearson, M. R., Brown, D. B., Bravo, A. J., & Witkiewitz, K. (2015). Staying in the moment and finding purpose: The associations of trait mindfulness, decentering, and purpose in life with depressive symptoms, anxiety symptoms, and alcohol-related problems. *Mindfulness, 6*(3), 645–653. https://doi.org/10.1007/s12671-014-0300-8
Rotter, J. B. (1966). Generalize D Expectancie S for Interna L Versus. *Malaysian Journal of Nutrition, 80*(1). https://doi.org/10.1037/h0092976
Schad, J., Lewis, M. W., Raisch, S., & Smith, W. K. (2016). Paradox research in management science: Looking back to move forward. *Academy of Management Annals, 10*(1), 5–64. https://doi.org/10.1080/19416520.2016.1162422
Shapiro, S. L., Carlson, L. E., Astin, J. A., & Freedman, B. (2006). Mechanisms of Mindfulness. *Journal of Clinical Psychology, 66*(4), 430–441. https://doi.org/10.1002/jclp
Sinha, J. B. P. (2014). Psycho-social analysis of the Indian mindset. *Psycho-Social Analysis of the Indian Mindset*. https://doi.org/10.1007/978-81-322-1804-3
Sinha, J. B. P., & Kanungo, R. N. (1997). Context sensitivity and balancing in Indian organizational behaviour. *International Journal of Psychology, 32*(2), 93–105. https://doi.org/10.1080/002075997400890
Sinha, J. B. P., & Kumar, R. (2004). Methodology for understanding Indian culture. *Copenhagen Journal of Asian Studies, 19*, 89–104. https://doi.org/10.22439/cjas.v19i0.27
Smith, W. K. (2014). Dynamic decision making: A model of senior leaders managing strategic paradoxes. *Academy of Management Journal, 57*(6), 1592–1623. https://www.jstor.org/stable/43589323
Spencer-Rodgers, J., Williams, M. J., & Peng, K. (2012). Culturally based lay beliefs as a tool for understanding intergroup and intercultural relations. *International Journal of Intercultural Relations, 36*(2), 169–178. https://doi.org/10.1016/j.ijintrel.2012.01.002

Sternberg, R. J. (1998). A Balance Theory of Wisdom to Understanding Wisdom, *4*, 347–365

Teasdale, J. D., Moore, R. G., Hayhurst, H., Pope, M., Williams, S., & Segal, Z. V. (2002). Metacognitive awareness and prevention of relapse in depression: Empirical evidence. *Journal of Consulting and Clinical Psychology, 70*(2), 275–287. https://doi.org/10.1037/0022-006X.70.2.275

Travis, F., Haaga, D. A. F., Hagelin, J., Tanner, M., Nidich, S., Gaylord-King, C., Grosswald, S., Rainforth, M., & Schneider, R. H. (2009). Effects of transcendental meditation practice on brain functioning and stress reactivity in college students. *International Journal of Psychophysiology, 71*(2), 170–176. https://doi.org/10.1016/j.ijpsycho.2008.09.007

Triandis, H. C. (1995). A theoretical framework for the study of diversity.

Upadhyaya, D. (1965). Integral Humanism20.pdf.

Ven, A. H. De, V., Meyer, A. D., & Jing, R. (2018). Opportunities and Challenges of Engaged Indigenous Scholarship, 1–14. https://doi.org/10.1017/mor.2018.28

Wallace, B. A., & Shapiro, S. L. (2014). Mental balance and well-being: Building bridges between buddhism and western psychology. https://doi.org/10.1037/0003-066X.61.7.690

Yama, H., & Zakaria, N. (2019). Explanations for cultural differences in thinking: Easterners' dialectical thinking and Westerners' linear thinking. *Journal of Cognitive Psychology, 31*(4), 487–506. https://doi.org/10.1080/20445911.2019.1626862

Chapter 3
The Buddha and Management: His Own Hands-On Experience

Koenraad Elst

Abstract Gautama the Buddha cannot be understood without being aware of his situation in life. The son of a very prestigious nation's President-for-life and former member of its Senate, he remained a much-sought-after political adviser to rulers till his death in high age, even more so because as the founding head of a monastic order, he had no stake anymore in the ongoing political intrigues and struggles. Political management was not his vocation, but we do get a glimpse of his ideals for public life from these forays into actual politics. Toward the end of his life, a minister of the Magadha kingdom sought the Buddha's help in his plans of conquest, viz an analysis of a state's secret for invincibility. On that occasion, the Buddha explained his "7 rules for non-decline," given to and applied by, both his order and the Vrjji republic, the one Magadha sought to conquer. These amounted to national consensus and respecting venerable persons and traditions. He also applied it to the organization that became his legacy to mankind: his monastic order. It is there we see a creation with an enormous staying power, demonstrating the Buddha's management skill.

Keywords Buddha · Consensus · Conservative · Ethical precepts · Subversion

Background Situation

Siddhartha Gautama was born around 500 (the year remains vague, a scholarly consensus around it has not been reached) as the son of President-for-life of the *Śākya* republic. This was situated in what is now the central border area between Bihar and Nepal. The delivery took place in the now Nepali village of Lumbini, where his mother was on the way to her parental home; but he grew up on the Indian side in Kapilavastu. For what it is worth, tradition explained this as the location given by the hermit Kapila (of *Sāṁkhya* fame) as habitat (*vastu*) to the refugee children of the patriarch Manu, the ancestors of the *Śākya* tribe.

K. Elst (✉)
KU Leuven, Leuven, Belgium
e-mail: koenraad.elst@gmail.com

© Jindal Institute of Behavioral Sciences 2022

S. P. Sahni et al. (eds.), *Spirituality and Management*,
https://doi.org/10.1007/978-981-19-1025-8_3

To maintain their prestigious bloodline, they practiced a strict endogamy with cousin marriage. This stood out among the local population because the Brahminical tradition imposed "forbidden degrees of consanguinity" and forbade cousin marriages. That is why some scholars, e.g., Michael Witzel and Jayarava Attwood, theorize that they may have been an immigrant tribe from Greater Iran, where cousin marriages were solemnized (with preservation of a prestigious bloodline only a made-up story). To this end, Śākya is explained as a variation on Śāka, "Scythian, an Iranian tribe. This would explain why among Biharis, Buddha stood out as tall and fair-skinned.

Siddhārtha Gautama's *Sitz im Leben* was a situation of privilege. Strictly speaking, his father was not a king, for the Śākya state was a republic (*gaṇarājya*). He was called a *rājā*, "ruler," but that term, unlike "king," does not necessarily mean a hereditary ruler. Consultation in assembly with an elective kingship (i.e., President-for-life) was an established practice in Indian republics. Everybody could attend, but only *Kṣatriya*s took part in the decision making, so it was an aristocratic republic. This was not a novelty; it must have been a Proto-Indo-European institution also in evidence outside India. The Athenian democracy equally limited participation in decision making to male citizens who had served as soldiers, no women or foreigners or slaves allowed. A distant example of elective rulership was the Holy Roman Empire, where the seven electors (*Kurfürsten*) chose an emperor from among themselves.

Usually described as a "prince," Siddhārtha was not automatically entitled to inherit the throne, though he certainly belonged to the upper class. His political savvy and character, together with his connections, would normally have made him the successor, if he had chosen so. He had a princely upbringing and was an elitist (*ārya*) par excellence. From the age of twenty, he served as a senator in the *Śākya* tribe's assembly. Though he broke with his administrator's vocation at 29 and became a spiritual teacher after his *Nirvāṇa* at 35, the kings and magnates from Northeastern India asked him for his advice on political and family matters until his death at 80.

Having grown up in this system, the *Śākya* republic, the Buddha upheld this model throughout his life, also in organizing his monastic *Saṅgha.* We should not view this as a modern democracy. Among the factors of inequality was seniority, exclusion of serfs and debtors, and once he had reluctantly agreed to allow nuns in his order, a strict subordination of even the senior most nun to even the simplest monk. Still, among the great spiritual leaders, he stood out as rather democratic.

Social Vision

In modern Western and Westernized-Indian sources, particularly in BR Ambedkar's Neo-Buddhism, it is routinely claimed that the Buddha was an egalitarian social revolutionary who rejected caste along with the Vedas. But if we turn to the primary sources, we find little evidence to substantiate this beatific vision.

As a spiritual leader, he totally focused on liberation, in the footsteps of the renunciate, whom he had seen during his fabled "four meetings" at age 29. This excluded any serious investment in social reform. People who say or write that the Buddha was also a social reformer willing to burden himself with enmity from the ruling class, only show that they do not take Buddhist spirituality seriously. Changing yourself and outgrowing your personal desires and limitations is already a full-time job; the far more demanding job of changing society is simply incompatible with a monastic spiritual career.

Yet his fellow aristocrats frequently consulted the Buddha about political matters. He was, after all, one of them. Even *Nirvāṇa* does not wash that off. The secret of his sect's spectacular success was not just the superiority of his message, as his followers and admirers might claim, but also down-to-earth access to finances. They sponsored his order and had their subjects, by way of taxes in kind (*corvée*, servitude), build and maintain monasteries for the Buddha's order.

Moreover, he was considered trustworthy. He knew the life of kings and the kind of dynastic, political, or military problems they could face. But at the same time, as a monastic abbot, unlike other aristocrats, he had no stake anymore in the rivalries between princes. He was trusted because he was deemed statecraft savvy, yet Impartisan.

On the occasion of these invited interventions in public life, he gave us a glimpse into his political views. We get to know him as ultimately a fallible human being, farsighted but not infallible.

Greatest Failure

The Buddha's friend, king *Prasenajit/Pasenadi* (where two forms of a name are given, the first is Sanskrit, the second Pali) of *Kosala*, repudiates his *Śākya* wife and son when he discovers she has deceptively been passed off to him as a *Kṣatriya.* In reality, when he had asked for the hand of a *Śākya* princess, the proud tribe had carefully considered the dilemma. As a powerful neighbor, they could not afford to offend him by refusing; but as an exceptional bloodline, they did not want to waste one of their precious girls on this non-*Śākya* interloper. So, they took a good-looking but illegitimate daughter of a maidservant and dressed her up as a princess. But later *Virūḍhaka/Viḍūḍabha*, the son born to the newlyweds, would, as a teenager, find out the truth of his ancestry. (See, e.g., the dictionary of Pali names www.palikanon.com, entry *Viḍūḍabha*).

When confronting his father about it, he finds himself and his mother promptly disowned. Humiliated and angry, *Prasenajit* consults the Buddha, who prevails upon him to take them back. Interestingly, if the Buddha had really been an anti-caste campaigner, this would have been the best occasion for an anti-caste tirade. Instead, he pleads for the older, purely patrilineal concept of caste. Since *Prasenajit* is a *Kṣatriya*, his son *Virūḍhaka* must be a *Kṣatriya* as well, regardless of his mother's status. We also find this patrilineal idea of caste in *Veda-vyāsa*, the Brahmin par excellence, editor of the Vedas, son of sage *Parāśara* with the non-Brahmin fisher-girl *Satyāvatī*.

But that was long ago and *Prasenajit* is aware of the new norm of endogamy: to be a *Kṣatriya*, both your parents have to be *Kṣatriya*. Against this new wave, the Buddha could not carry conviction. Prince *Virūḍhaka* retains a grudge and, using the cooperation of an unwitting Buddha, stages a *coup d'état* against his father. Indeed, when *Prasenajit* visits the Buddha and humbly leaves his regalia outside, his charioteer takes them and hurries back to the capital for the improvised coronation of *Virūḍhaka*. The Buddha is not clairvoyant enough to realize what is happening. Moreover, upon his lonely return, *Prasenajit*, in his civilian clothes is not recognized by the city guard and dies of misery.

Now that the prince has become the head of state, and he has an army at his disposal and vows revenge upon the *Śākya*s. The planned massacre of the *Śākya* tribe is known as the *Śākyahatya* (slaughter of the *Śākya*s). Initially, the Buddha manages to dissuade him; however, in *Virūḍhaka*'s next attempt, he expresses his disapproval but knowingly relents. He is reduced to explaining the ongoing massacre to his disciples as karmically preordained, i.e., merited by the victims. In their past life, the *Śākya*s had been the villagers who were insensitive to the pleas of fish, who, during the hot season, when the river had shrunk to a rivulet, begged them to be thrown into the remaining little bit of water. Now the fish had come back as the soldiers to take revenge. After the massacre was over, they went to sleep by the riverside, and it started to rain. Before the dawn, the river started flooding, and the soldiers drowned in it. In their previous incarnation, they had begged to be thrown in the water and now their wish was fulfilled.

Skeptics will seize upon this story. It proves that the Buddha's power of persuasion was limited and that he was not clairvoyant (which puts a question mark on his claim to know his own and even others' past lives). Because of the criterion of "admission against self-interest," historians reading this will judge in favor of its historicity. If Buddhists made these admissions, it is because the embarrassing facts were too well known among the audience to deny.

A Mixed Performance

Another failure in the secular field provides the context for his principal and laudable formulation of his political views. The Sanskrit *Mahāparinirvāṇa Sūtra* (1.1-5, Sanskrit), about the Buddha's final days and departure, and the *Satta-Aparihāniya-Dhammā*: "7 non-decrease duties" (*Aṅguttara-Nikāya* 7:21, Pali; translated by Thanissaro Bhikkhu 1997, online 2011) relate the *saptaśīla*, the "7 precepts" of non-decline.

The Magadhan king *Ajātaśatru/Ajātasattu* reveals to his prime minister, *Varṣakāra/Vassakāra*, his desire to annex the neighboring *Vṛjji/Vajji* republic but laments that the state seems invincible. Instructed on what to say, *Varṣakāra* in turn goes to the Buddha (then 79) to find out the secret of the republic's strength. The following conversation takes place:

"On approaching the *Bhagavān*, he offered his respects in a way as should be done, and sat down to one side. (…)." The *Mahāmātya* of *Magadha* further spoke, "O *Gautama, Vaidehī-putra Ajātaśatru, the king of Magadha, and the Vṛjji are not on mutual friendly terms, and the king desirous of invading them has so contemplated: 'I shall conquer the turbulent Vṛjji's. And I shall crush the Vṛjji's. And I shall put the Vṛjji's to rout, howsoever wealthy and valorous, noble and numerous, happy and gallant they might be.*" And having delivered the message as he was detailed for, the *Mahāmātya* of *Magadha* inquired, "*What does venerable Gautama say to this?*"

The Buddha now knows that anything he says will be used in a strategy of conquest. But still he gives a truthful answer. The republic's secret, he reveals, is its observance of the "7 Precepts of Non-Decline."

The scene develops as if made for theater performance. His disciple *Ānanda* is with the *Buddha*, and a dialog ensues: "Now at that time *Āyuṣmāna Ānanda* was standing behind *Bhagavān*, holding and running a fan for his comfort."

The first precept is unity. *Bhagavān* turned to venerable *Ānanda* and said, "*Say Ānanda, have you heard whether the Vṛjji's are united and the Vṛjji's stay united?'—'Yes Bhante, so have I heard that the Vṛjji's are united and that the Vṛjji's stay united', replied venerable Ānanda. 'Then, Ānanda, as long as they are united and remain united, consider them to be prospering and far from decline.*" This formula is repeated for every precept.

The second precept is decision making in mutual harmony. The *Vṛjjis* live together in harmony, progress together in harmony, plan their undertakings in mutual harmony, and carry out their plans in harmony with each other. "Then, *Ānanda*, so long as they are in harmony, consider them to be prospering and far from decline."

The third precept is to follow *Dharma*. The *Vṛjji's* establish the proper laws, do not violate the established laws, carry on and respect their *Sanātana Dharma,* and follow it. "Then, *Ānanda*, so long as they are establishing and following the proper laws, and respecting their *Sanātana Dharma*, consider them to be prospering and far from decline."

The fourth precept is to respecting the elders. The *Vṛjjis* have respect for their elders, teachers, parents, and the wise and honor, revere, venerate, and obey them.

The fifth precept is to respect women: among the *Vṛjji*s, the women and girls are respected and are not considered of little worth, are protected and treasured by their parents and brothers, husbands and in-laws, kinsmen, and neighbors, and do not suffer kidnapping and abduction, bondage, and confinement; the *Vṛjji* men do not lust after and seduce another's wife.

The sixth precept is to respect spiritual institutes: the *caitya's* [sacred place] in the city and outsides are revered, venerated, and respected by the *Vṛjji's*; they do not abandon the time-established tradition to provide the support to the *caityas.*

The seventh precept is to respect holy men: The *Vṛjjis* provide support and protection to the *Arhatas*; the *Arhatas* passing by their country are welcomed, looked after, provided necessary clothes, food, bed, and medicine.

These Seven Precepts were not thought up in the abstract, but given specifically to, of all people, the *Vṛjjis*: "*Bhagavān then (…) turned to the Mahāmātya of Magadha and addressed him, 'Brāhmaṇa, I was once staying at the Sāradandacaitya near*

Vaiśāli, and there I had addressed the Vṛjji's and given them these Seven Precepts of welfare. (…). And O Varṣakāra, know this, that as long as they continue to keep these 7 Precepts present in their minds and as long as they follow these 7 Precepts in their conduct, so long will the Vṛjji's only progress and prosper and not diminish and decline!'."

Surprisingly, *Varṣakāra* seems to have changed his mind: "*Hearing this, Brāhmaṇa Varṣakāra, the Mahāmātya of Magadha, addressed Bhagavān, 'O Gautama, I regard that if the Vṛjji's follow even any single one of these Seven Precepts, they would continue standing firm and Vaidehī-putra Ajātaśatru, the king of Magadha, would not be able to subdue them, what to say if they are following all seven of them! O Gautama, I do consider that it would be fruitless, and not proper, for Vaidehī-putra Ajātaśatru, the king of Magadha, to abandon diplomacy and go to war with the Republic of the Vṛjji's!'.*"

By this seeming change of mind in *Varṣakāra*, the Buddha is assured that his answer will not contribute to Magadhan aggression. This saves Buddhist commentators the pang of conscience over the Buddha's de facto cooperation with a scheming war strategist.

The Magadhan Prime Minister observes all diplomatic niceties: "*And Brāhmaṇa Varṣakāra further spoke, 'O Gautama, Alas! I must take your permission to leave now. I go, however, in much debt!' And Bhagavān replied, 'Then return, Brāhmaṇa Varṣakāra, if you must, for you know what is best for you.' Then departed the great Mahāmātya of Magadha, the Brāhmaṇa Varṣakāra, pleased with these words of Bhagavān.*"

But he has not changed his mind, and if Buddha got away with that impression, he was mistaken. *Varṣakāra* goes on his way to pursue his assigned task: weakening and ultimately defeating the *Vṛjji* republic. He had only said that there could be no aggression as long as the Seven Precepts are followed but this can change.

Filling in the Blanks

Varṣakāra then coordinates with king *Ajātaśatru* and stages a much-publicized quarrel in the *Magadha* cabinet. He pretends to be on the side of *Vṛjji* and gets fired. He is then offered the post of Education Minister in the *Vṛjji* cabinet, which he accepts.

It remains unclear how precisely *Varṣakāra* achieves it, but in the next few years, when the aged Buddha dies, he sows discord among the students, who contaminate their. His policies end up subverting the *Vṛjji*s' sense of unity.

Historian–publisher Sita Ram Goel imaginatively fills in the details in a Hindi historical novel: *Sapta-Śīla*, BibliaImpex, Delhi 1960; 2nd edition 1999. Incidentally, in the 1957 *Lok Sabhā* election, Goel stood as candidate for the opposition (anti-Communist, free marketeer) Swatantra Party in the Khajuraho constituency. Many readers noticed in the rendering of *Varṣakāra*'s conduct the mannerisms typical of Jawaharlal Nehru and connected this with Goel's politics. In the preface to the second edition, Goel tries to dispel this notion but settles for the assessment that such a likeness is inevitable. The saboteur *Varṣakāra* tries to subvert a society, corrupting it from within and taking away its commitment to its civilizational values, as a precursor to its eventual decay and defeat; and Nehru was often accused precisely of just such civilizational subversion.

Even a novelist cannot alter the well-known ending, so we resume the story as known. The councils are attended less frequently; the *Vṛjji* citizens are less public-spirited and neglect their customary observance of the Seven Precepts. Three years later, *Magadha* judges its neighboring state sufficiently weakened for conquest. It invades and annexes the republic.

The Buddha's Intention

Military conquest of a peaceful state could not have been Buddha's intention. It is moreover a case of a monarchy overpowering a republic, which apparently went against his convictions and pro-republic sympathies. All in all, his *Vṛjji*-against-*Magadha* episode was a defeat. But we shall see that this was not entirely a defeat.

When we ask Buddhists about this, they reluctantly admit that the Buddha was clearly not omniscient or clairvoyant, but make the best of it by asserting that this is a positive difference with, say, *Kṛṣṇa* or *Christ*: Their superstitious cults attribute miracles to them, whereas the Buddha was just a human being, thereby able to show the way to all other human beings. (In reality, miracles are traditionally imputed to the Buddha too, celebrated annually after the Lunar New Year in the Festival of Miracles, Tibetan *Chok-trul Du-chen*; with the knowledge of past lives as one of his Yoga-induced special powers; but in the West, he was received as rational, not based on blind belief nor anything supernatural, and this idealization has caught on (esp. among Ambedkarite neo-Buddhists).

They also try to whitewash the episode by speculating that the Buddha's cooperation with *Magadha* bought the *Vṛjji* republic time; though there is no mention of any strategic coordination, much less of the republic using that extra time to outwit *Varṣakāra*. Or alternatively, they assert that from the Buddha's superior vantage point, he just accepted the inevitable in this Vale of Tears, which we should not try to improve but only escape. This is in conflict with his assertion that he had given the worldly advice of the Seven Precepts to a worldly republic, with the worldly effect of its invincibility at least as long as it would live by these rules. But when pressed, they agree that it is a bit embarrassing: None of them has expressed pride in it, and the episode is omitted from most introductions to the Buddha's life.

His Political Views

Political views are only a tiny and occasional part of Buddha's teachings; but they are crystal clear. He never indulged in victimhood complaints, in "oppression" talk or in "class struggle." Neither did he care for social structures: He chose to focus on people's attitudes. He believed in the harmony model, with direct participatory "democracy," i.e., "consensus building." This meant collective decision making, not by majority vote (as in Athenian Direct Democracy or in Parliamentary Democracy) but by consensus. This might have been less practical, but it would leave no disgruntled minority against the republic's chosen course.

Further, a sense of coherence and unity must be fostered by a common culture: a common law-abiding attitude, a common participation in cultural and religious traditions. The Buddha's probable contemporary Confucius (both ca. 500, though the jury is still out on the Buddha's exact date) emphasized the role of music in a common culture; this element is not in evidence in the Buddha's teaching, but otherwise, the sense of respect and awe before elders, saints, and ladies are in common. With these positive attitudes, it will hardly be necessary to appeal to a repressive apparatus. We strengthen society not by draconian laws and "more blue on the streets," but by embedding in it a heartfelt care for its vulnerable yet precious members and a shared respect for ancestral (i.e., largely Vedic) tradition.

The distinctly conservative, anti-revolutionary streak in Buddhism belies the modern Ambedkarite view of the Buddha as "revolutionary." In society, he simply adapted to whatever institutions existed around him: imperial bureaucracy in China, military feudalism in Japan (with the Samurai class clinging systematically to Zen Buddhism), and casteism in India. Inside the order, caste and other worldly distinctions had no place anymore, but this implied no claim on worldly society's norms. This was a matter of time investment: You will not get far in your inward directed meditation practice if you foster ambitions for a worldly career, whether pursuing riches and honor for yourself or pursuing a utopia for the world at large. It was, though the Buddha never had reason to consider this, also necessary for the good of the monastic order: If worldly leaders were to notice that the *Saṁgha* was subversive of the existing social order, they might stop patronizing it and in a farther stage, even start persecuting it. The sheer success of the Buddhist monastic order in itself is a proof that it was not subversive of society.

If Buddha had practiced a kind of revolution, it was against the ordinary householder's life. He was not the first to require celibacy, but was unusually strict in his prohibition of any and every type of sexual activity. He broke up families, the cornerstone of Vedic (and many a) society, accepting novices of whom he knew they were leaving a wife behind, as he himself had done. This was against the traditional norm of paying off your debt (*Ṛṇa*) to your ancestors by procreating and continuing the life stream.

Invincible?

These Seven Precepts for non-decline may be a good thing, they may be desirable, they may eliminate the risk of disunity and social chaos; but do they make *invincible*? Does goodness make invincible? Disunity gives a handle to enemy forces to weaken and overpower your society, unity is certainly preferable to it, but does it make *invincible*?

This sounds a bit like the idealistic Gandhian belief in "soul force," or as the Mahatma said: "A *satyāgrahi* cannot be defeated." Possibly in the case of the *Vṛjji* republic and the *Magadha* kingdom, the power equation happened to be calibrated in such a way that unity vs. disunity made the difference between invincibility and defeat. But in general, among the numerous states throughout history that have been wiped off the map by more powerful neighbors, there must have been some with an admirable harmony seeking political system, fine while it lasted but unable to keep superior force at a distance. Certainly, "survival of the fittest" did not always mean that the best in quality carried the day. As Belgium's atrocious king Léopold II said: "God always sides with him who has the biggest cannon".

Moreover, the supposed force behind this supposed invincibility, *goodness* howsoever defined, in itself is hard-won, vulnerable, and susceptible to decline. Indeed, that is how, according to the Buddhist sources, the *Vṛjji* republic was defeated: It lost the will to keep up the Seven Precepts, then it lost the benefit of these Seven Precepts, became vulnerable, and was finally defeated. So, following them is more beneficial than an iron hand, but it is not all-powerful and does not make one invincible.

The Seven Precepts for the Monastic Order

If the benefit of the Seven Precepts for a state never gave proof of lasting very long, the experience of the Buddha's monastic order was better. Finally, a series of failures served as a step up toward lasting success. For the story continues:

After *Varṣakāra* has gone, the Buddha calls an assembly of the monks: "*Bhikṣus*/*Bhikkhus*, I will teach you the seven conditions for non-decline. Listen, *Bhikṣus*, pay close attention to it, I will speak." And then he gives the same Seven Precepts, slightly adapted for monastic use.

(1) "*Bhikṣus*, so long as the monks gather regularly and often, then, *Bhikṣus*, growth for the monks is to be expected, not their decline."

(2) "*Bhikṣus*, so long as the monks gather in fellowship, disperse in fellowship and do the *Sangha* duties in fellowship, then, *Bhikṣus*, growth for the monks is to be expected, not their decline."

(3) "*Bhikṣus*, so long as the monks do not authorize what has not been authorized, and do not abolish what has been authorized, but conduct themselves in accordance with the promulgated training rules, then, *Bhikṣus*, growth for the monks is to be expected, not their decline."

(4) "*Bhikṣus*, so long as the monks honour, respect, esteem and venerate the elder monks, those long-standing, long gone forth, *Saṅgha* fathers, *Saṅgha* leaders, and consider it worthwhile to listen to them, then, *Bhikṣus*, growth for the monks is to be expected, not their decline."
(5) "*Bhikṣus*, so long as the monks do not fall under the power of craving that arises in them, that leads to continued births, then, *Bhikṣus*, growth for the monks is to be expected, not their decline."
(6) "*Bhikṣus*, so long as the monks love to dwell in the forest, then, *Bhikṣus*, growth for the monks is to be expected, not their decline."
(7) "*Bhikṣus*, so long as the monks keep themselves up in mindfulness, so companions in the holy life of virtuous conduct who have not yet come would come, and that they who have come would dwell in comfort, then, *Bhikṣus*, growth for the monks is to be expected, not their decline."

The *Saṅgha* is the Buddha's main tangible achievement. Here his organizing capacity was put to the test. The result was to prove long lasting, world spanning and on balance, highly beneficial. The soft power of a gentle organizational approach is a large part of this success formula.

Again, this *Saṅgha* was not exactly invincible. Islamic invasions wiped it out from central, South, and parts of Southeast Asia. But it persisted in Mongolia, China, Tibet, Japan, and Indochina; while it maintained itself in Sri Lanka and from there spread to Myanmar and Thailand. It certainly survived until today, some 25 centuries, and is thereby one of the oldest institutions in the world.

Conclusion

Let us sum up the "Seven Precepts" briefly: (1) regular assembly meetings attended by all; (2) decision making by consensus; (3) holding fast to ancient laws and traditions; (4) respect and care for the elderly; (5) protection of women and girls; (6) maintaining sacred sites and upholding ancient rituals and sacrifices; and (7) veneration and hospitality to wandering ascetics. These rules form a much-neglected synopsis of the Buddha's sociopolitical views.

On the one hand, as far as governing structures are concerned, they can serve as justifying a form of direct participatory democracy; and on the other, in terms of the spirit animating a society, they underpin a Confucius like conservatism that seeks to fortify civil society by embedding in it a heartfelt care for its vulnerable but precious members and a shared respect for ancestral tradition. There can be little doubt that it is a *good* formula for managing a society and in that sense *successful*: It achieved certain happiness within the society concerned.

Whether it was successful in the sense of being robust and having staying power *vis-à-vis* the challenges coming from the outside world, is more questionable. Possibly, states *de facto* applying some of the Seven Precepts may be found to be more long lasting than others: This would necessitate (but deserves) a large-scale investigation. The one political case available to the Buddha, the *Vṛjji* republic, seems to provide a perfect correspondence between following them with flourishing and between neglecting them with courting defeat. Such, at least, is the message that the primary Buddhist sources, committed to writing some two centuries after the event, try to convey.

The only other instance available to him was more properly his own domain, fully under his control, where he could give his precepts an enduring validity. And here, the application of these precepts has proven more unequivocally successful: his monastic order. Here he gave mankind a lasting example of great management, resulting in an impressive longevity without indication of an imminent ending.

Chapter 4
Spirituality Models of Management and Leadership with Roots in Ancient Wisdom

Subhash Sharma

Abstract This paper presents some spirituality models of mangement and leadership rooted in ancient Indian wisdom. These modesl include OSHA model, Theory K, Negergy-Synergy grid. "MBA" model of decision making and Corporate Rishi model. The paper presents discussion on these models and also implications of these models for orgnaizations and their management.

Keywords OSHA model · Theory K · Negergy-Synergy grid · "MBA" model of decision making · Corporate Rishi · Western windows eastern doors

During recent times, the idea of spirituality in management and leadership has gained academic acceptability and acceptance by practitioners. In order to implement this idea in organization context, we need specifc models to help practitioners to practice these ideas. Accordingly, this paper drawing upon ancient Indian wisdom presents some models of spirituality in management and leadership.

Search for Indian models of management and leadership with roots in ancient wisdom and Indian experiences of building world class corporation and institutions has been a part of the academic pursuit of many Indian scholars. Prominent among them are Profs. Chakraborty (1995, 2001, 2003), Athreya (2002), Sinha (2000), Sharma (1996, 2007, 2013), Gupta (1991, 2002), Chatterjee (1998), Sharma and Rupali (2018) and others.

Ancient Indian wisdom includes ideas "such as Triguna theory, Vasudhaive kutumbkam, transforming tamas/darkness to sattava/light and Raj-rishi" (Chakraborty, 1995). Based on these ideas, Sharma (1996, 2007, 2013) suggests the following models of management and leadership:

I. "OSHA Model of Management and Leadership
II. Theory K of Enlightened Leadership;
III. Negergy-Synergy Grid of Leadership;
IV. 'MBA' Model of Decision Making;

S. Sharma (✉)
Indus Business Academy, Bangalore, India
e-mail: prof.subhash.sharma789@gmail.com

© Jindal Institute of Behavioral Sciences 2022

S. P. Sahni et al. (eds.), *Spirituality and Management*,
https://doi.org/10.1007/978-981-19-1025-8_4

V. Corporate Rishi Model of Leadership."

These models along with their significance for spirituality in management especially Indian management are discussed below:

Model I: OSHA Model of Management and Leadership

OSHA (Oneness, Spiritualistic, Humanistic, Animalistic) model of management in an leadership is rooted in "Triguna theory of Tamas, Rajas and Sattava qualities of nature and human beings" (Sharma, 1996). This model identifies "following four levels of human behavior."

"O: Oneness.
S: Spiritual.
H: Humanistic.
A: Animalistic/Aggressive."

Accorinding to this moel, "there are four types of persons, viz. 'O,' 'S,' 'H,' and 'A' depending upon the presence of the most dominant component. In this model, S element has its close equivalent in sattva. H in rajas and A in tamas" (Sharma, 1996). Figure 4.1 represents this model in diagrammatic form.

"O" level or oneness is metaphorically described through "Oceanic experience." It implies oneness with self and oneness with nature. This may find its manifestation in an individual's inner quest for SOS—Search Of Shanti. O level also incorporates within itself mystical meaning of shunya and its counter part ananta (infinite). Experience of such "fullness of void," i.e., experience of infinite at O level is variously described in spiritual literature. It is interesting to know that in mathematics such fullness of void is represented by O/∞ leading to indeterminate quantity known as brahm (brahman) in spiritual literature. Symbolically, O also stands for a circle—a circle of consciousness. As an individuals' circle of consciousness expands, creativity shows its continuous natural flow. For an atheist, "O" level simply implies oneness

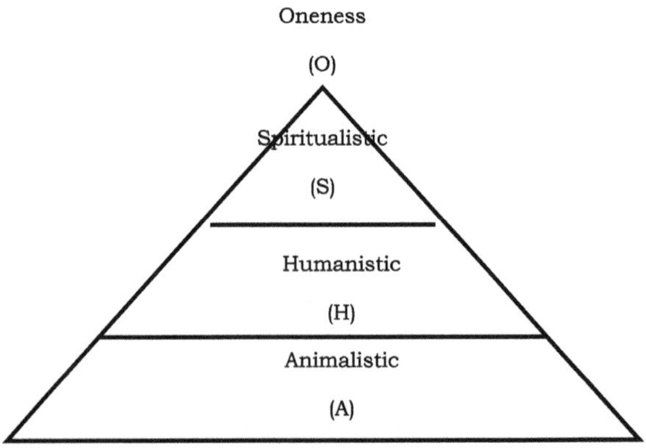

Fig. 4.1 OSHA model for self-awareness (Sharma, 1996, p. 127)

with nature. When oneness with nature is disturbed, ozone layer disappears and acid rain becomes a reality!

"S" level indicates the "spiritual aspect indicative of supreme goodness in human nature, represented by values of love, amity mercy and so on" (Sharma, 1996). These arise as a result of seeing self in others and seeing SELF in everyone. This also represents the connecting thread between various spiritual philosophies influencing the human psyche.

"H" level stands for the humanistic dimension and is represented by humanistic values such as empathy, dignity, liberty and so on.

"A" level "stands for "animalistic" or aggressiveness aspect of human nature that can be easily seen in many conflict situations" (Sharma, 1996). "A" level also stands for authoritarian as well as "asuri" (fascist/demonic) tendencies.

It may be observed that depending upon the emphasis given to O, S, H, and A element, there are diffenent types of personalities.

OSHA Interaction Matrix

OSHA model can also be used as a framework for analysis of inter-personal behavior. For this purpose, an inter-personal interaction matrix as presented in Fig. 4.2 could serve as an analytical framework. This matrix represents interaction of two persons in their various modes, viz. the spiritualistic, humanistic, or animalistic mode. These modes are: (S, S), (S, H), (S, A), (H, H), (H, A) and (A, A). Notation (S, S) represents interaction between two persons at S (Spiritual) level. Similarly (A, A) represents

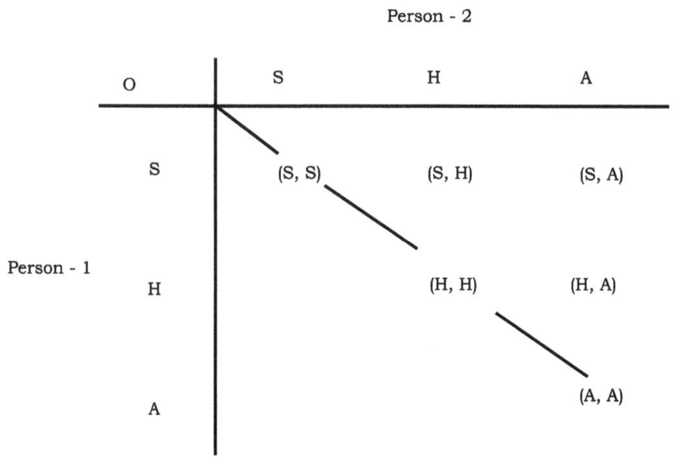

Fig. 4.2 OSHA interaction matrix (Sharma, 1996, p. 128)

interaction between two individuals both dominant in "A," i.e., animalistic or aggressiveness level. (H, A) represents an interaction between two persons with one person dominant in H level and other person dominant in "A" level.

When (S, S) type of interaction dominate synergy is generated. When (A, A) type of interactions dominate, negergy (negative energy) gets generated. An upward movement from (H, H) type interactions toward (S, S) type leads to synergy, while a downward movement from (H, H) type to (A, A) type leads toward negergy. At times, (A, A) type interactions can also induce an individual toward higher achievement; however, this achievement is likely to be at the cost of peace of mind. (H, H) and (S, S) type interactions would lead to achievement coupled with peace of mind. A difference between achievement with peace of mind and achievement without peace of mind is needed for holistic approach to individual's self-development and personal effectiveness.

This model has implications for managing and leading organizations, society and nations. If (A, A) interactions dominate organizations, society or nation, there will be lot of conflicts leading to high energy dissipation that takes away attention from achieving goals. This can be reduced through (H, H) and (S, S) interactions as such interactions will create lot of positive energy and synergy in organization, society or nation.

According to this model, there are four types of leaders viz.

(i) Oneness types who create oneness in organizations through vision and Higher-Order Purpose of Existence (HOPE);
(ii) Spiritual types who use spiritual and non-violent approach in decision-making approach;
(iii) Humanistic leaders who focus on human side of management and leadership;
(iv) Aggressive types who use aggression and violence in managing and leading organizations.

Humanistic side of management has been in practice since many years. This is combined with democratic style of leadership. Now, there is also appreciation of spiritualility in management and thereby for spiritual side of management in combination with human side. Because of ecological concenrs and climate change enlightened corporations are also moving toward oneness style in their management practice.

Model II: Theory K of Enlightened Leadership

Theory K is "rooted in the Indian idea of "vasudhev kutumbhkam," i.e., entire world is our family. In corporate context, a corporation can be viewed as a community/kutumb of stakeholders" (Sharma, 1996).

Theory K implies use of "a combination of approaches which may include use of theories, X, Y, or Z depending upon the situational requirements. Hence, theory K is a combination theory where K is a combination of X, Y, and Z" (Sharma, 1996).

Theory X refers to authoritarian style of management and leadership. Theory Y refers to democratic style and theory Z refers to team building approach to management and leadership. Theory X and theory Y are also referred to as American style of management, and theory Z is known as Japanes style of management. In practice, a mix of the three can be easily seen in operation depending upon the social and cultural upbringing. Experience indicates that societies that promoted colonialism were high on theory X in its X^- form. Similarly ideologies that are rooted in violence are more likely to promote theory X. However, long-term implications of exclusive use of theory X particularly in its X^- form have been witnessed in the collapse of colonialism as well as the Russian empire. This collapse occurred because "need for freedom" has always been very strong. In history, it has been manifested in the form of freedom struggles.

We represent the theory K in the form of following equation:

$$K = X + Y + Z.$$

Theory K can also be represented by following equation:

$$K = X^a Y^b Z^c$$

wherein the powers a, b, and c represent the intensities with which theories X, Y, or Z are used.

These equations indicate that theory K is an appropriate blend of X, Y, and Z depending on the situational requirements. Indeed theory K can also be referred to as XYZ theory of motivation and management wherein X, Y, and Z appear in various combinations. It may be indicated that in theory K, use of X appears in its X^+ form and not in its X^- form.

The equation $K = X^a\ Y^b\ Z^c$ also represents a personality theory. Depending upon the values of a, b, and c, an individual's personality would have X, Y, or Z tendencies or orientations.

It may be indicated that each individual consists of all the three types of qualities viz. X, Y, and Z. If X is dominant in an individual with Y and Z having secondary and tertiary intensities, then the individual can be referred to as X oriented. If Y is dominant with Z and X having secondary and tertiary intensities, then the person is Y oriented. If Z is dominant with X and Y having secondary or tertiary intensities, then the individual is Z oriented.

In organizational contexts, the complexity of inter-personal conflicts gets enhanced because of the X, Y, and Z personality mix of various individuals. Extending the above discussed interaction approach to three levels viz. managers, supervisors and workers, we can get a better understanding of complexity of inter-personal interactions in organizations. A manager could be X, Y or Z oriented. His/her supervisor could be X, Y, or Z oriented. Similarly his/her worker could be X, Y, or Z oriented.

Fig. 4.3 Theory K in matrix form (Sharma, 2007, p. 195)

Leader's Style \ Situational Requirements	X	Y	Z
X	(X, X)	(X, Y)	(X, Z)
Y	(Y, X)	(Y, Y)	(Y, Z)
Z	(Z, X)	(Z, Y)	(Z, Z)

Theory K in Matrix Format

According to theory K, different situations may demand different treatments. A situation may demand consultation or formation of teams. However, if manager/leader does not display style flexibility, he/she may use theory X in such a situation. This would obviously lead to a mismatch between the style and the situational requirements. Through experience managers and leaders learn to fine tune their styles to the situational requirements. Thus, theory K suggests that the situational requirements may demand style flexibility. Use of theory K is like the car driving. Changes in situations may require the change in the gears. Thus, theories X, Y, and Z can be considered as gears. Effective managers are able to make changes in the gears depending upon the requirements. Thus, they are able to get best performance from their work force. This idea of theory K can be presented as a matrix given in Fig. 4.3.

"The situations (X, X), (Y, Y), and (Z, Z) represent the style fit. In other situations given in the matrix here, there is lack of congruity between the style and the situation" (Sharma, 2007).

In the discussion, so far we have outlined the key aspects of theory K. It is essentially a combination theory wherein the theories X, Y, and Z are used in a blend form depending upon the situational requirements. In the discussion below, we provide comparison of the theories X, Y, and Z with similar Indian theories that are thought widely used yet not written about in management text books.

Ethical Dimension in Theory K

One of the limitations of the theories X, Y, and Z has been lack of emphasis on the ethical aspects as they are considered to be value-neutral. This also accounts for the appeal of these theories and makes them appear scientific in contrast to earlier traditional concepts that tend to be tilted in the value-positive direction. The seeming value neutrality of the theories X, Y and Z is not entirely true because they do tend to have certain ideological moorings. To twenty-first century managers, it may appear strange that the admired intellectual giants like Weber, Freud, and Taylor were indeed advocates of theory X.

In management literature, the "need for justice" has not received much attention. Kautilaya was perhaps the first scholar to give emphasis to the need for justice through his metaphor of the matasya-nyaya. Similarly, the "need for freedom" has not received due recognition. It may be indicated that the idea of "need for freedom" is derived from Tilak's famous quote "freedom is my birthright." In organizational contexts, need for freedom finds its expression in autonomy coupled with accountability.

Theory K, by emphasizing the justness in management actions. gives due importance to the "need for justice" and the ethical dimension. In addition, theory K also recognizes the "need for freedom." Hence. it emphasizes a shift away from X^- to other styles. The framework of theory K is both integrative and holistic because it not only integrates X, Y, and Z theories but also takes a holistic perspective by incorporating the ethical and justness dimension in social and managerial actions. Indian managers usually practice theory K in their managmetn and leadership styles.

Model III: Negergy-Synergy Grid of Leadership

Negergy represents negative energy. "Tamsoma jyotirgamaya" from darkness to light, is a well known mantra (Sharma, 1996). It forms the basis of the Negergy-Synergy grid. In organization context this is represented by negative energy, i.e., negergy and light representing synergy.

"Negergy-Synergy Grid is a combination of two axis. First axis views humans in terms of the authoritarian-democratic modes of decision making and action. Second axis is derived from the lessons about human nature from *Gita* as indicated in chapter XVI. This chapter identifies human beings in terms of two types, viz. the divine like and the demonic like" (Sharma, 2007). It may be indicated that both strands make certain implicit or explicit value judgements as reflected in their assumptions about human nature or the "models of humans."

"Divine like and demonic types qualities have been elaborated in this chapter. The divine-like human qualities include truthfulness, gentleness, modesty and steadiness, freedom from anger, forgiveness, freedom from malice and excessive pride, (*Gita*, XVI, 2 & 3). The demonic-like display arrogance, excessive pride, anger, harshness and manipulation (*Gita*, XVI, 4, 10)" (Sharma, 2007). In popular consciousness these two types of qualities are depicted through Ram-Ravana metaphor. Ram is "*maryada purushottam*" (best among humans for his human qualities) and Ravana is master of *vidhya* ("technology" and "science") and had his "*Sone Ki Lanka*," but his mental cast is demonic like. The demonic qualities could be referred to as savage like and divine like qualities could be referred to as sage like.

"When we put the two axis representing these two approaches to human nature, we arrive at a typology of humans indicating their mental cast and decision-making

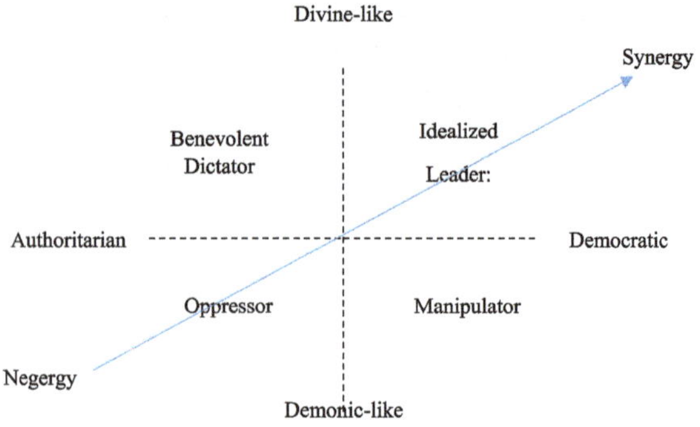

Fig. 4.4 Negergy-synergy management styles and leadership grid (Sharma, 1996, p. 176)

styles" (Sharma, 2007). This management styles and leadership grid is presented in Fig. 4.4.

The grid discussed here identifies four types of managers and leaders. These are as follows:

(1) Democratic and divine like;
(2) Authoritarian and divine like;
(3) Democratic and demonic like;
(4) Authoritarian and demonic like.

The democratic and divine like can be considered as an "idealized" type of manager or leader. The authoritarian and divine like is the typical benevolent-dictator. Democratic and demonic like is the typical manipulator type of manager. This type uses the democratic process as a facade to cover up his/her manipulative tactics. This person is a typical manipulator putting up a double face. Authoritarian and demonic like is an oppressor as depicted through many mythological characters.

The grid discussed here has implications for organizations in general and organization-culture in particular. While expectations from managers and leaders vary from culture to culture, certain idealized archetypes play important role in determining these expectations. In this new age, a new idealized archetype is emerging. This is the democratic and divine-like leader/manager. Transformational leadership is likely to belong to this category.

The grid presented here can be further refined. Instead of using the divine like and demonic extremes, we could use the classification of *gunas*. Thus, on Y-axis, we can have four segments viz., *sattavik*, *rajasik* positive, *rajasik* negative, and *tamasik* qualities.

The grid discussed here can be used as a framework for introducing change in the organizations. If an organization's culture is authoritarian-demonic type, there is likely to be high levels of negergy (negative energy). The energy dissipation coefficient will be high, thereby leading to high frustration levels and at times even revolts. The revolts may be manifested through subaltern processes of day to day resistance. If synergy is to be achieved, then a change must occur. This change should be in the direction of democratic–divine-like leadership. It implies that the leader should be a demoocratic and divine like person.

Model IV: "MBA" Model of Decision Making

In the "MBA" model of decision making, "the individual letters stand for *Manas*, *Buddhi* and *Ahamkaar*. According to this model, in any decision making, there is an interplay of all the three "internal sense organs" (Sharma, 1996). *Manas*, *buddhi* and *ahamkaar* are also referred to as *anthakaran* (internal sense instruments). As these terms are non-translatable in English, we will use them as they are. However, close English translations could be indicated. *Manas* refers to the mind, *buddhi* refers to the intellect and *ahamkaar* refers to self-sense/ego. However, it may be indicated that the term *manas* does not correspond exactly to the term "mind." Hence, the term "mind" is only an approximation. The term "*manas*" may include an emotive content of the decision-making situation, like the term "heart." So "*manas*" is a sort of blending of the "mind" and the "heart" (Sharma, 1996). *Buddhi* is the subtle sense of all mental processes, and *ahamkaar*, the self-sense, i.e., the principle of "individualism," arise from *buddhi*. *Ahamkaar* also leads to *abhimana*, i.e., the self-love in the individual.

"*Manas* acts as a "gatekeeper" to filter and process the sense data. It is involved in a preliminary screening of the information presented to the senses. It is also suggests different courses of action. Further, it also plays the role of intuition. The external senses (*indriyas*) and the *manas* present the experiences to *Buddhi* the intellect, which in turn undertakes a rational analysis of the data. However, this rational analysis is interfered with by *ahamkaar*, the self-sense or the ego" (Sharma, 1996). This is because *ahamkaar* creates a frame of reference in the individual in the form of the ego. Out of this, interplay emerges the final decision, which leads to action. This interaction is also influenced by *vritti* and *sanskaar*. *Vritti* is defined as fluctuations in the mind, that operate at the conscious level, while *sanskaars* are the subliminal impressions stored in the subconscious or the unconscious (*Karamasaya*, i.e., the *saya* or the storehouse of impressions resulting from karmas or the actions). *Vritti* and *sanskaar* also interact, and thus link the conscious and subconscious or unconscious. "While *Vrittis* operate at the conscious level, the *sanskaars* operate at subconscious or unconscious level. Both *Vritti* (mental orientations) and the *sanskaars* moderate the interplay of *manas*, *buddhi* and *ahamkaar*. Given his mental orientations and *sanskaars* (i.e., 'repertoire of experiences'), a manager may display a greater reliance on one of the three 'instruments' of *manas*, *buddhi* and *ahamkaar*" (Sharma, 1996). Figure 4.5 presents the "MBA" decision-making process.

In an increasingly "rational" society, decisions tend to be more "*buddhi*" and "*ahamkaar*" driven. In fact, the reality of organizational life indicates that a number of decisions are "*ahamkaar*" driven.

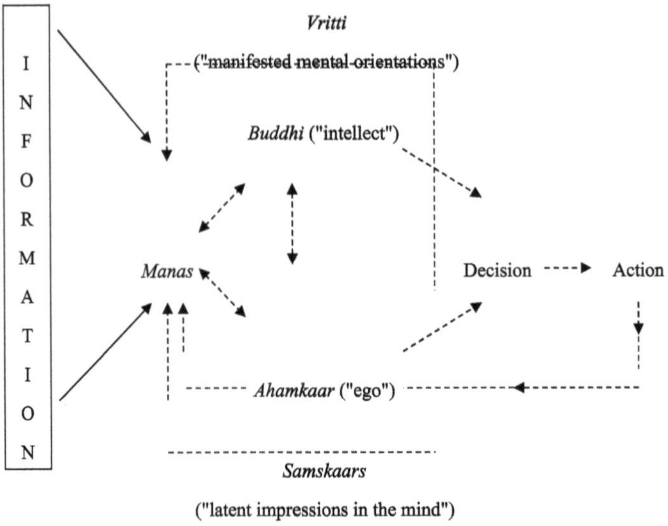

Fig. 4.5 The "MBA" model of decision making (Sharma, 1996, p. 136)

Model V: Corporate Rishi Model of Leadership: Rishi as Resee

"Corporate *Rishi*" is "an individual who has the ability to resee events, visions, strategies and action plans in new perspectives and new forms. A Corporate *Rishi* combines reason, intuition and business wisdom to sharpen his/her ability to see and resee the reality in new ways. Individuals evolve to the resee level, through education, experience and continuous learning—wherein they acquire the abilities to make use of reason, intuition and practical wisdom in varying combinations and thereby provide enlightened leadership to their organizations. Their 'Resee competence' is very high" (Sharma, 2006).

Sharma (2006) identifies "following tools that help a Corporate *Rishi* to resee events, threats, and opportunities in new perspectives including" (Sharma, 2006):

(1) "Continuous learning through 3D approach of discussion, dialogue, and ddiscourse;
(2) Communicative interaction through action-reaction-interaction processes;
(3) Acquiring practical wisdom through grounded praxis, i.e., relating theory to practice and practice to theory. This is further refined through action-reflection-contemplation.
(4) Empowering others by providing them dignity, liberty, and freedom through divine–democratic approach;
(5) Integrating intelligence quotient (IQ), emotional quotient (EQ), and spiritual quotient (SQ).

(6) Using creativity and imagination as a basis for charting out new path and a new direction."

A Corporate *Rishi* uses "these tools for fomulating his company's Vision, Strategies and Action plan (ViSA)" (Sharma, 2007). This approach is used to motivate employees to achieve extraordinary results.

Indian examples of Corporate Rishi include J. R. D. Tata, N. R. Narayanmurthy, and Azim Premji. These industry leaders have reseen events, threats, and opportunities in new ways and offered new directions to their organizations. Other managers and leaders can also learn from their experiences.

It may be indicated that the Indian models of management and leadership presented above can be empirically tested. This author has tested them with managers in his Management Development Programs. Managers find them practical, useful, and implementable. However, wider testing is needed. It may be further indicated that they "have also become part of the 'received knowledge' in the field of Indian Management" (Sharma, 2007). These have been cited in academic by various research scholars in their academic papers. Further, these models are interrelated, e.g., animalistic dimension of OSHA model has equvilance in theory X aspect of theory K and Ahamkar in "MBA" model and animalisitic approach, theory X approach and ahmakar approach to management create negative energy (negergy) at work place. Hence, need to shift toward synergy approach that represents the essence of spirituality in management and leadership. As these models have practical application, they can be used to create positive energy and synergy at work places and in organizations.

References

Athreya, M. B. (2002). Indian dimension in management. In S. Siddharth (Ed.), *Indian Management for Nation Building: New Ideas for New Millennium.* (pp. 61–69). WISDOM.

Chakraborty S. K. (1995). *Ethics in Management: Vedantic Perspectives.* Oxford University Press.

Chakraborty, S. K. (2001). *Wisdom Leadership.* Wheeler Publishers.

Chakraborty, S. K. (2003). *Against the Tide: The Philosophical Foundations of Modern Managemen.* Oxford University Press.

Chatterjee, D. (1998). *Leading Consciously: A Pilgrimage to Self Mastery.* Viva Books.

Gupta, R. K. (1991). Employees and organization in India; Need to move beyond American and Japanese models. *Economic and Political Weekly, 26*, M68–M76.

Gupta, R. K. (2002). *Towards Optimal Organization: Indian Culture and Management.* Excel Books.

Sinha, J. B. P. (2000). Integrative indigenous management in India: Practices and prospects. *Indian Journal of Industrial Relations, 97*(4), 439–460.

Sharma, S. (1996). *Management in New Age: Western Windows Eastern Doors.* New Age International Publishers.

Sharma, S. (2006). *Management in New Age Western Windows Eastern Doors.* 2nd edition. New Age International Publishers.

Sharma, S. (2007). *New Mantras in Corporate Corridors: From Ancient Roots to Global Routes.* New Age International Publishers.

Sharma, S. (2013). Three paradigms in management: American, Japanese and Indian. *International Journal of Organization Theory & Behavior, 16*(1), 30–41.

Sharma, R., & Rupali, P. (2018). Convergence of western and eastern perspectives into spirituo-humanistic leadership. *3D…IBA Journal of Management & Leadership, 10*(1), 15–25.

Chapter 5
Guiding Models from some Traditional Indian Philosophies for the Contemporary Worldview

Rekha Navneet

Abstract The chapter emphasizes on drawing the prototypical models from those traditions of Indian philosophy, which despite being centuries old can still provide prudential and viable guidelines to the contemporary worldview. The chapter has primarily focused on ethical and humanistic spiritualism as put forth in Kathopanishada, Vedanta-Upanishadic tradition, Sankhya and Yoga Philosophy, and the Bhagvad Gita, also referred as The Gita/Bhagvadgita which forms a part of the epic, Mahabharata. This chapter focuses on the traditional Indian wisdom as explicated in the philosophical and scriptural traditions of the aforementioned sources having a critical significance in influencing both the local and global socio-cultural, moral, and spiritual ethos in the present-day world. These theories have a detailed, structured, and conceptual clarity about: the meaning of self-identity and psyche, the meaning and nature of truth and reality, a clear guideline on the righteous way to lead life, and a holistic perspective to reflect and act. Another significant point of this chapter is noting that these traditional theories are quite apposite in the context of the "new normal" worldview as ensued by the COVID-19 pandemic. Another significant point of this chapter is noting that these traditional theories are quite apposite in the context of the "new normal" worldview as ensued by the COVID-19 pandemic. One of the primary issues of concern in the present-day world, even before the COVID-19's presence, has been sustaining the mindfulness and emotional stability in all domains of life and living. The chapter concludes with the view that these traditions of wisdom as propagated in the Schools of Indian Philosophy and Scriptures are viable guiding models addressing these twenty-first-century issues and concerns an enabling introspective analysis and finding meaning and purpose even in an adversity like a pandemic.

Keywords Philosophy · Indian tradition · Pandemic · Worldview · Wisdom · Holistic · Self-identity · Psyche · Mindfulness · Emotional stability

---

R. Navneet (✉)
Associate Professor, Department of Philosophy, Gargi College (University of Delhi), B-13, IFS Apartments, Mayur Vihar-1, Delhi 110091, India
e-mail: rekha.navneet@gargi.du.ac.in

© Jindal Institute of Behavioral Sciences 2022

S. P. Sahni et al. (eds.), *Spirituality and Management*,
https://doi.org/10.1007/978-981-19-1025-8_5

The chapter has primarily focused on ethical and humanistic spiritualism as put forth in *Kathopanishada* (from Vedanta-Upanishadic tradition) (Krishnananda, S. **Lessons from the Upanishads**. https://www.swami-krishnananda.org/katha1/Commentary_on_Katha_Upanishad.pdf. Accessed for the first time on 23/01/2021), Sankhya and Yoga philosophy (Radhakrishnan, 2008), and the *Bhagvad Gita,* also written as *The Gita or Bhagvadgitā (but I have written as the Gita),* which forms a part of the epic, *Mahabharata* (Radhakrishnan) (Dasgupta, 2002). These traditions, according to this chapter, form timeless model guidelines to follow a course on life skills in any epoch. The chapter has drawn sustenance from these Indian philosophies which are known to cover the common underlying thoughts of the *Shruti* and *Smriti* traditions (Gautam, 2013). The meeting point of these ancient traditions, as noted in the chapter, was a focus on humanistic spiritualism that implied (a) following a righteous living through actions done with a meaningful *telos*/purpose and, therefore, divested of trivial pleasures (*nishkāmakarma, the focal point in the Bhagvad Gita*), (b) having emotional–mental stability (*sthihtprajña,* the recurring thought in *Yoga* School), and (c) realizing the true meaning of one's spiritual identity gained through the knowledge of true nature and meaning of soul (*ātma-jñāna* or *Brahma-vidyā*—main theories of almost all Upanishads.).

All these aforementioned traditions have been found resonance in the present-day discursive narratives and theories that contemplate and deliberate on the meanings of self-identity, psyche, truth, post-truth, opinion and seek a clear guideline on the righteous way to lead life and a holistic perspective on living meaningfully.

Another significant point of this chapter is noting that these traditional theories are quite apposite in the context of the "new normal" worldview as ensued by the COVID-19 pandemic. The pandemic has, in an unprecedented way, impacted the inter-personal communications and work–life dynamics. Lockdowns, quarantines, work from home, social distancing, etc. have caused quite a distress to people across the globe. Hence, it becomes pertinent to problematize and contextualize the new meaning of active engagement with professional and personal spaces. The variants of the contagion as manifested in different waves and causing long-drawn pathological disorders and deaths have further challenged people across the globe in remaining emotionally stable and feel mentally agile and robust.

One of the primary issues of concern in today's world, even before the COVID-19's presence, has been sustaining the mental well-being and emotional stability both at the personal level as well as in the professional and public spaces, and a model to practice serenity and mindfulness can be drawn from this traditional Indian wisdom. References to the traditional Indian philosophies, as mentioned above, can both contextualize and problematize the worldview that is becoming digitally/technologically determined and has life issues in relation to it.

Methodology and the Aim

This chapter has been divided into two parts. In the first part, a brief explication of the traditional Indian philosophies has been delineated, and these have been referred as the philosophical models. The main tenets of philosophies like the ones advocated by the proponents of Vedanta/Upanishad, (with specific emphasis on *Kathopanishad*) *Sānkhya, Yoga*, and by the scripture like the *Bhagvad Gita. Katho-Upanishad* has been often referred to as *Kathā-Upanishad* and sometimes as *Kathā* by various scholars. Likewise, *Bhagvad Gita* is generally mentioned as the *Gitā* or the *Bhagvadgitā. However, I have mentioned it as The Gita or Bhagvad Gita here.* The synonymous usage has been part of the resources cited here as well as in available scholarly works.

In the second part, I have articulated my interpretations of these traditional theories as being viable and applicable as guiding thoughts for managing contemporary worldview and addressing life issues and challenges like COVID-19. I have also used phrases like empathy, unity, collective oneness, and inter-connectivity synonymously with inter-personal connectivity. These inferences are drawn in support of the thesis that has been propagated by this chapter, viz., the real and true knowledge of the self as the spiritual essential is different from being identified with the physical and material adjuncts. The understanding of this distinction between the spiritual and physical meaning and nature of one's self and thereby gaining self-awareness become the basis of managing emotional crisis and sustaining wellness and mindfulness.

My resource material has been from Scholarly Works on Indian philosophy like those of S. Radhakrishnan (2008), Surendranath Dasgupta (2002) A.K. Warder (2009), A.C. Bhativedanta's *Bhagvad Gita* (2006), Paul Deussen (1979), Namita Kar (1989), Roshen Dalal (2018), and online resource material, especially Internet encyclopedia, e-sources like e-gyankosha, e-newspapers, and various relevant Web sites, besides other research resources available online. All of these have been duly acknowledged and cited. I have sparingly referred to an earlier publication of mine and cited it, wherever I have used it (Navneet, 2020).

Traditional Indian Philosophies: An Exposition of the Main Tenets of These Model Theories

In the current chapter, the philosophies of Vedanta which are also alluded as the phase of Upanishads have been dwelt on first, thereafter the philosophies of Samkhya/Sankhya and Yoga, then references to *Kathopanishada,* and finally references to some aphorisms from *Bhagvad Gita* have been made for enunciating the philosophical models.

Vedanta System

Vedanta is one of the ancient systems of thought that agrees with Vedic testimony and is thereby known as one belonging to the orthodox systems of Indian philosophy. Vedanta school of thought emphasizes on gaining or realizing the knowledge of the ultimate reality or the truth and thereby in achieving spiritual liberation. On the other hand, this system decries those who lead themselves toward the pursuits ensnared in *māyā* (the phenomenon which is decried as concealing the truth) by deluding themselves to follow the path of egoistic attachments, or in having an insatiable aspiration for selfish desires, being led by obstructed reasoning and hence in suffering of pain and pleasure. 'Vedanta system does not have a singular interpretation, and hence, various schools within the same tradition differed about the conceptions and approaches with respect to the analysis of the nature of relationship and a degree of identity between the eternal core of the individual self (*jiva*) and the absolute (concepts of *ātman* and *Brahman,* respectively). These theories have been designated as- absolute non-dualistic (*advaita*) as propounded by the *eighth*-century philosopher Shankaracharya, popularly known as Shankara (and the most popular commentator on Vedanta) to the theistic one (*Vishishtaadvaitavāda;* or the qualified non-dualism) of the eleventh–twelfth-century thinker *Ramanujacharya*, referred to as Ramanuja, and the dualism (*dvaitāvāda*) of the thirteenth-century thinker Madhava.' (Paraphrased from *Encyclopedia Britannica* 2015, March 5 *Vedanta*) (T. Editors of Encyclopaedia, 2015).

A cursory review of the Vedantic period is that there are three fundamental texts that have been associated with this system of thought: "the Upanishads (some of these are longer and older ones like the one addressed in this chapter, the *Katha-Upanishad*); the *Brahma-sutras* compiled by Bādrāyana (also called *Vedanta Sutras*), which are very brief, even one-word interpretations of the doctrine of the Upanishads; and the *Bhagvad Gitā* (Song of the Lord)." (Paraphrased from *Encyclopaedia Britannica* 2015, March 5 *Vedanta).*

It needs to be noted that *Bhagvad Gita*, though combined with *Shruti* (Vedanta and Upanishads and has been adjudged to have used Samkhya and Yoga philosophical references too), is also considered a *Smriti* (*Smriti. Encyclopedia Britannica*) (Britannica, T. Editors of Encyclopaedia, 2013).

Upanishads: The Philosophical Current of Vedanta—The Documents/Dialogues During the Vedanta Period

"The Upanishads are among the oldest philosophical documents as the earliest texts are thought to have been composed between 800 and 500 BCE. Among the documented 180–200 Upanishads, the best known are about thirteen. *Katha-Upanishad,* which is also referred as *Kathopanishad* is one of these thirteen." (Paraphrased:

Mark, J. J. (2020, June 10). "Upanishads". *World History Encyclopedia*)) (Mark, 2020).

The Upanishads are generally identified with *Vedanta* and described as the concluding phase of the Vedas or the phase delineating pure philosophical description of the state of realizing spiritual knowledge. "These are basically documented discourses, which were composed mostly in the form of philosophical dialogs relating to the concepts expressed by the Vedas. Upanishads are also considered by orthodox tradition as being a part of *Shruti* since the wisdom and insight they contain appear too profound to be comprehended easily. As a matter of fact, the term *Upanishad* literally means to sit closely near a teacher for comprehending a sacred or an esoteric knowledge." (Paraphrased from *Encyclopaedia Britannica* 2015, March 5 *Vedanta).*

For the present chapter, **the focus is only on the *Kathopanishad*** to enunciate an example of ethical discourse in Vedantic philosophy. **This chapter has flagged the point** that the Vedantic philosophy, which is considered esoteric, since most of its discourse has been on metaphysical aspects of enunciating the meaning and nature of the self, did have some examples that detailed out a path of morality required to reach the stage of *mukti* (state of liberation). In other words, the chapter highlights that not all Upanishad explicated only on the metaphysical aspect of reality, but some, like *Kathopanishad,* stressed upon the moral aspects of living. So, *karma-mārga* (the path of action) was not altogether subtracted from the *jñāna-mārga* (the path of knowledge) from the Vedantic literature. However, the debate between the two paths is not considered here.

Also, as pointed out earlier, the chapter has noted that a significant common current of the ethically correct path or *karma* as a *Yoga* or a disciplined way to achieve *Brahmvidyā* or *ātma-jñāna* (cosmic knowledge about the soul or the self) has been followed up both in the *Bhagvad Gita* which assimilated the theory of Samkhya as expounded by Ishvarkrishna. It emphasized on explicating the discrimination of spiritual and physical aspects of individuals' moral life and spiritual aspirations as well as in the main tenets of Yoga philosophy as enunciated by Patanjali (Radhakrishnan: 2008 edition. Volume-2). However, this chapter has also pointed out the differences between them. Well-known scholar like Warder and some other scholars like Kar, Namita, and the cited online resources have also referred to this connection and contrast between this Upanishad and its contrast with philosophies of Samkya and Yoga. A brief overview of the philosophies of Sankhya and Yoga would substantiate these points.

An Overview of Sāṁkhya and Yoga Philosophies

Sāṁkhya Philosophy

'Sāṁkhya system (also spelled as Sāṅkhya) is one of the major schools of what was referred to as the orthodox system (*āstika*) in traditional Indian philosophies. It is also known to be one of the oldest schools, probably two millennia old. The oldest version is associated with Kapil Rishi, and the later version or the popularly known one is found in Īśvarakṛṣṇa's *Sāṅkhya-Kārikā* (350 C.E.), which has a condensed version explained through seventy-two verses. The renowned Indian epic, the *Mahābhārata,* apparently written during the first half of the first millennium BCE, refers to the Sāṅkhya system as already quite old. This school expounds a strict dualism between the eternal realms of physical reality or the nature (known as *Prakriti/* natural) and the spiritual (*Purusha* or the pure consciousness). At the same time, it advocates atheism. Nature according to this tradition is singular, while persons (Purushas) are numerous.' (Paraphrased: *Samkhya. Encyclopeadia Britannica.* https://www.britannica.com/topic/Samkhya) (Britannica T. Editors of Encyclopaedia, 2020).

Sāṅkhya, as is clear from the above, treats both the realities as **eternal and independent of each other.** *Purusha*s/spiritual entities or liberated persons are essentially unchangeable, inactive and refer to the pure and liberated entities, but due to the contact with *Prakriti,* i.e., the nature these entities can become bound by the ego, mind, and intellect that are the ingrained features of Prakriti or nature. Creation according to Sāṁkhya comes about by a conjunction of nature and principle of consciousness.

'*Prakriti* or nature is explicated as the constituent of three strands known as *guṇa*s (which is similar to the meaning that the word quality implies in English language). These qualities are known as *Sattva, Rajas, and Tamas.* The three qualities or *gunas* are in a state of equilibrium in an uncreated state of universe, but represent three kinds of nature in the created world and the bound persons or Purushas. In the state of creation, the homogeneity of the *gunas* becomes heterogenous, and one of the qualities becomes the dominant trait of the created/embodied Purusha. A **kind of a hierarchy is indicated in terms of the nature of these qualities.** The highest among the three is *sattva* (essence), the principle of light, goodness, and intelligence. *Rajas* (dynamism) is the principle of change, energy, and passion, while *tamas* (darkness) implies inactivity, dullness, heaviness, and despair.' (Paraphrased: https://iep.utm.edu/sankhya) (Ruzsa, F. *Sankhya.* https://iep.utm.edu/sankhya. First time accessed on 30/01/2021.).

Samkhya School has clearly distinguished between the concept of *Purusha* as the referent of individual person(s) or embodied persons and the *Purusha* who is enumerated as one of the two eternal realities that Samkhya system has explicated. The other reality is Prakriti composed of three *gunas,* as has been detailed in the preceding paragraph. It would be appropriate to refer to the embodied state of the Purusha/individual souls to clarify about Sankhya or correct knowledge of the distinction between the real nature and not the real nature of the self. Nature or *Prakriti* though explicated as the unconscious principle is, however, designated the purposive or teleological role to serve the goal/*telos* of the individual *Puruṣa* or persons. *Prakrti* is supposed to enable the life experience for the individual person/*Purusha* and should also lead his/her liberation from all material forms of individual's embodied existence by liberating him/her from itself.

'Besides being existent in the physical universe, the individual *Purusha* comprises the gross body and subtle aspects of a *Purusha* (the principle of consciousness or spirituality). The subtle aspects contain, among other things, the epistemological apparatus of embodied beings (such as the mind and the intellect). The subtle aspects of a *Purusha* transmigrate after the death of the gross body. An embodied Purusha is reborn into another gross body according to past merit. An escape from this endless circle is possible only through the realization of the fundamental difference between nature/*Prakriti* and persons/*Purusha*, whereby an individual *Purusha* loses interest in nature and is thereby liberated forever from all bodies, subtle, and gross.' (Paraphrased: https://iep.utm.edu/sankhya/).

It is argued by the Samkhya that 'these three *gunas* are present in all the objects of the world. None of them exists alone. Among them each *guna* tries to dominate the other two. Hence, they can't exist in a tranquil state. As a result, they can't remain pure for a single moment since they are changing continuously. Variation and diversion is their nature. However, the liberated *Purusha* (the principle of spirituality) remains the onlooker without either being part of any change or experiencing any changes.' (Paraphrased: Radhakrishnan, 2008 edition. p. 237–238 and 267–269).

Scholars like Warder have pointed out that Sāṅkhya concepts and terminology frequently appear in the portion of the Vedas known as the Upaniṣhads, like in the *Kaṭha-upanishad.* "It is significant to note that the philosophical texts such as the *Katha-Upanishad i*n verses 3.10–13 and 6.7–11 describe a well-defined concept of *puruṣha* and other concepts of Samkhya and *Bhagavad Gita.* In Book 2, it provides axiological implications of Samkhya, thereby providing textual evidence of Samkhyan terminology and concepts." (Warder: 2009, 63–64).

Yoga Philosophy of Patanjali

Yoga philosophy has historically received its theoretical sustenance from Saṅkhya philosophy which, as aforementioned, means right knowledge, i.e., knowing difference between the principle of spirituality and the eternal physical side of the worldly reality of varied experiences.

'Patanjali's Yoga, unlike the literal meaning of Yoga (union), does not imply any kind of union between the individual self and some other reality like God or the Absolute, rather the aim here is to prevent the self from identifying itself with mental modifications' (Radhakrishnan, S: 2008 edition. Volume-2 P. 309–10 paraphrased).

Patanjali in his *Yoga-Sutra* expounded the cessation of mental functions or modifications of mind as being the connotation of Yoga. Yoga is defined by Patanjali as "*cittavṛttinirodha*, which implies the cessation of mind's diversion. The *citta* is compared to mind by Patajali. There are five *vṛttis* (modifications or diversions or distortions of the mental or psychical dispositions)." (https://iep.utm.edu/yoga) (Edwin, B. *The Yoga Sutras of* Patanjali. https://iep.utm.edu/yoga. First time accessed on 30/01/2021.). The mind or the *citta*, according to Patanjali, is the locus of the emotional dispositions and expressions and is characterized by controlling the senses which becomes feasible through regulating the senses and experiences or impressions associated with them. At the same time, it also serves as the connecting link between the emotional states and *buddhi* (intelligence). Hence, *citta* has been used, in Patanjali's *Yoga-Sūtras,* to refer to any sensual impression and an engaged mental state.

According to Patanjali's *Yoga-Sutra,* the distinction between the individual self and the supreme reality is not realized as long as the self has not realized its distinction from the mind/*citta.* His thesis of Yoga really stands for the cessation and negation of all mental modifications or diversions due to association of the self or spirit with ego and psychological obstructions. The *Purusha,* or the embodied self (similar to the concept of individual person, as delineated in the Samkhya School), is layered in these psychical-intelligence aspects prior to becoming the embodied self. 'The Yoga School has used the terminology of *buddhi, ahaṁkāra,* and *manas* as used by Sankhya but differ, somewhat, from them in conceiving these as rather interacting functions singularly of the *citta* or the mind. Hence, *citta* becomes the focal term in Patanjali's *Yoga-Sutra.* In Patanjali's philosophy of Yoga, five possible modifications or diversions (*vrttis*) of the mind are mentioned. These five *vṛttis* are: right knowledge, error, metaphor, deep sleep, and memory. A cessation of these changes or diversions of the mind have been called Yoga.' (Paraphrased: https://iep.utm.edu/yoga).

For the purification and enlightenment of *citta* or the mind, his Yoga suggests following the eightfold means. These have been enumerated as: "(a) *yama* or restraint, (b) *niyama* or culture, (c) *āsana* or posture, (d) *prānāyama* or breath control, (e) *pratyahara* or withdrawal of the senses, (f) *dhārana* or attention, (g) *dhyāna* or meditation, and (h) *Samādhi* or concentration. *These are known as aids to Yoga. When practiced regularly with devotion and dispassion, they lead to the attainment of calmness, the meditative state—both samprajnata and asamprajñātā*". (https://iep.utm.edu/yoga). "There are two main kinds of yoga or Samadhi or the ultimate state of calmness, viz., the *samprajñata*and the *asamprajñāta.*" (Radhakrishnan: 2008 edition, Volume 2, p. 317). The former kind of samadhi discusses the state of minimum material modification of the mind, but the latter represents that state of Samadhi or meditation where all mental modifications stop and, hence, represents an absolute placid state of mind. 'Both these kinds of Samadhi are known by the common name of *Samadhi-Yoga* or the cessation of mental modifications, since both conduce to self-realization, and thereby liberation from all sensuous desires.' (Paraphrased, Radhakrishnan: 2008 edition, Volume 2, p. 317 and 329).

Yoga philosophy analyzes the five conditions or levels of the mental life (*cittabhumi*) in details matching the methods of psychology. "The *citta* is constituted by the elements of *sattva, rajas,* and *tamas* (the three *gunas* constituting the reality of nature or Prakriti as in Samkhya) or purity, activity, and sloth, respectively. Its different conditions are determined by the predominance in which these elements are present and operative in it. These conditions are states of restlessness, or of pleasure, or of distraction, or of focus, and of restrain." (Paraphrased: Radhakrishnan: 2008 edition, Volume 2, p. 317).

'Though there have been references to Yoga even as early as 4000 years ago, it is in the late Vedic age, marked by the philosophical speculations expressed in the Upaniṣads like the *Kaṭha-Upaniṣad* that ethical practices that can be clearly related to classical Yoga are first articulated in literary sources. While the Upaniṣhads are primarily concerned with *jñāna* (knowledge of or understanding *Brahman*, as the cosmic and absolute truth, there are also several references to a technique or the methods or the paths for realizing *Brahman* (in the individual's context of *ātman*) called Yoga. The *Mahābhārata Epic,* which is the largest literary epic in the world, also preserves significant material representing the evolution of Yoga, by referring to the paths of gaining the wisdom as yoga and the agents practicing these as the Yogi. *Bhagvad Gita*, which forms a part of the epic, *Mahabhārata*, recurrently refers to this tradition.' (Paraphrased: https://iep.utm.edu/yoga/).

Kathopanishad: Enunciation of Two Paths—*Shreyas* (Good) and *Preyas* (Pleasant)

"The *Katha-Upanishad* also referred to as the *Kathopanishad* is one of the primary Upanishads found in the last short eight sections of the *Kaṭha* School of the Krishna Yajurveda." (Krishnaanda, Swami, **Lessons on the Upanishads.** Most of my references are from this source, which has been **duly cited earlier** in the chapter, unless specified otherwise).

"*The* Katha-Upanishad *is considered as one of the major Upanishads, since Sankara Bhagavatpäda has commented on it. It belongs to the Kathaka-Säkhä of* Krshna-Yajurveda. *Although tradition considers Shruti as timeless, scholars place it belonging to the Sütra period of Vedic Sanskrit literature. It figures as third Upanishad in the list of 108 Upanishads in* Muktikä Upanishad (Muk.- Up.*-30). It consists of two chapters (*adhyāyas*), each divided into three sections (*vallis*) that contain a total of 119 mantras. In volume, it comes third after* Chändogya *and* Brhadranyaka *Upanishads. Many mantras of Kathopanishad have been repeated in the* Bhagavad Gitä *in verbatim/or adapted.*" (https://www.speakingtree.in/blog/kathopanishad-i-231976) (Atmaprajananda, 2013).

This Upanishad is a dialogical narrative between Nachiketa—the son of Sage Vajsravasa (and is a young boy) and Yama (the God of Death). Their conversation primarily focuses on the themes of the essential nature of individuals, real nature of *Brahmvidyā* or the knowledge of *ātman*/Brahman (soul, self), and *moksha* (spiritual liberation) following the righteous or ethical path of Shreyas (good).

The background to this dialog is the story that Nachiketa had enraged his father, King Vajasravasa by not acknowledging his acts of generosity as selfless actions. 'In his rage to the response and queries made by his son about donations, which Nachiketa feels have no value for the recipients, the king (his father) wills his son to the lord of death, Yama. In the dialog between Yama and Nachiketa, one of the main points of *Kathopanishad* emerges. It dealt with the way or the path to gain the true knowledge about self (*ātmajñāna*). Nachiketa asks Yama to grant him the knowledge of supreme spiritual principle or *brahmavidyā* as his third boon. The first two boons being, wellness of his father and a cordial relation with him when Nachiketa goes back to his palace. The first *adhyaya* of the second valli (which has 6 verses) *of*

Kathopanishad teaches the concept of *Shreyas* and *Preyas*, where Yama talks about how the discerning power of the mind enables man to take either the path to worldly prosperity or to immortality.' (Paraphrased: Krishnaanda, Swami, **Lessons on the Upanishads**).

The Upanishad states that Yama in an attempt to dissuade Nachiketa who is a teenager from seeking the knowledge of self and secrets of death and allures him by offering pleasures of life, kingship, wealth, progeny, and livestock. However, Nachiketa resiliently stands his ground to seek the higher level of truth and knowledge. This earnestness from Nachiketa impresses Yama, and he explains to him the nature, meaning, and the correct path to attain and realize spiritual wisdom or the highest knowledge.

The Upanishad explicates that the ethical path of treading wellness or good in itself *(shreyas)* and the pleasurable way of acquiring worldly gains (*Preyas*) are available to all individuals. The wise person examines and is able to distinguish their worth and treads on the righteous one. "The wise one prefers *Shreyas* (wellness), but people of poor intellect accept Preyas (pleasures) since they are lured by vanity. One preferring *Shreyas* over *preyas* follows the path of *Nivritti* or *moksha* (spiritual liberation). On the other hand, a person possessing poor intellect, lacking in discrimination opts for *Pravritti* and seeks the pleasures of the body." (Paraphrased: Krishnaanda, Swami, **Lessons on the Upanishads**). *Nivrittimarga* or the path pursued through good or righteousness implies that the focus is on the welfare of the *ātmā* and not of the body. This realization (*Moksha*) about seeking good of the soul rather than the body is reached through detachment from the worldly gains. Nachiketa symbolizes this path of righteous discrimination.

Hence, in choosing *Shreyas* and thereby *nivrttimarga*, Nachiketa chooses the path *of ānanda*, the path of untainted bliss which also means *nishreyas. Ananda* literally means bliss or happiness that comes with the end of the cycle of rebirth and makes the individual self-aware and, hence, spiritually elevated and wise.

As noted in the preceding paragraphs on Upanishads, 'the knowledge of Brahman is not easily attainable by many even when taught by an expert. Rarely does a soul become a knower, after being instructed by a proficient teacher.' ("*Katha-Upanishad" in* R Dalal: 2018, p. 212–213).

The point regarding *Kathopanishad* emphasizing equally on *karma* and *jnana*, and thereby reflecting upon the humanistic spiritualism, has been commented upon by Shankara as well. According to Shankara, 'this Upanishad emphasizes on the ethical principles of practice of oneness following the path of goodness, and this is in consonance with the epistemological–metaphysical principle of non-dual conception of Brahman as being the only reality.' (Paraphrased, Kar, N.: 1989, p. 42–46.)

Both paths that of duty and of desire—that of the good and of the pleasant—were examined by Nachiketa. It became clear to him that there was no plurality and separateness between the essence of "I" and "others," between the essence of "nature" and "spirit." Hence, a seeker of the essential knowledge about soul, like Nachiketa, ignores the superficial individuality of others and accepts the essential cosmic identity of everyone.

Kathopanishad, Sankhya, and Yoga Philosophies: Similarity and Contrast

As stated earlier, I have inferred that there are running common threads of thoughts in the *Kathopanishad*, as well as Sankhya and Yoga philosophy. Yet, the two stand out through their propagation of their respective conceptions about spiritualism and correct knowledge. In final verses of the second valli, the *Katha-Upanishad* asserts that *ātman-knowledge*, or self-realization, is neither attained by instruction nor through arguments or through reasoning from scriptures. It is comprehended by oneself through meditation, introspection, and self-realization. It is not attained by those who are restless and not composed, not also by those whose mind is not calm and tranquil, but only by those who live ethically, are composed, tranquil, internally peaceful, search within, and introspect and become Prajapati (self-aware).

The *Kathopanishad*, according to Shankara's commentary, states that 'the highest goal is attainment of Brahman, which is gained only by that knowledge which is completely purged off by *adhyasa*/maya/the phenomenon concealing the truth and thereby leading to ignorance. An individual should holistically unify one's tempered senses and mind with their intellect, all these with one's *Atman* (Soul, great Self), and unify one's great Self with the Self of the rest, the tranquility of oneness with the *avyaktam* and cosmic unity of the soul.' (Paraphrased: Kar Namita: 42–46).

However, the differences between Sankhya-Yoga and *Kathopanishada* are clear to a person with a nuanced understanding of these traditions. It becomes clear to such a person that "beyond the senses, mind, and intellect is the great soul that is unmanifest; beyond the unmanifest is the cosmic soul, and beyond this is nothing. That is the end, the final goal." (Paraphrased, Krishnaanda, Swami, **Lessons on the Upanishads**). These verses clearly separate the *Katha-Upanishad* from Sankhya-Yoga tradition. In the Samkya and Yoga, the unmanifest soul remains separate forever from the senses, mind, and body.

The *Bhagvad Gita*: A Syncretic Philosophy

'The *Bhagvad Gita* (literally meaning The Song of the God or of the Divine One, where Lord Krishna is the denotation of the divine consciousness) is also referred to as the *Gitā* and has been a part of the epic *Mahabharata.* Lord Krishna is the narrator of the *Bhagavad Gita* where the verses are written in a poetic form, and these are traditionally chanted; hence, the title. The teachings of the *Gitā* are narrated as a conversation between Lord Krishna and Arjuna, a warrior prince, taking place on the battlefield of Kurukshetra just prior to the start of a climactic war. Responding to Arjuna's emotional turbulence and moral about going to war with his cousins who have taken to the path of deceit, Krishna explains to Arjuna his duties as a warrior and a prince.' (Paraphrased: Mark, J.J., 15th June 2020 "Bhagvad Gita") (Mark, 2020).

Krishna elaborates on a number of philosophical tenets for everyday living, with examples and analogies. *Bhagvad Gita* is generally considered a *Smriti* text, but much like *Shruti* traditions (Gautam, P.K. February 12, 2013 "Shruti and Smriti") focus on the fundamentals of the eternal truths like the concepts of *Ātmā* and the concept of detachment to gain spiritual realization. The central thought of this scripture as a Smriti is to elucidate that knowledge about the spiritual principle and following the ethical path of duty or detachment/*nishkama* from the fructified result of one's action enables a person to remain emotionally and mentally stable in adverse circumstances. *Bhagvad Gita* has been also described as the guide book exemplifying the concept of responsible acts or dutiful actions done by an individual person without desiring for the results thereof (*nishkama-karma*). According to the *Gitā,* 'the ownership of action needs to have the moral intent of performing it without claiming any beneficial entitlements that accrue. Hence, the *Bhagvad Gita* which consists of 18 chapters can be described as a concise guide to Hindu philosophy and also as a practical, self-contained guide to life skills to the contemporary humans despite its historical antiquity.' (Paraphrased: Mark, J.J. 15th June 2020 "Bhagvad Gita").

The explanation of a mindful and emotionally stable person, a *sthitprajnña,* has been made feasible in the *Gitā* due to its syncretic philosophy of giving equal emphasis to the three paths (*karma, bhakti, and jñāna*). It is advocated here that the spiritual elevation or well-being follows in achieving the stability of the mind, and this is the key to realizing one's true identity, life's meaning and purpose. With this wisdom, achieved through mindfulness and emotional stability, a *sthithprajnña* can clearly discern things, know the truth from falsehood, reality from delusion, and escape from the confusion and delusion of *māyā*' or the alluring web of competitions, material, and consumerist gains. It may be noted that the scripture has dextrously combined the traditions of Sānkhya, Yoga, and Vedānta philosophies, like the *Kathopanishad*, in analyzing the relationship of being intellectually elevated (or being mindful) and in gaining the spiritual wisdom by following the righteous path. Chapter 3 (between verses 3.6 and 3.17) of *The Gita* has explicated the primary traits of a *karma-yogi* (a dutiful agent), who knows the importance of controlling one's senses and of engaging with work with a focus on duty (Referred, here, to the chapters as put in Bhaktivedanta's Bhagvad Gita As It Is). So, a person who overcomes the desires to compete is calm and performs one's actions without craving to win and prove oneself better than the others. Such an approach not only liberates human beings from the struggling and striving ensued earlier by pandering to their egoistic dispositions, but also greatly reduces their anxieties and frustrations, thereby facilitating on a permanent basis—a stable, peaceful, and contended life.

'The *Bhagvad Gita* has explained the state of mind's tranquility and physical wellness by taking a philosophical sustenance from Patanjali's Yoga philosophy and to some extent from the monistic tradition of Vedanta. The wisdom in the *Gita* as imparted between Chaps. 2 and 18 makes it feasible to pursue any of the three paths (*karma, bhakti, and jñāna*) without feeling constrained to follow any one in particular or even follow each exclusively' (Paraphrased, Dasgupta, Surendranath: 2003 edition, "The Philosophy of Bhagvadgītā.",) (the cited source, Dasgupta has used these spellings of Bhagvad Gita).

The *Bhagvad Gita*, as is clear from the preceding paragraphs, has drawn from philosophy of Sankhya and Vedanta. There is certainly a significant change by referring to the cosmic principle as a theological one, i.e., Lord Krishna. "God, in the theological sense, is referred to as the *avyakta*, the unmanifested. However, the difference from Samkhya is that while the Purusha in Sankhya remains avyakta, Krishna as the supreme lord/Purusha remains so till the person remains overpowered by the sensuous desires and attachments to the physical aspects of the world. He becomes manifested to the one who has elevated oneself spiritually, thereby making the case of a *jivan-mukta* possible, i.e., making the case of humanistic spiritualism and spiritual self-elevation feasible for individuals or humans." (Dasgupta, Surendranath: 2003 edition, paraphrased: "The Philosophy of Bhagvadgītā" (these spellings of Bhagvad Gita are from the cited work, i.e., Dasgupta's).

Application of the Traditional Models in the Contemporary Worldview

It would be appropriate to instantiate by referring to lessons on each philosophical model that this chapter has extensively delineated, and enunciating the lessons drawn from these in managing life issues in the present-day world, and also their relevance in the current state of the world besieged by the pandemic. These can be cited as denotations of the dictum—*from model to application.*

Specific Context of the Current Times and Life Skill Management Guidelines from the Philosophical Traditions of India

The running thought in the chapter has been to explicate and assess the feasibility of the traditional Indian philosophical theories and scriptural narratives in providing able guidelines in the twenty-first-century worldview. The current world situation has seen the decline of mental health and a widened gap in inter-personal relationships. The twenty-first-century ecosystem with its existential conditions being guided by a high level of dependence on technology and virtual world, competition rather than cooperation in inter-personal relations, fixation with body shape, physical features, and wrongly identifying these with the meaning of self-identity, and consumeristic consumption of resources could have led to the life issues just mentioned above. The traditional philosophies, according to this chapter, are viable models to address and suggest resolutions.

The chapter has specifically flagged current situation of pandemic and has advocated that this has made humans across the globe realize the critical significance of **empathy in inter-personal connection, importance of wellness in mind and**

body, valuing the ethical virtue of contentment and cooperation, and following good practice of hygiene. The **social distancing** which has become the **new normal** has made people more anxious about losing the connect that makes humans thrive as social and cultural species. The cases of mental ill-health are on the rise. Reminiscing and deliberating on oneness though intervened by a virtual mode has enabled some reassurance in people's mind. The emphasis of this chapter has been that the traditional Indian philosophies, explicated here, have facilitated this positive reaffirmation.

Life Lessons from Kathopanishada and Vedanta: The Impact of Vedantic Theory of Oneness/Empathy/Cosmic Unity

The teaching of Upanishads centered on establishing the concept of essential commonness of the human beings has been termed, in almost all Upanishads as being synonymous with *atman or Brahman* (soul or cosmic consciousness). "*Brihadaaranyaka Upanishad*, for instance, says in this regard: *ahambrahmaasmiiti, tasmaat tat sarvamabhavat*; which means realizing one's true self as Brahman, one becomes everything" (Swami, 2020). This *jñana / Knowledge* or awareness about the essential identity of each one of us needs to be the highest goal of a human being that can easily be the guiding value in managing life issue of competitive strife. The welfare of the world depends upon the welfare of all which makes us respect the significance of inter-personal connectedness or empathy.

The Vedantic/Upanishadic tradition, according to this chapter, can be understood as a significant wisdom guide on making us self-aware and in comprehending the meanings of spiritual realization, which in turn follow the knowledge of self-identity, being informed about the truth-Brahman/atman and its distinction from the fake. The digital/online world or the reference to the world (*jagat*) as a virtual truth (*māyā*) can be contextualized in today's scenario of the world being monitored by social distancing, yet, being inter-connected simultaneously via the virtual/online platform.

Kathopanishada's Impact: The Moral and Spiritual Elevation Due to a Discerning Attitude

The reference to emphasis upon *Shreyas* as the right choice for a moral action on leading a virtuous life based upon rational discrimination (*Vivek*) and seeking oneness with everyone can be easily compared with Samkhya School, which propagates the discriminatory knowledge between the physical and spiritual nature of reality as the correct awareness. Our worldly engagements as experienced at the level of physical reality can never determine our essential truth. These are all capable of change and impermanence. So, they should neither deter us nor exhilarate us. These are experiences of psychophysical side of our living which keep changing with the changing material conditions and are thereby not to be accounted for our spiritual growth. Our essential truth transcends this level, and at the transcendental level, we are **inter-connected**. We are cosmically united as one or sharing the same essence.

***Shreyas*, in today's time,** will be exemplified by a person who is compassionate, emotionally mature, spiritually aware, and follows the path of non-consumerist way of life. *Preyas,* on the other hand, will denote anxiety ridden people who are never satisfied with what they have and keep yearning for more and more of selfish and personal material gains. The Upanishad's guiding lesson is that the more we realize the inter-connectedness and harmony of being, the closer we are to the concept of spirituality. The more the separation between one person and the other, the greater is the assumption of the individual, hence, more the anxieties and imprudence.

Hence, *Kathopanishada,* through Nachiketa's example of seeking self-growth and remaining consistent with this aspiration despite being in the center of the most adverse circumstance, that of being in the house of the God of Death, teaches the significance of remaining steadfast/Sthitprajna in one's aims. This can be surely understood as an important life lesson for the current state of living through the pandemic: facing threatening situations with a calm mind and emotional maturity.

Effects of Yoga Philosophy in the Present-day World Amid the COVID-19 Challenges

While the *asamprajñāta* kind or the focused and absolutely detached meditation or a state of absolute mindfulness may not be feasible in the fast multi-tasking modern world of today, the COVID-19 pandemic has forced us to look in the directions, which the contemporary worldview has been avoiding to seek a mindful, holistic view of mental and physical wellness. Health and Yoga experts say that meditating on a regular basis helps improve the immunity system, thus creating a shield in a fight against this highly infectious disease.

To substantiate my thesis about **Yoga philosophy lending pragmatic guidelines to holistic wellness,** (mental as well as physical), I have quoted from an article published in *Indian Express,* e-chapter, published on July 2020, as cited below:

> In an article published in the International Journal of Recent Scientific Research, several medical doctors have drawn a comparison between stress and immunity and how too much of mental agony can decrease the healing powers of mind and body. That's when the ancient practice of meditation can help build a wall around the human immunity system. The studies say that meditation increases telomerase activity and lengthens telomeres and thus promotes immune cell longevity. Beneficial effects of meditation also include reducing the activity of nuclear factor - kB, which is a mediator in the pathogenesis of certain types of cancer, arthritis, asthma, and neurodegenerative diseases. Talking more about the benefits of meditation, Hyderabad-based yoga trainer Harshita Soni shares, out of 195 Yoga Sutras, only three talk about physical asanas. The rest is all about the mind and its power, almost magical in nature. We can say that Patanjali was the first psychologist in the world. While one meditates the goal is to pluck the mind out of the problem. Why people experience more

pain while suffering is because their focus is on the pain, which multiplies its intensity. Meditation techniques do boost immunity especially if one exhales properly and deeply; that alone empties the lungs bringing purification. Even five minutes of Pranayam every day is very good especially in these times when everyone is experiencing extreme anxiety. She??? operates from a Somajiguda centre, which is now restricted only to children with special needs or senior citizens. A team of researchers from the University of Wisconsin Madison conducted a study on a group of 25 healthy employees, who practised meditation for eight weeks. The finding revealed that meditation activated an important immune linked region in the brain as it showed a good antibody response. Any disease finds its way in our body more easily if we are under stress, which also means that our mind isn't calm. It's all about experiencing the 'now', and meditation facilitates it, bringing its own treasures" (Saima, 2020).

Bhagvad Gita and the Twenty-First-Century Worldview and the Situation of the Pandemic

In relation to the *Gitā* and the context of present-day crisis amid the pandemic, it becomes imperative to further explicate how this scripture focuses upon the current dynamics of the blurred boundary between the personal domestic space and the duty-bound professional domain, i.e., **work from home.** This kind of situation has added anxiety and restlessness besides the challenge of keeping oneself safe from the virus and its afflictions. Also, most people have felt emotional turmoil with the guilt of not being able to physically be with the aggrieved sufferers of this disease.

However, the *Gitā* can be a valuable guide to provide to work in this new normal way of life and living. *Bhagavad Gita* provides a guidance to comprehend an appropriate meaning of inaction and action. The correct meaning of *nishkāma* as gathered from the scripture emphasizes on doing the duty responsibly and righteously whether in the public domain or the private one. So, the undefined space between two domains will also need to be worked upon with the same sense of duty which is not based upon the hierarchy of spaces where public space has been considered superior hitherto. This sense of duty comes only by becoming self-aware/atma-*Jñāna* and realizing the significance of the impermanence and mortality of the experiences associated with the material side of life. Hence, the concept of *karma* as *nishkāma* and the concept of *self*-awareness in relation to it imply a correct methodology or the path of managing life skills in the current state of global distress.

'In the context of the current situation of the pandemic and feeling of helplessness associated with it, a *sthithaprajñya* an emotionally evolved and a mindful person, as defined in the *Gitā*, will have the knowledge that distinguishes between the real (the permanent; the cosmic oneness known through *atman* or the soul) and the unreal (the changing impermanent, worldly experiences).' (Paraphrased: Navneet, Rekha: 2020). Such a person realizes that genuine feelings and the affirmative meanings of human inter-connectedness matter more than just being there physically together. This kind of a person will have the empathy to feel connected and along with the knowledge of the correct meanings of duty with purpose will surely be able to sustain mindfulness and emotional stability despite there being social distancing and the blurred spaces of home and work place. 'This steadfast state of mind achieved through the right action can be used as a reference point for understanding the influence of The *Gitā* in addressing present-day issues of mental health following the emotional upheavals.' (Paraphrased: Navneet, Rekha: 2020).

Conclusion

Traditional Indian Philosophical Discourse: Wisdom Guideline for the Present Times

The philosophies, explicated in the chapter, separately and collectively advocate that our worldly experiences based upon our interactions with worldly existence are ever changing and ephemeral. These experiences are representative of our psychophysical identity and, hence, different from our spiritual nature. We are often deluded into believing this to be our true identity and fuel our anxiety to protect it. These philosophies have guided on making us aware of this mistaken notion of self and thereby of the self-centered or ego-centered concepts of I, me, mine, myself, etc. Hence, these philosophical theories guide us toward the path of right knowledge by enabling us to discriminate between the narrow or an incorrect meaning of "I" as opposed to its essential meaning as the soul, and thereby identify ourselves with our essential self-identity (*ātmā*), thus, making us realize our cosmic unity (as in identifying our individual self with *Brahman*).

These philosophies, therefore, act as model guidelines that facilitate ourselves seeking the right knowledge (*vedanta/upanishads*), acting upon the awareness of the difference between physical and spiritual (Samkhya and Yoga), in following the righteous path to realize the spiritual awareness of one's self/*ātmā/Brahman* (*Kathopanishad*) and in synthesizing/processing of all of these along with the devotion to the concept of a Supreme *Purusha* or soul in the form of Lord Krishna (*Bhagvad Gita*). These philosophical treatises lead us to become mindful, morally righteous, spiritually elevated and thus help us in becoming emotionally stable and realizing the critical significance of inter-personal connectivity. Together, these philosophies prepare one to follow the ethical path of wellness (*shreyas*) and detach from superficial pleasures.

These traditions can, hence, be used as a reference to the concept of interconnectedness as part of living life meaningfully, mindfully, and ethically. People internalizing these philosophical guidelines become spiritually elevated, feel calmness of mind and fitness of body, can discern between the fake and the real, conserve more and consume less, and can certainly empathize more through their compassion. These practices enable an individual to be self-aware and have a calm mind and emotional stability at the individual level, thereby sustaining a genuine inter-personal fellowship in the public domain.

Following the cues from the aforementioned theories, it may be stated that the following ways could, and in some cases have, enabled putting things in a

better perspective and managing life in these adverse times in an exemplary way.

Some examples like those of using the period of isolation and quarantine to contemplate and deliberate on meaning and purpose of life. The second wave of pandemic surge in India led to fatalities among younger and otherwise healthy population. Yet, some people were able to manage grief of losing their loved ones so suddenly with a commendable sense of equanimity, specifically in conducting death rituals. Strangers cooperated and reached out during the emergency situations despite the physical distancing. A new sense of cooperation and empathy emerged among people, and transcended the parochial boundaries of caste, class, and religion. Various practices, that have now started gaining momentum, like maintaining hand hygiene, of following fitness of the body rather than vanity and buying essentials instead of unbridled consumption resonate with the precepts advocated in the traditional Indian wisdom, and clearly situate guidance from these Philosophies in the present-day life-issues.

References

Afreen, S. (July 9th, 2020). *Meditation in the time of COVID-19*. The Indian Express. e-chapter, Accessed on 22/02/2021.

Atmaprajananda, S. (2013 November 12). Kathopanishad. https://www.speakingtree.in/blog/kathopanishad-i-231976. First time accessed on 30/01/2021.

Britannica, T. Editors of Encyclopaedia (2013, October 4.). *Smriti. Encyclopedia Britannica*. https://www.britannica.com/topic/Smrit.

Britannica T. Editors of Encyclopaedia. (2020, December 2). *Samkhya. Encyclopeadia Britannica*. https://www.britannica.com/topic/Samkhya.

Dalal, R. (2018). *The 108 Upanishads: An introduction*. Penguin.

Dasgupta, S. (2002 edition). *Volume II. A history of Indian philosophy*. Motilal Banarsidass Publishers Private Limited. This has been my Primary resource material for discussion on the *Bhagvad-Gita* in the present chapter besides the others as cited here and in-text citations.

Dasgupta, S. (2002 edition). *Volume II. A history of Indian philosophy*. Motilal Banarsidass Publishers Private Limited.

Deussen, P. (Re-printed edition 1979). *The philosophy of the Upanishads*. Munshiram Manoharlal Publishers PVT, LTD.

Edwin, B. *The Yoga Sutras of Patanjali*. https://iep.utm.edu/yoga. First time accessed on 30/01/2021.

Gautam, P. K. (February 12, 2013). *Shruti and Smriti: Some issues in the re-emergence of Indian traditional knowledge (IDSA)*, New Delhi. https://www.files.ethz.ch/isn/159912/IB_ShrutiandSmriti.pdf. Accessed for the first time on 23/01/2021.

Kar, N. (1989). *Humanistic trends in some principal Upanisads*. Ajanta Publications.

Krishnananda, S. **Lessons from the Upanishads**. https://www.swami-krishnananda.org/katha1/Commentary_on_Katha_Upanishad.pdf. Accessed for the first time on 23/01/2021. This has been my Primary resource material for the present chapter besides the others as cited here and in-text citations.

Mark, J. J. (2020, June 10). "Upanishads". *World History Encyclopedia*. Retrieved from https://www.ancient.eu/Upanishads/. Accessed for the first time on 23/01/2021.

Mark, J. J. (2020 June 15). "Bhagvad Gita" in World History Encyclopaedia. First time accessed on 30/01/2021.

Navneet, R. (October. 2020). Relevance of the philosophical wisdom as drawn from the *Bhagvad-Gitā* during adverse circumstances like a pandemic. *IOSR Journal of Humanities and Social Science (IOSR-JHSS), 25*(10), 52–58. Series 3. e-ISSN 2279-0837, p-ISSN 2279-0845. www.iosrjournals.org. https://doi.org/10.9790/0837-2510035258. https://www.iosrjournals.org/cfp.html.

Prabhupāda, A. C. B. S. (2006 edition). *Bhagavad-Gītā As It Is*. Bhaktivedanta Book Trust.

Radhakrishnan, S. (2008 edition). *Indian philosophy-with a new introduction by J.N. Mohanty.* Oxford University Press. I have used mainly for Philosophical References on Sankhya and Yoga besides the ones cited here and in text citations.

Radhakrishnan, S. (2008 edition). *Volume-2 Indian philosophy-with a new introduction by J.N. Mohanty.*

Ruzsa, F. *Sankhya*. https://iep.utm.edu/sankhya. First time accessed on 30/01/2021.

Swami, V. (August 22 2020). What does the pandemic teach us? https://www.esamskriti.com/author/Swami-Vireshananda.aspx. Accessed for the first time on 30/01/2021.

T. Editors of Encyclopaedia. (2015, March 5). *Vedanta. Encyclopedia Britannica*. Accessed for the first time on 23/01/2021.

Warder, A. K. (2009). *A course in Indian philosophy*. Motilal Banarsidass.

Chapter 6
Environmental Management in Transition: Lessons from Tantra

Tatjana Kochetkova

> *The most beautiful thing we can experience is the mysterious. It is the source of all true art and science. He to whom the emotion is a stranger, who can no longer pause to wonder and stand wrapped in awe, is as good as dead; his eyes are closed.*
> Albert Einstein

Abstract This paper analyzes the ideational factors behind the inefficiency of mainstream environmental management. The causes of the environmental crisis are here related to a mechanistic, utilitarian world view that includes rationalization, and "the iron cage of modernity," as well as what Max Weber calls disenchantment (a lack of non-naturalistic elements in our vision of nature), with consequences such as insufficient and inefficient conservation policies. In search of an alternative framework, capable of overcoming Weber's disenchantment and motivating environmental action, we review the lessons of Tantric Spiritual Ecology, one of the several inspiring nature-centered spiritual practices, for restoring the balance within the human psyche, which, according to ecopsychologists, is a precondition for healing the earth. We further discuss the potential of Tantric spirituality to be translated into ecological action and contribute to changes in environmental management.

Keywords Environmental crisis · Environmental management · Rationalization · Tantric spiritual ecology

Introduction

Even a cursory look at the historical balance of success and failure in environmental management will not fail to reveal an urgent need for improvement. To mention an example, the reduction of carbon dioxide emissions, as described, e.g., in the Paris Agreement on Climate (2015), is one of the most important and pressing issues in

T. Kochetkova (✉)
O. P. Jindal Global University, Sonipat, India
e-mail: tatjana@jgu.edu.in

© Jindal Institute of Behavioral Sciences 2022

S. P. Sahni et al. (eds.), *Spirituality and Management*,
https://doi.org/10.1007/978-981-19-1025-8_6

today's international agenda. Yet, despite the interest and degree of commitment of many stakeholders, the resulting level of success has been modest at best.

What can be done to improve this level of success? The main thesis of this article is that a psychospiritual component is necessary, perhaps even crucial, for real success to be reached in environmental management. A purely utilitarian approach, deprived of the intrinsic meaning derived from a "reenchantment" of nature (to use Max Weber's well-known formulation), will always fall short of its own goals. As a defense of this viewpoint, after a quick view of the controversies surrounding environmental management, the psychospiritual practices of Śākta Tantra, an Indian tradition with several aspects that can assist in deepening the perception and thus improving the results of all agents involved in environmental management will be examined. Here are some of these aspects:

1. Tantra sets nature as a cultural value, cherished both in art and in daily life.
2. Tantra has a tradition of "sacred geography" which can be efficient as a means of protecting local biodiversity.
3. Tantra enables personal transformation and spiritual development in directions that make environmental management more viable.

In conclusion, the chapter will discuss how personal and cultural transformation, involving the extension of personal identity toward planetary citizenship, is a part of successful environmental management, both for its durability and sustainability.

The Controversy Around Environmental Management

The unprecedented environmental degradation associated with the Industrial Revolution of 1780s–1830s and the arrival of anthropocene threw a serious challenge to humanity. In response to this challenge, environmental management emerged—an umbrella of legislative, economic, and regulatory policies aiming to conserve biodiversity and prevent environmental pollution. Environmental management is an intentional activity aiming to "maintain and improve the state of an environmental resource affected by humans."[1] It originated in the USA and Europe, the epicenters of environmental degradation in the previous century.

During the period from 1880s till the 1940s, environmental degradation had become an obvious issue in the West, much so that state-based environmental regulation became a necessity. The concept of environmental management appeared at this point. Among its pioneers were Gifford Pinchot, the chief of the US forestry service and his opponent, nature writer John Muir.

Already in the debate between Muir and Pinchot, the major dilemma of environmental management was formulated: should nature be treated as a resource, as "environment" or "surroundings," or, on the contrary, as an intrinsic value, as an entity to be preserved for its own sake, or even as sacred?

[1] https://westcoastdm.co.za/about/environmental-management/.

John Muir argued for the latter, fiercely opposing the construction of a dam in the magnificent Hetch Hetchy valley in California, which he believed to be at least as sacred as any church and cathedral. On the opposite side, Pinchot claimed that the biosphere is primarily a resource for humans and that national forests can be used for logging and grazing cattle, albeit in a scientific way to maintain their future capacity and prevent deforestation.

A compromise between these two conflicting approaches was achieved in Teddy Roosevelt's environmental policy. His love for wildlife made him an outstanding figure in this area. Being the first politician to establish a national park and implement important green legislation, Teddy Roosevelt managed to design a balanced policy combining the benefits of both preservation (the protection of nature for its own sake) and conservation (the protection of nature as a sustainably usable resource).

The controversy between these viewpoints, variously termed as anthropocentric and ecocentric or "shallow" versus "deep" ecology, persists until today. Though, the debate has changed its form. The preservationists of today or "deep" or "radical" ecologists share some of the assumptions of ancient, traditional approach to nature, while Pinchot's anthropocentric followers claim that nature can and should be used for developmental purposes. The latter argues that natural ecosystems should be protected primarily for the sake of human needs and to the extent to which they are needed by present and future human generations. Human well-being is the end goal of the anthropocentric approach at the base of the concept of sustainable development. Even though the Pinchot-Muir debate was not resolved and continues till today, it provided the foundation for contemporary state environmental policy.

As a result of environmental policies, in most industrialized countries, the quality of air, soil, and water improved since 1960s, posing no more immediate threat to their citizens' health. The shock of events such as the great smog of London in 1953 or the Minamata disease in Japan in 1956 seems to have been left behind. Of course, these problems still exist in other countries: booming new economies like India and China, to say nothing of emerging economies in Asia, Africa, and Latin America; have come with massive environmental damage and pollution of air, water, and soil. People wearing anti-smog masks in New Delhi, Mumbai, or Shanghai can be cited as an example to fight such existing problems. Still, for the developed world, the situation has improved dramatically when compared with that of the first half of the twentieth century.

Since it was first introduced, the concept of environmental management grew and evolved from goals such as clean air, water, and soil to include biodiversity conservation and thriving ecosystems. These goals, alas, have not been reached: Ecosystems are losing space and the number of extinct species is increasing. In addition, another urgent problem has appeared: anthropogenic climate change, solutions to which are still debated and contested and have only been partially, if at all, implemented.

This weakness entails that, as the atmospheric concentration of greenhouse gases keeps rising, the overall state of the planetary environment continues to deteriorate. For instance, the heatwaves in Canada and heavy flooding in several Western European countries in the summer of 2021 highlight the urgent need for climate action.

Six years after the Paris Agreement, the desired CO_2 emission reductions have not yet been achieved. According to UN environmental program:

"If we rely only on the current climate commitments of the Paris Agreement, temperatures can be expected to rise to 3.2 °C this century. Temperatures have already increased 1.1 °C, leaving families, homes, and communities devastated" (Emissions cap report 2019—UN environmental program).[2]

It would appear that current environmental management and the politics that has been created around it cannot replicate the initial success in combating pollution in the sphere of broader, worldwide issues.

Why is Current Environmental Management Failing?

One of the policy-creating ideas that have sprung from the concept of environmental management was "sustainable development." The classical definition of sustainable development, from the Brundtland Report, defines it as "meeting the needs of the present generation without undermining the needs of the future generations" (Report of the World Commission on Environment and Development: Our Common Future 1987). The paradigm of sustainable development was well intended, but it failed to achieve its objectives.

As we have seen so far, environmental management and related ideas like "sustainable development" are clearly not working as well as had been initially intended. They are not fulfilling the promises they made and one is left to wonder about the reasons for their failure to reach their own goals. Is it a pragmatic question of organizing and setting the right goals and the measures to achieve them, along with the necessary resources and support from various entities and governments? Or is there some deeper problem?

Let us start by considering Max Weber's aforementioned concept of "disenchantment," which he introduced while writing about the "rationalization of our worldview." According to Weber, our current worldview is based on "[...] knowledge or belief that if one but wished one *could* learn at any time. Hence, it means that principally, there are no mysterious incalculable forces that come into play, but rather that one can, in principle, master all things by calculation. This means that the world is disenchanted." (Weber, 1971, p. 138). In other words, Weber's "disenchantment" comes from the removal of "mystery" from nature, from the devout trust in "calculations" that trap people in an "iron cage" or "shell as hard as steel." In the conclusion of his *Protestant Ethics*, he predicted that this rationalization would eventually lead to the loss of meaning and freedom in our civilization.[3]

[2] https://www.unep.org/interactive/emissions-gap-report/2019/.

[3] Similarly to Weber's critique of rationalization, Dostoyevsky inquired in his *Notes from Underground*: "Indeed, if there really is some day discovered a formula for all our desires and caprices—that is, an explanation of what they depend upon, by what laws they arise, how they develop, what they are aiming at in one case and in another and so on, that is a real mathematical formula—then,

It is the main thesis of this chapter that this "disenchantment," this view of the world as understandable and manageable via "calculations," is a deeper cause for the failure of environmental management to reach its goals. Beyond the more superficial problems of mismanagement and miscalculations (to say nothing of the influence of actors whose selfish interests oppose many necessary policies), there is a more profound "philosophical" or "spiritual" disconnect that poisons our relation with nature and leads to policies that can at best, be only partially or unsatisfactorily successful.

Weber's concept presents this disconnect very clearly. The same mechanistic ("calculations") worldview implicit in the rationalization of our worldview leads to a transactional relationship with nature in which there is no reason not to see it as a resource to be used, in which wisdom is simply learning how to use it intelligently and sustainably. This, however, leaves out the entirety of our own subjective relationship with nature, as beings that have evolved in it and have deep physical and psychological roots in it. By removing the "mystery," the "enchantment" of nature, the current worldview diminishes the emotional and numinous aspects of our connection to it and leaves us orphaned from that which is ultimately an integral part of ourselves. It is thus not difficult to accept that policies based on such a worldview would leave us all less involved, less motivated, less connected to the whole effort, thus achieving results that, while good in themselves, end up being at best disappointing and at worst insufficient to prevent further damage to our world.

This disenchantment of nature must thus be overcome if our environmental policies are to progress beyond their current state. It cannot be simply dismissed: It must be actively overcome by science itself, via the rediscovery of the more "mysterious" or "sacred" side of nature. The aim is to sublate this disenchantment, to "reenchant" nature with more than simple rationality, to account both for our own feelings in relation to it and create a climate in which further environmental action can become a real success. Some efforts to integrate this reenchantment of nature with scientific and rationality have already appeared among scientists, albeit in a discussable way (e.g., David Bohm's concepts of "hidden variables" and a "holographic universe," Whitworth's "virtual reality," and Lazlo's "zero-energy field") will hopefully lead to science undermining the "iron cage of modernity" from inside (Bohm & Hiley, 1993; Whitworth, 2008: Lazlo, 2004).

Overcoming the Disenchantment of Nature

Here, I analyze the phenomenon of "disenchantment of nature" in relation to environmental destruction. Several scholars (Adorno, Horkheimer, and, more recently, McGrath), claim that disenchantment is associated with the *ethical devaluation* of nature, i.e., with its reduction to resources for humans, deprived of intrinsic value

---

most likely, man will at once cease to feel desire, indeed, he will be certain to. For who would want to choose by rule?".

(Bernstein, 2000; Luque-Lora, 2020; McGrath, 2003; Merchant, 1980; Shiva, 2016; Stone, 2006; White, 1967). Further, these scholars associate the devaluation of nature with environmental degradation.

The devaluation of nature goes along with an anthropocentric perspective that implies that environmental policy should have humans in view as its final goal: Nature is valuable as a resource for human well-being.

One may object that an anthropocentric view does not automatically lead to the destruction of the environment. Indeed, a mechanistically minded manager may still aim to protect nature as an important resource for human well-being—the way Gifford Pinchot intended nature conservation.

However, in practice, resource management based on an anthropocentric viewpoint has often led to decreasing biodiversity (Plumwood, 2002). I think this is not just a technical mistake or "poor management," because the needs of wild species or ecosystems systematically often clash with economic interests. Such clashes are resolved differently from the anthropocentric and from the biocentric viewpoint. For instance, climate change is an obvious threat to the economy and to human health, yet anthropocentrically minded managers would rather search for cheaper technological fixes to save humans rather than take all the necessary steps to eradicate the root cause of excessive CO_2 emissions by replacing current technology with a carbon neutral one.

The anthropocentric/utilitarian approach to nature follows from the mechanistic model of the universe, as is elucidated by E. A. Burtt:

> The gloriously romantic universe of Dante and Milton, that set nobounds to the imagination of man as it played over space and time, had now been swept away. Space was identified with geometry, time with the continuity of number. The world that people had thought themselves living in, a world rich with colour and sound, redolent with fragrance, filled with gladness, love and beauty, speaking everywhere of purposive harmony and creative ideals—was crowded now into minute corners in the brains of scattered organic beings. The really important world outside was a world hard, cold, colourless, silent, and dead; a world of quantity, a world of mathematically computable motions in mechanical regularity. The world of qualities as immediately perceived by man became just a curious and quite minor effect of that infinite machine beyond. (Burtt, 2003)

The mechanistic view lacks a first-person perspective. It is limited to a third-person view, or the perspective of "it," seeing everything as a collection of objects. Therefore, this vision of nature deprives it of "meaning, purpose, and agency," according to Luque-Lora (2020). Remarkably,

> the enlightened thinking has liquidated enchantment [sense of mystery, awe -TK] by removing the particular and experiential contents of specific objects (Luque-Lora, 2020).

The disenchantment of nature resulted in the current view of the universe as a collection of objects governed by mathematical laws. Importantly, the disenchantment has *invalidated our direct experiential perception*, or the immediately perceived qualities of various entities, whether they are natural or social. The implication is that natural and social objects are altogether reducible to elementary particles. They can be calculated, predicted, and manipulated by means of science and technology for any specific goal.

Also, humans themselves have become "disenchanted." This is because humans in this paradigm are reducible to the elementary particles. They are complex yet intelligible machines. For instance, in this context, humans appear as "survival machines—robot vehicles blindly programmed to preserve the selfish molecules known as genes." (Dawkins, 1989). In this view, the human body and mind are also entirely "makeable," i.e., it can be created and manipulated through technology. This framework equally rejects a notion of intrinsic value or meaning: All values are mere constructs.

I think that portraying a living body as entirely makeable leads to disregarding the uniqueness of living beings because this viewpoint contains no concept of life as qualitatively different from non-living entities, no sense of nature's intrinsic value and autonomy. Indeed, the mechanical universe of objects contains homogeneous space and time, and the atoms they are made of are replaceable. According to it, any object, including plants, animals, and ecosystems can in principle, be manipulated, exchanged, or repaired if we have enough know-how. Hence, they are neither unique nor intrinsically valuable.

As a logical consequence of such a view, the biosphere becomes a utilitarian resource to satisfy human desires. The environmental implications are that ecosystem, and the entire biosphere can be altered to satisfy human ends. For example, some proposals for geo-engineering climate contain large-scale interferences in the functioning of the biosphere, such as seeding oceans with iron to promote the growth of plankton, which will absorb carbon dioxide, or injecting sulfur in the atmosphere to diminish solar radiation.

But the mechanical paradigm, which has been implemented since the seventeenth century by means of technology and economic growth, has so far mostly caused environmental degradation as their side-effect (Merchant, 1980; Plumwood, 2002). McGrath (2003) argues that the mechanistic view won acceptance by simply dismissing its rivals—organic models—as primitive superstitions, not by proving them wrong:

> Yet in reality, these organic models of nature were merely suppressed, not defeated, by the mechanical model of nature. Although the 'mechanistic' analysis of reality has dominated the Western world since the seventeenth century, the 'organismic' perspective has stubbornly remained in movements such as Romanticism, American transcendentalism, the German Nature philosophers… (McGrath, 2003, p. 119).

Applied to society, it leads to the reign of "instrumental rationality." According to Habermas, everything is seen as a resource, and nothing has a meaning or purpose of its own (1984). Humans are in principle not different from the rest of nature. Hence, the disenchantment of nature is also the disenchantment of humans with themselves. In the final count, if you accept this vision, human existence will appear meaningless, just like the rest of the universe. This is because, according to it, any self-created meaning can ultimately be reduced to neurons and electric signals in the brain, which have no intrinsic value in this perspective.

Becoming aware of all implications of disenchanted, mechanical universe may have extremely disappointing effect to the extent of even pushing one to despair.

Perhaps under the impression of the Weberian rationalization of society, the famous German author Hesse (2011, reprint of 1957) once claimed:

> ...despair is the result of each earnest attempt to go through life with virtue, justice and understanding, and to fulfill their requirements. Children live on one side of despair, the awakened on the other side.

How can one awake on the other side of despair? One cannot simply dismiss the mechanistic worldview or "the iron cage," as Weber called it. It is important to find out where it goes wrong and overcome it from inside, using dialectical reason. This task is still unresolved. In my view, a solution lies neither in an artificial reenchantment of nature as "valuable creation," as suggested by McGrath (2003), nor in an "animated materialism" or some other interpretation of the mechanistic universe. Because, in my view, the problem is not with the interpretation, but with the mechanistic paradigm's claim to be the one truth and held universally valid.

Perhaps, Feyerabend (2010) came close to transcending the mechanistic worldview with his critique of the scientific method. He argues that scientists historically did not follow a single method, rather used a variety of them. The mainstream scientific method is one among many ways to construct plausible and effective theories; hence, its products do not have a monopoly on truth.[4]

To overcome disenchantment, I think one does not need to construct meaning artificially or to cover up superficially for the vacuum of post-modern life because meaning is not made up, but discovered and experienced. To see meaning in life, we need to have trust in the validity of the immediate experience, which is the same as to trust ourselves, our own reason, senses, and intuitions.

In my opinion, rationalization and the mechanistic worldview do not give us real reason to despair or even lose our ontological optimism, i.e., positive attitude to reality as such. On the contrary, they motivate us to understand the limitations of the mechanistic view of the universe and to transcend it by means of more complete or integral rationality.

In addition, rivals of the mechanistic world model—alternative visions—are alive today, as will be seen in the sections below. The alternative which we discuss here—Tantric spirituality—concerns the restoration of the validity of experiential perception. Reality appears to our direct perception as an infinite mystery in its core. Already Einstein and Goethe insisted on the uncanny character of reality.[5] Every scholar or scientist has experienced this fundamental sense of wonder, characteristic of reality as such. But social programming causes many of us to forget this fundamental wonder and perceive the world through the internalized conceptual framework of so-called ordinary reality.

---

[4] Furthermore, the mechanistic paradigm currently faces the problem of accumulating extra-paradigmatic evidence, i.e., of phenomena that do not fit into it (Feyerabend, 2010; Kuhn, 1996).

[5] As Goethe puts it: "The world of spirits is not closed:
Your senses are: your heart is dead!".
In Goethe's view, the genuine enchantment follows from opening one's heart and mind to the reality as it is (1951).

While searching for a new environmental paradigm, many ecologists emphasize the need to adjust our worldview toward an ecocentric perspective, which will enable changes inecological policy (Naess, 1989; Sherma, 1998; Shiva, 2016; Starhawk, 1999). While these changes are important, still more is needed to inspire ecological action. According to various sociological insights, in a democracy, environmental policy is an outcome of a sociocultural process, rooted in values, worldviews, and daily practices. Therefore, the following steps seem logical as the basis for sound environmental policy:

1. For an ecological policy to be crystallized at the national or global level, it must start with changes in ecological consciousness and individual motivation.
2. For the desired ecological consciousness to change, the individuals shall form ecological movements and NGOs. These must take collective action to impact civil society.
3. Civil society in a democracy must take its demands to the government and achieve state directed changes in policy and legislation that represent environmental concerns and translate it into action.

Inherent Cultural Values and Environmental Policy: *A Case Study*

Here, we look at the potential of ecospirituality in combination with active civil society to generate green policy. For this, I would refer to a case study of Japan. The cultural value of nature, as embedded in Buddhism and Shintō, inspired the rapid ecological transformation in Japan. Its moving force was not the ruling party or the Liberal Democrats, but instead citizens' protests and the pressure from the opposition. The Japanese government "was forced to confront pollution" by their own people (Harney, 2013).

Behind the twentieth-century greening of Japan, we find its local governments, who have power and autonomy to pressurize business to comply with environmental regulations (Kojima, 2010). The primary causes were the citizens, their values, actions, and pragmatic thinking.

The role of the Shintō religion, "the root of Japanese values," provided an important source of inspiration for environmental action in Japan. One of its traits is the centrality of nature in Japanese art and literature. An example of its pervasive impact is a case from 1970s, involving a 700-year-old tree, named the Big Kusu. The government wanted to have it removed because it stood in the way of building a new train station in Neyagawa, a small city in Osaka Prefecture. But the tree was sacred to local people, who believed that a *kami* (a spirit or deity) resides in it. The local residents pressurized their government and successfully prevented it from cutting the Big Kusu. The project was adjusted, so that another more expensive train platform design was implemented, surrounding the Big Kusu without damaging the tree (Earls, 2018).

The values inherent in a culture tend to shape its environmental policy (Plumwood, 2002). Hence, a way to achieve green culture is establishing a living connection to nature, developing biophilia through art and daily practices like gardening, walking in parks, and in forests. In the long run, these values are among the factors that will determine the outcome of the anthropocene endeavor.

The conclusion of the above example is that ecological consciousness does not consist of rational concerns alone. Knowledge about the detrimental effects of CO_2 emissions at greenhouse effect and global warming or toxic pollution, albeit necessary, is not sufficient to motivate environmental action. There are other concerns besides the scientific ones that motivate human behavior toward nature. The biggest problems appear because of conflicts between economic growth and conservation. The desire for unlimited economic growth on a limited planet results into clash with nature.

It seems that the problem of environmental action is not the simple lack of conceptual understanding of the importance of a healthy biosphere and respect for the ecosystem's boundaries for planetary survival, but rather the psychological boundary between self-interests and nature, the boundary that makes one's own pragmatic short-term interests prevail over ecological concerns, as one can see in case of Nyamgiri hills controversy, (Sethi, 2014). In other words, the problem is self-centeredness, separate self, and the disconnectedness of individual minds from their own bodies as well as from the living nature around us.

The mental construct of separate self and separate individual interests grounds environmental exploitation—the externalization of environmental costs for profit, a short-term drive to reap immediate benefits at the expense of nature. For a separate self, the individual body appears as if it existed apart from the rest of the biosphere.

In fact, this is about going beyond the concept of separate self to the self embedded in the one universe of which we all are a part of. Ecospiritual practices offer one of the ways to see how self is embedded in the universe.

Many people understand that the separate self is a social construct but keeps behaving as if it were real. To overcome this construct, one needs to change, among other things, the living experience of own body and of nature, so as to develop a sensitivity to the web of life, to the interwovenness between the body and nature.

To arrive at an adequate level of ecological awareness, one needs to restore the connection to nature within the psyche, including the collective psyche. This implies increased sensitivity to our immediate natural surrounding—to the quality of air and water, to the state of animals and plants near us. While the human psyche belongs to nature even today, the problem for ecoaction is the loss of awareness or of this belonging.

Lessons from Tantra: An Inspiration for Environmental Action

The argument here is that Tantra may be a source for new ecological consciousness and possibly an inspiration for ecofeminism.[6] Thus, Tantrism is sensitive and detailed about experiential perception, which is crucial to overcome the "iron cage" of rationality and disenchantment. Evidence to this is the growing interest for Tantrism among neurologists and their search for a complement to their own third person perspective in Tantric descriptions of the body.

There is a risk that Tantra can be misused for sectarian or power-oriented goals unrelated to ecological restoration or spiritual awareness, as was mentioned by Sherma and Lidke (Lidke, 2009; Sherma, 1998). However, this risk is external to Tantra, having no impact on its insights, wisdom, and experience.

Tantra embraces both Hindu and Tibetan Buddhist streams. When Shakti worship entered Hindu practice, in the fifth century BC, "tantras" was simply the name of the sacred books and doctrine of Shaktism. It flourished from the eighth to the fourteenth century in India and spread to Tibet. Among its representative, thinkers are Abhinavagupta (*c.* 975–1025 ce) and his follower Jayaratha, both Shaivists who integrated various practices into a stream that strives to awaken and realize the transcendent subject within human consciousness (Abhinavagupta & Shastri, 2015; Padoux, 2017).

Tantra is mostly a practical discipline, or "*sadhana*," which puts little weight into theory, while striving to embrace, awaken, and "rise" the inner spiritual power of *kundalini.* Scholars of *Tantra* define *kundalini* as a supernatural, yet biologically active energy, "a sleeping dormant potential force in the human organism and it is situated at the root of the spinal column" (Saraswati, 2002, p. 10).

Various threads of Tantra present a path to liberation, emphasizing the experiential, or "bodily felt, lived-through experience." It is a path that celebrates life, perceives the numinous as present in the here and now, and embraces all beings without regard of social or gender categories.

What is Tantra?

Tantra is an umbrella term for some Indian philosophies, rituals, and yogic practices. Tantra is present in several schools of Hinduism and in Vajrayana Buddhism. The earliest appearance of the word "Tantra" is in hymn 10.71 of the Rigveda (Padoux, 2017).

The discussion about what differentiates Tantra from non-Tantric approaches in Hinduism and Buddhism still goes on today. According to Andre Padoux, a Hindu

---

[6] Tantra is one among several inspiring nature-centered spiritual practices, every of which contains important lessons for ecological management. Here, we focus on Tantra alone because including all of them would extend this paper beyond the current limits.

Tantra scholar, Tantra entails a divergence from the Vedic tradition via the application of *Kundalini* Yoga, different from classical Patanjali's Yoga (Padoux, 2017).

The aspects of Tantra that make it especially applicable for ecological consciousness change include the ontology of immanent divine nature, the Tantric vision of embodiment and psychosomatic spiritual practices, and sacred geography, which involves engagement with sacred natural places and their protection.

In ŚāktaTantra, the ontology is based on the worship of Śākti, "the power or energy of the divine nature in action" (Padoux, 2017, p. 6). Sherma (1998), in her discussion of the relevance of ŚāktaTantra for ecological action, outlined its vision of nature as hierophany, and its theology of the Divine Mother.

> The vision of the earth as a sacred hierophany and material form of the divine is perhaps most dramatically displayed in Goddess theology, first crystallized in the sixth century text, a part of the *Markandeya Purana called*, the *Devi Mahatmya* or "Glorification of the Goddess". (Sherma, 1998, p. 89)

In her inquiry, Sherma (1998, p. 89) shows Tantra as a viable source of inspiration for the development of ecofeminist theology.

As Sherma and Lidke argue, Tantric ontology and practice share the following key points with ecofeminism:

> (1) celebration of all aspects of life (2) elevation to ultimacy of a feminine principle linked to materiality; (3) possibility for liberation of female gender from constraints of 'fertility and nurturance alone'; (4) affirmation of phenomena as Goddess; (5) articulation of a discourse of empowerment for the marginalized; (6) veneration of the body and its sensations; (7) absence of a spirit/matter dichotomy. (Lidke, 2009)

The Tantric ontology of sacred Goddess, immanent in nature and body, aligns with spiritual ecofeminism, such as represented in the writings of Starhawk or Vandana Shiva (Mies & Shiva, 1993). Indeed, "Tantra as 'theology of identification' is not only helpful for the cultivation of an earth-centered spirituality" but also a source of "inspiration" for "personal spiritual empowerment." (Sherma, 1998). Thus, "reconstruction of Śākta Tantra can become a channel through which Hindu nondualism can inspire a viable philosophy on which to base a transformed vision of the earth." (Lidke, 2009; Sherma, 1998).

While supporting Sherma's thesis that Tantra is a viable approach to restore human–nature unity and inspire body–mind continuity, leading to spiritual empowerment and to overcoming all sorts of marginalization; I would like to emphasize that its potential is not limited to ontology but extends to a unique practical approach to bodily awareness.

Tantra's ontology of Sacred Mother-Goddess is inspiring for ecological consciousness. Its core is shared by several traditions that venerate the hierophany of the World Soul through physical nature. Nature was perceived as hierophany by Gnostics and neo-platonics up to nineteenth century Romantic Vladimir Solovyov and his followers in theology of Divine Sophia, to Ralf Waldo Emerson and Native Americans' traditions, and to contemporary ecofeminists as Starhawk and Vandana Shiva.

Any ontology is inevitably expressed via concepts and words, yet the word as such is an inadequate instrument for understanding the ultimate reality. Because, as it was understood by Tantra, "any attempt to reduce ultimate reality to words, categories, and conventional logic would always end in paradox." (Venkatraman et al., 2019, p. 1189).

But the concepts alone may not suffice to transform practical human–nature relations. Another peculiarity of Tantra is also necessary: its practice of awakening sensitivity.

Tantric Embodiment. Implications for Human–Nature Relations

Tantric practice relies heavily not on verbal discourse but on a range of bodily and mental techniques: breathing, visualization, asana, mudra, and mantras.

The Tantric perspective on the body investigates how it appears in immediate experience or the "I-perspective." This differentiates Tantra from neurology, which studies the body as "it," from a third-person perspective, which is equally applicable to a living body and a cadaver. The gap between "I" and "it" illustrates the problem of "iron cage" rationality via its lack of comprehensiveness. In fact, the third person view of the body is one-sided. A comprehensive approach should integrate all three perspectives—first person (experiential), second person (hermeneutic, communicative) and third person (physiology, material body).

As we have seen, Tantra opens this possibility, which attracts growing attention from neurologists (Venkatraman et al., 2019, p. 1189). It focuses on *the body which we can sense within ourselves*, "through the inward direction of attention" or interoception (Venkatraman et al., 2019, p. 1189).

In Tantra terms, the "subtle body" is differentiated from the "gross body," and the experiential body is distinguished from the physical body. The "subtle body," according to Loizzo, reflects an "interoceptive map of the nervous system" (2016).

> Interoception can be broadly thought of as encompassing afferent signals about the state of the body through neural, immune and endocrine channels, the neural encoding and integration of this information, the influence of this information on other perceptions, and the psychological expression of these changes as presented to our consciousness. An interoceptive map therefore would be something similar to the somatosensory homunculus … but more comprehensive. It would incorporate internal sensations, such as those arising from heartbeat and lung expansion as well as other modalities such as taste and vision.

The yogic "subtle body" is envisioned by Tantra as a flow of primeval divine energy or Kundalini. It contains a set of "centers or nodal points" called chakras. They are connected by several channels named "nadi," the most important of which are Ida, Pingala, and the central Sushumna. Tantric yogic practices involve the raising of Kundalini from its most frequent location in the lowest chakra to the highest chakra in which it returns to the divine source.

According to recent scientific studies, "chakras" reflect "some experiential aspects of neurological functioning"; therefore they cannot be reduced to any physical objects. At the same time, Tantric ideas of subtle body, chakra, and nadi seem to have relevant correlates in neuroscience (Venkatraman et al., 2019, p. 1190).

"Subtle body" practice is efficient in some testable ways. First of all, there are associations between some physical organs and mental functioning, congruent with the chakra scheme, for example, "the connection between the nervous control of the heart and social behavior" or between Irritable Bowel syndrome and "a patient's reactivity to emotional words" (Venkatraman et al., 2019, p. 1190). This is the kind of body–mind connection which aligns with and follows from the chakra approach.

Furthermore, Tantric practice "can bring about sustained changes in the structure and function of the nervous system of practitioner."

Finally, advanced yogis and Tantric adepts can exercise conscious control over "what are thought to be 'autonomous' functions such as pulse and heart rate variability," as well as body temperature, and blood pressure (Venkatraman et al., 2019, p. 1190).

Tantric practice thus modulates the functioning of the nervous system, brain, and awareness, extending conscious control over the body beyond the ordinary to include functions not otherwise accessible to the subject.

Tantra and Biophilia

The effects of rising Kundalini include increased awareness of one's body's connectedness to nature. It envisions the cosmos as paradoxically contained within the body. This structure is akin to the Bohm's idea of a "holographic universe"—a model in which every part contains the whole, also known as Indra's net. Current research suggests that human health is to a large extent defined by environment (Institute of Medicine, 2001). Natural science expresses the health-environment connection through concepts which do not necessarily affect our experience. In contrast to this, Tantric Yoga allows one to feel the environment, turning the "subtle body"—field into a part of one's lived experience, which is conducive to an attachment with living nature. The practitioner experiences natural entities as full of colors, sounds, forms, and smells, which is essential to finding meaning and forming attachment. In the process, the boundary between self-care and care for nature dissolves, giving rise to biophilia, an "innate human affinity with nature" (Wilson, 1986). One can hardly imagine a stronger motivation for environmental action. According to the biophilia hypothesis, the human tendency to affiliate with nature and other living beings is innate (Wilson, 1986). Early evidence for biophilia was supplied by Ulrich's (1984) study, which showed that 23 patients recovered faster and with lower use of painkillers after gall-bladder surgery if they stayed in hospital rooms with "windows looking out on a natural scene," in comparison to those with "windows facing a brick wall." Interestingly, a physical view to a natural landscape was not the only way to boost recovery. According to later research, even images of green landscapes had beneficial effect on patients.

Biophilia is a primary motive for environmental action and citizens demands for conservation, as well as inherent green values in cultures. It might be possible to strengthen biophilia by training our awareness of sensory perception.

Tantric practice of Kundalini may be conducive to biophilia because it reconnects the individual mind with nature, as viewed by contemporary ecopsychologists. This is possible because, in the Tantric view, the universe is a unified energy field of Shakti or divine power. The body is an integrated part of this universal energy field and mirrors the structure of the universe. Thus, the "subtle body" is not an object at all, but rather a stream of energy within the universal "Šākti" field, and Tantric embodiment is part and parcel of the earth's biosphere and the larger cosmos.

The ecological challenge of our time is thus, also a psychological one—it requires a shift of mainstream personal consciousness from identification with the "skin encapsulated ego" (Watts, 1994, p. 76) toward a larger ecological self. Tantric practice is congruent with the ecopsychology of reconnection and transformation of individual consciousness "from ego to eco," through the process of personal growth (Danon, 2019).

The ecological self ("eco") is achieved via (1) downward reconnection to all living beings, (2) inward reconnection or "getting in touch with 'who I really am' and (3) upward reconnection to the ultimate, transhuman reality" (Danon, 2019, p. 10).

As one can see, the objective of the Tantric "sadhana" practically coincides with the "upward reconnection to ultimate reality" in ecopsychology. Despite differences in vocabulary and practice, the two approaches share their aim—to overcome the "skin encapsulated ego" or identity which regards otherness as merely instrumental value and to realize transcendent subjectivity. With some twelve centuries of practice of upward reconnection, Tantra is a great inspiration for the transformation of consciousness "from ego to eco."

Sacred Geography

The point under consideration here is the potential of sacred natural places, specifically Tantric sacred ecology, to promote conservation and complement secular environmental policy.

State-based environmental conservation is only the most recent attempt to keep the environment in optimal condition. Alternative, traditional ways to conserve biodiversity were practiced in most ancient civilizations, from India to Australia to South America. Sacred groves (of which there are over 13,000 in India alone, maintained by religious and tribal communities), mountains, lakes, or caves, despite having mostly other goals than conservation alone, were nevertheless efficient in protecting biodiversity and ecosystems, as well as maintaining cultural continuity and creating opportunities for spiritual realization.

Long before the Industrial Revolution, ancient civilizations made efforts to stay in equilibrium with their environment. From Japan to South America, from India to Tibet, people practiced a radically different approach to conservation. Even though nature was still a resource vital for their survival, it has never been merely reduced to its utilitarian value. Nature was envisioned as fundamentally sacred, as hierophany, and humans saw themselves in unity with nature, as we see in Shamanic practices, in Buddhism and Hinduism, Shintō or Daoism.

An essential feature of the ancient vision of nature is the correspondence between micro and marcocosmos, between the individual body–mind and the universe. This was as true for Plato as for ancient Indian philosophers:

> A body whose structure and life are simultaneously human, cosmic and divine is also a yogic body. The place and the role of the human body in Tantra are such that most aspects of the Tantric domain could be studied from the body's point of view (Pardoux, 2017).

When one studies a landscape from the subtle body's perspective, one encounters what we call here "the sacred geography." The microcosmos of Tantric body reflects and contain the earth and the entire universe—the macrocosmos. The goals of Tantric practice include the actualization of the unity of micro and macrocosmos, performed by practicing sacred geography. As twelfth century Saraha stated:

> Here [in my body] are the Ganga—and the Yamuna—...here are Prayaga and Varanası, here the Sun and the Moon. Here are the sacred places, the *pıthas*...Never have I seen a place of pilgrimage and an abode of bliss like my body (Padoux, 2017).

The land was covered with a net of sacred sites—groves, mountains, caves, or lakes—forming a mandala—the inner map of the land. Sacred sites were the most ancient form of biodiversity conservation and traditional environmental management.

For Tantra, "sacred geography" implies a categorization of natural environments that differentiate between sacred and profane spaces. Sacred meaning is attributed to mountains, lakes, rivers, or caves. Mountains are the abode of gods, while caves are the dwelling of spirits that live under the water or the surface of the earth.

The key elements of the sacred geography are sacred sites, called "*tirthas*" or "*pithas.*" The word "tirtha" means "crossing," and it signifies the passage from a human to a transhuman dimension. Some examples of *tirthas* are mount Kailash, and the entire Himalayan mountains chain, some rivers as Ganga, Yamuna, Sarasvati, Sindhu, Narmada, Godavari and Kaveri or groves, as Mawphlang Sacred Grove, located in National forest in Synrang Kaban, Meghalaya. The shared part of their worship is through pilgrimage to them, which may lead to a circumambulation of a mountain *tirtha* or taking a bath in a river *tirtha.*

"Tirtha is a place where one crosses over the river of samsara—this repeated cycle of birth and death—to attain a state of liberation. Many of the tirthas were places which were indeed a ford, i.e., where a river could be crossed safely" (Eck (2012: 34), Goswami).

Tirthas are nodes in the net of power flow, comparable to chakras—the nodes in the energy flow of the "subtle body." When performing "*nyasa,*" a ritual that means literally "placing," a rishi or "seer" performs a series of touches in specific locations on the body (Flood, 1993; Kularnava Tantra, 1983, 55–74). In "*nyasa,*" the Tantric practitioner reproduces the unity of the microcosmos of one's body with the macrocosmos of the universe, inhabited by gods and spirits and described in terms of "sacred geography." The nyasa ritual communicates the presence of the deity in the body.

By maintaining sacred places like tirthas, communities did not aim at species conservation apart from the protection of the sanctity of said places. The protection of biodiversity in sacred sites was a consequence of their perception as disclosures of the sacred in the ordinary. Tirthas are thus mostly forest spots of different sizes, protected by neighboring communities. Historically, ayurvedic medicinal plants were cultivated there, and today they are biodiversity hotspots.

Another Tantric way to experience the sacred in nature is pilgrimage. The desire of practitioners to be part and parcel of a sacred world was fulfilled through pilgrimage, where they can "live in a pure and holy cosmos" (Eliade, 1968; Goswami, 2016). Both in nyasa ritual and in pilgrimage, the individual ego reconnects with the sacred reality as present in natural sites.

In conclusion, Tantric sacred geography develops motives for environmental action by promoting reconnection with nature at various levels and facilitating the emergence of the "ecoself"—the current step in global consciousness transformation.

Sacred geography is an organic framework which perceives human body, nature, society, and entire universe as profoundly meaningful. Sacred sites are essential for maintaining various cultural identities. National or local cultures are closely tied to the landscapes within which they develop. Maintaining local ecosystems is thus essential for conserving cultural diversity.

In a secularized multi-cultural society, state-based environmental management is a steady point of reference for conservation. Yet it is not enough and they can benefit from being complemented by sacred ecology. Both the approaches promote biodiversity, albeit in a different way.

Conclusion

In which way ecocentric spirituality such as Tantra can provide a remedy for environmental crisis? It most probably can when combined with active civil society and democracy. The entire spectrum of nature-centered spiritual traditions presents a valuable resource to transform our consciousness, culture, and policy to overcome environmental crisis.

Ecocentric spirituality can tackle the dysfunctional relationship of humanity with nature, which is the root cause of current environmental management's inability to resolve the ongoing climate crisis.

Arguably, the causes of such dysfunctionality lie in the utilitarian view of nature as only instrumental to human needs. The utilitarian treatment of nature is connected to the mechanistic nature vision, rationalization, disenchantment, and "iron cage of modern rationality," followed by industrial and technological revolution.

The reason for this is that the human treatment of nature depends on the values and type of identity that are prevalent in a culture. In my view, the physical degraded condition of the biosphere is indicative of the inner state of human civilization (Kochetkova, 2008). Our external physical condition (biosphere) reflects the mental turmoil of today's humanity. The source of this idea lies in the most ancient times, in the realization of the micro and macrocosmic correspondence. As my colleagues and I have argued before (2013), "The ecological crisis cannot be resolved with technical means alone. The ecological crisis is the manifestation of the deeper underlying crisis, frequently understood as a crisis of the worldview" (*translation from Dutch mine—TK*) (Boersema et al., 2013). To restore the biosphere, the global culture needs to overcome its limitations, such as "iron cage rationalization" (Weber) and "skin encapsulated ego" (Watts), which see otherness as merely instrumental value.

The problems of the "skin encapsulated ego" can be resolved by moving to the next stage of personal development, or eco—an identity which is reconnected with nature. The urges of our current historical moment—the shift from ego to eco, finding a new scientific paradigm, overcoming disenchantment and the mechanistic worldview—may receive a boost from Tantric practice. This is because the final goal of Tantric practice—spiritual liberation—overlaps to an extent with the tendencies of our current historical moment and the emergence of a planetary identity.

The Tantric emphasis on experiential perception, its sadhana of awareness tuning, contains the following lessons for ecological consciousness and environmental management:

1. The experience of the natural world as permeated by divine energy, the unity of the immanent and the transcendent, or sacred immanence. This is congruent with the celebration of life, with emphasis on mindfulness and happiness in the here and now.
2. The Tantric perception of embodiment contains a methodology for shifting from the "skin encapsulated self" to a broader human identity as a member of an ecological community and a microcosmos. The Tantric embodiment is valuable in bridging the first- and third-person approaches to the study of nervous system. According to recent neurological studies, it "may open up new avenues for cognitive enhancement and treating neurological diseases." (Venkatraman et al., 2019). In fact, Tantric methods of consciousness training are proven to impact cognition, emotions, and neural functioning. However, their way of operation and their very nature is little understood. More studies of Tantric "sadhana" and its effects on body–mind remain necessary.
3. Our present historical moment involves a profound cultural and spiritual transformation, involving the extension of personal identity toward planetary citizenship, associated with mundialization and the increase in virtual communication, enabling us to form communities independently from our physical location. The awareness tuning element in Tantric psychospiritual practice facilitates this expansion, thus responding to our current historical needs.
4. The Tantric tradition of sacred groves, currently threatened by modernization and in need of revitalization, is another beneficial contribution to the protection

of biodiversity by offering a path toward reconnecting individual consciousness with ecosystems. It would be a welcome complement to secular policies and legislation for environmental protection.

To conclude, here, we have discussed *Tantric* tradition as a possible remedy for the failure of mainstream environmental management. Tantra, being a form of Spirituality in its core, seems capable of bringing valuable contributions to environmental protection. The problem is that current mainstream environmental management *fails to reduce carbon dioxide emissions to the extent, necessary to keep global temperature under control—which is below 2 °C rise*. This means that current environmental management cannot guarantee the safety and continuity of the planetary civilization. As it has been extensively argued above, behind the inefficiency of mainstream environmental management is the utilitarian world view and "the iron cage of modern rationality" described by Weber as "disenchantment." As a result, the current forms of management, including environmental management, are not comprehensive enough to save the planet, and lack of spiritual inspiration is one of their problems. Thus, the involvement of spirituality into environmental management can help to make it work. Tantric spirituality has potential to contribute to changes in environmental management, bringing efficient environmental action.

Acknowledgements I would like to express my deepest thanks to Dr. Sérgio Meira for his insightful feedback on the draft of this paper.

References

Abhinavagupta, R., & Shastri, M. R. (2015). *The Tantrasara of Abhinava Gupta*. Bibliolife DBA of Bibilio Bazaar II LLC.

Bernstein, J. M. (2000). Re-enchanting nature. *Journal of the British Society for Phenomenology, 31*(3), 277–299.

Boersema, J., Bolsenbroek, A., Kochetkova, T., Henstra, A., Pedroli, B., Schouten, M., Egmond Van, K., & Meeuwesen, L. (2013). Sustainability comedy (in Dutch). Retrived from: https://sociologiemagazine.nl/artikel/de-duurzaamheidskomedie

Bohm, D., & Hiley, B. J. (1993). *The Undivided Universe*. Routledge.

Brundtland, G. (1987). *Report of the World Commission on Environment and Development: Our common future*. United Nations General Assembly document A/42/427.

Burtt, E. A. (2003). *The metaphysical foundations of modern physical science*. Dover Publications.

Danon, M. (2019). "From Ego to Eco": The contribution of ecopsychology to the current environmental crisis management. *Visions for Sustainability, 12*, 8–17.

Dawkins, R. (1989). *The selfish gene*. Oxford University Press.

Earls, A. (2018). *Trees that fight back: Shinto and the environment in Japan*. Retrieved at https://digpodcast.org/2018/05/20/trees-that-fight-back-shinto-the-environment-in-japan/

Eck, D. (2012). *India: A sacred geography*. Harmony Books.

Eliade, M. (1968). *The sacred and the profane: The nature of religion*. Mariner Books.

Feyerabend, P. (2010). *Against method*. Verso Books.

Flood, G. (1993). *Body and cosmology in Kashmir Śaivism*. Mellen Research University Press.

Goethe, J. W., & MacNeice, L. (1951). *Goethe's Faust: Parts I and II*. Faber and Faber.

Goswami, A. (2016). Pilgrimage as imagined site: A study of Prayag tirtha. *International Journal of Religious Tourism and Pilgrimage, 4*, 16–22. https://doi.org/10.21427/D7212X

Habermas, J. (1984). *The theory of communicative action. Vol. I: Reason and the rationalization of society*. Beacon

Harney, A. (2013, February 15). Japan's pollution Diet. *New York Times*. Retrieved from https://www.lee.k12.nc.us/cms/lib03/NC01001912/Centricity/Domain/1464/Pollution%20in%20Japan.pdf

Hesse, H. (2011). *A journey to East*. Martino Fine Books.

Institute of Medicine. (2001). *Rebuilding the unity of health and the environment: A new vision of environmental health for the 21st century*. The National Academies Press. https://doi.org/10.17226/10044

Kochetkova, T. (2008). On the intellectual origins of the environmental crisis: Toward a gestalt solution. *Ethics, Place and Environment, 8*(1), 95–113.

Kojima, S. (2010). *Green growth and green economy in Japan*. In *Event: 2010 NISD conference on "Green Growth and Green Economy" [PDF document]*. Retrieved from https://www.iges.or.jp/en/pub/green-growth-and-green-economy-japan/en

Kuhn, T. S. (1996). *The structure of scientific revolutions*. University of Chicago Press.

Kularnava-Tantra. (1983). Sanskrit text with English translation by Ram Kumar Rai—Prachya Prakashan, Varanasi. Retrieved from http://vishnudut1926.blogspot.com/2019/04/kularnava-tantra-sanskrit-text-with.html

Lazlo, E. (2004). *Science and the Akashic field: An integral theory of everything*. Inner Traditions International.

Lidke, J. (2009). Towards a theory of tantra-ecology. In C. K. Chapple (Ed.), *Yoga and ecology: Dharma for the earth: Proceedings of two of the sessions at the fourth Danam conference, held on site at the American Academy of Religion, Washington, DC, 17–19 November 2006*. Deepak Heritage Books.

Loizzo, J. (2016). The subtle body: An interoceptive map of central nervous system function and meditative mind-brain-body integration. *Annals of the New York Academy of Science, 1373*, 78–95. https://doi.org/10.1111/nyas.13065

Luque-Lora, R. (2020). *The disenchantment and reenchantment of nature, and their environmental implications*. [PDF document]. Retrieved from ResearchGate Web site: https://www.researchgate.net/publication/340284376_The_disenchantment_and_reenchantment_of_nature_and_their_environmental_implications

McGrath, A. (2003). *The re-enchantment of nature: Science, religion and the human sense of wonder*. Hodder & Stoughton.

Merchant, C. (1980). *The death of nature: Women, ecology, and the scientific revolution*. Harper & Row.

Mies, M., & Shiva, V. (1993). *Ecofeminism*. Zed Books.

Naess, A. (1989). *Ecology, community and lifestyle*. Cambridge University Press.

Padoux, A. (2017). *Hindu tantric world—An overview*. University of Chicago Press.

Plumwood, V. (2002). *Environmental culture: The ecological crisis of reason*. Routledge.

Saraswati, S. S. (2002). *Kundalini Tantra*. Yoga Publications Trust.

Sethi, N. (2014, January 11). Government rejects Vedanta's bauxite mining plans in Niyamgiri. *The Hindu Business line*. Retrieved online from: https://www.livemint.com/Politics/RfscBlhoFhQDapFA6uU7UK/Government-rejects-Vedantas-bauxite-mining-plans-in-Niyamgi.html

Sherma, R. D. (1998). Sacred immanence: Reflections of ecofeminism in Hindu Tantra. In L. E. Nelson (Ed.), *Purifying the earthly body of god*. SUNY Press.

Shiva, V. (2016). *Staying alive: Women*. North Atlantic Books.

Starhawk (1999) *The spiral dance*. In 20th Anniversary Edition. Harper.

Stone, A. (2006). Adorno and the disenchantment of nature. *Philosophy & Social Criticism, 32*, 231–253.

Ulrich, R. (1984). View through a window may influence recovery from surgery. *Science, 224*, 420–421.

UN, Emissions cap report 2019—UN environmental program. Retrieved from https://www.unep.org/resources/emissions-gap-report-2019
Venkatraman, A., Nandy, R., Rao, S. S., Mehta, D. H., Viswanathan, A., & Jayasundar, R. (2019). Tantra and modern neurosciences: Is there any correlation? *Neurology India, 67*, 1188–1193.
Watts, A. (1994). *Eastern wisdom, modern life: Collected talk: 1960–1969.* New World Library.
Weber, M. (1971). *The sociology of religion.* Methuen.
White, L. (1967). The historical roots of our ecological crisis. *Science, 155*, 1203–1207.
Whitworth, B. (2008). The physical world as a virtual reality. http://www.cs.auckland.ac.nz/staff-cgi-bin/mjd/secondcgi.pl?serial
Wilson, E. (1986). *Biophilia.* Harvard University Press.

Chapter 7
Horizontal and Vertical Business Models and their Relation with Ida and Pingala Concepts in Yoga

Kamini Desai

Abstract This chapter makes a connection between Pingala/Ida, Ha/Tha, dynamic/receptive balance, which is espoused as the basis of health and spirituality in Yoga. Pingala is more authoritative while Ida is more inclusive. One quality without the other manifests unhelpful extremes such as being overly controlling (Pingala) or collapsing under stress (Ida). The chapter discusses both Ida and Pingala characteristics, their strengths and weaknesses, and how to use the opposing energetic principle to return to balance. With this understanding, the discussion furthers on how to practically apply these yogic principles in the workplace to create optimal communications, interactions, and leadership. Finally, the relationship between Ida, Pingala, and the horizontal versus vertical business organization model has been discussed. The Pingala organization tends to be more of a "chain of command" business model. However, without an appropriate Ida (horizontal) organizational balance, this management style may encounter certain pitfalls. The Ida model alone is not the answer either. The horizontal organization is strong at collecting input, considering all points of view, and making sure everyone is happy. Without the vertical (Pingala) balance in an organization, this can quickly devolve into inertia, lack of action, and indecisiveness. Just as in Yoga, these two together create an organizational structure that is balanced and optimally effective.

Keywords Inclusive · Emotional intelligence · Stress · Burnout · Communication · Productivity · Balance · Leadership · Job satisfaction · Yoga · Self-evaluation

Yogic Cosmology

According to Tantric philosophy of Yoga, we may understand that existence or source is called *Brahman*. *Brahman* has two components: time bound and timeless. The timeless aspect of source is never born and never dies. It is eternal.

K. Desai (✉)
Seabiscuit Trail, Tallahassee, Florida 32309, USA
e-mail: kamini@iameducation.org

© Jindal Institute of Behavioral Sciences 2022

S. P. Sahni et al. (eds.), *Spirituality and Management*,
https://doi.org/10.1007/978-981-19-1025-8_7

Out of this timeless source emerges multitude forms—just as multitude waves arise out of an undifferentiated ocean. Each wave is unique, with differing qualities and characteristics, yet all arising out of the one ocean—timeless source.

The manifest aspect of source is composed of energy called *Shakti*. Everything in form is composed of this *Shakti* (energy). *Shakti* is considered to be the building block of all existence, just as Einstein says that everything in existence is made up of varying degrees of dense energy.

Form and the formless, from which form arises, are inextricably intertwined and interconnected. This verse from the ***Mahanirvana Tantra*** (Woodroffe, 2013) captures the essence of this principle:

> *In the beginning there was the One. It willed and became many. Ahab bahu syam—"mayIbe-many."In such manifestation of Shakti, the Brahman is known as the lower (apara) or manifested Brahman, who as the subject of worship, is meditated upon with attributes. It is embodied in the forms of all Devas and Devils and in the worshipper himself. And in fact to the mind and sense of the embodied spirit (jiva) the Brahman has body and form. Its form is that of the universe and of all things and beings therein (p.7).*

From Unity to Polarity

When formless source manifests into the world of form, it does so via the principle of polarity. This means, at the level of form that which is born will die. That which has a beginning will have an end.

However even though forms may live and die, the formless from which they come remains eternal. *The eternal aspect of source has no beginning or end. It exists in unity.*

By contrast, *the manifest aspect of source exists in polarity—complementary opposites*, which together create unity. In form, polarity makes up all aspects of manifest existence from the largest (birth and death) to the smallest. Night follows day, breathing in follows breathing out, relaxation follows tension, and pleasure follows pain.

Neither one is better than the other. Both are essential for life. These polarities, although appearing to be opposite, together create perfect harmony and balance through their qualities and actions.

This principle is clearly depicted through the *Yin/Yang* symbol, which is made up of complementary halves, which together make up one whole. Together they create *manifested unity*. Breathing in cannot happen without breathing out. Both together create the whole of life.

Duality

However, the human mind is capable of dividing this polarity into what we call duality. Let us take pain and pleasure. The truth is that pleasure is only revealed in contrast to pain, just as up is only revealed in contrast to down. If we experienced only pleasure and more pleasure, with no contrast of pain—we would not even call it pleasure. Pleasure does not exist except in contrast to pain. Up does not exist except in contrast to down. It is only because we are down that we know what up is.

Yet the human mind often fails to see this. Instead, the mind chooses for one—wanting it to last forever. The mind wants to live and never die. It wants to be up and never down. It wants to experience pleasure and never pain.

In choosing for one, however, the mind makes an enemy of its opposite. As soon as we choose pleasure, we become afraid of pain. When we choose success, we become afraid of failure. We fail to see the underlying unity and, instead, choose for one side of polarity. This creates a split in the *Yin* and the *Yang*. The underlying unity of existence is cleaved into two, depriving us of the experience of harmony and balance in the midst of the changing experiences of life.

Life will have successes and failures. If we can allow both as part of one whole, we can be in harmony with the natural flow of life. But the moment we choose for one type of experience, and not another, we pit ourselves against the natural inherent harmony in life. *When we choose for success, we are bound to feel fear, conflict, and stress when the part of polarity that we have divided from (failure) appears.*

Ida and Pingala

This same polarity principle exists within the human body in the form of two complementary elemental energies. The timeless manifests into the body as polarity via two main energy channels (*nadis*), which are opposing, complementary energies those together power bodily functions. These two energies are called *Pingala and Ida* and are said to correspond to what science calls the autonomic nervous system.

The autonomic nervous system functions through the sympathetic and parasympathetic nervous system. The sympathetic nervous system deals with the *fight and flight* response. The parasympathetic nervous system deals with the *rest and digest* response. The *Pingala* energy described in Yoga corresponds to the sympathetic nervous system. *Ida* energy corresponds with parasympathetic nervous system function. The *Pingala* energy in the body is the dynamic and active energy. Think of it as the energy of the Sun. It is like the positive pole of a battery. *Ida* energy is receptive, non-doing and Moon energy. It is like the negative pole of a battery. These two energies together, in balance with one another, power the functions of the body. Whenever one is out of balance with the other, it creates a state of stress in the body and sets the stage for disease. When these two are operating in unified function, it creates an optimum environment for physical health. It is also said to be the point at which the third and central channel of the body (the *Shushumna*) opens. Energy ascends toward the seventh energy center (*Chakra*) at the crown of the head and back to the timeless source consciousness from whence it came (Fig. 7.1).

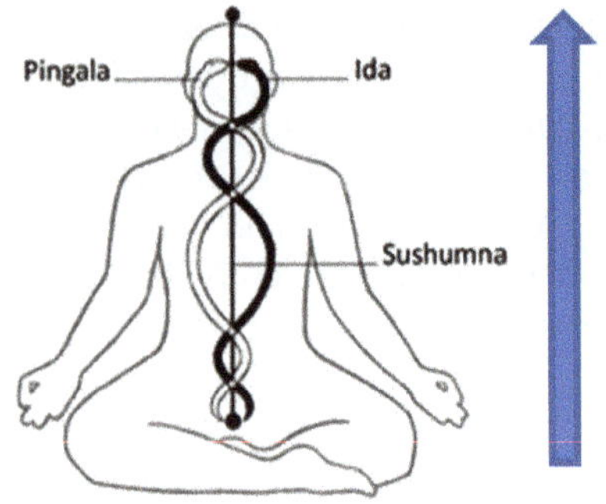

Fig. 7.1 Ida and Pingala artwork by JoEl James

Ida and Pingala: Why is Balance Important?

Just as *Ida* and *Pingala* allow the body to create physical balance, they also contribute to our mental and emotional balance. Based on our upbringing, environment, and innate character, we tend to gravitate toward *Pingala* or *Ida* qualities in different measures. These qualities may also change according to the environment we are living in and how we have habitually learned to respond in certain situations and with certain people.

Ida qualities represent softer, more emotionally intelligent sides of our nature. At best, *Ida* qualities have to do with caring, nurturing, and the ability to see things from others perspective and even put another's needs before our own. It is the quality within us that is oriented to being of service.

However, when we act from extreme *Ida* qualities (not sufficiently balanced by *Pingala*), we may become indecisive or feel paralyzed. Instead of being in service, we may be excessively driven by approval seeking and give up our own needs and boundaries as a result. Unbalanced *Ida* qualities can cause an individual to question themselves rather than challenging others and may tend to avoid conflict.

Pingala qualities represent the dynamic and achieving aspect of our nature. At best, *Pingala* qualities give us motivation, drive, focus, and determination. This energy allows us to stay focused on a given goal and helps to achieve it. However, when *Pingala* is taken to its extreme and not balanced out by its complementary pole, single-pointedness can become tunnel vision; unable or unwilling to see things from another point of view. Without the softer side to balance it, the individual with *Pingala* qualities may appear selfish, rigid, and controlling. When following excess *Pingala* qualities, an individual can be so devoted to the task at hand that she/he might fail to take into consideration other people's needs or opinions. Getting to the goal becomes so important that everything else takes second place. *Drive becomes demand. Doing becomes controlling* in order to get to the desired outcome—even at the cost of others.

When these polar aspects of our nature are properly balanced, we function and interact with life from a state of wholeness, with all parts of ourselves acting in cocreation. The whole person is able to care for others as well as care for themselves.

They not only have determination and drive, but also gain fulfillment from connection and interaction. The person strives for achievement, but not at the cost of connection or healthy relationships with others.

Whenever we find ourselves expressing one extreme of *Ida* or *Pingala* qualities, we can find balance by bringing in enough of the complementary opposite to move us back to center. For instance, an individual who has found themselves on the *Ida* extreme, allowing their well-being to depend on others' approval, can consciously cultivate more *Pingala* qualities, such as greater self-reliance and self-assurance. Once balanced in the center, that individual will do their best to meet everyone's needs, but will also recognize it is not always possible. They will be able to move forward securely with this in mind.

Ida and Pingala Communication Styles in the Corporate Environment

The Ida Pattern at the Workplace

There is tremendous opportunity here to apply these Eastern principles to the corporate environment where interpersonal interactions are a major source of stress (Frone, 2000, pp. 246–255). Such simple yet powerful principles put to use in this manner can help the individual navigate in a better way on the corporate ladder and help create a context for understanding oneself, one's colleagues, and even the culture of the organization itself.

As applied to the workplace, *Ida* communication styles include compassion, inclusivity, listening, and encouragement. An *Ida* communicator wants to make sure every voice is heard and that everyone feels good. These qualities create a safe psychological environment and positive relationships among coworkers.

However, an extreme *Ida* will shift toward *depending* on others' approval and *needing* everyone to feel happy in order to feel worthy of themselves. If the other does not feel good, they will become anxious, distraught, and may even make decisions based on pleasing their coworker or employee rather than acting in the best interests of the organization.

An employee or coworker with this pattern may tend to override their own boundaries—working late or longer than what is healthy or committing to work more than they can really handle. In the long run, such type of individual may end up in burnout or feeling resentful. Initially, such an individual may say "yes" to numerous projects and commitments in order to be liked. However, at some point, this becomes too much. Because to say "no" would mean to risk not being liked, they do not speak up. Instead they may either continue to drive themselves beyond their natural limits or they may let commitments go—letting things pile up so much that they become paralyzed and overwhelmed with being unable to keep up. Or they may end up feeling resentful and angry, "Why am I stuck here doing all this?" What they may not see is that their *Ida* pattern has put them in such a situation.

Someone who recognizes themselves in this position can employ the principles we have outlined to begin to bring this back into balance. A person who is too much on the *Ida* side needs to move toward the *Shushumna*, the balance point between *Ida* and *Pingala.* They can do this by incorporating more *Pingala* energy and qualities into their communication styles and habitual behaviors. Instead of always saying "yes" to projects, they need to consider, as a *Pingala* would, if this is actually in their own best interests. *Pingalas* are good at caring for themselves, and *Idas* may be so busy caring for others or organizational needs that they forget their own needs. Instead of trying to please everyone, a *Pingala* would bring in a firm and definite answer, whether the answer is favorable or not.

The only thing to be cognizant of in this scenario is that *Ida* individual does not overbalance to the extreme opposite. Sometimes, as a counterbalance to taking on too much and saying yes to everything and everyone, *Ida* may swing to the other pole, becoming excessively rigid—thinking of their own needs and not considering others—feeling that they are now doing the right thing. However, they have not moved to a balanced situation but are at the opposite extreme. Now, they may be unwilling to take on any other projects, help colleagues, or take on extra and unexpected tasks. The principle is correct—to develop opposite qualities—it simply goes too far to the other pole.

More helpful would be for such an individual to consciously incorporate *some Pingala* qualities in order to move to the balance point *between* the two poles. Here, the individual is able to include *themselves* in the choices and commitments they make. *This supports mental, physical, and emotional health, while being of best service to the organization.* Though it may initially appear that individuals who are willing to overextend themselves in the name of work are desirable employees, over the long term, these qualities can also put them at risk for burnout. An individual who is able to attend to his or her own self-care while being motivated on the job is the one who will be productive for years to come. This is the principle of work–life balance (Sirgy & Lee, 2015).

Ida Suppresses Their Inner Fire

Ida individuals have often found themselves out of internal balance because they have suppressed *Pingala* qualities, which they are uncomfortable with. I will sum it up by suggesting that the *Ida* individual is often afraid of their inner fire. They may be afraid, sometimes due to socialization, of their own power, drive, or ambition. They may be conflict avoidant—wanting to agree rather than disagree. As a result, instead of speaking up, they may not speak up at all. They may bottle up emotions inside until eventually they become passive aggressive. Instead of speaking calmly and clearly about a challenging matter, they may tell others, but not the leadership about their concerns. Comments and hints about their displeasure may slip out, but they will not directly address the issue. This style of communicating can be destructive in an organization, especially as others are recruited into this communication style.

Often the one who displays *Ida* qualities is afraid of getting angry. Yet anger, when channeled in healthy ways, becomes conviction, clarity, focus, and drive. If this has been suppressed, there is little or no fire to drive one's life.

Most of us have areas where *Pingala* has been suppressed, and we tend to collapse. Instead of leaning forward in the situation, we feel powerless. This mental and emotional pattern combined with stress can create just the right environment for depression. In fact, many Western psychologists describe depression as resulting from suppressed anger (Sperberg & Stabb, 1998).

When we see such situations that are not working for us, we can consciously develop a relationship with our inner fire. Rather than suppressing it, we can begin to allow it—recognizing that if it is used consciously, it can be a tremendous asset. We do not deny the *Ida* side of the personality, but trust that our inner fire can pass through the more heart-centered *Ida*. We can begin to trust that we can speak up, allow our fire to be heard, but channeled through the kindness, skill, and compassion that *Ida* brings. When these two qualities come together, fire is transmuted to conviction and clarity.

Now the individual is able to voice their point of view without being overly dominating or aggressive. They are able to trust themselves and their contribution. They can speak clearly, but in a way that is not offensive or hurtful to others. They become someone who can have a big impact on the workplace environment just by developing a healthy relationship with these elemental energies within them. This is an important aspect of self-management, which is a key aspect of emotional intelligence (Goleman & Boyatzis, 2017).

The Pingala Pattern in the Workplace

Helpful *Pingala* qualities include decisiveness, the ability to get things done, and the ability to make logical and rational decisions rather than emotional ones. *Pingala* worries comparatively little about what others think—unless it will affect their bottom line. A *Pingala* will demand nothing less than the highest achievement from themselves and others. They will expect only successes and will not tolerate failure. Emotions may be seen as a nuisance and as having little or no part to play in business. At its extreme, a *Pingala* can be authoritarian, hypercritical, demanding, and micromanaging.

Generally speaking, *Pingala* qualities are highly valued in the workplace. Motivation, ambition, and perfectionism are all qualities that engender high performance. Someone who pushes oneself and others, who works for long hours, and who puts work above leisure is actually respected in many cultures.

However, excess of *Pingala* can manifest its negative qualities. For example, no matter what the employee does, a *Pingala* boss will always manage to find fault.

Acknowledgment or appreciation is extremely rare, if they occur at all. This is important because, according to an article published in *Strategic HR Review,* employees overwhelmingly prefer receiving words of affirmation as primary way to receive appreciation in the workplace (White, 2017).

While the *Pingala* drive may initially be inspiring, without encouragement and appreciation, energy and enthusiasm will flag. Excessive Pingala actions may alienate others. Instead of offering a guiding hand, the excess *Pingala* will try to improve performance by continually telling others what they did wrong. They will be quick to blame and short in patience. They may take over and undercut the work of others in the belief that they know best. They will impatiently assess a matter but may not take the time to truly listen and understand the whole picture before issuing commands again. When working in a team, such a pattern can wreak havoc.

In the absence of *Ida* energy to listen, encourage, support, assist, and shepherd, an employee or colleague may subtly give up and distance themselves, feeling that no matter what they do, it will never measure up anyway. Others will still strive to please their *Pingala* employer but will rarely feel the satisfaction of a job well done. Everyone needs both. We need to achieve a level of performance that we never could have imagined to be possible, but also mentored, guided, and nurtured to reach this potential. Blame and criticism alone will not work.

The solution is simple. When we see that we are expressing excess *Pingala* qualities, such as being hypercritical, autocratic, or fault finding, we can offset it with *Ida* qualities, such as taking time to appreciate others' work and empowering with a combination of both, direction and latitude, to carry out tasks. A balance is struck where the leader is at their best, able to access both the strong and soft skills, that bring out the best in their employees.

Pingala Suppresses Their Inner Vulnerability

The *Ida* dominant personality tends to suppress their inner fire while the *Pingala* dominant personality tends to suppress their *vulnerability*—their *Ida* side. Each individual exists on a spectrum between these two qualities and will therefore manifest through a range of behaviors. The *Pingala* dominant personality may be shut down to the more emotional sides of their nature. They may appear cool and a bit distant, reserved, or even disconnected. They will have more comfort with logic and reason than with emotions. Instead of relating to others as equals, because they want to hide their own insecurities, they may come across as a condescending—"know it all."

Actually, an extreme *Pingala* may be using these qualities to hide their deeper and softer sides, which they will perceive as weakness. They will try to use *Pingala* qualities such as performance and achievements to bolster the part of them that secretly feels unworthy and not good enough. *Outcomes are not just about ambition; they are used to trying to alleviate the lingering sense of not measuring up that arises from within.* External achievements are used as an antidote to this inner feeling.

In the presence of stress, the *Pingala* will try to suppress the feeling of fear, uncertainty, or worry through *control*, whereas *Ida* would have faced these with *collapse*. They will try to manage a fearful or uncertain situation by doing more and trying harder. They will tend to get angry and explosive—blaming others (while the *Ida* would more likely suppress and implode).

These strategies work as long as the *Pingala* continues to win, achieve, and succeed. But as soon as failure or loss comes, as it inevitably will, the inner feeling of not measuring up will again rise to the surface. This is why the *Pingala* must continue to win, to succeed, and will do everything to do so—all in an effort to vanquish the demon within.

The control strategy can throw the *Pingala* individual into extreme action and long hours, with devotion to the job that far exceeds the body's ability to keep up. *Ida* patterns can do the same thing but arise from a different underlying cause. Combined with internal factors such as perfectionism and holding oneself up to impossibly high standards, *Pingala's* excess demand on the sympathetic nervous system may set the stage for *anxiety*. If living in this state over a long period of time, eventually it will not take much for the body to move from a state of sympathetic arousal to an experience of pure fear, which eventually will arise unbidden—even without an apparent trigger. The body has simply learned to go to anxiety in the presence of prolonged physical and emotional stress (Desai, 2017).

The *Pingala* strategy is considered one that we learned early in life and therefore has become a part of the core personality. These qualities are often rewarded in many cultures the world over, so it is not surprising that we develop them. However, with attention, it can be shifted to a healthier and more balanced pattern.

Instead of denying, hiding, or suppressing one's apparent weaknesses or insecurities, we can channelize them. The first step is allowing for these parts of us to be present without fear that we will fall victim to them. These are simply the sides of our energy patterns, which need to be channeled and directed in a healthy way. The extreme *Pingala* can channel their so-called *Ida* vulnerabilities toward the heart energy—compassion, caring, and nurturing of others. This is the higher octave of *Ida*. Instead of being afraid of that softness, we can use it and direct it in a way that is helpful to those around us. Instead of, "I'm afraid I'm not good enough," we redirect that same Ida energy to a higher octave of itself—perhaps, "I am here to care for others." In the act of caring about others, the old story is healed. We pull out of the extreme *Ida* that collapses on itself and back to its extraordinary emotionally intelligent qualities. Our heart opens to our own vulnerabilities and from that place we are truly able to give to the other, from the heart, in a meaningful way.

As the extreme *Pingala* individual develops these qualities, they begin to find more peace within themselves. Instead of finding fulfillment only in achievement, they will also feel fulfilled by being of service to others. They will listen, interact, mentor, and guide. They will still have the magnificent leadership that *Pingala* has given them, but with the heart to use that power well. *They will become someone who just does not tell others what to do, but will become the embodiment of a true leader.*

This is an environment where colleagues, coworkers, and employees can begin to blossom. In an environment of safety, with room to learn and grow along a path to excellence, individuals can develop at an exponential rate. When unafraid to speak up, they will feel safe to bring new ideas to the table. Given room to experiment, they will succeed on behalf of the organization as well as learn from their mistakes. These are the qualities that foster *intrapreneurship;* a positive learning environment and empowerment model that allow individuals to use their entrepreneurial skills for the benefit of the company. This kind of safe environment actually increases the ability of individuals to learn and develop at a faster rate (Carmeli, Brueller, & Dutton, 2009). It also creates more job satisfaction and sense of accomplishment. In fact, studies show a strong relationship between employee satisfaction, intrapreneurship, and firm growth (Auer & Antoncic, 2011). Balanced leadership, beginning with internal energetic equilibrium, creates the right environment for these to occur.

Swinging Between Ida and Pingala

Most commonly, we find aspects of both extreme *Ida* and *Pingala* within our individual personalities. Whenever and wherever we see these patterns are not serving us, we can use these principles to move back to center.

To demonstrate this further, let us say an individual has just received a promotion that many others in the department were hoping for. There is an atmosphere of jealousy surrounding this newly promoted individual along with hopes they will fail. Perhaps they begin on the *Pingala* side, their inner voice says to them, "I have to do this." "I have to succeed, I cannot fail." This leads to the next thought, "I just have to do more and try harder." "I have to prove I am capable." "I will do whatever it takes." At some point however, the individual may push themselves to such an extreme that they try to find the antidote to the pressure by swinging to the opposite pole—*Ida*. The individual then gets into an *Ida* cycle, "What if it doesn't work?" "What if I fail?" "Why bother, I'm never going to succeed." "I wish I'd never gotten this promotion."

Then, what might this individual do? They might swing back *again* to the *Pingala* side, "No, I will make this work!" "All I have to do is to try harder!" "I am going to show them!" We can all swing back and forth like this using one side as the answer to the other.

While the principle is correct, we need to look to the middle line. We need to do the best we can (*Pingala*), give it all we have, and yet be surrendered to the results (*Ida*). *Bhagavad Gita* Chap. 2 verse 47 says (Mitchell, 2006):

> You have a right to your actions, but never to your actions' fruits. Act for the action's sake. And do not be attached to inaction.

This is essentially saying the same thing. We must learn to bring *both* the energies of effort *and* surrender into the equation rather than swinging from one side to the other. The individual with the promotion needs to *do their best and then let go.*

Once we have performed our best, there is nothing more left to do. There is nothing more that is within our control to do. Then it is time to let go. A wonderful phrase to remind oneself of this principle is: *I do my best and let go.*

This principle is also touched upon in Stephen Covey's book, *The Seven Habits of Highly Effective People*, where he discusses the power of working within our circle of influence. We each have a circle of concern, which are the things that matter to us—the state of the world, the economy, and politics. Here most of us have little power. However, *within that circle of concern, there is a circle of influence.* This is the place where we have concerns and are actually able to do something about those concerns. The more we can do our best *within* our circle of influence, the more empowered we feel to make the changes we *can* make (Covey, 2020). This is what *Pingala-Ida* balance looks like. We are doing what we can to the degree that we can in the areas where we *do* hold influence and control. But we are also able to let go in those areas where circumstances are outside of our control.

Complementarity Can Become Interpersonal Conflict

Stress and its effect on *Ida/Pingala* energies is a major factor that can imbalance working relationships. With bosses, colleagues, or in our home environment, we often initially gravitate toward individuals who complement us without even realizing it. We hire people who are similar to us in some ways as well as possess qualities that we do not have. In relationship, we not only appreciate someone who is similar to us, but also who brings something different to a relationship.

When we first enter into a professional partnership for example, we may find ourselves in an organic and complementary interchange—polarity. For example, one person is more driven and motivated, the other more laid back and relaxed—able to easily interact with clients, but less task oriented. Even though these are opposite qualities, they are complementary, and when in balance, they create a feeling of effortless unity—the *Yin* and *Yang* or *Ida* and *Pingala*, working together. Interactions flow, and each appreciates the other for the qualities they bring to the whole. The company functions well, and as a result, each individual fulfilling a key function draws on their unique skill sets for the benefit of the whole.

But, especially when under stress, we can move from this natural complementary polarity to conflict. Instead of looking to the other and appreciating the qualities they bring to the whole, we begin to see through the eyes of duality rather than polarity. The one who plays the more active role looks to the one who is opposite to them, and instead of appreciating their emotional intelligence and healthy perspective on life, they see someone who is "lazy" and "isn't pulling their weight."

The reverse is true as well. The easygoing person looks over to the one opposite to them and, instead of appreciating their drive and determination, sees someone who is overly controlling and demanding. Rather than perceiving the underlying unity behind the apparent opposites, we see someone who is different from us. We no longer view them as someone who is contributing their part to the whole. Instead of appearing as a welcome solution, the other person appears to be a problem. It now appears that the solution to that problem is to get them to be more like us.

In effect, each one is saying to the other, "Well, if you were just like me, everything would be okay." *Pingala* says, "If you would just plan your day, finish your tasks and fulfill your responsibilities, I wouldn't have to be so controlling." *Ida* says in response, "Well if you would just give me some space rather than finding fault with everything I do, I might actually be motivated to do my work." Complementarity has moved to conflict. What began, as an effortless easy interchange of skills becomes a power struggle, as each seeks to exert their work strategy on the other.

Sometimes the power struggle is overt, and sometimes it is covert. Sometimes, the struggle is never spoken about, but becomes an underground, unspoken resentment. Perhaps one feels so controlled that they simply withdraw and stop participating altogether. This is a pattern that most people will recognize in some area of their lives. It manifests in the professional as well as personal arena.

Conflict Affects the Organization from the Top Down

While this dynamic may seem relatively insignificant, it can play out in various detrimental ways within an organization. As managing partners, family-owned companies or directors within an organization move into duality, they will consciously or unconsciously begin to recruit people to their point of view. Assistants, colleagues, and even outside contractors may receive subtle cues that they need to take sides:

1. Anyone who sides with the "other" is the enemy. Instead of working together, competition and conflict buds *within* the organization itself.
2. Focus becomes on inter-organizational politics, backstabbing to make sure the other does not "win."
3. As leaders jockey for position, clarity and leadership are lost. Employees do not know who to listen to and take direction from.
4. The organization essentially has two organizations functioning within it, each headed by the two leaders who are in conflict.
5. Focus shifts from working together against outside competitors to fighting among one another.

Interpersonal conflict plays a very significant role in workplace stressors, attitudes, and behaviors (Jaramillo et al., 2011). On the other hand, quality relationships at work foster greater connectivity, mutuality, psychological safety, and greater ability to learn. These can all be shifted with honest self-evaluation, self-awareness, and the willingness to shift our personal patterns. These shifts are not just for our personal betterment or for our immediate team. They can actually have a significant impact on the bottom line (Cameron et al., 2003).

Considerations for Reversing the Dualistic Dynamic

First, we must recognize the key importance that leaders of an organization hold for the entire culture of an organization. Any dysfunction at the top rapidly multiplies and becomes a divisive force, a cancer, within the organization.

Corporate team building and the like can be very useful. However, if such efforts do not include top management, results will remain limited. Just as we can grow a plant by making sure its roots are healthy, we must work at the root of the organization—its top management—to ensure the health of the rest of the tree. Then, once the foundation is restored to health, the remaining structure built on this foundation will be steady and strong.

Shifting Perspective

Simple steps can be implemented to help reverse this invasive pattern. Shifting perspective by taking time to decompress on a regular basis is the key. When we are stressed, we are more likely to perceive from a divided perspective. Chronic stress increases the activity level and number of neural connections in the amygdala, the place where we perceive threat in the brain (Murgia, 2016). The more stressed you are, the more you will perceive people and situations as a threat.

To reverse this effect, practices such as taking a walk in nature or engaging in any right-brain creative activity will be helpful for shifting perspective. However, entering alpha brainwave and deeper states will be most effective. Alpha brainwave states take place when we are in restful wakefulness or in that twilight zone between waking and sleeping. Here the relaxation response or the parasympathetic nervous system is activated. Inducing a relaxation response on a regular basis will strengthen the part of your brain that dampens the fear response and helps to maintain your mental and emotional clarity (Hölzel et al., 2011).

Meditation

Practices such as meditation or Yoga Nidra (sleep-based meditation) not only induce alpha and deeper brainwave activity, but they also reduce stress hormones such as cortisol in the system, reduce activity in the threat center of the brain, and help you change your relationship to your thoughts. Even though you may have times that you do not appreciate your business partner or coworker, *meditation practices help you observe rather than participate in the thought.*

Thousands of thoughts are moving through the mind every day, but we become habituated to listen and act more on some than others. Some of these thoughts can act to our detriment. By creating a different relationship to these unhelpful thoughts through meditation, we no longer take them so seriously and are less likely to react to them. As human beings, our minds are made to have thoughts and opinions about everything, but we do not need to be run by them.

Yoga Nidra

Yoga Nidra is a type of meditation. Its advantage is that it is performed lying down and therefore removes much of the effort involved in seated meditation. This makes it ideal for the novice meditator. Yoga Nidra consists of a guided series of breath, body, and awareness techniques that allows the practitioner to progressively release any doing and enter into a profound state of rest where the body is able to deeply regenerate itself. Here, the brain is operating in virtual symmetry.

This is important because according to Yogic philosophy, the *Pingala nadi*, or meridian, corresponds to the left-brain while the *Ida nadi* corresponds to the right-brain. As Yoga Nidra creates a state of balanced brain activity, it is similarly balancing *Ida* and *Pingala* so that the individual has set the foundation to operate in life from balance.

In fact, Yoga Nidra practitioners report this change. They report feeling more balanced, able to maintain their calm in the midst of conflict and less triggered by others. Besides this, it is also simple to practice; Yoga Nidra is an excellent practical resource for those who want to develop both their strong and soft skills in a variety of situations.

In addition, Yoga Nidra works with the tool of intention. In Yoga Nidra, we can plant a seed, which will support the attitudes and behaviors we want to develop. If we find ourselves being excessively *Ida* or *Pingala* in a certain situation, we can set an intention in the form of words, an image or a felt sense during the Yoga Nidra. In this state, the intention can be deeply and profoundly received without any back talk from the mind.

In Yoga Nidra, this intention can be fully received. Your cells hear it, your body hears it, your emotions hear it, your mind hears it, and your spirit receives it. Your wh*ole being* can begin to move in that direction. Usually, we make a shift only at the *level of the mind*, but that does not mean the rest of our body is along for the ride. This is the reason why the intentions which we make with the conscious mind are limited and often do not work as well as those used with Yoga Nidra.

Once planted in Yoga Nidra, we can *reinforce* our intention in the waking state through repetition. We all have *Pingala* and *Ida* qualities, but in certain situations we may find ourselves continually thrown to one extreme or the other. When we see ourselves going into an undesirable pattern, we can bring the intention to mind and use it as a cue to redirect our thoughts and actions in the direction we want to go. In this way, we can progressively begin to shift from unconscious and automatic patterns to the conscious and deliberate outcomes we want to create.

Once each individual has created the best possible *internal environment,* employing tools such as above, they are in the best position to begin to build optimal *external* conditions for themselves and others. *Internal* tools combined with *classic external* techniques such as team building can help build the capacity of these relationships to withstand stressors and continue to hold partners and coworkers in mutual positive regard. With Eastern practices and self-awareness, we can consciously cultivate ways of being that truly serve the individual and the corporate environment in the long term.

Ida and Pingala at the Organizational Level

We have understood *Ida Pingala* dynamics in one's own personality and how this can affect workplace dynamics, communications, and conflict. Now let us look at how the elemental energies of *Ida* and *Pingala* can influence the entire culture of an organization and how each relates to horizontal and vertical business structures (Quinn, 2019).

What is the Horizontal versus Vertical Business Organization?

The *vertical* business organization is one in which the CEO and top-level executives give middle managers directives, which are then passed on to the bottom level of employees who execute on the directives that have come from upper management. In this business model, the employee is not expected to object or to give any input into how the organization operates. The chain of command is rigid and structured. Any input or feedback intended for upper management must happen according to formal procedure.

The *horizontal* model is a flat model in which there are fewer managers. Here employees are expected and encouraged to give input, collaborate, and take the initiative to improve workplace processes. Rather than only being told what to do by a manager, the horizontal model invites each individual to work toward the goals of the organization and gives them more authority and autonomy than in a typical vertical organization. This can improve workplace efficiency and morale.

In a vertical organization, communication from the top-down takes time; in a horizontal organization, communication flows more freely between individuals and upper management. At best, it allows everyone to be a "leader" in his or her area working for the same outcome. Because communication flows both ways and authority is more widely distributed, the business is able to shift more quickly according to the needs of the market.

Ida and Pingala Relate to Horizontal and Vertical Business Organizations

One could argue that there is a strong correlation between the *Pingala* dynamic and the vertical business organization (Aoki, 1986). The *Pingala* quality is more authoritative, linear, and hierarchical, while the *Ida* quality is more inclusive and collaborative. As we have learned so far, neither *Ida* nor *Pingala*, horizontal or vertical, is better than the other. Rather, I suggest it is the balance between the two where magic can happen (Han et al., 2019).

A classic Pingala or vertical business organization only receives input according to a regimented protocol from its employees. For the most part, they are simply told what to do. However, it is very often the rank and file employees who have the most interchange with the product or service and therefore have important information to contribute. Without an easy exchange of information, the business may take years to make changes that could have been made more efficiently.

Essentially, in the vertical/*Pingala* model, communication is running predominantly one way. There is little information feeding back to the top giving them valuable information on how to course correct. It is very much like having a brain that only sends signals to the limbs, but the limbs are only able to communicate limited sensory information back to the brain so that it can react and adjust accordingly.

Healthy two-way communication is as essential for the body of an organization as it is for our own physical body. Incorporating *horizontal Ida* qualities into a Pingala organization can create more opportunities for effective two-way communication. Rather than just *telling*, there is *listening* and responding.

In addition, the Pingala organization expects orders to be obeyed to the letter, with very little room for creativity or discussion. This can disempower employees from taking initiative, not bringing out the full extent of their skills and thereby leaving no sense of satisfaction in them.

It might sound like the horizontal *Ida* organization is the more desirable; however, it has its own pitfalls when not balanced by the structure and direction *Pingala* can provide. While a horizontal *Ida* organization can be good in many respects, sometimes such a business can spend too much time in making sure everyone feels good and is heard. However, when it comes to reaching consensus on just what ideas need to be executed, this can be difficult. Enormous amounts of time can be spent in getting input and making sure everyone is heard, but little or nothing may be done with it. Mired in discussion, information may not make its way from ideas to implementation. *Without the vertical (Pingala) balance in an organization, this can quickly devolve into inertia, lack of action, and indecisiveness.* Here, *Pingala* decision-making authority is the key. Once all the information has been gathered, it is helpful to have someone make the final call and be the driving force to putting ideas into action. These are the *Pingala* qualities that will bring the equation into balance.

Furthermore, *Pingala* structured businesses will tend to have a lot of layers with accompanying protocols, policies, rules, and responsibilities for each individual.

This is often less clear in an *Ida* organization resulting in redundancies and lack of clarity about who is doing what. Foundational structures, policies, and procedures may be lacking and only introduced as needed. This can keep the *Ida* organization fundamentally disorganized and scattered. Such an organization may develop policies and procedures on the fly rather than at the outset. This can create confusion as employees struggle to keep up with these changes.

While a *Pingala* business will motivate employees and increase performance by providing a clear structure for advancement into management, an *Ida* organization will motivate and inspire *now* by encouraging creativity and providing opportunities for success through teamwork, collaboration, and a certain scope of authority within any position they may hold. Too much *Pingala* will limit individuals' ability to truly contribute to the organization unless they are in some kind of a leadership position. It may even crush ideas, inspiration, and a sense of being a part of something larger. By the same token, too much *Ida* may give away too much authority. Without proper oversight, empowered individuals may make faulty choices for which the business pays the price. Appropriate *Pingala* managerial oversight to *Ida's* openness and empowerment strategy is the optimal balance, allowing people to bring their ideas to someone who has a larger picture of the overall scheme of things and can discern from a larger perspective what will best serve the overall vision.

What Might a Balanced Ida Pingala Business Organization Look Like?

Imagine that an organization has clear direction and vision. Each person has well-defined roles and responsibilities. They may or may not have individuals below them to assist with their mandates. This is a somewhat *Pingala* structured organization, but with less middle managers who can slow the lines of communication.

Within that structure is *Ida* flexibility. Support staff collaborates and interchanges their ideas with their bosses, working together to help achieve the goals of the organization. Staff may be empowered to take a project and run with it within certain parameters and scope of authority, while reporting back periodically on what they are doing, so that the boss can keep them on track. *Ida* gives the space to do the work; *Pingala* makes sure the work done is in keeping with the overall goals of the organization.

Direction is coming from the top-down, but there is space for ideas to come from the bottom-up as well, with less protocols and formal channels in place for feedback to occur. Ideas and creativity can flow on all sides. Individuals from many different levels of the organization contribute to the whole and work together to make things happen. Yet everyone knows and agrees on who the final decision-maker is.

To me, this is an example of an organization in *Ida Pingala*, horizontal and vertical balance. In this way, the disadvantages we see at either extreme may be mitigated or even neutralized by working from the center. The organization can make the best of *both* inclusive and directive qualities. This is an organization that is truly whole—alive with inspiration, able to shift with the tides of changing demands quickly and efficiently with an "all hands on deck" approach. It not only makes the best of everyone's skills, but it also has the forward momentum, drive, and focus that *Pingala* energy brings.

Conclusion

Self-awareness at the individual level is a powerful tool. As each individual seeks to balance his or her inner *Pingala* and *Ida* qualities, this will naturally begin to make shifts in how that individual completes their tasks, communicates, and interacts with others. *Ida and Pingala qualities do not just affect the individual's inner world; it affects their behaviors and choices, which will eventually impact the work environment and even the business organization itself.* Cultivating an awareness of the *Ida Pingala* principle in one's professional life can lead to great gains and provide simple but powerful points of awareness to create optimal productivity and outcomes for the business organization. This is no longer a spiritual ideal but a practical application of yogic principles to business organizations.

References

Aoki, M. (1986). Horizontal versus vertical information structure of the firm. *The American Economic Review, 76*(5), 971–983. Retrieved July 26, 2021, from http://www.jstor.org/stable/1816463

Auer Antoncic, J., & Antoncic, B. (2011). Employee satisfaction, intrapreneurship and firm growth: A model. *Industrial Management and Data Systems, 111*(4), 589–607. https://doi.org/10.1108/02635571111133560

Cameron, K. S., Dutton, J. E., Quinn, R. E., Dutton, J. E., & Heaphy, E. D. (2003). In *Positive organizational scholarship: Foundations of a new discipline essay* (pp. 263–278). Berrett-Koehler Publ.

Carmeli, A., Brueller, D., & Dutton, J. E. (2009). Learning behaviours in the workplace: The role of high-quality interpersonal relationships and psychological safety. *Systems Research and Behavioral Science, 26*(1), 81–98. https://doi.org/10.1002/sres.932

Covey, S. R. (2020). *The 7 habits of highly effective people*. Simon & Schuster UK Ltd.

Desai, K. (2017). *Yoga nidra: The art of transformational sleep*. Lotus Press.

Frone, M. R. (2000). Interpersonal conflict at work and psychological outcomes: Testing a model among young workers. *Journal of Occupational Health Psychology, 5*(2), 246–255. https://doi.org/10.1037/1076-8998.5.2.246

Goleman, D., & Boyatzis, R. E. (2017, February 6). *Emotional intelligence has 12 Elements. which do you need to work on?* Harvard Business Review. https://hbr.org/2017/02/emotional-intelligence-has-12-elements-which-do-you-need-to-work-on.

Han, J. H., Kang, S., Oh, I.-S., Kehoe, R. R., & Lepak, D. P. (2019). The goldilocks effect of strategic human resource management? Optimizing the benefits of a high-performance work system through the dual alignment of vertical and HORIZONTAL FIT. *Academy of Management Journal, 62*(5), 1388–1412. https://doi.org/10.5465/amj.2016.1187

Hölzel, B. K., Carmody, J., Vangel, M., Congleton, C., Yerramsetti, S. M., Gard, T., & Lazar, S. W. (2011). Mindfulness practice leads to increases in regional brain gray matter density. *Psychiatry Research: Neuroimaging, 191*(1), 36–43. https://doi.org/10.1016/j.pscychresns.2010.08.006

Jaramillo, F., Mulki, J. P., & Boles, J. S. (2011). Workplace stressors, job attitude, and job behaviors: Is interpersonal conflict the missing link? *Journal of Personal Selling and Sales Management, 31*(3), 339–356. https://doi.org/10.2753/pss0885-3134310310

Mitchell, S. (2006). *Bhagavad Gita: A new translation*. Three Rivers Press.

Murgia, M. (2016, November 9). *How stress affects your brain*. TED. https://www.ted.com/talks/madhumita_murgia_how_stress_affects_your_brain.

Quinn, S. (2019, January 31). *The Difference Between Vertical and Horizontal Business Organizations*. Small Business–Chron.com. https://smallbusiness.chron.com/difference-between-vertical-horizontal-business-organizations-24915.html.

Sirgy, M. J., & Lee, D.-J. (2015). Work-life balance: A quality-of-life model. *Applied Research in Quality of Life, 11*(4), 1059–1082. https://doi.org/10.1007/s11482-015-9419-6

Sperberg, E. D., & Stabb, S. D. (1998). Depression in women as related to anger and mutuality in relationships. *Psychology of Women Quarterly, 22*(2), 223–238. https://doi.org/10.1111/j.1471-6402.1998.tb00152.x

White, P. (2017). How do employees want to be SHOWN APPRECIATION? Results from 100,000 employees. *Strategic HR Review, 16*(4), 197–199. https://doi.org/10.1108/shr-06-2017-0037

Woodroffe, J. G. (2013). *Mahanirvana Tantra: Tantra of the great liberation*. Theophania Publishing.

Chapter 8
Developing an Indigenous Thick Description: *Tapas* in the *Bhagavadgītā*

Dharm P. S. Bhawuk

Abstract In this paper, the construct of *tapas* is derived from the Bhagavadgītā. By analyzing the 36 verses that refer to *tapas*, nine themes were identified. First, *tapas* is a *daivik sampadā*, and it is presented in a nomological network of 26 virtues. Second, *tapas* can be *sāttvika*, *rājasika*, or *tāmasika*, and thus, it is a part of the typology of *sāṅkhya darśana*. Third, *tapas* can be *mānasika*, *vācika*, or *kāyika*, and it is presented in three additional nomological networks with other constructs. Fourth, *tapas*, *yajña*, *dāna*, *karma*, and *śraddhā* are closely associated and presented in the sixth nomological network. Fifth, Kṛṣṇa is present as *tapas* in *tapasvīs* or *tapas* is Kṛṣṇa personified in *tapasvīs*. Sixth, *tapas* is presented in a typology of *yajña*, making it a type of *yajña*. Seventh, *tapas* is necessary for *sādhakas* of *adhyātma*, but not sufficient, and *bhakti* needs to be cultivated. Eighth, *tapas* is an attribute of a *brāhmaṇa* showing that those who want to lead others by being exemplars must cultivate *tapas*. Finally, Arjuna is presented as an exemplar of a *tapasvī* or ascetic. The themes are infused with many insights and behavioral outcomes of *tapas* presenting a rich indigenous thick description of the construct. Implications for global psychology are discussed.

Keywords Indigenous thick description · *Tapas* · *śraddhā* · *Yajña* · *Dāna* · *Bhagavadgītā* · Indian psychology · Indigenous psychology

---

The paper is gratefully dedicated to Dr. Om Prakash Sharma for it was inspired by the simple question he asked me, "What is *tapas*?" Some parts of this paper were presented as a keynote address in the symposium—Thriving in difficult times with Bhagavad Gita—organized by Vedic Indian Psychology Research & Application (VIPRA Division), Department of Clinical Psychology, National Institute of Mental Health & Neurosciences (NIMHANS) Bengaluru, India, February 26, 2021. Also, some parts of the paper were presented as a part of Dr. Vedavyas Memorial Online Lecture Series, International Institute of Vedic Sciences, sponsored by Vedavyasa Bharati Trust, USCEFI and Yoga Brotherhood of America, on May 2, 2021. I would like to thank Professors Jai B. P. Sinha and Avi Karan for their critical comments that helped me improve the paper.

D. P. S. Bhawuk (✉)
Management and Culture and Community Psychology, University of Hawai'i at Mānoa, Honolulu, USA
e-mail: bhawuk@hawaii.edu

© Jindal Institute of Behavioral Sciences 2022

S. P. Sahni et al. (eds.), *Spirituality and Management*,
https://doi.org/10.1007/978-981-19-1025-8_8

This paper builds on the recommendations that Marsella (1998) presented for the development of global-community psychology. He emphasized the need to pay attention to how culture shapes human behavior. He also proposed that research in indigenous psychologies should lead to the replacement of monolithic Western psychology, which is presented as a universal psychology. Indigenous psychologies are more amenable to multilevel and multicultural perspectives and can synthesize various levels of variables from individual to the level of the planet as a whole (see Bhawuk, for an illustration of this). Bhawuk (2009) adopted narrative analysis and discourse analysis (Bhawuk, 2019d) to demonstrate how indigenous models could be developed. This paper contributes to global-community psychology by presenting a novel indigenous construct, *tapas*, which will further enrich our understanding of *adhyātma* or spirituality.

Bhawuk (2011) drew our attention to many fundamental indigenous psychological constructs like *manas, buddhi, ahaṃkāra,* and *ātman,* which cannot be translated into English. Other indigenous psychological constructs include *cit* or consciousness (Bhawuk, 2014), *lajjā* (2017a, 2019c), *lokasaṃgraha* (2008b, 2019e), and *adhyātma* or spirituality (Bhawuk, 2019a, 2019b) that are grounded in the Indian culture. Employing qualitative methodology like textual analysis, Bhawuk (2008a, 2017b20112005) developed various models of expanding and contracting. Analyzing the verses of the *Bhagavadgītā,* Bhawuk (1999, 2011) demonstrated how peace and harmony could be modeled at the individual level. Employing multiple texts and other qualitative methodology, Bhawuk (2017a, 2019c) presented the construct of *lajjA,* which allowed him to question the Western paradigm that there are shame and guilt cultures. He was also able to synthesize a spirituality-based theory of creativity (2019d; Bhawuk, 2003) by analyzing the dialogues of saints, bridging life world and scientific world. Following the recommendations of Marsella (1998), Bhawuk has employed a number of qualitative methodologies including autoethnography (, 2017c, 2019c; Bhawuk, 2009), case analysis (Bhawuk, 2003; Bhawuk et al., 2009), historical analysis (Bhawuk, 2003), lexical analysis (Bhawuk, 2017a, 2019a, 2019b; 2019e) and literary analysis (Bhawuk, 2017a).

In this paper, the construct of *tapas* is drawn from the *Bhagavadgītā.* By developing indigenous constructs like these, we are able to reduce our dependence on Western constructs. Not to fall into the trap of the pseudo-etic (also called imposed etic) approach in which ideas are derived from one culture, often the Western culture, and presented as universal constructs, the indigenous constructs are presented as thick descriptions that are embedded in a specific culture. This approach helps enrich indigenous psychology literature and also informs the extant literature that draws heavily from the Western cultures. A synthesis of indigenous constructs and Western constructs could lead to a richer global psychology as suggested by Marsella (1998).

Method

Tapaḥ appears in the *Bhagavadgītā* 15 times in 14 verses of five cantos, specifically, 7.9, 10.5, 16.1, 17.5, 17.7, six verses from 17.14 to 17.19, 17.28, twice in 18.5, and 18.42. Other forms of the word are used 12 times (in 13 verses), namely *tapantam* (11.19),[1] *tapasā* (11.53), *tapas* (17.27), *tapasyasi* (9.27),[2] *tapasvibhyaḥ* (6.46), *tapasviṣu* (7.9), *tapaḥsu* (8.28), *tapāmi* (9.19), *tapobhiḥ* (11.48), *tapoyajñaḥ* (4.28), *taptam* (17.17, 17.28), and *tapyante* (17.5). Also, *tapa* is used in *parantapa* as a name of Arjuna, and it appears nine times in verses 2.3, 2.9, 4.2, 4.5, 4.33, 7.27, 10.40, 11.54, and 18.41. The text of all the 14 verses that refer to *tapaḥ*, 13 verses that refer to other forms of the word *tapas*, and nine verses that use *parantapa* as a name for Arjuna were analyzed to decipher the meaning of the construct.

Results

The nine themes derived from the analyses of all the 36 verses in the *Bhagavadgītā*. referring to *tapas* in some form are presented below. All these themes are interrelated and together provide an indigenous thick description of the construct (Bhawuk, 2020).

Theme 1: Tapas *is a* Daivik Sampadā: *The First Nomological Network*

In verses one to three of Canto 16[3] of the *Bhagavadgītā*, *tapas* is presented as one of the 26 *daivīka sampadas* (or virtues). The development of all the 26 virtues can be traced to *sattvaguṇa*, which would shape thoughts, feelings, and actions that arise in the *manas* or mind.[4] These virtues need to be cultivated by effort into daily living. In the fourth verse,[5] six negative qualities are listed as *āsurīka* (*asuras*are presented as cruel people in the Indian worldview and texts). They are *dambha* (deceit), *darpa*

---

[1] Verse 11.19: *anādimadhyāntamanantavīryamanantabāhuṃ śaśisūryanetram, paśyāmi tvāṃ dīptahutāśavaktraṃsvatejasā viśvamidaṃ tapantam.*

[2] Verse 9.27: *yatkaroṣi yadśnāsi yajjuhoṣi dadāsi yat, attapasyasi kaunteya tatkuruṣva madarpaṇam.*

[3] Verse 16.1: *abhayṃ sattvasaṃśuddhirjñanayogavyavasthitiḥ, dānaṃ damaśca yajñaśca svādhyāyastapa ārjavam;*verse 16.2: *ahiṃsā satyamakrodhastyāgaḥ śāntirapaiśunam, dayābhuteṣvaloluptvaṃ mārdavaṃ hrīracāpalaṃ;* verse 16.3: *tejaḥ kṣamā dhṛtiḥ śaucamadroho nātimānita, bhavanti sampadaṃ daivīmabhijātasya bhārata.*

[4] In Saṃskṛt, *manas* is the agent for thought-feeling, and action (Bhawuk, 2008, 2011). It cannot be translated into English. Mind is a poor translation for *manas*. Mind cannot capture feeling and action. Therefore, *manas* is used throughout the paper.

[5] Verse 16.4: *dambho darpo'atimānaśca krodhaḥ pāruṣyameva ca, ajñanaṃ cābhijātasya pārtha sampadamāsurīm.*

(pride), *atimāna* (seeking much respect), *krodha* (anger), *pāruṣya* (harshness), and *ajñāna* (ignorance). They are *tāmaskia* (negative) in nature and should be weeded out in daily living. Since *tapas* is associated with the other 25 virtues, we have to appreciate it in the nomological network of these 26 attributes or virtues.

The 25 virtues are *abhayam* (without fear), *sattvasaṃśuddhi* (purification of the inner self), *jñānayogavyavasthiti* (being situated in the spiritual self), *dānaṃ* (charity), *damaḥ* (restraint of senses), *yajñaḥ* (all activities that purify the self are considered *yajña*), *svādhyāyaḥ* (daily study of scriptures), ā*rjavaṃ* (being straightforward), *ahiṃsā* (complete absence of violence), *satyaṃ* (acting truthfully in thought, speech, and action), *akrodhaḥ* (complete absence of anger), *tyāgaḥ* (without attachment), *śāntiḥ* (complete peace of *antaḥkaraṇa*), *apaiśunaṃ* (non-calumny), *dayābhuteṣu* (compassion for all beings), *aloluptvaṃ* (absence of greed), *mārdavaṃ* (gentleness toward all), *hrīḥ* (internal sense of appropriateness), *acāpalaṃ* (absence of fickle-mindedness), *tejaḥ* (personal effulgence), *kṣamā* (forgiveness), *dhrītiḥ* (resoluteness), *śaucaṃ* (purity), *adrohaḥ* (absence of offense), and *nātimānitā* (not seeking importance). The word *tapas* refers to keep *mauna* (silence), fasting, getting up early morning, sticking to a rigorous daily schedule and so forth. Such practices help one to control actions, speech, and the subtlest of thoughts.

Since the 26 *daivīka sampadas* are to be cultivated, it is reasonable to assume that each of them will grow upon the person with practice. Since *lajjā* is socially learned, it guides the practitioner such that he or she performs the actions that one ought to do (*karaṇīya*) and never neglects them. Also, *lajjā* guides one not to perform actions that one ought not to do (*akaraṇīya*). Thus, *lajjā* is necessary for the cultivation of all the 25 virtues. Also, since the practice of cultivating any virtue itself is *tapas*, it becomes the most fundamental *daivika sampada* along with *lajjā*. *Lajjā* comes with *viveka* and a calmness of *buddhi*, which becomes stronger with growing *tapas*. Thus, *tapas* is not only associated with the other 25 *daivīka sampadas*, but also necessary for mastering the others (see Fig. 8.1, Panel 2).

At the end of Canto 16, Kṛṣṇa emphasizes that those who violate the injunctions of the *śāstras* and act willfully achieve success neither in this world nor beyond, and happiness eludes them. He strongly recommends that one should follow the *śāstras* in performing various activities. To quote Saint Sitārām Dās Omkārnāth, "Who says human beings have written the *śāstras*? Man is surely the recollector of *śāstras*, but the creator is God alone. God published these scriptures in the hearts of *RSis* absorbed in profound meditation" (Jeeyar, 2008, p.184). He illuminated the purpose of the *śāstras*—"The role of *śāstras* is to help one determine the truth and be one-pointed with the great unity. People cannot lift themselves up with a single leap; they can gain peace by steadily walking on the path of *śāstras*. If it were possible to attain everything through *nAm* [name of God] alone, what is the use of *vedas, upaniSads, samhitAs, purANa, tantra*, etc.? Their purpose is to develop loving devotion to *nAma*. How can you develop loving devotion to *nAma* without reading the *śāstras?* (p. 185). Human mind craves for newness, which is why so many texts have been composed (p. 192)."

Sitārām Dās Omkārnāth further stated, "To make the mind flood with religious feeling, it is necessary to read a religious text daily—a book that will melt the heart.

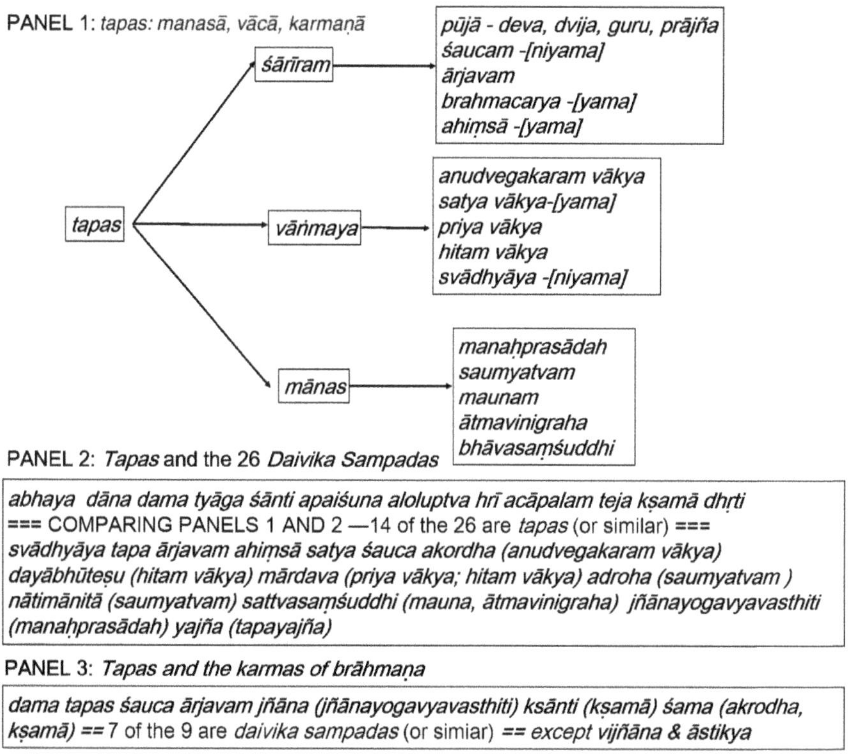

Fig. 8.1 Nomological networks of *Tapas*

sitārām reads divine drama daily; and reading, in its wake, brings about great thrill in the body. I derive more pleasure in reading scriptures than in meditation (p. 185).” Thus, saints of India continue to exemplify the injunctions of the *śāstras* in their lives, and the *śāstras* are not obsolete texts but embodiment of cultural wisdom that permeate people’s daily living.

Theme 2: Tapas *Can Be Sāttvika, Rājasika, or Tāmasika: The Second Nomological Network*

In the beginning of Canto 17, Arjuna asks Kṛṣṇa about the consequences faced by those who have *śraddhā* but do not follow the *śāstras* in performing various activities. In response, Kṛṣṇa presents the *sāṅkhya darśana* and how the three gunas of *sattva, rajas*, and *tamas* can be employed to understand *śraddhā, āhāra* (or food), *tapas, yajña,* and *dāna.* This shows how deeply embedded *tapas* is in the Indian *śāstra* and worldview. A typology of *tapas* is presented in three verses (verses 17.17 to 19) by employing the classification system of *sāṅkhya-darśana.*

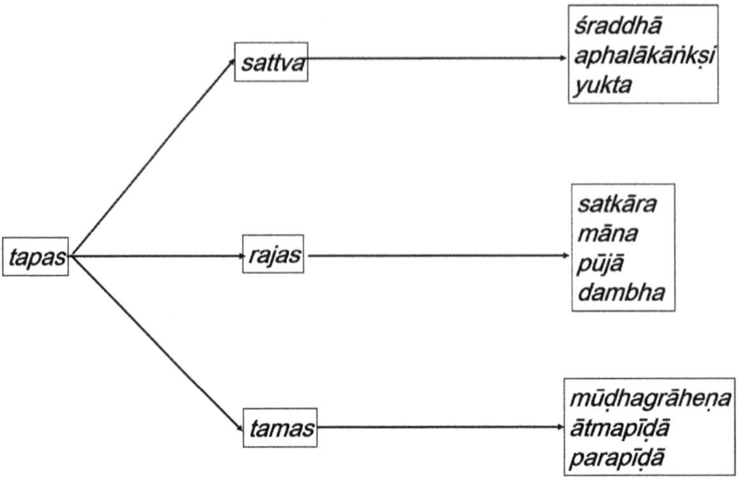

Fig. 8.2 *Tapas* and *Triguṇas*

In verse 17. 17,[6] *sāttvikatapas* is presented as one in which people practice three kinds of *tapas* (*manasā-vācā-karmaṇa*) with the highest *śraddhā,* with equanimity of *manas* or mind and also do not hanker after the fruits of their actions.

In verse 17.18,[7] *rājasika tapas* is said to be one, which is done to receive praise, respect, and honor from others or done with ostentation. It is emphasized that the fruits of such *tapas* are transitory and uncertain, thus making it lower in quality to *sāttvika tapas.* Finally, in verse, 17.19,[8] *tāmasika tapas* is said to be one that people undertake based on an unwise decision (by consulting neither a *śāstra* or scripture nor knowledgeable teachers), and it is performed by causing pain to oneself or for the purpose of hurting or destroying others (see Fig. 8.2). This framework is instructive in that people should strive to follow *sāttvika tapas*, and not the other two types, which is consistent with the Indian worldview in which people are supposed to pursue *dharma* or duty, *artha* or wealth (*gītā* verse 4.28 presents a category of *yajña* that is called *dravyamayoyajña*, or a *yajña* for which much resources are needed; thus, wealth is to be pursued for auspicious activities), *kāma* or pleasure (in *gītā* verse

[6] Verse 17.17: *śraddhayā parayā taptaṃ tapastattrividhaṃ naraiḥ, aphalakaṅkṣibhiryuktaiḥ sāttvikaṃ paricakṣate.* When people who practice the aforementioned three kinds of *tapas* with the highest *śraddhā* and do not hanker after the fruits of their actions, then that *tapas* is said to be *sāttvika.*

[7] Verse 17.18: *satkāramānapūjārthaṃ tapo dambhena caiva yat, kṛyate tadiha proktaṃ rājasaṃ calamadhruvam.* That *tapas* which is done to receive praise, respect, and honor from others or for done with ostentation is called rājasika, whose fruits are transitory and uncertain.

[8] Verse 17.19: *mūḍhagrāheṇātmano yatpīḍayā kṛyate tapaḥ, parasyotsādanārthaṃ vā tattāmasamudahṛtam.* When one undertakes a *tapas* based on an unwise decision (by consulting neither a *śāstra* or scripture nor knowledgeable teachers), and it is performed by causing pain to oneself or for destroying others, it is called *tāmasika.*

7.11 Kṛṣṇa proclaims that he personifies pleasures that do not go against *dharma—dharmāviruddho kamo'smi;* thus, one should only engage in pleasures that follow *dharma*) *and mokṣa* or liberation.

Theme 3: Manasā-Vācā-Karmaṇa and Tapas*: Three Additional Nomological Networks*

A typology of *tapas* is presented in three verses (verses 17.14 to 16) by employing the classification system often used in Indian *śāstras* about the levels of purification of one's behavior. Behavior purification at the grossest level starts with the physical activities. One's actions must be pure. The next level is to purify one's speech. What one speaks should be pure. Finally, one has to purify one's *manas* or mind. One's thoughts should be pure. In verse 17.14[9] *tapas* related to the physical body are enumerated. First, four people are identified who should be revered and served, God, *brāhmaṇa* (or people who help perform *yajñas), guru* (or teacher), and learned people. Serving them is considered physical *tapas.* Further, it enumerates *śaucam* (or purity of the body), *ārjavam* (or straight forwardness), *brahmacarya* (or being in the presence of *brahman* in whatever activity one may be performing; *brahmacarya* is also interpreted as celibacy for monks and being faithful to one's spouse for householders), and *ahiṃsā* (or nonviolence).

In verse 17.15,[10] *tapas* related to speech is enumerated. This includes speech that is non-agitating (or not being hurtful to all), truthful, and mellifluous. Further, one should be well-meaning toward the person with whom one is speaking. According to *Śaṅkara,* the absence of any of these four attributes will amount to a failure in the *tapas* of speech. Therefore, all *sādhakas* or spiritual aspirants must cultivate these four attributes in their speech, which automatically applies to *sādhus* or monks. Finally, regularly studying the scriptures or chanting *strotras* (or encomiums) like *viṣṇusahasranāma, lalitāsahasranāma, śivasahasranāma, ādityahṛdayam, rudra-aṣṭādhyāyī,* and so forth is a part of *svādhyāya* and is considered *tapas* of speech.

In verse 17.16,[11] the five practices that are considered the *tapas* of *manas* are enumerated. They include, first, tranquility of the *manas*, which comes from purity of mind that is achieved by weakening the drives for material objects that one experiences while interacting in the world. Second pertains to cheerfulness and gentleness

[9] Verse 17.14: *devadvijaguruprājñapūjanaṃ śaucamārjavam, brahmacaryamahiṃsā ca śāriraṃ tapa ucyate.*

[10] Verse 17.15: *anudvegakaraṃ vakyaṃ satyaṃ priyahitaṃ ca yat, svādhyāyābhyasanam caiva vāṅmayaṃ tapa ucyate.* Non-agitating, truthful, mellifluous, well-meaning, self-study, and practice are the *tapas* of speech.

[11] Verse 17.16: *manaḥprasadaḥ saumyatvaṃ maunamātmavinigrahaḥ, bhāvasaṃśuddhirityetattapo mānasamucyate.* Tranquility of the *manas*, cheerfulness of the *manas*, silence of speech through silence of *manas*, complete control of the *manas*, purification of all thoughts and feelings are called the austerity of the *manas.*

of the *manas*, which is achieved by wishing everyone well and not desiring what is improper. Third is associated with silence of *manas*, which is achieved when one has no desire to engage in speech with anybody for any reason. This comes with years of practicing silence, recognizing one's desires to express and letting them go. Fourth pertains to the complete control of the *manas*, which means one has quenched the *vṛttis* or propensities of the *manas* to go toward elements of the material world for seeking pleasure or avoiding those that cause pain. Finally, purification of all *bhāvas* or feelings means that has to get over anger, greed, passion, and so forth. According to Śaṅkara, one is able to do this only when there is complete absence of trickery in interactions with other people. These five are called the *tapas* or austerity of the *manas*, and it is quite obvious that each of these will require conscious effort over years or all of one's life (see Fig. 8.1, Panel 1).

Theme 4: Tapas, *Yajña, Dāna, Karma, and Śraddhā: The Sixth Nomological Network*

In verse 17.1[12]Arjuna asks a question about people who do not follow the method given in *śāstras*, but worship with *śraddhā.* He states, "Are these people by nature, *sāttvika* (calmness or illumination), *rājasika* (or dynamism) or *tāmasika* (or inertia)?" In response, Kṛṣṇa synthesizes *āhāra* (or food), *yajña, tapas,* and *dāna* with *śraddhā* and the three *guṇas* of *sāṅkhya darśana.* In verse 17.2,[13] *śraddhā* is said to be *sāttvika, rājasika,* or *tāmasika,* as the function of the basic nature of a person. In verse 17.3,[14] *śraddhā* is said to characterize people, and a person becomes whatever is the nature of his or her *śraddhā.* Therefore, *śraddhā* not only reflects the most basic nature of people, but also personifies him or her (Bhawuk, 2020).

In verse 17.4,[15] it is stated that people who are *sāttvika* in nature worship various forms of Gods, whereas those of *rājasika* nature worship demigods (or living supernatural beings like *yakṣa*, e.g., *kubera*) and ogres (or *rākṣasa*). People who are *tāmasika* in nature worship ghosts and spirits. Thus, the basic nature of people can be determined by examining whom they worship. In verse 17.5,[16] other characteristics of those whose basic nature is *tāmasika* are enumerated as people who have *dambha* (or religious ostentatious), *ahaṃkāra* (or pride), passionate attachment to desire (or *kāmarāgabalānvitāḥ*), and who perform severe austerities (*ghoraṃ tapas*) that are

[12] Verse 17.1: *ye śāstravidhimutsṛjya yajante śraddhayānvitāḥ; teṣāṃ niṣṭhā tu kā kṛṣṇa sattvamāho rajastamaḥ.*

[13] Verse 17.2: *trividhā bhavati śraddhā dehināṃ sā svabhāvajā; sāttvikī rājasī caiva tāmasī ceti tāṃ śṛṇu.*

[14] Verese 17.3: *sattvānurūpā sarvasya śraddhā bhavati bhārata; śraddhāmayo'yaṃ puruṣo yo yacchraddhaḥ sa eva saḥ.*

[15] Verse 17.4: *yajante sāttvikā devānyakṣarakṣāṃsi rājasāḥ; pretānbhūtagaṇāṃścānye yajante tāmasā janāḥ.*

[16] Verse 17.5: *aśāstravihitaṃ ghoraṃ tapyante ye tapo janāḥ, dambhāhaṅkārasaṃyuktāḥ kāmarāgabalānvitāḥ.*

not sanctioned in the *śāstras* (or scriptures). Further, in verse 17.6,[17] it is stated that the people whose basic nature is *tāmasika* are not conscious and engage in *tapas* that amounts to brutal torturing of the body and the Divine that resides in the self. These verses are meant to clarify what one ought not to do and refer to the ā*suri vṛtti* (or demoniacal tendencies), which is presented at length in Canto 16.

In verses 17.7 to 17.22, Kṛṣṇa also presents a typology of food,[18] *yajña* (or sacrifices), *tapas* (or austerities), and *dāna* (or charitable giving) according to the three *guṇas,* further illustrating that one's *śraddhā* shapes everything—the type of food one eats, the *yajña* one *carries out*, the austerities (*tapas*) one performs, and what one donates to others (*dāna*). Thus, *śraddhā* constitutes the substratum of *yajña, tapas, dāna,* and actions. This is further ascertained in verse 4.40[19] by stating that the absence of *śraddhā* makes everything inauspicious. Kṛṣṇa tells Arjuna that those who are ignorant, those who are without *śraddhā,* and those who are skeptical, completely miss out both in this world and beyond, and also do not find happiness. In this verse, the absence of *śraddhā* is equated to lack of knowledge, which is not surprising, since in 4.39 it is stated that only those who have *śraddhā* obtain knowledge (*śraddhāvān labhate jñānam*). Further, the absence of *śraddhā* is equated to being skeptical as well as a precondition of happiness.

In verse 9.3,[20] Kṛṣṇa emphasizes the value of *śraddhā* by stating that the absence of *śraddhā* is not conducive to *mokṣa.* Thus, whereas the presence of *śraddhā* leads to *jñāna* or knowledge and that in turn leads to *mokṣa* (verse 4.39), the absence of *śraddhā* leads to the cycle of life and death.

Further, in verses 17.11, 17.12, and 17.13, the three types of *yajña* are described. Verse 17.13 specifically describes a *tāmasika yajña*as one that is performed with no *śraddhā.* Another characteristic of a*tāmasikayajña* is not using proper *mantras.* If *dakṣinā* (proper remuneration) is not given to the priests, a*yajña* is said to be *tāmasika.* Further, if *prasādam (*food) is not distributed to people attending the *yajña,* it is considered *tāmasika.* And finally, if proper procedure, as presented in the *śāstras,* is not followed, it is considered *tāmasika.* It is clear that verse 17.13 enjoins people to perform *yajña* with *śraddhā* following the *śāstras.*

In verse 17.24,[21] it is instructed that the followers of the *vedas* should always start the performance of a *śāstra* (or scripture) prescribed *yajña* (sacrifice), *dāna*

---

[17] Verse 17.6: *karśayantaḥ śarīrastham bhūtagrāmamacetasaḥ, mām caivāntaḥ śarīrasthaṃ tān viddhayāsuraniścayān.*

[18] Verse 17.7: *āhārastvapi sarvasya trividho bhavati priyaḥ, yajñastapastathā dānaṃ teṣām bhedamimaṃ śṛṇu.*

[19] Verse 4.40: *ajñaścāśraddadhānaśca saṃśhayātmā vinaśyati; nāyaṃ loko'sti na paro na sukhaṃ saṃśayātmanaḥ.*

[20] Verse 9.3: *aśhraddadhānāḥ puruṣā dharmasyāsya parantapa; aprāpya māṃ nivartante mṛtyu-saṃsāravartmani.*

[21] 17.24: *tasmādomityudāhṛtya yajñadānatapahḥkriyāḥ, pravartante vidhānoktāḥ satataṃ brahmavādinām.* Therefore, the followers of the *vedas* should always start the performance of a *śāstra* (or scripture) prescribed *yajña* (sacrifice), *dāna* (charity), and *tapas* by saying *om.*

(charity), and *tapas* by saying *om*. And in verse 17.25,[22] it is stated that those who aspire *mokṣa* (liberation) should perform *yajña* (sacrifice), *dāna* (charity), and *tapas* after uttering *tat* (referring to *brahman*) without desiring the fruits of their actions. In verse 17.26,[23] it is stated that *sat* (a synonym of *brahman*) is used for existence, goodness, and auspicious activities. In verse 17. 27,[24] it is stated that *sat* (a synonym of *brahman*) is used for *yajña, tapas*, and *dāna,* as well as all activities associated with them. In verse 17. 28,[25] it is emphasized that not only *yajña,* but also *dāna, tapas,* and *karma* when performed without *śraddhā* are futile. In verses 17.26 and 17.27, the word *sat* is used in conjunction with *om tatsat,* which has deep cultural meaning as all auspicious activities are started by saying *om tatsat.* In the Upaniṣads, *tat* is used to refer to *brahman* (verse 17.23[26]). Later in Canto 18 (see verses 18.3[27] and 18.5[28]), it is emphasized that we should always perform *yajña, dāna, tapas,* and *karma.* However, when we perform them without *śraddhā,* they become *asat* or inauspicious. Therefore, it is *śraddhā* that makes them virtuous. This emphasizes the virtue of *śraddhā* in no uncertain terms, and presents a nomological network of *śraddhā*, *yajña, dāna, tapas*, and *karma* (see Fig. 8.3).

Theme 5: Kṛṣṇa is Present as Tapas *in* Tapasvīs

In verses 7.8 to 7.12, Kṛṣṇa tells Arjuna that he is the essence of all elements and components of creation. He is the taste of water, sound in space, *om* in the *vedas,* effulgence of the moon and the Sun, and masculinity of men (verse 7.8); fragrance of earth, heat of fire, life of all beings, and *tapaḥ* (or austerities) of ascetics (verse

[22] 17.25: *tadityanabhisandhāya phalaṃ yajñatapaḥkriyāḥ, dānakriyāśca vividhāḥ kriyante mokṣakaṅkṣibhiḥ.* Those who aspire *mokṣa* (liberation) should perform *yajña* (sacrifice), *dāna* (charity), and *tapas* after uttering *tat* (referring to *brahman*) without desiring the fruits of their actions.

[23] Verse 17.26: *sadbhāve sādhubhāve ca sadityetatprayujyate; praśaste karmaṇi tathāsacchbdaḥ pārtha yujyate. sat* (a synonym of *brahman*) is used for existence, goodness, and auspicious activities.

[24] Verse 17.27: *yajñye tapasi dāne ca sthitiḥ saditi cocyate; karma caiva tadarthīyaṃ sadityevābhidhīyate. sat* (a synonym of *brahman*) is used for *yajña*, *tapas*, and *dāna,* as well as all activities associated with them.

[25] Verse 17.28: *aśraddhayāhutaṃdattaṃtapastaptaṃkṛtaṃ ca yat; asadityucyatepārthana ca tatpretya no iha.*

[26] Verse 17.23: *om tatsaditi nirdeśo brahmaṇastrividhaḥ smṛtaḥ; brāhmṇāstena vedāśca yajñāśca vihitāḥ purā.*

[27] Verse 18.3: *tyājyaṃ doṣavadityeke karma prāhurmanīṣiṇaḥ; yajñadānatapaḥkarma a tyājyamiti cāpare.*

[28] Verse 18.5: *yajñadānatapaḥkarma na tyājyaṃ kāryameva tat; yajño dānaṃ tapaścaiva pāvanāni manīṣiṇām.*

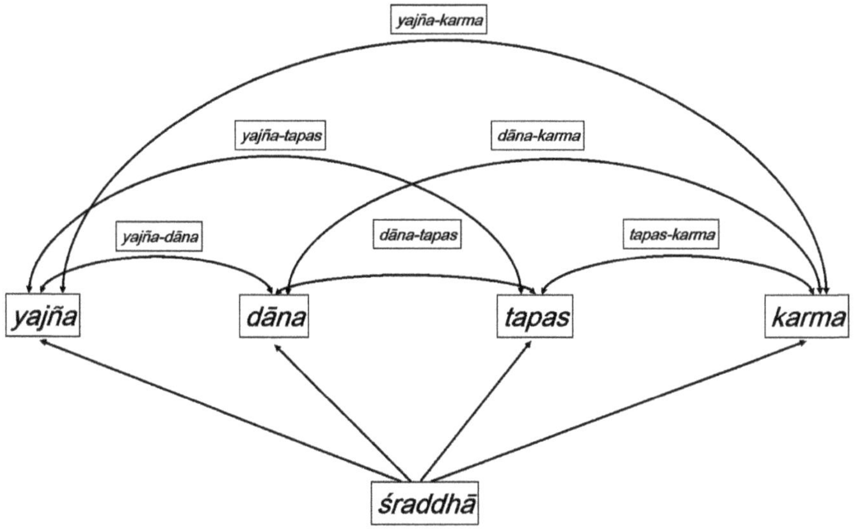

Fig. 8.3 Interaction of *śraddhā, yajña, dāna, tapas, and karma*

7.9[29]); *sanātana* (or eternal) seed of all beings, *buddhi* of the wise, resoluteness of the resolute (verse 7.10); strength devoid of desire and attachment of the strong, and the desire of all beings that is not contrary to *dharma* (verse 7.11). He summarizes by saying that all the *bhāvas* arising from the three *guṇas* arise from him (verse 7.12). When Kṛṣṇa enumerates attributes that personify him, he picks *tapas*, which highlights the importance of this construct.

Later in Canto 9, Kṛṣṇa again elaborates how he is present in the elements of the universe in verses 9.16 to 9.19 and emphasizes that he is all dualities, the one who burns (*tapāmi*) as the Sun and showers as rain (draws and releases rain), death and no-death, and truth (or what is real) and non-truth (or what is unreal) (verse 9.19[30]). He employs *tapas* as the essence of Sun, which he himself is. Thus, *tapas* appears again as a fundamental element of the universe.

[29] Verse 7.9: *punyo gandhah prthivyam ca, tejas casmi vibhavasau; jivanam sarva-bhutesu tapaścāsmi tapasvisu.* I am the unpolluted fragrance of earth, heat of fire, life of all beings, and *tapas* (or austerities) of the ascetics.

[30] Verse 9.19: *tapamyahamaham varṣam nigrhnāmyutsṛjāmi ca, amṛtam caiva mṛtyuśca sadasaccāhamarjuna.* I burn as the sun and shower as the rain. I am death and immortality; real and non-real.

In Canto 10 (verses 10.4[31] and 10.5[32]), Kṛṣṇa continues to elaborate how all the essential attributes of living beings emanate from him and lists *buddhi* (discriminating faculty), *jñāna* (knowledge), *asammohaḥ* (non-delusion), *kṣamā* (forgiveness), *satya* (truth), *damaḥ* (control of senses), *śamaḥ* (pacification of *manas*), *sukham* (happiness), *duḥkham* (sorrow), *bhavaḥ* (birth), *bhāvaḥ* (existence), *bhaya* (fear), *abhayam* (fearlessness), *ahiṃsā* (nonviolence), *samatā* (harmony), *tuṣṭi* (contentment), *tapas*, *dāna* (charity), *yaśaḥ* (fame), and *ayaśaḥ* (infamy). Thus, *tapas* is an important construct, not to be left out in any discourse.

Theme 6: Tapas *in the Typology of Yajña*

In verse 4.28, Kṛṣṇa enumerates five types of *yajñas*, namely, *dravyayajña* (or sacrifice through wealth), *tapayajña* (austerities presented in 17.14–16 noted earlier), *yogayajña* (sacrifice through the eightfold path of yoga, namely *yama, niyama, Asana, prANAyAma, pratyāhāra, dhAraNa, dhyAna,* and *samAdhi*), *svādhyāyayajña* (or study of the *śāstras* as a daily spiritual practice), *jñānayajña* (or pursuing the spiritual path of knowledge that includes self-examination or *Atma-cintan* by constantly asking who am I or *kvo'ham*, and following *neti-neti* or I'm not this—I'm not this). This again places *tapas* in the nomological network with *yajña*, and *tapas* becomes classified as a *yajña*.

Theme 7: Tapas *as Necessary but not Sufficient Condition for Adhyātma*

In verses 11.53[33] and 11.54, Kṛṣṇa presents a limitation of all paths of spiritual practice, namely, studying the *vedas*, doing *tapas*, giving *dāna* (or charity), or doing *yajñas* (the sacrifices noted above in 4.28 and other verses in Canto 4). None of these paths allows a practitioner to see *Viṣṇu* in his *caturbhuja rūpa*[34] (with four hands holding *śankha*, *cakra*, *gadā*, and *padma*). It is the path of devotion alone that allows

---

[31] Verse 10.4: *buddhirjñānamasammohaḥ kṣhamā satyaṁ damaḥ śhamaḥ, sukhaṁ duḥkhaṁ bhavo'bhāvo bhayaṁ chābhayameva cha. buddhi* (discriminating faculty), *jñāna* (knowledge), *asammohaḥ* (non-delusion), *kṣamā* (forgiveness), *satya* (truth), *damaḥ* (control of senses), *śamaḥ* (pacification of *manas*), *sukham* (happiness), *duḥkham* (sorrow), *bhavaḥ* (birth), *bhāvaḥ* (existence), *bhaya* (fear), and *abhayam* (fearlessness), which all beings experience come from me.

[32] Verse 10.5: *ahiṁsā samatā tuṣhṭistapo dānaṁ yaśho'yaśhaḥ, bhavanti bhāvā bhūtānāṁ matta eva pṛithagvidhāḥ. ahiṃsā* (nonviolence), *samatā* (equanimity), *tuṣṭi* (contentment), *tapas, dāna* (charity), *yaśaḥ* (fame), and *ayaśaḥ* (infamy), which all beings experience come from me.

[33] Verse 11.53: *nāhaṃ vedairna tapasā na dānena na chejyayā, śany evaṃvidho draṣṭuṃ dṛśṭavānasi māṃ yathā.*

[34] Verse 11.46: *kirīṭinaṃ gadinaṃ cakrahastamicchāmi tvṣṃ draṣṭumahaṃ tathaiva, tenaiva rūpeṇa caturbhujena sahasrabāho bhava viśvamūrte.* O Thousand-handed One! I want to see you in your

such a vision. In these verses it is clarified that the three that ought to be done—*yajña, dāna,* and *tapas* (also noted in verse 18.5)—are necessary but not sufficient for spiritual practitioners; they must cultivate *bhakti* or devotion to receive the grace of the Divine.

The importance of *bhakti* is also emphasized in verses 6.45–47. In verse 6.45,[35] it is stated that by applying oneself with effort over many lives a yogi is able to purify the accrued sins and achieves the highest goal (of *mokṣa*). In verse 6.46,[36] it is stated that such a yogi is superior to those who are engaged in action, austerities, or knowledge; and Kṛṣṇa encourages Arjuna to strive to become a yogi. In verse 6.47,[37] it is stated that even among such yogis, those who constantly contemplate on the Divine (*bhajate*) with their *antaḥkaraṇa* (or internal organ which includes *manas, buddhi,* and *ahaṅkāra*), and with *śraddhā*, are the best. In verse 8.28, it is stated that those who know (and knowing always means translating knowledge in behavior employing the threefold process of *śravaṇa, manana,* and *nididhyāsana*) *brahman, adhyātma, karma, adhibhūta, adhidaiva, adhiyajña,* and the process of knowing the Divine at the time of death (see the seven questions raised in verses 8.1 and 8.2, which are addressed in the discourse in Canto 8; for a discussion see Bhawuk, 2019) transcend the *puṇya* or merits of studying the *vedas*, making sacrifices (*yajña*), practicing austerities (*tapas*), and giving charity (*dāna*), and reach the primordial supreme state. This verse also points out that *tapas* (and *yajña, dāna,* and studies of *vedas*) is necessary but not sufficient, and that one has to be constantly engaged in yoga as noted in verse 8.27.[38]

Theme 8: Tapas *as an Attribute of a Brāhmaṇa*

In verse 18.42,[39] the nature of work of a *brāhmaṇa* is enumerated. It includes *śama, damaḥ, tapaḥ, śaucaṃ, kṣāntiḥ, ārjavam, jñānam vijñānam,* and *āstikyam.*

---

four arm form with crown, *gadā* (or mace) and *cakra* (or disc). In this verse, *śankha* and *padma* are not mentioned, which are held by V*iṣṇu* in the other two arms.].

[35] Verse 6.45: *prayatnādyatamānastu yogī saṃśuddhakilbiṣaḥ, anekajanmasaṃsiddhastato yāti paraṃ ganim.*

[36] Verse 6.46: *tapasvibhyo'adhiko yogī jñānibhyo'pi mato'dhikaḥ, karmibhyaścādhiko yogī tasmādyogī bhavārjuna.*

[37] Verse 6.47: *yogināmapi sarveṣāṃ madgatenāntarātmanā, śraddhāvanbhajate yo māṃ sa me yuktatamo mataḥ.*

[38] Verse 8.27: *naive sṛtī paratha jānanyogī muhyati kaścana, tasmātsarveṣu kāleṣu yogayukto bhavārujua.* O *Pārtha*, the yogi who knows these two paths (one that leads to the rebirth and the other that leads to *mokṣa* or liberation) never gets deluded. O Arjuna, therefore, be engaged in yoga at all times.

[39] verse 18.42: *śamo damastapaḥ śaucaṃ kṣāntirārjavameva ca, jñānaṃ vijñānamāstikyaṃ brahkarma svabhāvajam.*

They are all mentioned as a part of *sāttvika tapas* (verses 17.14–16 and 17.17–19) or *daivi-sampadā* (verses 16.1–3) discussed above. Thus, *tapas* characterizes a *brāhmaṇa,* which is also supported in other *śāstras. In the Manusmṛti, it is said—sammānadbrāhmaṇo nityamudvijeta viṣādiva, amṛtasyeva cākaṃkṣhed avamānasya sarvadā*—a *brāhmaṇa* should get agitated when praised as if he has been given poison, and should always desire insult as nectar (for insults test the success of his *tapas*). In the *Mahābhārata* (*śānti-parvam,* 245, 12) it is said—*yena kenacidācchanno yena kenacidāśitaḥ, yatra kvacanśāyi syattaṃ devā brāhmaṇaṃ viduḥ*—the Gods call him a *brāhmaṇa* who wears whatever he is given, eats whatever he is offered, and sleeps wherever he is asked to. Again, in this description of a *brāhmaṇa,* we find a person who is contented in self (*ātmanyeva saṃtuṣṭaḥ, Bhagavadgītā 3.17*) and does not care about the material existence. It is also said in another *śāstra*— *yatīnāṃ praśamo dharma niyamo vanavāsinaṃ, dānmeva gṛhasthānāṃ śuśruṣā brahmacāriṇām—the dharma of a sannyāsin is śama or the controlling of the antaḥkaraṇa or internal organ, the dharma of a* forest-dweller *is to follow niyama (śauca, santoṣa, tapaṣ, svādhyāya, and īśvarpraṇidhāna), the dharma of a householder is charity, and the dharma of a brahmacārī is service (to God, brāhmaṇa, guru,* and the wise ones). What is prescribed for each of the four phases of life is taken voluntarily by a *brāhmaṇa* in whatever phase of life she/he may be (see Fig. 8.1, Panel 3).

Theme 9: Arjuna as an Exemplar of Tapas

A word is defined by a living example, an exemplar, or a person, for such a person stands as a *pratyakṣa* or direct experience for the one who is trying to learn the concept. From the second to the 18th canto Kṛṣṇa addresses Arjuna as *paraṃtapa* nine times, which is natural since there is much evidence in the *Mahābhārata* to support that Arjuna was a *paraṃtapa,* an ascetic par excellence. He worked hard to become an excellent archer, zealously wanting to be the best in the world, and following extremely hard discipline for it. He learned to shoot in the darkness by practicing assiduously when he was inspired by an experience of eating in the dark when the wind blew out the lamp. When *Droṇa* wanted to give some extra time to his son, *Aśvathāmā,* and gave everybody pots with smaller opening so that they would be delayed in filling up the pot and fetching it back to the *aśrama,* Arjuna used his archery to fill the pot and would return even before *Aśvathāmā,* earning the love of *Droṇa* and getting extra lessons from him along with *Aśvathāmā.* He was the only one who had conquered his senses to such perfection that he could focus on the decoy's eye, when all others failed and could shoot it without missing the target. This was demonstrated again in shooting the eye of the fish at *svayamvara* or wedding contest organized by king *Drupada* for his daughter *Draupadī.*

Arjuna was so capable that he was invited to purge the Khāṇḍava forest of the serpents, which he successfully accomplished with Kṛṣṇa as his charioteer, which took place before the battle of *Mahābhārata.* For doing this assignment he received the indestructible bow, Gāṇḍīva, which remained with him for the rest of his life. He did such *utkṛṣṭa* or high quality of *tapas* that it led *Śiva* to give him his favorite weapon, the *pāśupatāstra.* After the battle of *Mahābhārata,* he also spent a year away from the palace roaming around as a medicant, because he had violated the code that none of the five *Pāṇḍavas* would enter the palace of *DraupadI* when she was with one of the other four brothers. He had to go there to pick up his *gāṇḍīva* to protect a *brahmaṇa* when it was *Yudhiṣṭhira*'s turn to be with *DraupadI*. He also got into an unpleasant situation of fighting Kṛṣṇa because *Subhadrā* had given shelter to a person who was to be punished by Kṛṣṇa, and *Subhadrā* forced him to stand against Kṛṣṇa in a duel, which resulted in a draw. He was versatile and also learned to dance from the *apsarās* in heaven and was so accomplished that he became the dance teacher of *uttarā* when he was spending a year in disguise in the kingdom of *Virāṭa.* Clearly, all of Arjuna's achievements were the result of his discipline and *tapas* or austerities suggesting that *tapas* is about self-discipline and making concerted effort and sacrifices to acquire excellence in the chosen skills.

It should be noted that one of the names of *Viṣṇu* in the *sahasranāma* is *mahātapāḥ* (whose *tapas* is great, number 122), and *śiva* is also called by seven names that are a variant of *tapas*, namely *tapasvi* (an ascetic, number 34), *mahātapasi* (a great *tapasvi,* number 74 and 175), *ghoratapasi* (an extreme *tapasvi,* number 75), *paramatapasi* (a great *tapasvi,* number 81), *tapaḥsakta* (one who is attached to *tapas*, number 729), *tapaḥnidhiḥ* (whose asset is *tapas*, number 778), and *tapaḥmaya* (filled with *tapas*, number 969). Thus, the importance of *tapas* as an attribute of a person can hardly be overemphasized.

Discussion

The comparison of the 26 *daivika sampadas* and the typology of *tapas* based on *manasā* (practices of the *manas* or mind), *vācā* (practices of speech), and *karmaṇā* (actions or practices of the body) show that 14 of the 26 virtues fall in the category of *tapas* (see Fig. 8.1, Panels 1 and 2). Of these six appear on both networks, namely *svādhyāya tapa ārjavam ahiṃsā satya* and *śauca.* Eight others are quite similar in meaning. For example, *akordha* is captured by *anudvegakaram vākya, dayābhūteṣu* is captured by *hitam vākya,* and *mārdava* is captured by *priya vākya* and *hitam vākya,* which are all *tapas* of speech. Similarly, *adroha* and *nātimānitā* are captured by *saumyatvam, sattvasaṃśuddhi* by *mauna* and *ātmavinigraha,* and *jñānayogavyavasthiti* by *manaḥprasādah,* which are all *tapas* of *manas.* Finally, *yajña* is captured by *tapayajña.* The overlap of these 14 *daivika sampadas* with *tapas* indicates that *tapas* is a fundamental *daivika sampada.*

As noted above, the process of cultivation of virtues itself is *tapas*, and so cultivating the other 11 virtues, namely *abhaya, dāna, dama, tyāga, śānti, apaiśuna, aloluptva, acāpalam, teja, kṣamā,* and *dhṛti,* will amount to doing *tapas. Hrī* is the only one that is fundamental enough to stand by *tapas* as a partner, if not an independent construct, since cultivating any virtue requires having a sense of what one ought to do and what not to do. This sense is *lajjā* or *hrī*. However, with the increased strength of a practice or *tapas* for a virtue, *lajjā* also becomes crystallized and stronger. An advanced *sādhaka* or practitioner engaged in cultivating these virtues is likely to catch the thought itself as it arises in the *manas* and thus prevents any lapse at the speech and action level.

Similarly, the comparison of the *daivika sampadas* and the nine natural duties of a *brāhmaṇa* shows that four of them appear on both lists, namely *dama, tapas, śauca,* and *ārjavam.* Two of them are different simply in formation of the words, e.g., *jñāna* or *jñānayogavyavasthiti* and *ksānti* or *kṣamā.* The seventh one, *śama,* means quietening of the *antaḥkaraṇa.* If the *antaḥkaraṇa* is not calm, one gets angry whenever a desire is not fulfilled (*gītā* 2.62). Thus, cultivating *śama* is similar to cultivating *akrodha.* The only two duties of a *brāhmaṇa* that are not on the list of *daivika sampadas* are *vijñāna* and *āstikya.* Therefore, *brāhmaṇas* are supposed to be *tapasvis* and lead an austere life. As the exemplars of *daivika sampadas*, they are supposed to lead others in the society by example, and pursue *jñāna* and *vijñāna* (or wisdom) rather than status and positions of power. This idea is also found in Western philosophy in the work of Plato when he discusses a Philosopher King (Republic V.473d).

The importance of *śraddhā* is clear in the typology of *tapas* based on the three *guṇas* of *sattva, rajas*, and *tamas*, since it only appears in the category of *sattvika tapas* (see Fig. 8.2). Since *śraddhā* also defines *sattvika yajña,* and the absence of *śraddhā* makes all actions, *yajña, dāna*, and *tapas* futile; it is clear that *śraddhā* is necessary for performing anything worthwhile (see Fig. 8.3). *Tapas* can become mechanical, and the practitioner can lose perspective and becomes what is called *śuṣka* (or vain) *tapasvi*, someone who revels in the austerities and forgets that the purpose of *tapas* is to not get attached to the material world. Thus, *tapas* is necessary but not sufficient (discussed above in Theme 7, verses 11.53 and 54), and cultivating *śraddhā* keeps the *sAdhaka* or spiritual aspirant focused on self-realization. In *Pātañjali Yogasūtra* 1.20 *śraddhā* is presented as the first *upāya* or method for the practitioner. The *vyāsa bhāṣya* explains the *sūtra* as follows: From *śraddhā* (*manas* filled with delight) follows *vīrya* (or enthusiasm for *sādhanā* or spiritual practice), *smṛti* (or recollection of *īśvara* and his attributes), *samādhi* (or concentration or one-pointed *manas*), and *prajñā* (or insight). With *prajñā*, the practitioner gains direct experience, and with the practice of *viveka* (discrimination) and *vairāgya* (detachment), he or she achieves *asamprajñāt-samādhi* or self-realization. Thus, śraddhā is emphasized in yoga *darśana* also. However, it is quite clear that there is no other way but to cultivate *tapas*, since it is the source of all virtues.

The importance of *tapas* is unequivocally emphasized in all Indian *śāstras* or texts. For example, in the *Manusmṛti* in Canto 11 *tapas* is discussed in much detail in 13 verses (verses 11.234 to 11.246). In verse 11.234, it is stated that *tapas* or austerity is source of all happiness for men and *devas* in its entirety, the beginning, the middle, and the end. In verse 11.235, *tapas* is defined for the four *varṇas,* namely *jñāna* or knowledge for the *brāhmans*, protection of others for the *kṣatriyas*, agriculture for *vaiśyas*, and service for *śūdras*. In verse 11.236, it is stated that through *tapas* of living on fruits and roots (i.e., restraining what is eaten) the self-controlled sages are able to see all mobile and immobile beings of the three worlds. In verse 11.237, it is stated that *tapas* is the means of acquiring all knowledge—of medicines, drugs, and science—and *siddhis* or Divine powers, and *tapas* alone leads to their acquisition. In verse 11.238, it is stated that all—(i) what is hard to traverse, (ii) what is hard to attain, (iii) what is hard to reach, and (iv) what is hard to do—is accomplished by *tapas,* which is itself irrepressible. In other words, *tapas* alone is the means of achieving all desirable outcomes.

In verse 11.239 of the *Manusmṛti*, it is stated that well-performed *tapas* is the means of becoming free of all, little or heinous, sins. Austerity, therefore, is the way to mend one's ways. Verse 11.240 praises *tapas* as the means for even other beings—insects, snakes, moths, animals, birds, and immobile beings—to go to heaven. In verse 11.241, it is stated that *tapas* absolves all sins—whether committed by thought, word or deed —and so it is the sole wealth of people. In verse 11.242, *tapas* is presented as a precondition or preliminary step for all auspicious activities. One must be purified by practicing austerities before performing *yajñas* or sacrifices for them to bring in the desired results. Verse 11.243 recounts the creation of the universe and the *vedas* as a result of *tapas* of *prajāpati* or the creator God and the *ṛṣis* or sages, respectively. Thus, *tapas* is the core of creativity in the Indian worldview, and anybody desirous of creating something monumental must perform suitable *tapas*. Verse 11.244 sums up the praise of *tapas* by nodding that even the Gods, what to talk of humans, view austerity as pious, for it is behind the creation of the universe. Verses 11.245 and 11.246 refer to the virtue of studying the *vedas* for dispelling the minor or major offenses committed by people. Though the word *tapas* is not used in either of the verses, it is implied that studying the *vedas* is a type of *tapas* that helps absolve sins as mentioned in previous verses.

The *Yogasūtrastapas* is presented as one of the five *niyamas*, namely *śauca* (external pertaining to food, etc.; and internal pertaining to cleansing of the *manas*), *saṃtoṣa* (only seeking resources enough to support the body), *tapaḥ* (to tolerate duality, e.g., hunger, thirst, hot and cold, wood-like silence, and various types of fasting), *svādhyāya* (studying the *śāstras* pertaining to *mokṣa* orchanting *praṇava*), and *īśvarapraṇidhāna* (resting in *īśvara* or the controller of the Universe or offering all actions to *īzvara*). What is interesting is that *tapas* also includes three of the five *yamas* or restraints, namely *ahiṃsā, satya*, and *brahmacarya* (see Fig. 8.1, Panel 1). Only *asteya* (non-stealing) and *aparigraha* (non-possession) are not captured in the *manasā-vācā-karmaṇā* typology of *tapas* presented in the *Bhagavadgītā*. Thus, *tapas* includes both *yamas* and *niyamas* presented in *Pātañjali Yogasūtra* and constitutes the foundation of all *sādhanā,* which is consistent with the *Manusmṛti* that notes *tapas* as a prerequisite for performing other pious activities.

The following meanings of the word *tapas* are found in *saṃskṛtam* dictionaries by Apte and Monier-Williams: religious austerity, bodily mortification, penance, and severe meditation. *Tapas* refers to heat of fire in the *pañca tapāṃsi.* When a person is practicing this austerity, he or she stands or sits in the middle with four sets of fire burning on the four quarters, with the Sun burning above. In the *Ṛgveda* (verse vii, 82, 7) *tapas* stands for pain or suffering. *Tapas* is so important in the Indian worldview that one of the seven *lokas—bhuḥ, bhuvaḥ, svaḥ, mahaḥ, janaḥ, tapaḥ,* and *satyam*—is called *tapaḥ*. This *loka* is the sixth highest and has the abode of the *devas*, which is called *virāja* according to *Śrī Viṣṇu Purāṇa* (2.7.14). The first verse of *bhūmi-sūtra* in *atharva-veda* (12.1.1[40]) states that earth is held by *satya* (or truth), *ṛta* (or principles of natural order including *yamas* and *niyamas*), *ugra* (*tejas* or power), *dīkṣā* (initiated or skillfulness), *tapas* (or austerities), *brahman* (one that permeates everything), and *yajña* (or sacrifice). It is significant that *tapas* is identified as one of the seven qualities that nurtures earth, and it is listed along with *brahman, satya, ṛta,* and *yajña,* which are the most important constructs in the Indian worldview.

To summarize, *tapas* as a practice entails following a set of rules. The major rules are captured by *yama* and *niyama.* The minor rules are integrated into daily living, and though they have textual support in texts like the *Manusmṛti,* they are often taken for granted as cultural wisdom. Such rules include waking up early morning before sunrise in what is called the *brahman muhurta.* Some such rules come from *Ayurveda,* which includes practices like not drinking water while eating food, not eating yogurt at night, eating before sunset, and so forth. Dancers and musicians are known to lead extremely disciplined lives for both the acquisition and mastery of their professional skills, called *abhyAsa* or practice, which is also referred to as *tapas.* This also applies to wrestlers and other sportsperson, and in general to any practice that leads to tangible or intangible achievements of skills and material success.

It is clear from the nine themes that analyses of texts provide meaning spaces that are richer than what can be obtained from the synonyms and antonyms that dictionaries can provide for a word. We can see that taken together, many of the verses of the *Bhagavadgītā* coalesce as a semantic unit, and jointly they have a unity of meaning (see Lemke, 1991 for a discussion of semantic unit and text). As Halliday and Hasan (1976) noted, texture is the semantic property of texts, and texts are not clauses put together randomly. The nine themes presented above also demonstrate that indigenous thick descriptions (Ryle, 1949, 1971; Geertz, 1973) provide interrelationships of constructs that go beyond the dictionary meanings of a word. It is recommended that people study texts like the *Bhagavadgītā* everyday as a part of *svAdhyAya,* which consists of reflective self-study. When engaged in *svAdhyAya,* we experience the texture in some spiritual depth, which goes beyond what can be captured in words. The experience cannot be objectified in a fixed sequence and would have nuanced subjective meanings that could vary across people, yet have some common expressions. As the examination of the verses on a theme progresses, the texture becomes a web of meaning, as can be seen in the presentation of the six nomological networks of *tapas* and its relationships with other constructs, which is beyond what a thick description has come to stand for according to Geertz (1973) or Ryle (1949, 1971). Such a contribution is only possible if indigenous researchers themselves examine constructs in their own culture systematically.

---

[40] Verse 12.1.1: *satyaṃ bṛhadṛtamugraṃ dīkṣā tapo brahman yajñaḥ pṛthiviṃ dhārayanti; sā no bhūtasya bhavyasya patnyuruṃ lokaṃ pṛthivi naḥ kṛṇotu.* The earth is held by *satya* (or truth), *ṛta* (or principles of natural order including *yamas* and *niyamas*), *ugra* (*tejas* or power), *dīkṣā* (or initiated or skillfulness), *tapas* (or austerities), *brahman* (or one that permeates everything), and *yajña* (or sacrifice). The earth has taken care of living beings in the past and will do so in the future too. May such a generous earth provide us space for living.

References

Bhawuk, D. P. S. (2020). *śraddhā*: Construct definition from the *Bhagavad-Gītā*. *Psychology and Developing Societies, 32*(1), 1–16.

Bhawuk, D. P. S. (2019a). *Adhyātma* or spirituality: Construct Definition and elaboration using multiple methods. In S. K. Mishra & A. Varma (Eds.), *Spirituality in management: Insights from India* (pp. 19–41). Palgrave-Macmillan.

Bhawuk, D. P. S. (2019b). *Adhyātma* or spirituality: Indian perspectives on management. In P. S. Budhwar, R. Kumar, & A. Varma (Eds.), *Indian business: Understanding a rapidly emerging economy* (pp. 256–266). Routledge.

Bhawuk, D. P. S. (2019c). *Lajjā*: Learning, unlearning, and relearning. In E. Vanderheiden & C.-H. Mayer (Eds.), *The bright side of shame: Transforming and growing through practical applications in cultural contexts* (pp. 35–49). Springer.

Bhawuk, D. P. S. (2019d). Toward a spirituality-based theory of creativity: Indigenous perspectives from India. In K.-H. Yeh (Ed.), *Asian indigenous psychologies in the global context* (pp. 139–168). Palgrave MacMillan.

Bhawuk, D. P. S. (2019e). *Lokasaṃgraha*: An indigenous construct of leadership and its measure. In S. Dhiman, & A. D. Amar (Eds.), *Managing by the Bhagavad Gita: Timeless lessons for today's managers* (pp. 273–297).

Bhawuk, D. P. S. (2017). *Lajjā* in Indian psychology: Spiritual, social, and literary perspectives. In E. Vanderheiden & C.-H. Mayer (Eds.), *The value of shame—Exploring a health resource across cultures* (pp. 109–134). Springer.

Bhawuk, D. P. S. (2017). *Cultivating meditation for leading a peaceful life.* Foundation for Human Values in Management and Society.

Bhawuk, D. P. S. (2017). Developing theories and models to serve: A manifesto for indigenous psychologists. *Asian Journal of Social Psychology, 20*(2), 155–160.

Bhawuk, D. P. S. (2014). *Citta* or Consciousness: Some perspectives from Indian psychology. *Journal of Indian Psychology, 28*(1 & 2), 37–43.

Bhawuk, D. P. S. (2011). *Spirituality and Indian psychology: Lessons from the Bhagavad-Gita.* Springer.

Bhawuk, D. P. S. (2009). Humiliation and human rights in diverse societies: Forgiveness & some other solutions from cross-cultural research. *Psychological Studies, 54*(2), 1–10.

Bhawuk, D. P. S. (2008). Anchoring cognition, emotion, and behavior in desire: A model from the *Bhagavad-Gita"*. In K. R. Rao, A. C. Paranjpe, & A. K. Dalal (Eds.), *Handbook of Indian Psychology* (pp. 390–413). Cambridge University Press.

Bhawuk, D. P. S. (2008). Toward an Indian organizational psychology. In K. R. Rao, A. C. Paranjpe, & A. K. Dalal (Eds.), *Handbook of Indian Psychology* (pp. 471–491). Cambridge University Press.

Bhawuk, D. P. S. (2005). A model of self, work, and spirituality from the *Bhagavad-Gita:* Implications for self-efficacy, goal setting, and global psychology. In K. Ramakrishna Rao, S. B. Marwaha (Eds.), *Toward a spiritual psychology: Essays in Indian psychology* (pp. 41–71). Samvad Indian Foundation.

Bhawuk, D. P. S. (2003). Culture's influence on creativity: The case of indian spirituality. *International Journal of Intercultural Relations, 27*(1), 1–22.

Bhawuk, D. P. S. (1999). Who attains peace: An Indian model of personal harmony. *Indian Psychological Review, 52*(2 & 3), 40–48.

Bhawuk, D. P. S., Mrazek, S., & Munusamy, V. P. (2009). From social engineering to community transformation: Amul, Grameen Bank, and Mondragon as exemplar organizations. *Peace & Policy: Ethical Transformations for a Sustainable FutuRe, 14*, 36–63.

Geertz, C. (1973). *The interpretation of cultures: Selected essays.* New York: Basic Books.

Halliday, M. A. K., & Hasan, R. (1976). *Cohesion in English.* Longman.

Jeeyar, T. S. M. R. (Ed.) (2008). *Cloudburst of thousand suns*. [English rendering of Sri Sri Omkar Sahasra Vaani]. Translated into English by Raj Supe (Kinkar Vishwashreyananda). Delhi, India: Jai Guru Sampradaya.

Lemke, J. L. (1991). Text production and dynamic text semantics. In E. Ventola, (Ed.) *Functional and systemic linguistics: Approaches and uses* (pp. 23–38). Mouton/deGruyter (Trends in Linguistics: Studies and Monographs 55).

Marsella, A. J. (1998). Toward a global-community psychology: Meeting the needs of a changing world. *American Psychologist, 53*(12), 1282–1291.

Ryle, G. (1949). *Concept of the mind*. Hutchinson and Company.

Ryle, G. (1971). Collected papers. Volume II collected essays, 1929–1968. Hutchinson.

Chapter 9
sAdhu mArga: an Indian Model of Living and Leading

Dharm P. S. Bhawuk

Abstract This paper attempts to draw the management style of pujyapramukha swAmi mahArAja who provided leadership to bocAsanvAsI zrI akSar puruzottama swAmInArAyaNa saMsthA (BAPS) from 1950 to 2016. The definition of the word sAdhu is derived from the bhagavadgItA and the BAPS sampradAya (or tradition). Examining the vows of a sAdhu of BAPS sampradAya and reflecting on how pramukha swAmIjI carried them out in his life while performing all activities, it becomes clear that he led by example. Implications for leadership are discussed.

Harvard-Kyoto protocol for transliteration for devanagarI is used for all saMskRta and hindI words and names, and the first letters of names are not capitalized. All non-English words are italicized.

अ a आ A इ i ई I उ u ऊ U ए e ऐ ai ओ o औ au ऋ R ॠ RR ऌ lR ॡ lRR अं M अः H क ka ख kha ग ga घ kha ङ Ga

च ca छ cha ज ja झ jha ञ Ja ट Ta ठ Tha ड Da ढ Dha ण Na त ta थ tha द da ध dha न na प pa फ pha ब ba भ bha म

ma य ya र ra ल la व va श za ष Sa स sa ह ha क्ष kSa त्र tra ज्ञ jJa श्र zra

This paper is dedicated to *pUjaniya bhadreza sAdhu* who has been a constant inspiration and guide to me and has provided support for taking on this project. I am grateful to *munivatsal swAmiji* who has hosted me at the New Delhi *akSardhAma* temple many times and showered his unconditional love on me. I am also grateful to *ArSa puruSa swAmiji* for his generous support. *bholA bhAi* stands out as the exemplar *hari-bhakta* who is always there to help me and inspire me. *swAmI maGgalnidhi dAsajI* and *ajinkya navArejI* provided constructive comments that helped me improve the paper. I am grateful to them for their generosity. I would also like to thank *sAgarjI* for his generous help on this project. Working on this project in association with *bhadreza swAmIjI* has significantly shaped my personal *sAdhanA*, and I am grateful to BAPS *samsthAna* for being a support group to me. I follow most of the practices recommended for *hari-bhaktas*. The author is grateful to many authors whose works helped him develop a rich understanding of the life of *pramukh swAmIjI*, and acknowledges the following sources: Amrutvijaydas (2003), Anandswarupdas (1998), Brahmaswarupa Yogiji Maharaj (1999), Dave (1996), Divine Memories (1997a, 1997b), Gems from Shikshapatri (2002), Ishwarcharandas (2002), Keshavjivandas (1997), Patel (1995), Priyadarshandas (1995), Shantipriyadas (1998), Vasu (1894), Vivekpriyadas (2005a, 2005b), and Viveksagardas (2004).

D. P. S. Bhawuk (✉)
Management and Culture and Community Psychology, University of Hawai'i at Mānoa, Honolulu, USA
e-mail: bhawuk@hawaii.edu

© Jindal Institute of Behavioral Sciences 2022

S. P. Sahni et al. (eds.), *Spirituality and Management*,
https://doi.org/10.1007/978-981-19-1025-8_9

Keywords BAPS · Pramukh Swami · Sadhu · Leadership · Indigenous psychology · Indian psychology

sAdhu mArga: An Indian Model of Living and Leading

If we are to learn how a general manages his brigade, we will need to examine his or her worldview about nation and how to protect it from aggression. If we want to see how a doctor manages a hospital, we will need to examine his or her philosophy of health and wellness. If we want to examine how an academic manages an institution of learning, a school, a college, or a university, we will need to examine his or her ideology of education and pedagogy. If we want to comprehend how a *sAdhu*[1] manages a *saMpradAya* or *AdhyAtmika saMsthAna*, we would need to study the person in a historical context since he draws from the traditions of the *saMpradAya* and also his personal practices since he is an embodiment of the principles of the *saMpradAya*.

All managers are specialists in some profession, but become generalists as they rise in the organizational structure beyond the boundaries of their specialty departments. An engineer, accountant, or sales person continues to do engineering, accounting, or sales and manage his or her specialty department until he or she becomes the head of a division that includes other specialties. The head of an organization necessarily has to manage multiple specialties and becomes a generalist. However, it is not uncommon to hear that the person has remained at his or her core an engineer, an accountant, or a sales person. Professional specialties of managers often define their management philosophy and style. This is especially true for a *sAdhu* or monk who has renounced the world, yet lives and serves in it.

So, to understand the management style of a *sAdhu*, especially the head of a *saMpradAya* (an *AdhyAtmik* or spiritual organization), we must examine his *sAdhuttva* or *sAdhu bhAva*. In this chapter, an attempt is made to study how *pujyapramukha swAmi mahArAja* provided leadership to *bocAsanvAsI akSar puruzottama saMsthAna (BAPS)*. Various activities performed by *pramukha swAmi mahArAja* are examined and reflected on to decipher the management principles he employed. The history of the *sampradAya* is reflected upon when necessary to understand the practices. The definition of the word *sAdhu* is derived from the *bhagavadgItA* and the BAPS *samsthAna*[2] (or tradition).

---

[1] Since the paper is about a man and *sAdhu* is a masculine word, the paper uses gender neutral language when appropriate.

[2] BAPS is an independent organization that is a part of the *swamInArAyaNa sampradAya*. This is the position of the organization today, as it always has been from the time it was founded by *zAsgrIjI mahArAja*. *bhagatji mahAraja* never even imagined leaving the *sampradAya*, even when he was personally humiliated on occasions (Atmatruptadas, 2005). He also never wanted *zAstriji mahArAja* to leave the *sampradAya* when they were both insulted by others in the *sampradAya*. However, *bhagatji mahArAja* was clear that *guNAtitAnanada mahArAja* was the *akSara avatAra,* who was to be worshiped along with *swAmI sahajAnanada*, the *parabrahman avatAra* (Atmatruptadas, 2005). BAPS follows this principle from the beginning, and it is fundamentally different from the original

sAdhu in the *bhagavadgItA*

sAdhu appears in the *bhagavadgItA* four times, in verses 4.8, 6.9, 9.30, and 17.26. In verse 4.8,[3] *kRSNa* tells *arjuna* that he appears on earth in every age for the all-round protection of the righteous (*sAdhu*), the destruction of the evildoers, and for the establishment of righteousness (*dharma*). *sAdhu* is contrasted with *duSkRta* (those who act inappropriately) in this verse, providing insight that the *sAdhus* do *sukRta* or positive activities. *Adi zaGkara* interprets *sAdhUnaM* as *sanmArgasthAnaM* or those who are situated in the path of *sat*.[4] Thus, a *sAdhu* is one who is *sukRta* (righteous) or situated on the path of *sat*.

In verse 6.7,[5] *kRSNa* tells *arjuna* that a person who has control over the self and who is in deep peace engages with *paramAtmA* (or *brahman* or the supreme self). *Adi zaGkara* interprets it as *sakSAd AtmabhAvena vartate* or engaging with everything as the self. Therefore, such a person is engaged in all dualities—hot and cold, happiness and sorrow, praise and insult—while being engaged with *brahman* or the supreme self. In verse 6.8,[6] *kRSNa* further elaborates other characteristics of such a person: such a person is content with knowledge of self-learned from the *zAstras* or external sources (*jJAna*) and their internalization within the self (*vijJAna*); is always unperturbed (*kuTaStha*); has controlled the senses (*vijita-indriya*); is engaged with *brahman* (*yukta*); and such a *yogi* sees no difference between a lump of earth, stone, and gold.

Finally, in verse 6.9,[7] *kRSNa* lists some more characteristics of such a person as the one who is equally disposed to, or one who does not take sides (*udAsIna*) of, an altruistic person (*suhRd*), a friend, or an enemy. Such a person wishes well to people who are opposed to each other (*madhyastha*). Such a person is equally disposed to a vindictive or envious person, a relative, a *sAdhu* (*Adi zaGkara* interprets sAdhu as *zAstrAnuvartiSu* or those who follow the *zAstras*), or a sinner. In verse 6.9, *sAdhu* is contrasted with sinner (*pApI*), which is consistent with verse 4.8 where *sAdhu*

---

sampradAya on this principle. Therefore, I think it is appropriate to call it a *sampradAya*. But, that would clearly not be acceptable to BAPS because that would go against the wishes of *bhagatji mahAraja and zAstriIjI mahArAja*. An incident supports this position. A scholar offered *sAstrIjI mahArAja* an opportunity to challenge the main branch of the *sampradAya,* which he turned down by emphatically stating that he would never do a *zAstrartha* or debate with anybody from the other branches of his own *sampradAya* (Vivekpriyadas, 2005).

[3] Verse 4.8: *paritrANAya sAdhUnAM vinAzAya ca duSkRtAM; dharmasaMsthApanArthAya sambhavAmi yuge yuge.*

[4] The meaning of *sat* will become clearer as a thick description will be developed in the paper. To begin with, *sat* refers to *brahman* or the true being, that which really is. Therefore, it is the essence of everything.

[5] Verse 6.7: *jitAtmanaH prazAntasya parmAtmA samAhitaH, zItoSNasukhaduHkheSu tathA mAnApamAnayoH.*

[6] Verse 6.8: *jJAnavijAAnatRptAtmA kUtastho vijitendriyaH, yukta ityucyate yogI samaloSTAzmakAJcanaH.*

[7] Verse 6.9: *suhRinmitrAryudAsInamadhyasthadveSyabandhuSu; sAdhuSvapi ca pApeSu samabuddhirviziSyate.*

was contrasted with *duSkRta* or those who act inappropriately. Therefore, *sAdhus* are associated with many virtues and act in accordance with the *zAstras* following *dharma,* which is established by *zAstras* and *avatAras* (or incarnations of the divine).

In verse 9.30,[8] *kRSNa* tells *arujna* that even if a person of bad conduct worships him with one pointed devotion, then such a person is to be considered a *sAdhu* for he or she has the right resolve. This verse provides an interesting insight into who a *sAdhu* is—a *sAdhu* is one who has a firm resolve and worships God with single-minded devotion. The past activities of the person are not important. In the verse 9.31,[9] *kiRSNa* assures *arjuna* that such a person quickly becomes righteous (*kSpraM bhavati dharmAtmA*), attains everlasting peace (*zazvacachAntiM nigacchati*), and that a *kRSNa* devotee never perishes (*na me bhakta praNazyati*). This further emphasizes the importance of firm resolve, single-minded devotion, and worshiping God, which are the characteristics of a *sAdhu.*

In verses 17. 26,[10] *kRSNa* tells *arjuna* that the word *sat* is used in three contexts, namely *sadbhAva* (or the state of existence), *sAdhubhAva* (or the state of goodness), and *prazasta karman* (or auspicious activities like the 16 *saMskAras* that include *garbhadhAna* or conception, *upanayana* or the sacred thread ceremony, *vivAha* or marriage, *vAnaprastha* or preparation of the third phase of life in which one lives in a forest as a hermit, *sannyAsa* or the beginning of the fourth stage of life when one becomes a monk, and *antyeSTi* or cremation, to name a few. In verse 17.27,[11] *kRSNa* further elaborates that *sat* is also used for the *sthiti* or steadfastness in performing *yajJa, dAna, tapas,* and *karma* that is done for *brahman* (*tadarthIyam*). *Adi zamkara* and *zrijJAnadeva* (see *zrIjJAnezvarI*, 17. 380–17. 405, and 17. 406–17. 431) interpret that the word *sat* is a name of *brahman* and it is capable of not only removing the defects of *asat* and *asAdhu,* but also remove the defects of *yajJa, dAna, tapas,* and activities that have some demerit. Further, *sat* is also capable of making them auspicious. These verses complement the previous verses, 17.23–17.25, in which the value of *om* and *tat*, two other words used for *brahman*, is emphasized. Together verses 17.23–17.28 emphasize the value of *om-tat-sat*, each of the three words that are used to symbolize *brahman.* What is pertinent here is that the word *sAdhu* is closely associated with *sat* and, therefore, *brahman,* though it is not etymologically derived from *sat.*

sAdhu is derived from the *dhAtu* or root, *sAdh,* which belongs to *svAdi* group of *dhAtus.* Both *rAdh* and *sAdh* are used to mean *saMsiddhau* or to guide straight; to guide well; to direct someone to a goal; to go straight to any goal, aim, or objective; to attain an object; to be successful; to accomplish; to succeed; or to prosper (see Apte, 1890; Monier-Williams, 1899). The *dhAtu, sAdh*, according to *dhAtupAth,* give

---

[8] Verse 9.30: *api cetsudurAcAro bhajate mAmananyabhAk; sAdhureva sa mantavyaH samyagvyavasito hi saH.*

[9] Verse 9.31: *kSipraM bhavati dharmAtmA zazvacchAntiM nigacchati; kaunteya pratijAnIhi na me bhaktaH praNazyati.*

[10] Verse 17.26: *sadbhAve sAdhubhAve ca sadityetatprayujyate; prazaste karmaNi tathA sacchabdaH pArtha yujyate.*

[11] Verse 17.27: *yajJe tapasi dAne ca sthitiH saditi cocyate; karma caiva tadarthIyaM sadityevAbhidhIyate.*

us the following words: *sAdati, sAdhyati, sAdhnoti, and sadhnoti, sasAdha, asAtsIt, sAddhA, sAtsyati, sAddhum, sAdhitum, and sAdhase.* The word *sAdhu* is *made by adding uNa pratyaya*[12] to the *dhAtu sAdh,* which means guiding or directing others. Therefore, *sAdhu is* a person who accomplishes the object of another, works for the benefit of others, and guides them straight on *sadmArga* or the path of truth. Therefore, a *sAdhu* is completely virtuous.

To summarize, in the *bhagavadgItA*, a *sAdhu* is (i) closely associated with *sat*, which is a synonym of *brahman*; (ii) a person with firm resolve, one pointed devotion, and devoted to the worship of God; (iii) a person who follow the *zAstras* (*zAstrAnu-vartin*); (iv) a person who engages with everything as the self (*sakSAd AtmabhAvena vartate*); (v) contrasted with *duSkRta* (those who act inappropriately), providing insight that the *sAdhus* do *sukRta* or positive activities, or *sAdhus* are those who are situated on the path of *sat*; (vi) contrasted with *pApI* or sinner; and (vii) also associated with characteristics like *jitAtmanaH, prazAnta, parmAtmA samAhitaH, samabhAva* in *dvandva* (*zIta-uSNa, sukha-duHkha, mAna-apamAna*), *jJAna-vijJAna tRptAtma, kuTaStha, vijita-indriya, yukta, yogi, sama-loSTa-aSma-kAJcana, suhRd, udAsIna,* and *madhyastha.* It would be appropriate to add that a *sAdhu* is also an embodiment of the 26 *daivika sampads* presented in verses 16.1-3 (see Bhawuk, 2017 for a discussion).

pramukh SwAmIjI: A Brief Biographical Profile

pramukh swAmijI was born on December 7, 1921, as *zAantIlAl patel*, in *chAnsad, gujarAt*, India. He left the world or returned to *akSardhAma* on August 13, 2016, when he was visiting *sAraGpur, gujarAt*. He was blessed by *zAstrIji mahArAj*, his *adhyAtmika* or spiritual guru, at birth, and showed interest in pursuing a monastic life from early years. He was invited by *zAstriji mahArAj* to join the monastic order on November 7, 1939, and with the permission of his parents, he left home right away. He received his *pArzad dikSA* at *amblivADI pol* in *amdAbAd* on November 22, 1939, and was called *zAnti bhagat*. He later received *bhAgvati dikSA* and was initiated as a *sAdhu* on January 10, 1940, at the *akSar Deri* in *gonDal, gujarAt*. He received the name *nArAyaNaswarUpadAs* (Shelat, 2005).

He was appointed *pramukh* or President of BAPS by *zAstrIji mahArAj* on May 21, 1950, at the age of twenty-eight, despite his multiple refusals, out of humility, in the past. His austere practice of the vow of *nirmAna* could be seen when he was cleaning utensils in the evening the day he was appointed *pramukh* (*akSarvatsaldAs*, 2007). He worked under the guidance of *yogiji mahArAj* as *pramukh*, and after *yogiji mahArAj's*

[12] Other words formed using the same principle are as follows: *kR* (to make) + *uN* = *kAruH* or an artisan; *vA* (blow) + *uN* = *vAyuH* (the wind); *pA* (to drink) + *uN* = *pAyuH* (the organ of excretion); *ji* (to overcome) + *uN* = *jAyuH* or a drug, which overcomes disease; *mi* (to scatter) + *uN* = *mAyuH* or the bile; *svad* (to be pleasant to the taste + *uN* = *svAduH* or sweet; *aZ* (to pervade) + *uN* = *AzuH* or quickly (see 3.1.1, Vasu, 1891, Volume 3, p. 483).

return to *akSardhAma*,[13] both as *guru* of the *sampradAya* and *pramukh* from January 23, 1971, until he returned to *akSardhAma* on August 13, 2016. During his tenure as *pramukh*, BAPS became an international organization with 3850 centers all over the world, and over a million devotees who are vegetarians, practice fidelity, and do not take alcohol or other addictive substances. The devotees begin their day with *pujA* and *japa* (chanting), serve regularly as volunteers, and many donate ten percent of their income to support the temple and its service activities. Many biographical accounts of *pramukh swAmijI* are available, which profited this writer in learning about him (see Bhawuk, 2019 for a discussion of *AdhyAtma and pramukh swAmIjI*).

sAdhu in the BAPS *sampradAya*

The *zikSApatri* is a book that has 212 verses in *saMskRtam* that provides a code of behavior for the members of the BAPS *sampradAya*. The *sAdhus* of BAPS *sampradAya* take five vows for life, namely *niSkAma* (vow of celibacy and non-lust), *niHsneha* (non-attachment or affection for anybody; offer complete servitude and love to God), *nisswAda* (or having control of the palate; or find flavor only in God), *nirmAna* (not have pride; practice humility), and *nirlobha* (free of greed; practice of *aparigraha* or non-accumulation).

The first one, *niSkAma* (or a life free of sexual desires), is elaborated in *sikSApatrI* at length (175-195) and pertains to a complete non-interaction with women. A *sAdhu* should not look at women intentionally (175), let alone talk to them or touch them (175), talk or listen to talks about them (176), go to places like wells, ponds, and riverbanks frequented by them (176). A *sAdhu* should not even look at pictures or carvings of women, except of goddesses (177), let alone draw them (178).

A *sAdhu* should not touch women's clothes (178). A *sAdhu* should not look at animals and birds having intercourse (178). A *sAdhu* should not even look, touch, or talk to a man dressed like a woman (179). A *sAdhu* should not give discourses to women or sing *bhajans* addressed directly or indirectly toward them (179). A *sAdhu* should not even obey the commands of his guru if they would contradict the vow of *brahmacarya* (180).

Should a woman forcibly approach a *sAdhu*, she should be advised against or even reproached for coming near (181). In the extreme situation when a life of a woman or a *sAdhu* is endangered, then a *sAdhu* may speak to a woman or touch her to save life (182). A *sAdhu* should not go beg for alms where they are distributed by women (184). A *sAdhu* should keep away from effeminate men, just like they keep distance from women (185).

All *sAdhus* should avoid any type of contact, verbal, or non-verbal, with women (188). A *sAdhu* should never allow a woman to enter his place of residence (190).

---

[13] The passing of a guru is referred to as returning to *akSaradhAma*, and so I use this expression as a sign of respect. Personally, I have no difficulty in believing the wisdom passed on in the tradition for generations.

A *sAdhu* can go to a householder's home and have meals cooked by women, but it must be served by men, and women should not come in the sight of the *sAdhu* at any time (195). If that is not possible, then the *sAdhu* should take raw materials from the householders and cook for himself, offer it to God, and then eat (195).

Should a *sAdhu* touch a woman by chance, then he should fast for a day as penance. For example, *yogIjI mahArAja* blessed a baby girl when he was visiting a *satsaGgi's* home, thinking that the child was a boy. The householders were apologetic for allowing that to happen. Though it was only a baby and Yogiji Maharaj was in his seventies, he still started the fast immediately. When a devotee pleaded that the rule should not apply since he was a senior citizen and the guru of the *sampradAya*, Yogiji Maharaj said that it was all the more reason that he should fast. He fasted the next day.

On another occasion, a younger *sAdhu* told me how a woman came and sat next to him and said hello to him on a flight. A male cabin attendant explained to her about the vow of the *sAdhu* and helped the woman passenger switch seats. She apologized and gracefully moved to another seat. The *sAdhu* started the fast from that moment and fasted until the next day as per the tradition.

The *sAdhus* of BAPS *sampradAya* take this vow seriously, because it has been followed by all the *sAdhus* from the very beginning since the *sampradAya* was founded. *pramukh swAmIjI* has said many times that this vow will never be relaxed for any *sAdhu*, including the *guru* of the *sampradAya*. Many public figures pleaded with him that for an advanced *sAdhu* like him, it would not matter if he met the women devotees and female dignitaries. Some even argued that it was discriminatory to women. He would explain that the *sAdhus* were neither anti-women nor disrespectful of them. On the contrary, their respect for women was without any bias or blemish.

In the BAPS *sampradAya*, women visit the temples and *satsang sabhAs* without any restrictions. If they have questions, they write them down, pass it on, and the *sAdhus* answer their questions. Women are not treated differently in any way in the temple or the *sampradAya*. Different times are allotted to men and women to visit the temple in small areas with large crowds, such as in *akSaraDerI*. However, this is generally not the case in large temples, where there is ample space for male and females to do *darzana*. At the *Arati*, men sit behind the *sAdhus*, and women sit at the back. After the *Arati*, the *sAdhus* leave and then the women come to the front for *darzana* of the deities. It is no surprise that more than half of the members of BAPS are women. Mothers have no remorse in allowing their sons to become *sAdhus,* who would never see them in life again. I met a woman who had allowed all her three sons to become *sAdhus*.

When *pramukha swAmIjI* was visiting an African country, the President of the country requested him to bless his elderly, ailing mother. The devotees thought he should make an exception and visit the President's mother. But, *pramukh swAmIjI* explained to the President about the vow and said that he could not do that. The President understood and did not mind it at all. His sincerity about the vow had endeared him to the women devotees even more.

I interviewed a group of women devotees in Rajkot in December 2018. I must say that I was curious about their view on this vow of the *sAdhus*. When I asked a woman devotee if she felt bad about not being able to see *pramukh swAmIjI* face to face like the men devotees did, she said that she had no complaints. She remarked that she was happier about never sitting with him in person, because this way there was nobody between him and her! This feeling had developed over decades of association with *pramukh swAmIjI*.

She told me that she was not from a *satsaGgI* family. Her parents were not devotees of BAPS *sampradAya*. She had told her parents that she would be happy to marry a *gujarAti* man, but they should make sure that he was a sophisticated urbanite. Her wish came true. She married an officer of the Indian Force. The condition she had laid out brought a lot of restraints in her life, because he was a devotee of BAPS. For example, I asked her how she had survived the fancy parties of the Indian Air Force; I know about them because my brother-in-law is in the Corps of Electronics and Mechanical Engineers (EME). She told me that she had eaten plain rice and curd at all the parties all her life. She was visibly happy about it, and the restriction did not bother her.

When her husband was posted on the battlefront during the *kArgil* war, the Indian Air Force informed her that her husband die in the battle, her husband's last wishes were to send his *pujA* items to her. She wrote to *pramuh swAmIjI* about it, and he wrote her back, "Do not worry. Your husband will come home with his *pujA* setup." And that is what happened. It is relationships like these that make women not mind missing the face-to-face interactions with BAPS *sAdhus*.

She narrated another incident. When her mother passed away, her father was in deep depression. Her brother requested his father to meet *pramukha swAmIjI*, but since he did not believe in meeting *sAdhus*, he declined the request. But, her brother mentioned it to *pramukh swAmIjI* and also told him about his father's health condition. Swamiji readily agreed to meet with his father the next day. He came home and told his father that *pramukh swAmIjI* would meet with him the next day in the morning.

On being told about this, the father berated his son for fixing a meeting against his will. Her brother simply left it at that. The next day morning, her father thought it would be rude not to meet a *sAdhu*, even if he did not believe in meeting *sAdhus*. Since an appointment was already arranged, he went to see *pramukh swAmIjI*. Being a heavy smoker, he continued to do so while waiting to meet Swamiji. When he was asked to go in, he left the packet of cigarette on the table, as a courtesy to the *sAdhu*.

He had a long conversation with *pramukh swAmIjI*, who commiserated with him about the loss of his wife. Toward the end of the conversation, *pramukh swAmIjI* asked him if he would mind accepting *tulasi-mAlA*. Altough he did not wear a *mAlA*, he accepted it from *pramukh swAmIjI*. *pramukh swAmIjI* put a *tulasi-mAlA* around his neck. When he came out, he did not care to pick-up his pack of cigarette. He had quit smoking from that moment. When the brother shared this story with his sister, she could not believe it. She thought that perhaps her father was smoking secretly, since he was a heavy smoker and had been smoking for over fifty years. But, he had actually quit smoking completely, just like that. Experiences like this makes the women devotees appreciate the affection the *sAdhus* have for them. So, they are accepting the vow that prevents them to meet the *sAdhu* in person.

niHsneha or Non-attachment

This vow looks simple for a *sAdhu*, since the precondition of becoming a *sAdhu* is to have no attachment to anybody or any object (*zikSApatrI* 188: Conquer the base instincts of desire, anger, greed, and pride; 189: Control all sense organs). Having no attachment for anybody also is interpreted as offering complete servitude and love to God. There are many incidents that speak volumes of *pramukh swAmIjI*'s complete surrender to *bhagavAna swAminArAyaNa* and love for him. Once while traveling to the USA, he acted with deep concern that *ThAkorjI* was not traveling well. He made sure that he was placed properly on his *gaddi*. *ThAkorjI* was not an idol for him but a living being. When the President of Kenya, Jomo Kenyatta, asked him whether it was a symbol of God, he explained that it "was God," not a symbol (*akSarvatsaldAs*, 2007). When he was requested to stand in the British parliament to be acknowledged, he asked the *sAdhu* who was holding *ThAkorjI* to stand. There was not an iota of doubt in his mind that it was not he but *ThAkorjI* who was being honored by the British government. When asked by a journalist about what talent he had, he said as a matter of fact, "I have God." These support his total surrender to God and that his love for God was constant and continuous at all times and in all places.

pramukh swAmIjI showered so much love on both the *sAdhus* of the *sampradAya* and the *hari-bhaktas* that it would be impossible to say he was without *sneha*. When a young *sAdhu* did not cover the top part of his body with the *gAtro*, some people complained to *pramukh swAmIjI* about it in the evening. He threw his own *gAtro* and said, "I am a *sAdhu*. I have no bondage. I am ever free of all bindings." The young *sAdhu* felt quite relieved that *pramukh swAmIjI* defended him in front of everyone. The next day, when *pramukh swAmIjI* saw the young *sAdhu* without covering his upper body, he approached him and gently told him, "I know you must be feeling hot and that is why you do not cover your body. But it is not appropriate for a *sAdhu* to show his upper body uncovered. As a *sAdhu*, you must train yourself to adjust to the heat and cold." The young *sAdhu* never broke the rule after that. Such was the *sneha* of *pramukh swAmIjI*.

On another occasion, he himself made tea for a student who was not able to give up the habit of drinking tea. The student was so overwhelmed by his love that he quit drinking tea after that. When the team of *sAdhus* returned from a long international trip, *pramukh swAmIjI* came out of his room and prostrated in front of them to welcome them. A woman whose son met with an accident and was injured called *pramukh swAmIjI* and described to the *hari-bhakta* attendant how her son needed his blessing. He conveyed his blessing without delay and without caring about the time of the evening. She prayed to him that her son should not have to go through surgery, and he blessed her that it would be so. Her son got well without surgery, rather miraculously. His concern and care for the *hari-bhaktas* and their troubles and pieces of advice sent to them would match a mother's love for a child. His care for the *sAdhus* and for the *sampradAya*, and his frequent long letters to them, would pale a father's love and care for his children. Such a caring behavior is possible only when *niHsneha* so blossoms that it becomes pure spiritual *sneha* or love, and one sees *ThAkorji* within the devotees. It is no surprise that in his last days in *sAraGpur* temple, he went to have a *darzana* of swAmi*nArAyaNa* everyday, when the devotees came to bask in his presence. I must note that the *sneha* (or love) I have received from the *sAdhus* and *hari-bhaktas* of the *sampradAya* is unparalleled, and that every interaction with them remains indelibly etched in my mind. As a *sAdhaka* or practitioner of spirituality, I aspire to cultivate such non-attachment, which can best be described as pure and unconditional love for everybody in our lives, which leads to expressions of care in all domains of interaction.

nisswAda or Having No Taste

One of the vows taken by the *sAdhus* of BAPS is to cultivate the control of the palate (*zikSApatrI*, 189: Control all sense organs. Control tongue or *rasanA* especially). This is also interpreted as finding flavor only in God. The *sAdhus* take different food items in a bowl and mix them all so as not to taste different food items individually. Then, they add three *anjulis* (or cups of palm) of water in the food, which is done to take the taste away from the food. When a young man was serving *pramukh swAmIjI* in Ahmedabad, he was so inspired by observing how *pramukh swAmIjI* practiced *nisswAda* while taking his food that his own hankering for food died without any effort. Before this transformation, he was an impatient young man who wanted his food to be in a certain way. If it were not to his liking, he would throw tantrums, would not eat, or even throw away the food. He was a pain for his mother when it came to food. Being in the presence of *pramukh swAmIjI* completely transformed him.

It should be noted that there is long tradition in the *sampradAya* of feeding people. *bhagatji mahArAja* fed a group of young *sAdhus* one day when they were visiting him. Young *zAstriji mahArAja*, who was used to eating one-half of a *rotI*, had to eat two large *rotis,* and he did with great difficulty for the pleasure of his *guru.* As a visitor, I have experienced the love of the *hari-bhaktas* and *sAdhus* who fed me like my mother, with utmost care and love. It is important to note that though the *sAdhus* practice the vow of *nisswAda*, they are generous in feeding the *hari-bhaktas* and guests and are also great cooks. The food served at the BAPS temple cafeterias is the most delicious vegetarian food that one can get anywhere. The *hari-bhaktas* involved in the cooking do it with full devotional service. All food served in the temple is *prasAda* or offerings made to *bhagavAna swAminArAyaNa.*

nirmAna or Not Have Pride

The vow of *nirmAna* or having no pride also is the practice of humility (*zikSApatrI* 188: Conquer the base instincts of desire, anger, greed, and pride; 189: Control all sense organs). BAPS sAdhus have a long tradition of cultivating this vow. For a period of time, *sahajAnandaswAmI* encouraged the *sAdhus* not to go to villages where they were showered with praise and welcomed generously. He also demanded that they keep going back to villages where insults were hurled at them; they should keep doing so until the villagers started to welcome them. At that point, they should stop visiting the village. This is consistent with *manusmRti* (2.162), where it is stated, *sammAnAd brahmaNo nityamudvijed viSAdiva, amRtasyaiva cAkAGkSeda avamAnasya sarvadA.* When *bhagatji mahArAja* asked *guNAtItAnanda swAmIji mahArAja* what the *sAdhu*'s *kasab* was, he had elaborated some practices, and *nirmAna* was the very first one on his list. *Bhagatji mahArAja* and *zAstrIji mahArAja* suffered much insult in their lives, but did not ever react with anger.

pramukha swAmiji mahArAja knew about the insults that his guru, *zAstriji mahAraja* endured in his youth for following *bhagatji mahArAja* in putting forth the foundation that *swAmIsahajAnanda* was the incarnation of *para-brahman,* and *swAmI guNAtItAnanda* was the incarnation of *akSar brahman. zAstriji mahAraja* had even been demoted to wearing white garments that *pArsAds* wear despite having been a *sannyAsi* for many years. But, he followed the order of *bhagatji mahArAja* and did not leave the *sampradAya. pramukha swAmiji mahArAja* practiced humility in daily life. He was known to clean toilets, pick-up used plates, clean the premise of used *datans* (or bamboo sticks used for brushing teeth), and so forth. He always followed the orders of *yogiji majArAja,* which allowed him to practice humility. He also showed deference not only to the senior *sAdhus* of the *sampradAya,* but also to all others. He never took credit for anything, but gave it to the *sAdhus* and *hari-bhaktas* for all the activities that were organized by the *sampradAya.* He always said that all the temples that were built while he was the *pramukh* were following the vision of *yogiji mahArAja*; he simply carried them out. He created a culture in the *sampradAya* where everybody gives credit to other people and practices humility or *nirmAna.*

nirlobha (or Free of Greed; Practice of *Aparigraha* or Non-accumulation)

One could wonder why *nirlobha* would even be a vow for a *sAdhu* who has already renounced the world (*zikSApatrI* 188: Conquer the base instincts of desire, anger, greed, and pride; 189: Do not hoard money or goods by oneself or through others; 190: Do not keep others' money). With renunciation, *aparigraha* is concomitant. Therefore, one needs to examine aspects of *lobha* or greed. First, greed is related to wealth or money. It is for this reason that the *izopaniSad* warns right at the outset, *mA gridhaH kasya sviddhanam,* do not hanker after wealth, for whose is it? While one does not hanker after wealth, one may still be attached to material things. A scholar may be attached to books; a warrior may be attached to weapons; and so forth. Holding on to anything that is not necessary for supporting the existence of the physical body in the present moment is considered appendage to self, and the practice of *nirlobha* guides the person to avoid accumulating anything. This also allows one to surrender to God and accept difficulties as opportunities to grow in *sAdhanA*. Finally, there is attachment to place, as one wants to stay in a place where one has become comfortable. The practice of *nirlobha* calls for not becoming comfortable in any place. Another way of understanding *nirlobha* is by examining the three attachments, *putreSNA*, *zAstreSaNA,* and *lokeSNA*, which refer to desire for children or procreation, pursuing knowledge of *zAstra* or texts and desiring recognition from other people. We will see that *pramukh swAmIjI mahArAja* had risen above all of these forms of *lobha*.

He became a *sAdhu* at the tender age of 17, and so clearly, he did not have *putreSNA* (desire for children), which is not easy, but a requirement for *sannyAsins*. It also captures what we already discussed above under *niSkAma* or *brahmacarya.* He wanted to study *saMskRtam*, but somehow it did not come his way because of his responsibilities as the head of the temple and then as the head of the *sampradAya* at a young age of 28. So, he did not have *zAstreSaNA* or the attachment for knowledge of *zAstras* or texts. Finally, it is fame that even *sAdhus* can get entangled with. An incident from his life toward the end of his journey is illustrative to prove that he had conquered *lokeSNA* or the desire for adulation. In his senior years, there was a time when he was in wheelchair. Devotees wanted to visit him or even get a glimpse of him. So, a special glass room was designed for him to sit in so that devotees could sit in his presence. Every time he was taken to the room, he would tell the attendant *sAdhu*, it is time for *hari-darzana*. He was not giving a *darzana*, but getting a *darzana* of *nArAyaNa* in all the devotees who came to be in his presence. Such was his accomplishment of *lokeSNA* or *nirlobha*—he saw *nArAyaNa* in all!

There are other events sprinkled all over his life, which show that he had mastered *nirlobha* from an early time and was always alert not to succumb to *lobha*. When he went to buy marbles, to *rAjasthAna*, his contingency had to overstay by days. Since the ration of food was planned for fewer days and they could not cook food, he would eat the least to make sure others got enough food. Another time at a *kumbha melA*, a similar situation of food shortage arose when he met some devotees who had not planned ahead and stocked food. He instructed the attendant *sAdhus* to part with the food they had brought and lived with little or no food himself.

When he was offered Presidency by his guru, he turned it down twice, in writing. I often thought that it was not being consistent with the Indian order of being a good disciple. But, even *lakSamaNa* said no to *rAma* when he was offered *yuvarAja pada* (crown prince), so *rAma* had to appoint *bharata* to the position.[14] It is a not an often heard or cited story, but definitely a powerful example. Of course, both *lakSamaNa* and *sitA* are known not to agree with *rAma* when they were asked not to accompany

[14] *vAlmikI rAmAyaNa*, verse 6.128.92-93: *AtiSTh dharmajJa mayA sahemAM gAM oUrvarAjAd-hyuSitAM balena; tulyaM mayA tvaM pitRbhirdhRtA yA tAM yauvarAjye dhurmudvahasva. Oh, dharmajJya lakSamaNa!* Just as many other kings of the past and our ancestors ruled this land, join me as crown prince to rule this land. *sarvAtmanA paryanunIyamAno yadA na saumitrirupaiti yogam, niyujyamAno bhuvi yauvrAjye tato'bhyaSiJcad bharataM mahAtmA. rAma* tried to convince *lakSamaNa* in all possible ways, but when *lakSamaNa* did not accept the position, he appointed *bharata* as the crown prince.

him to the forest. So, the Indian tradition does allow to disagree with the elders, but only to a degree. He did finally accept the order of his *guru* and served as the head of the *sampradAya.* He faithfully served the orders and wishes of *yogiji mahArAja* as instructed by *zastrIji mahArAja* until *yogIji mahArAja* returned to *akSardhAma* on January 23, 1971.

There are many interesting incidents that capture *pramukh swAmIjI mahArAja*'s relationship with *yogiji mahArAja. yogiji mahArAja* always called him the *pramukh,* and *pramukh swAmIjI mahArAja* always considered him the guru and the leader of the *sampradAya.* Once *pramukh swAmIjI* was leaving after a celebration and went to take the permission of *yogIjI mahArAja.* He asked him how he was going to make the journey. *Pramukh swAmIjI* told him that he was taking the train. *yogiji mahArAja* told him that since he was the *pramukh* of the organization, he should go by a car or a jeep. But, there was no vehicle available. *yogiji* asked him to wait and leave only when the jeep was available. It became a long, arduous, and wasteful day. The jeep came late, and it broke down on the way. It took them more than 24 *h* to get to the destination. Besides, they suffered much due to rain, bad road conditions, and breakdown of the jeep. *pramukh swAmIjI* never expressed any displeasure about *yogiji mahArAhja*'s decision to send him by jeep. He never sought physical comfort, which would be a form of *lobha.* He also never questioned *yogiji mahArAja*'s decisions, whatever the cost. He was not affected by the *lobha* of efficiency.

Discussion

I think the most important theme that emerges from the above observations is that five vows guided *pramukh swAmIjI's* daily behavior, which inspired others to emulate him. It is no surprise that a child requested her parents to give money for the *pujA* at the temple, instead of celebrating her birthday. The little girl's sacrifice inspired the parents and her brother to do the same on their birthdays. Her brother took a vow in the presence of *pramukh swAmIjI* that he would not watch movies or eat out at the age of fifteen and has been maintaining it for seven years at the time of writing this. A security guard at the temple told the author that he used to drink alcohol from morning to evening, but also had a gift of singing *bhajans.* When his friend invited him to sing at a *sabhA* or gathering at his village home that evening, he did not feel like drinking at all. There was a photograph of *pramukh swAmIjI* at the *sabhA,* and he felt good that he had not drunk that day at all. He just stopped drinking from that day and got involved in the *sampradAya.* Today, there is a temple in his village, and he works at the temple in the city far away from his home, but is still at home in the temple. There are hundreds and thousands of such stories of life-changing events associated with people around *pramukh swAmIjI.* He inspired people to change by being an exemplar, by living the change he wanted to see, to quote *gAndhIji.* By living a pious life of a *sAdhu,* he created *sat-mArga* that people could tread on. He led by living, which was his management and leadership style.

When we discuss leadership processes, we invariably recognize that a leader has a vision and never loses sight of that vision. In the case of *pramukha swAmIjI*, we find that he was an embodiment of a *sAdhu*. The vision came from being a *sAdhu*, to always follow *sat-mArga*, even when people get carried away with growth of the *saMsthAna* with the number of temples and devotees. The temples are created for the devotees to find a place to connect with God, and in that, it provides the path of *sAdhanA*, which is *sat-mArga. pramukha swAmIjI* never lost an opportunity to remind people that the purpose of the *saMsthAna* was not to build temples and organize activities to show the world how well the *saMsthAna* was doing, but for the devotees to lead a simple life guided by simple rules that kept them making progress on the *sat-mArga* that would take them to the *dhAma* of *bhagavAna swAminArAyaNa*.

The *padhramanis* were not merely a tool of fund raising or recruiting members for the organizations or creating a following, but a method for *pramukha swAmIjI* to offer presence in the homes of the devotees. The *padhramanis* created channels that inspired the devotees in far flung villages to start and continue righteous living. The *padhramanis* constituted personal tracks for individual devotees that connected to the *sat-mArga* of the *sampradAya*, the highway that would lead devotees to the *dhAma* of *bhagavAna swAminArAyaNa*. The *padhramanis* were *AdhyAtmika* irrigation channels for *sat* or mother *gaGgA* to flow to each house of the devotee. They also served as the channels of communication between the highest level of the organization, *pramukha swAmIjI*, and the masses of devotees working in thousands of worldly organizations and occupations.

The celebrations organized for a day or the longer ones that went on from a week to a month to a year, which *pramukha swAmIjI* created by the droves, created temporary *tirthas* all over the world in space and time, which were positive events that allowed people to reboot and recharge themselves so that they could go back to the worldly organizations and occupations with a renewed connection with *bhagavAna swAminArAyaNa*. It also allowed devotees to serve each other and develop a spirituality-based network. Service propels people on *sat-mArga*, spirituality-based network provides support group when they return to the hustle-bustle of material pursuits, and the *utsavas* or celebrations are positive events that provide the much needed booster.

The analyses of *pramukha swAmIjI*'s life and activities have allowed us to discover an indigenous model of leadership, which is unique to India and its culture. A *sAdhu* lives a life that is guided by many vows. By following his vows, he becomes an exemplar not only for other *sAdhus* but also for the householders. Householders follow their own vows of eating pure food, keeping *satsaGga* or good company and doing *sevA* for the *sampradAya* through its many charitable activities carried out for the community at large. The householders continue to earn their living, and from the simple farmers to the wealthy industrialists, they all have *sAdhanA* or practice that keeps them making spiritual progress while still living in the world of incessant actions. We find that the *sAdhu mArga* helps integrate spirituality in daily living and offers a way or model of leadership and followership hitherto missing in literature. This is one of the many intellectual contributions of *pramukh swAmIjI*, which he made by living rather than pronouncing it; for the sage takes credit for nothing and so everything, even the impossible, gets done around him (Daodejing, Chap. 2; see Ames & Hall, 2003). Therefore, though the model derived from the life of *pramukh swAmIjI* is indigenous to India, and it is also applicable to China and perhaps the rest of the world by leading a life guided by *sAdhanA* or spiritual practice.

References

akSarvatsaldAs, S. (2007). *Portrait of inspiration: Pramukh Swami Maharaj*. (Trans. by Sadhu Vivekjivandas). Swaminarayan Akshparpith.
Ames, R. T., & Hall, D. L. (2003). *Dao de Jing: Making this Life Significant: Translation and Philosophical Interpretation of the Dao de Jing*. Ballantine Books.
Apte, V. S. (1890). *The practical Sanskrit-English dictionary*. Shiralkar & Co.
Atmatruptadas, S. (2005). *Brahmaswarupa Bhagatji Maharaj: Jivan aur karya*. Ahmedabad, India: Swaminarayan Akshparpith.
Amrutvijaydas, S. (2003). *Divine memories, Part III*. Swaminarayan Akshparpith.
Anandswarupdas, S. (1998). *Divinity: A voyage into the Divine world of Pramukh Swami Maharaj* (2nd ed.). (Trans. by Sadhu Paramtattvadas). Swaminarayan Akshparpith.
Bhawuk, D. P. S. (2017). *lajjA* in Indian psychology: Spiritual, social, and literary perspectives. In E. Vanderheiden, & C. H. Mayer (Eds.), *The value of shame—exploring a health resource across cultures* (pp. 109–134). Springer. https://doi.org/10.1007/978-3-319-53100-7_5
Bhawuk, D. P. S. (2019). *adhyAtma* or Spirituality: Construct definition and elaboration using multiple methods. In S. K. Mishra, & A. Varma (Eds.), *Spirituality in management: Insights from India* (pp. 19–41). Palgrave-Macmillan. https://doi.org/10.1007/978-3-030-13984-1_3
Brahmaswarupa Yogiji Maharaj (1999). Ahmedabad, India: Swaminarayan Akshparpith.
Dave, R. M. (1996). *Shikshapatri ke suktiratna: Bhagavan Swaminarayan rachit dharmasamhita*. Ahmedabad, India: Swaminarayan Akshparpith.
Divine Memories, Part I; Sadhu disciples share inspiring moments about Pramukh Swami Maharaj (1997a). Ahmedabad, India: Swaminarayan Akshparpith.
Divine Memories, Part II; Sadhu disciples share inspiring moments about Pramukh Swami Maharaj (1997b). Ahmedabad, India: Swaminarayan Akshparpith.
Gems from Shikshapatri (2002). Ahmedabad, India: Swaminarayan Akshparpith.
Ishwarcharandas, S. (2002). *Aksharbrahmad: Gunatitanand Swami*. Ahmedabad, India: Swaminarayan Akshparpith.
Keshavjivandas, S. (1997). *Divine memories, Part IV:* A personal account by Pujya Mahant Swami as he has seen and experienced Pramukh Swami Maharaj. Swaminarayan Akshparpith.
Monier-Williams, M. (1899). *A Sanskrit-English dictionary*. Oxford, UK: Oxford University Press. Reprinted in 1960.
Patel, M. (1995). *In the joy of others: A life sketch of Pramukh Swami Maharaj. Translated by BAPS Sadhus*. Swaminarayan Akshparpith.
Priyadarshandas, S. (1995). *Pramukh Swami Maharaj: An introduction*. (Trans. by Sadhu Yogavivekkdas). Swaminarayan Akshparpith.
Shantipriyadas, S. (1998). *Pramukh Swami Maharaj*. Ahmedabad, India: Swaminarayan Akshparpith.
Shelat, K. N. (2005). *Yug Purush: Pujya Pramukh Swami Maharaj*. Ahmedabad, India: Shri Bhagwati Trust.
Vasu, S. C. (1891). *The aSTAdhyAyI of pANini*. Calcutta, India: Published by Sindhu Charan Bose.
Vasu, S. C. (1894). *The aSTAdhyAyI of pANini* (*Volume 3*). Allahabad, India: Satjnan Chaterji.
Viveksagardas, S. (2004). *Yogiji Maharaj ki satsang kathae* (parables of Yogiji Maharaj). Ahmedabad, India: Swaminarayan Akshparpith.

Vivekpriyadas, S. (2005a). *Brahmaswarupa Shastriji Maharaj: Jivan aur karya*. Ahmedabad, India: Swaminarayan Akshparpith.

Vivekpriyadas, S. (2005b). *Vachanamruta: Ek parichaya* (An introduction to Vachanamruta). Ahmedabad, India: Swaminarayan Akshparpith.

Chapter 10
Yogic Leadership Approach: Linking Spirituality and Management for Harmonized Human Responses

Shiv K. Tripathi and Wolfgang Amann

Abstract Harmonized human responses are considered to be pivotal in shaping successful organizations. From Henry Fayol to Peter Drucker and Kaoru Ishikawa to Philip Crosby, most scholarly contributions in management appear to agree on an essential unity of "organization excellence and dedicated human action" with both these dimensions driving each other in a unique evolutionary configuration. Despite the volume of research on the related themes, the invisible source of organizational excellence still remains a mystery for organization theory scholars, perhaps, due to the high variation in the organization's characteristics as an entity. In other words, the organizations can technically look similar but at the same time have significant inherent differences in terms of responses, actions, and decisions. Philosophical traditions, particularly the righteous action philosophy emerging from Srimad Bhagwadgita, explain the fundamentals behind excellence in individual human responses and combining the same at organizational level. It gives some interesting perspectives on synchronizing the organizational efforts for excellence despite the huge variation in the characteristics of different types of organizations. The chapter, which is partly based on the review of literature, yet mostly on decades of practical experience, builds a generic "Yogic Leadership" approach for linking spirituality and management through harmonized human responses in the organizations. It intends to inspire and enable reflection. The chapter also provides a trigger for researchers to further explore and expand the framework through focused studies across different organizational contexts, irrespective of geography and culture.

Keywords Yogic Leadership · Humanistic management · Transcendental leadership · Indian wisdom

S. K. Tripathi
Atmiya University, Rajkot, Gujarat, India

W. Amann (✉)
HEC Paris, 5825, Doha, Qatar

© Jindal Institute of Behavioral Sciences 2022

S. P. Sahni et al. (eds.), *Spirituality and Management*,
https://doi.org/10.1007/978-981-19-1025-8_10

Introduction

Reviewing business environments as well as established phases of organizational development over the life cycle of an organization, it is more likely to face, deal with, or recover from a crisis than operating in quieter times. These VUCA years, characterized by volatility, uncertainty, complexity, and ambiguity, challenge leaders and managers alike. The difference between these two groups is that managers work in a box assigned to them, while leaders attempt to work on the box. Leadership, as a function, is involved in all managerial roles; however, the extent may vary depending on the contextual factors. Leaders ought to be transformational and transcendental leaders in a modern way of understanding their role. They share the need in these challenging VUCA times to have and convey psychological safety. They have to be role models for their teams and enable conducive working conditions for peak performance.

Spirituality can help endow individuals with psychological safety when adopting a safe base perspective on leadership and management. In other words, by eliminating the "psychological insecurity" through spiritually aligned leadership, the organizational environment can be significantly improved for better performance and well-being of its employees. Being able to rely on one constant in one's life encourages leaders and managers to not merely play it safe in their roles but play to win.

However, looking at the existing parading of leadership roles, the influence of a "balance sheet" orientation appears to be a dominating force in shaping "how a leader acts." The decisions of the corporate boards, which, in most cases, overemphasize the growth and profit need of the organization create a never-ending chain of "Greed Mixed Pride (GMP)" in accomplishing the set targets. The glitter and intoxication GMP is at such a high level that gradually converts the leaders into "pseudo- leaders" who work for numbers at all levels starting from self to the unit and organization at large. The multiplier effect of such a pseudo-leadership makes the situation quite challenging as it starts at all levels and functions and thereby taking the ethics, wisdom, and empathy at corner. The knowledge development in the field, which is also aligned to the "market need," appears more to satisfy the client requirement than bringing the ethically desired improvements. References for every argument are required.

The Yogic Leadership approach is based on Indian wisdom, drawn from Shrimad Bhagwadgita and Shri Ramcharitmanas. The "leadership as Yoga" was first introduced in the work "Corporate Yoga" (Tripathi & Amann, 2017). The framework was developed using summarized hermeneutics (Hunter, 2004). Later, the concept was periodically presented and refined with a group of 25–30 international management program participants, with different nationalities and executive experiences, for four consecutive years before first publication and four years post-publication.

While developing the approach, we follow the three-step approach: addressing the WHAT question (what are the issues?) before proceeding to the SO WHAT question (so what does it mean for organizations, leaders, and managers), and finally concluding with clear recommendations on the NOW WHAT question (distilling clear recommendation for the practitioners).

Why Yogic Leadership Approach is Needed?

Given the hundreds (if not thousands) of leadership development models and frameworks, one may question why another one is required? One answer could be that not many leadership development approaches touch the "spirituality" dimension. However, we can come across a number of leadership development models and approaches, developed by different spiritual leaders who have diversified in the area of corporate leadership development. Most of these models or frameworks emphasize on prescriptive set of do's and don'ts. Another significant challenge in most the existing prescriptive models is the connection between "theory and practice." The analysis of existing leadership development approaches indicates the two issues:

A. Separation of knowledge, science, and Ethics;
B. Over-dependence between economics, commerce, and knowledge;

The scientific knowledge without ethics cannot contribute to the larger goal of desired "good." The existing efficiency or effectiveness focus in most of the leadership development approaches hardly leaves any room for incorporating the ethical considerations in leadership decision and actions. Similarly, in last two centuries, the industrial revolution caused "commerce and economics supremacy" trend globally. This trend has influenced the state of "knowledge development" also. Most of the research happening today is to meet the requirements of the growing industries and economies. However, unless we judiciously apply the ethical considerations of "what is right" in the context, it is very difficult to reach the body of knowledge that will produce good. Across all the disciplines ranging from life science to commerce, management, and development studies, we often find examples of "deliberate ignorance of ethics" in the knowledge body. Flyvbjerg (2001) looks at this trend as a problem research methodology. There could be different possible reasons/causes behind this trend. However, analysis show that both A and B above together, i.e., "separation of knowledge, science, and ethics" as well as 'over-dependence between economics, commerce, and knowledge" is causing a SAD-SAD or lose-lose situation in organizational context, which is presented in Fig. 10.1. This requires interventions in terms of leadership development that will help in preventing such a situation arising in the organizations.

This is important to clarify that the SAD-SAD (Fig. 10.1) is not a generalized explanation; rather, it aims to highlight the challenges caused by the existing leadership development approaches. This is also to clarify that this analysis is not based on any specific sample or cases; rather, it reflects the observation and experience based on common trends across different organizational types and contexts. Also, when we refer to the organizations, we are not only pointing at the businesses but rather

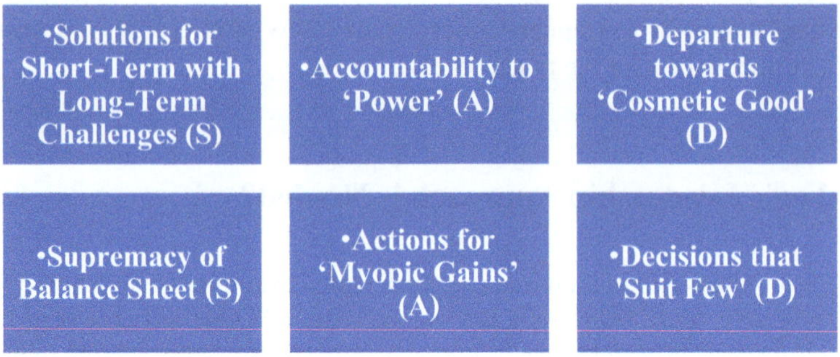

Fig. 10.1 Existing leadership environment and SAD-SAD?? situation

including all such organizational contexts (profit or non-profit or government) where the leadership development approaches can be applied.

One of the most pressing challenges in the organizations we find is the tendency to restore to short-term solutions, which can create long-term problems. In other words, what could have been solved with a simple solution, why create a complex design to solve that and spend resources? For example, during the time of COVID-19 crisis, we have seen many CEOs and leaders, supporting the immediate salary reductions of the employees to balance the losses from the business. Many organizations, small and with no cash power, might not be having other options. However, we know many such big organizations with good cash reserve and/or not very significant (or no) business loss yet cutting the salary of their employees. There could be many ways to avoid such situations which would eventually result in maintaining long-term motivation of the employees as well as the image of the organization as a whole. The tendency to develop short-term solutions is perhaps due to the separation of knowledge and ethics in practice, which leads to a situation with "quick-fix" solutions rather than looking at the larger pictures. These quick-fix solutions can only be temporary in nature, but the focus is necessarily to be on long-term strategies.

The leaders are considered to be accountable to wider group of stakeholders to whom they directly or indirectly serve. However, it has been observed that the internal environment in most organizations encourages the behavior of satisfying the "centers of powers," and therefore, the accountability toward rest of the stakeholders either only becomes theoretical or just a cosmetic display. CEO only focusing on board members, a leader focusing only on his/her superior, or someone who can benefit (or harm) him/her is some common examples of this type of problem. Such organizations show lack of ethics which could be ruinous for responsibility toward the stakeholders that should be uppermost in their functioning.

Another major challenge, which is found common with many leaders, is the presentation of the short-term accomplishments in such a way that reflects the long-term success toward meeting stakeholder expectations and legitimate needs. Not to say that the marketing, branding, and public relations units play an important role in painting such a picture which reflects the situation that is far from reality. While highlighting the achievements is always desirable, false (or manipulated) presentation of information with the intention to create good image often creates challenging situations in the long term.

A very common trend in most of the organizations is "supremacy of balance sheets," i.e., everything in the organization starts from and ends at the financial figures. Whether it is top-down planning or bottom-up flow, most of the targets and goals revolve around the financial performance the organization wants to achieve in the given time. This creates a pressure situation in the organizations and often leads to ignorance of ethical considerations. The leaders have an important role in creating the orientation within their respective units/functions/organizations regarding the balance between "financial targets" and "quality of performance and results," failing which the organization may start evolving with a culture of chasing numbers instead of making a significant impact.

Linked to the tendency to develop short-term solutions, there is another challenging area of focusing on "myopic gains." By saying "myopic," we mean ignoring the potential of long-term bigger picture of growth by focusing on some short-term gains that satisfies the immediate interest but costs the organization dearly in long terms. For example, sometimes, by entering into partnership with a vendor for saving some quick money but ignoring the quality, speed, and customization requirements in the supply could be considered as a classic example of that. Similarly, sometimes, one may find HR team working on head count reduction by targeting such people who have played significant role in growth of the organization and can be a great source of mentoring for new staff. But because they appear to not have required utility value, they can be targets for the myopic gains in the organizations.

The stakeholder power politics is quite alarming for the growth of any organization. Those who are powerful stakeholders in organizations try to influence the decisions in such a way that suits them. It becomes responsibility of the leader to avoid such a situation in which decisions are made to suit the interest of a few powerful stakeholders. However, the challenges arise when the leaders have tendency to be accountable to only the "sources of power" in the organizations instead of looking at the bigger picture and serving to the larger group of stakeholders for long-term growth of organizations.

It is important to note that most of these challenging factors (Fig. 10.1) do not operate in isolation and, therefore, cannot be considered as mutually exclusive. In fact, in practice, it is very difficult to identify which of these factors are more dominant in any organization than others. For example, the tendency to work for short-term solutions can be quite linked to the actions for "narrow gains." Similarly, one can find many such examples in which two or more of these factors are working in combination. Therefore, the SAD-SAD framework is suggested for explaining and understanding the challenges with the organization, instead of taking it as an absolute model with prescriptive applications. We saw with the help of SAD-SAD framework the type of challenges being faced by the organizations because of the fact that leadership development is not addressing these issues in a pragmatic way. Another possible explanation behind such a situation could be the lack of suitable leadership development interventions with potential for transforming the leaders for the greater good. The Yogic Leadership approach helps in dealing with existing challenges in terms of addressing identified gaps in the leadership development approaches.

The Genesis of Yogic Leadership Concept

The concept of Yogic Leadership is based on Indian wisdom regarding roles and functions of different people in the society. More specifically, we have referred to the translated version of Srimad Bhagwadgita to draw further insights. While selecting the translation and interpretation, we referred to the available versions, which suit more to the context of leadership and management. The management as we understand it in context of modern knowledge body of the subject has been defined in a holistic manner in Srimad Bhagwadgita.

अधिष्ठानंतथाकर्ताकरणंचपृथग्विधम्।
विविधाश्चपृथक्चेष्टादैवंचैवात्रपञ्चमम्।।

SrimadBhagwadgita||18.14||

"The basis, as well as the agent, diverse instruments and distinct activity of various kinds and Destiny, are certainly the fifth" (Translation by Dr. S. Sankarnarayan). In other words, there are five factors responsible for effective accomplishment of any tasks: context + basis; doer/leader; tools; different means; and the nature/unforeseen destiny, which are the missing link in modern text of management. The characteristics of a good *"karta"* or doer/leader has been explained in detail in Srimad Bhagwadgita, which forms the basis of developing "Yogic Leadership" concept. The concept was first presented in a research work (Tripathi, 2002); later it was modified and presented to a group of 25–30 international management cohort of executives in a European University. Based on the suggestions, it was modified and presented again. This continued for four consecutive years before it was first published in 2017 (Tripathi & Amann, 2017, op. cit.). Now, while further modifying the concept, we referred to *Shri Ram Charitmanas*, which also offers great wisdom for ethical leadership in any context. The work is conceptual in nature and based on the wisdom of ages. Therefore, we have not tried to test it using modern methodologies, which we encourage other researchers to do.

The presented approach is called "Yogic Leadership" because of the following reasons:

- We combine three types of Yoga suggested in *Srimad Bhagwadgita, i.e., gyan Yoga* (knowledge focused), *karm Yoga* (action focused), and *bhakti Yoga* (devotion focused). The approach emphasizes on synthesis/integration of the three different yoga types;
- The concept works with the ultimate objective of achieving the collective joy through holistic well-being and included economic, social, psychological, and

spiritual well-being of an individual, organization, community, and society, which are considered always to function in harmony with each other rather competing for narrow gains;

- The approach aims at generating continued efforts toward achieving "sustainability (economic + social + environmental)" for the infinite time horizon, i.e., "*sustainafinity.*" The focus on infinity gives an opportunity for continuous improvement with aim for greater good;

Here, it is important to note that we do not mean Yoga to be only a set of physical activities but rather as a set of leadership actions that leaders perform.

Fundamental Pillars of Yogic Leadership

As mentioned earlier that the "Yogic Leadership" approach is not prescriptive in nature. It suggests certain conditions for improving the leadership practices and, therefore, is more generic in approach, which can be adopted by the leaders who trust in the approach and want to practice it. The main conditions for achieving "Yogic Leadership" are presented in Fig. 10.2.

The "empathy" is considered as one of the pre-conditions for practicing Yogic Leadership. In this context, we consider "empathy" as the ability to understand and see the situation from the viewpoint of the stakeholder(s) to whom we are serving. The Southern African Ubuntu philosophy best explains this by emphasizing *"I exist*

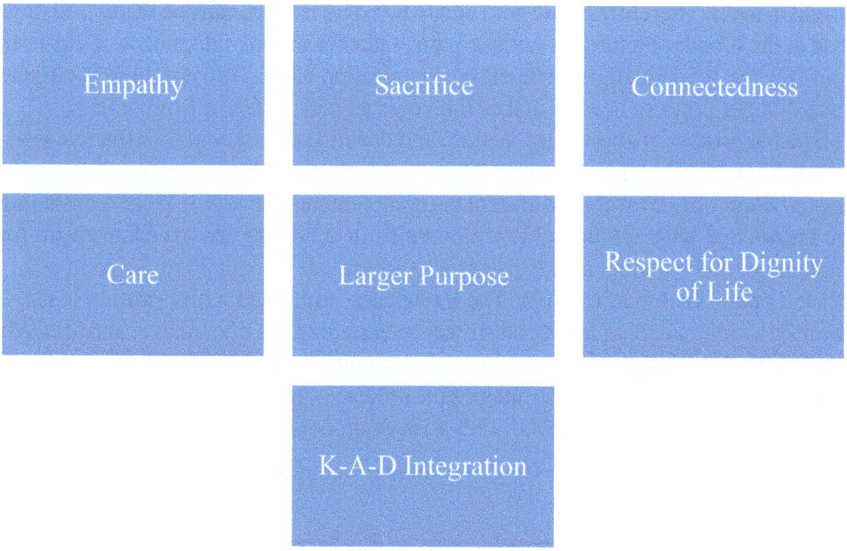

Fig. 10.2 Yogic Leadership—fundamental pillars (Tripathi, 2021)

because, you exist, and, therefore, we all are" (Tripathi, Amann & Kamuzora, 2013). The sense of (and willingness to) sacrifice is another important condition for Yogic Leadership. It is quite evident that unless one is willing to go that extra mile to solve the challenges faced by others, it is very difficult to achieve a situation where no one loses. It is not easy to develop and practice "sacrifice," and therefore, it requires consistent efforts in this direction.

The appreciation toward connectedness between organization, individual, and society is one of the important conditions for developing leadership for overall good. The individual who works in the organization is also a member of the family and society. Therefore, while making decisions and actions in the organizations, one must consider the inter-connectedness and long-term implications of the decisions. The inter-connectedness leads to another important and related consideration "caring orientation." The more we care about our people, the more they will reciprocate it not only in the organization but also beyond, i.e., in family, community, and society at large. Bob Chapman (Chairman and CEO of Barry Wehmiller) observes:

> *We can't separate organizational role of the individuals from their respective roles in family and society...More we care, more they reciprocate, caring is contagious.*[1]

As highlighted in a three-stepped approach of humanistic management (HMN, n.d.), the respect toward "dignity of life" is also an important consideration in mastering Yogic Leadership approach. Unless one develops the inherent respect for dignity of life, it is very difficult to practice leadership, which is based on "good for all." The passion toward the larger purpose, i.e., "common good" is another important consideration in practice of Yogic Leadership. The organizational success is considered as a means to achieve the larger purpose of "good" rather than considering it as an end in itself. Therefore, those who aim to be yogic leaders must be ready to always look at the broader picture for holistic gains rather than look into narrow short-term gains for the individual, department or organization alone. The continuous passion toward larger purpose is what makes the yogic leaders different from others.

The integration of knowledge, action, and devotion is essential for effective practice of Yogic Leadership approach. These three elements have been emphasized in *Srimad Bhagwadgita* as three different but complementary paths of Yoga. Combining the knowledge with action and devotion helps in achieving the excellent result for producing good without any adverse effect (Tripathi & Mukhi, 2013; Tripathi et. al., 2014; Tripathi & Amann, 2017). The knowledge combined with devotion leads to superior action, which in turns contributes to enriching the knowledge, and all these three elements continue to work in cyclic manner with synergistic effect toward good in the long term. K-A-D integration reflects a unique combination of theory and practice for driving the good with a focus on continuous improvements in the efforts.

---

[1] Bob Chapman in "Leadership Gold" series talk with Dr. Ernst von Kimakowitz on April 22nd, 2021, humanistic management network. Details available: www.humanisticmanagement.network.

Challenges in Effective Implementation of Yogic Leadership

The knowledge building in the discipline of management has been questioned by different scholars in the past (Chakraborty, 1990, 2003; Mintzberg & Gosling, 2002; Ghoshal, 2005; Sharma, 2006; Amann et. al., 2011). Most of the scholars agree that the current approach to knowledge development in the discipline of management focuses more on the scientific tradition of knowledge building and, in most cases, ignores the relevance of knowledge being produced.

The major challenge in academic system is the "scientific orientation," which in case of disciplines like social sciences including business has not yet produced the path-breaking innovations that the world needs. Global warming, rising inequality due to COVID-19, or unresolved ethical questions related to AI represent just a few examples. The knowledge built by using the assumptions and methodology of natural sciences cannot be relevant in social sciences, which is often quite contextual in nature (Flyvbjerg, 2001).

Some of the limiting factors in implementing Yogic Leadership have been summarized in Fig. 10.3. The universities and B-schools, which continue to chase and produce scientific knowledge without adequately ensuring relevance, may not easily accept such approach which do not confirm to the so-called test of "scientific wisdom." Similarly, the overall "greed factory"-type environment, which hardly

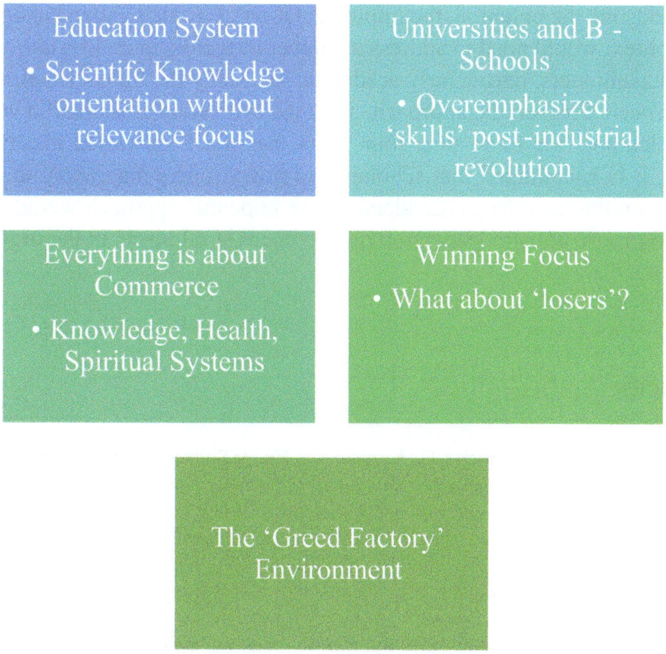

Fig. 10.3 Factors limiting the implementation of Yogic Leadership

encourages values of "care" and "empathy" may not be very effective in accepting and practicing Yogic Leadership. There appears to be an over emphasis on meeting technical skills development needs in universities, and therefore, often the issues dealing with human skills get ignored. Too much commerce orientation in different types of organizations and a blind race for winning without understanding the consequences are two other major constraints that may create challenge in effective implementation of Yogic Leadership approach in organizations.

Conclusion

The existing challenges in our organizations, both profit or non-profit, require a fresh thinking about how human value-oriented leadership can be developed and promoted in the organizations. The Yogic Leadership approach, which is based on the wisdom drawn from Indian scriptures, offers a generic alternative to the existing leadership development frameworks. The Yogic approach is based on humanistic orientation and aims to produce larger good by developing "doers/leaders" who act like yogis in achieving a broader purpose, which is beyond the immediate financial results of the organizations. The Yogic Leadership approach is likely to add a fresh perspective in leadership development by taking a holistic view of the organizations and individuals instead of considering them as an isolated part in the larger system. However, despite the potential, the implementation of Yogic Leadership approach in modern context would need to address a number of factors including convincing the different stakeholders, particularly academia, regarding the transformational power of the approach. Further, the approach, although evolved in consultation with global executive learners for more than four years, has not been tested in any context. Therefore, it is encouraged that scholars and practitioners may adapt the different suggested conditions of Yogic Leadership. We hope this approach would be helpful in achieving more holistic leadership development at all levels in the organizations for larger good.

References

Amann, W., Pirson, M., Dierksmeier, C., Kimakowitz, Ev., & Spitzeck. H. (2011). *Business schools under fire: Humanistic management education as the way forward*. Palgrave Mcmillan.

Chakraborty, S. K. (1990). *Human response development*. Wiley Eastern.

Chakraborty, S. K. (2003). *Against the tide: The philosophical foundations of modern management*. Oxford University Press.

Flyvbjerg, B. (2001). *Making social science matter: Why social inquiry fails and how it can succeed again*. Cambridge University Press.

Gentile, M. C. (2010). *Giving voice to values: How to speak you mind when you know what's right*. Yale University Press. Available at http://www.givingvoicetovaluesthebook.com/.

Ghoshal, S. (2005). Bad management theories are destroying good management practice. *Academy of Management Learning and Education, 4*(1), 75–91.
HMN. (n.d.). Foundations of humanistic management. Available http://humanisticmanagement.network/publication/the-foundations-of-humanistic-management/. Retrieved 04/20/2021.
Hunter, L. M., Kasouf, C. J., Celuchc, K. G., & Curry, K. A. (2004). A classification of business-to-business buying decisions: Risk importance and probability as a framework for e-business benefits. *Industrial Marketing Management, 33*(2), 145–154.
Lassch, O., & Conaway, R. N. (2013). *Principles for responsible management: Global sustainability, responsibility and ethics*. Cengage Learning.
Mintzberg, H., & Gosling, J. (2002). Educating managers beyond borders. *Academy of Management Learning and Education, 1*(1), 64–76.
Sharma, S. (2006). *Management in new age: Western windows eastern doors*. New Age International Publishers.
Tripathi, S. K., & Amann, W. (2017). *Corporate yoga: A primer for sustainable and humanistic leadership*. Information Age Publishing.
Tripathi, S. K., & Mukhi, U. (2013). The spiritual triology of human action for ethical business responses: Moving towards corruption-free zone. *International Journal on Spirituality and Organizational Leadership, 1*(2), 107–117. Academy of Value Based Management, India.
Tripathi, S. K., Amann, W., & Kamuzora, F. (2013). Towards a humanistic and responsible managerial decision making model: The corporate Ubuntu approach. In K. Shiban, & W. Amann (Eds.), *World humanism: Cross-cultural perspectives on ethical practices in organizations* (pp. 122–134). Palgrave Macmillan.
Tripathi, S. K., Amann, W., Pandey, P., & Mukhi, U. (2014). The philosophy and science of corporate yoga: Some perspectives on responsible management action. *International Journal on Vedic Foundations of Management*, *1*(2), 68–81. ISOL Research Foundation, India.

Chapter 11
Values in the Workplace: Avoiding Dual-Life Syndrome

John E. Simms

Abstract This essay examines a case of cognitive dissonance phenomenon (Festinger L in A theory of cognitive dissonance, 1957) resulting in dual-life syndrome in which an individual maintained and acted upon two incompatible value systems. The incompatibility created an irreconcilable internal conflict leading to psychological strain (Zhang in Chinese Mental Health Journal 19:778–782, 2005; Zhang et al. in Developing the Psychological Strain Scales (PSS): reliability, validity, and preliminary, 2014), culminating in his suicide. The essay presents the case of Cliff Baxter, formerly Chief Strategy Officer for Enron, in the time leading to his tragic suicide in January of 2002.

Keywords Ethics · Values · Cognitive dissonance · Psychological strain · Enron · Dual-life syndrome

It seems natural to compartmentalize aspects of our life, separating the personal from the professional. In *The Godfather,* Abe Vigoda's character Salvatore Tessio realizes his betrayal has been discovered and he is about to be executed. Tessio says, "Tell Mike it was only business. I always liked him" (Coppola 1972). Tessio's betrayal was only possible by the complete separation of his business practices from his personal feelings. Viewers may tell themselves that *The Godfather* is only a movie based on a work of fiction, but there is often profound human truth presented in stories without factual basis.

Kohlberg (1958, 1984) divided moral development into three stages: preconventional (driven primarily by self-interest), conformity (driven primarily by approval from others), and principled (focused primarily on the interests of others). Massey (1986) divides the development of values into a similar triad: The Imprint Period (to the approximate age of 7), The Modeling Period (ages 8–13), and the Socialization Period (13–21).

J. E. Simms (✉)
University of St. Thomas, Houston, TX, USA
e-mail: simmsj@stthom.edu

© Jindal Institute of Behavioral Sciences 2022

S. P. Sahni et al. (eds.), *Spirituality and Management*,
https://doi.org/10.1007/978-981-19-1025-8_11

One commonality between Kohlberg (1958, 1984) and Massey (1986) is that many (perhaps most) have fully developed values systems in place by the time they reach adulthood.

Pastin (1986) introduced what he called *ground rule ethics* to describe the way an individual's behavior informs others' as to the individual's fundamental values.

When a single individual has internalized two values systems that are in conflict, the resolution to the conflict involves either changing one or both of the values systems, or else change the external situation that is creating the conflict.

The Merriam Webster Unabridged Dictionary (2021) defines a *syndrome* as "a group of signs and symptoms that occur together and characterize a particular abnormality or condition." The signs and symptoms are described in the background sections of *cognitive dissonance* and *strain.* Dual-life syndrome is created by cognitive dissonance and characterized by the symptoms of psychological strain. Fundamentally incompatible value systems come into conflict and create a need to either accept the dichotomy by rationalization, redefining the external situation, changing the internal value system to match external reality, or devise a means to change the situation by addressing the external source of the problem at its root cause.

The Institute of Management Accountants (IMA) presents the IMA Statement of Ethical Professional Practice (2017). After presenting and defining the professional mandates of competence, confidentiality, integrity, and credibility, the statement provides guidance on resolving ethical issues. The latter section is a hierarchy of resolution strategies. The first is to follow established organizational policies. If the organization's policies do not provide a means of addressing the issue, the next possibility is to present the problem to one's immediate supervisor. If that is not feasible or the supervisor is possibly involved, one should approach the next higher level of authority. The IMA then proposes the next step of calling anonymous ethics helplines. Unfortunately, in 2002 when the case to be presented takes place, ethics "hotlines" did not exist. In fact, it is in large part because of the case presented that they exist today. The next step is to call one's personal attorney to ascertain various options and the associated risks. If none of the above proposed steps are acceptable, the IMA states "If resolution efforts are not successful, the member may wish to consider disassociating from the organization" (2). However, for many people, the organization itself becomes a significant part of their identity, tied into self-image and self-esteem. In some cases, it could become extremely difficult to imagine or actualize leaving the firm. The remainder of this essay uses as an example the case of a senior executive at Enron, J. Clifford "Cliff" Baxter. The rest of the essay is organized as follows: First, the case of Cliff Baxter, Chief Strategy Officer at Enron, is introduced. Second, the background of the theories of cognitive dissonance and strain is presented, and the model of dual-life syndrome is introduced. Following after is the application of strategies to avoid dual-life syndrome and its deleterious effects, including an individual's initial selection of an employer, followed by examples of the use of faith-based strategies for internal conflict resolution and achieving a work/life balance that incorporates spirituality and professionalism. Successful incorporation of an individual's spirituality into the workplace environment can be achieved by finding commonalities between spiritual guidance or mandates and professional codes of behavior. The example presented uses the paper written by Pope Saint John Paul II *Ex Corde Ecclesiae* (ECE) and the Code of Ethics provided by the American Institute of Certified Public Accountants (AICPA). The example is based on the work by Simms (2019). This is followed by the conclusion of the paper.

The Case

J. Clifford "Cliff" Baxter committed suicide at or around 2:20 a.m. on January 25, 2002. He was the Chief Strategy Officer for Enron and acted as a sounding board and friend of the CEO, Jeffrey Skilling. Baxter had agreed to testify before congressional committees after being subpoenaed regarding his knowledge of the Enron scandal. The note he left for his wife, Carol, said in part, "I feel I just can't go on. I have always tried to do the right thing but where there was once great pride now it's gone."

Baxter's suicide was included during the opening credits of the movie *Enron: The Smartest Guys in the Room* (Gibney 2005), based on the book of the same name by *Fortune* magazine writers McLean and Elkind (2003).

By all accounts, Baxter was a good father and faithful husband. He was born in Amityville, NY, earned his bachelor's degree from NYU, then entered the military and achieved the rank of captain in the U.S. Air Force. After the military, he received an MBA from Columbia. Baxter was no stranger to pressure, so what drove him to take his own life?

Of course, we cannot know precisely what his thoughts and feelings were, but his note does provide a major clue. "…where there was once great pride now it's gone."

One can easily surmise that what he saw going on in Enron was in direct conflict with the principles and values that he had accepted, developed, and by which he lived.

Background

This section examines theories of *cognitive dissonance* and *strain* and then introduces a related phenomenon, *dual-life syndrome.*

Cognitive Dissonance Theory

The Oxford English Dictionary (2021) defines *cognitive dissonance* as "the state of having inconsistent thoughts, beliefs, or attitudes, especially as relating to behavioral decisions and attitude change."

Festinger's (1957) theory of cognitive dissonance has been revised during the subsequent three decades (Beauvois & Joule, 1982; Greenwald & Ronis, 1978; Joule,

1986) but continues to be relevant despite considerable controversy and criticism; it is still one of the most important theories in social psychology according to Cooper and Croyle (1984). Cognitive dissonance theory has been characterized as "the most important development in social psychology" by Aronson (1997).

The Strain Theory

The strain theory of suicide was first presented by Zhang (2005) and posits that strain results from at least two stressors which may result from conflicts created by two differential cultural values, discrepancies between hopes and reality, perceived status differences, and the lack of coping abilities in crisis situations. Zhang, Lu, Zhao, Lamis, Li, Kong, Jia, Zhou, and Ma (2014) developed psychological strain scales (PSS) which were shown to be correlated with suicidal ideation (Zhang & Lester, 2008; Zhang et al., 2009).

The outward manifestation of frustration-aggression strategies of criminal behavior is shown to fit the model (Agnew, 2006; Durkheim, 1951; Merton, 1957), as well as the inward manifestation of suicidal ideation (Freud 2002).

Strain theory is closely related to, but not the same as, cognitive dissonance, as Zhang et al. (2014) explain:

> As the cognitive dissonance theory suggests, strain is a psychological frustration or even suffering that one struggles to find a solution to reduce or eliminate. But in truth, it is more serious, frustrating, and threatening than cognitive dissonance because major cultural value systems may be involved. (338)

Festinger (1957) presented cognitive dissonance as a conflict between two inconsistent ideas or by a discrepancy between behaviors and values. Festinger and Aronson (1960) elaborated by categorizing the strain into four types: value strain, aspiration strain, relative deprivation strain, and coping strain. Festinger and Aronson (1960) posit the problem as follows:

> Strain, in its psychological impact, could be even more pathogenic, powerful, and devastating than the cognitive dissonance, and the reduction of strain may require something beyond the above three options for cognitive dissonance. Again, the built-up strains and their consequent tensions, if not timely reduced or released otherwise, could lead to crime (outward releasing) or mental disease (including suicide). (339)

Festinger and Aronson (1960) list three survivable options available: change our behavior, attempt to justify our behavior through changing one of the dissonant cognitions, or attempt to justify our behavior by adding new cognitions.

Dual-Life Syndrome

Each person adopts universal principles and develops personal values which become the primary drivers of their behavior. Research has shown that the two primary sources of values are family and faith (Bussey, 2006; Miller, 2002; Roccas, 2005). In philosophy, ethics is concerned with how these principles become personal values. Ethics in business is about *behavior*. Specifically, business ethics is how an individual resolves conflicts between personal values and professional norms or expectations.

Dual-life syndrome occurs when the conflicting value systems remain unresolved. It is characterized by behavior wherein individuals apply, demonstrate, and perhaps enforce different sets of values for different aspects of their life. All too often, someone is accused or convicted of a crime and those closest to him or her find it difficult to accept. "*I can't believe that. He was such a kind, caring man. He would never do such a terrible thing.*" Clearly, Cliff Baxter was conflicted. He suffered from both value strain and coping strain. Zhang et al. (2014) define value strain as "two or more conflicting and internalized values" (341). Coping strain, on the other hand, is "a psychological frustration for an individual facing some crisis but being unable to deal with it. It can be measured by lack of coping skills when one encounters a crisis life event" (342). Baxter held himself to very high standards of performance, as well as personal and professional behavior, but his knowledge of, and perhaps participation in, the deceit that was Enron created the necessity for alternate views of his world, his job, and himself that were fundamentally incompatible with the values he had incorporated into his own identity.

According to Carbonell (2015), the resolution of these incompatibilities sometimes involves a *sacrifice of self,* "Certain activities change us. We emerge from them altered, out of touch, diminished, or even morally corrupted" (53).

These types of changes have been observed in many human activities and challenges, including criminal psychology (Agnew, 2006; Durkheim, 1951; Merton, 1957), post-traumatic stress disorder (PTSD) in combat veterans (Carbonell 2015), and business (Cruver, 2002).

Application

The avoidance of dual-life syndrome requires first a thorough understanding of your own values and those of the prospective employer.

The Fit of Personal Values and Organizational Culture

If the organization has a culture that is in fundamental conflict with your values, sooner or later you will be faced with a dilemma that requires you to change your values, change the organization, or leave. When someone is looking for employment, there are two basic questions that need to be answered: First, *Do I want to work in this industry?* And, if the answer is yes, then the second question is addressed: *Is this the company I want to work for?*

Answering the first question may be easy. For example, if you are a vegetarian, you may not wish to work in a meat-packing plant. If you are an adamant pacifist, the armaments industry may not be the place for you. The idea here is that you need to *believe in what you are doing.* The first compatibility has to be with the product—whether the product is goods or services. Intuition is supported by the research that tells us that people perform better doing what they enjoy. "If you love your job, you'll never work a day in your life," the old adage says.

Answering the second question may be more challenging. In every industry, there are good companies and not so good ones. Be careful, though—just because a firm is good at making a profit, that does not necessarily mean it is a good place to work. There are some firms that are very good at making a profit because profit is the only priority.

When you are interviewing for a job, remember that you are also interviewing the company. If there is not a cultural fit, then there might come a time when the incompatibilities become manifest and you are forced into either sacrificing your values, changing the organization, or resigning.

The initial step is for an individual to choose to work for a firm that espouses, demonstrates, and enforces values that match those of the individual. The six basic *hypernorms* of honesty, fairness, compassion, integrity, predictability, and responsibility (Berenbeim, 1999) might be a good place to start. The two-part question becomes what are *your* values and what values does the *firm* state, live, and enforce?

QUESTION: Which values do you consider so important that they are essential to your well-being, or perhaps to your very identity?

Finding the right fit involves knowing the prospective employer as well as knowing yourself. Take the time to conduct a personal inventory of your values and priorities. It works best if you make a specific list ranked from most important first.

Next, track your time. This is done to examine how you use the most precious resource you have, time. Rank the activities from most time spent first.

Third, compare the two lists. Ask yourself if you are *living your values.* The activities are not mutually exclusive, of course. In fact, the integration of your values with *all* aspects of your life is essential for a healthy psychoemotional life.

What Are the Priorities of the Firm?

Select a group of firms that produce a product that is in line with your values and that you believe are successful enough to provide a sufficient income for your needs. Eliminate firms from the list that have a bad history or reputation. Take the time to do the research. It can save years of misery, angst, and lost sleep. Narrow the list down to no more than three.

Communicate your goals clearly to the firm you finally select as the preferred employer. *During the interview, do not be afraid to ask the hard questions.* Remember that every firm will say they are very moral and have a commitment to ethical practices. Again, do the research. Read social media, look at profiles on professional sites. Search individuals in leadership positions. Most importantly, talk to people who worked there previously, if possible. Understand that former employees might not have an unbiased opinion.

Example Before and during the interview process, the representative tells you the firm has a firm commitment to diversity, equity, and inclusion. However, your research reveals past or pending lawsuits for hostile workplace environment, discrimination, or unfair practices.

Question: Does the firm live by the stated values?

Again, do the research. Are there pending lawsuits? Some companies seem unable to integrate mission, vision, and values in a way that creates and maintains a healthy organizational culture. Any statement of values becomes merely "words on the wall."

The Case—Reexamined

Arthur Andersen (AA) was considered by many to be the premier accounting firm in the world. The integrity of the founder is a matter of legend. He refused to "fudge" the numbers, and he would not budge from his opinion regardless of the monetary rewards at stake. Until its fall, Enron was one of AA's clients, when the accounting treatment provided by the partner in charge of the Enron account, David Duncan, was challenged by the partner in charge of quality control, Carl Bass. The CEO, Joe Berardino, instructed Duncan to bypass QC and send everything directly to him (USHECC 2002a 2002b). He approved Duncan's recommendations, and the rest is history. A firm almost 90 years in the making was gone.

J. Clifton Baxter was not interviewing for a job. He was a top-level executive for Enron. What strategies can be used to resolve a profound ethical dilemma for an individual in a decision-making position? The following section provides some models for ethical decision making.

Ethical Decision-Making Models and Their Applications

Cardijn (1982) developed the "See-Judge-Act" model of ethical decision making during his many decades in the development and application of liberation theology in Latin America. Sands (2018) documents the application of the "See-Judge-Act" model in Africa, documenting Nelson Mandela's praise of the Young Christian Workers (1995).

The emphasis on putting values into action is still an essential part of the Christian value system. The Roman Catholic Church is the largest Christian denomination according to World Atlas (Bada, 2018) with approximately 1.3 billion followers. In *Ex Corde Ecclesiae*, Pope Saint John Paul II outlined the essential nature of ethical behavior as sometimes necessarily confrontational: "…confronting the great problems of society and culture…" (¶13), and focusing on the human aspect of the situation: "It is essential that we be convinced of the ethical over the technical, the primacy of the person over things, of superiority of the spirit over matter" (¶18).

He also points out his understanding of the need for courage that is to be found by looking to the future: "…open to the promise of future achievements that will require courageous creativity and rigorous fidelity" (¶8). He explicitly states that institutions and individuals must "have the courage to speak uncomfortable truths which do not please public opinion, but which are necessary to safeguard the authentic good of society." (¶32).

He also builds a case for the current need for ethical leadership. Individuals "should be ready to shoulder society's heavier burdens…" (¶9). He emphasizes the necessity to integrate professional competence with wisdom (¶22) and to put values into action through a "…leadership of service" (¶24).

In the bigger picture, he enumerates multiple areas of opportunity for addressing.

> *serious contemporary problems* in areas such as the dignity of human life, the promotion of justice for all, the quality of personal and family life, the protection of nature, the search for peace and political stability, a more just sharing of the world's resources, and a new economic and political order that will better serve the human community at a national and international level. (¶32, emphasis in original)

Most of the above are areas that were applicable to Baxter's position, and the community may well have profited from his significant personal and professional influence.

Unlike the individual interviewing for a position with a firm, Baxter was a top-level executive at Enron. He was faced with the choice to either accept the status quo or attempt to change it. Following Festinger and Aronson (1960), to accept the status quo, Baxter would have had to change the way he perceived the situation (decide the deception was not that bad, or the bad was outweighed by the good being achieved) or change the situation (fix the financials or become a whistleblower). His suicide note implies he knew the situation was bad, and he was not able to rationalize it. It would have been impossible to fix the financials since the executives who were required to sign off on the financial statements were the ones perpetrating the fraud. The last option was to become a whistleblower. That would have meant the end of his career and very public humiliation for himself and his family. By committing suicide, he assured a large insurance payout for his family and avoiding the negative publicity. The biggest problem with the suicide solution is that it ignores the effect on others. Make no mistake—Baxter was financially adept. He knew the truth would come out eventually. He probably understood the devastating effect it would have on the share price. Also, he was almost certainly aware of the pressure tactics used by management to ensure employees had retirement portfolios loaded heavily with

Enron stock far beyond common sense and basic diversification strategies. When the fraud became known, all those retirement portfolios would lose value—which is exactly what happened. He protected his family with an insurance policy and allowed thousands of other families to suffer terrible losses.

Brooks and Dunn (2018) break down the components of ethical analysis into four principles: consequentialism, deontology, virtue ethics, and justice.

Consequentialism is based on teleology (the focus on end results)—essentially to try to do the most good (or the least harm) for the most people. In the corporate world, for example, consequentialism is characterized by cost/benefit analysis and risk assessment to make decisions. Deontology focuses on *duty*. Deontology is sometimes (mistakenly) used as a filtering mechanism to determine which individuals or groups should be included in the consideration of end results. Stakeholder analysis (Freeman 1983, AACSB 2004) is a method of ensuring that *all affected parties* are included in the decision-making process. Baxter did not include the effect on thousands of people holding Enron stock in his decision.

Virtue ethics involves an analysis of the virtues expected. Its origins go back to Aristotle's *Nicomachean Ethics* (trans. by Ross, 1999). Virtue ethics has as it focuses the moral character of the decision-maker and is, therefore, independent of the consequences on others or the motivation of the decision-maker. It is a purely subjective analytical methodology. It is based on the idea that the decision-maker, as a whole person, is made up of a unique set of virtues that act as a guide and as a set of mandates and constraints in the decision-making process.

Justice is a construct with which humankind has struggled since the dawn of history and still struggle today. Establishing an objective definition of justice is almost impossible. Most people, when asked to define justice, reply with a statement that includes the idea that people get what they deserve. When asked who decides what an individual deserves, most people have no reply. The two models of legal justice are distributive justice and procedural justice.

In Aristotle's *Nicomachean Ethics* (1999), he introduces the concept of *distributive justice*, wherein a convicted perpetrator of a crime who was of high status in society would pay less of a penalty than a person of low status who committed the same crime. The logic was that the infraction and its negative effects should be weighed against the positive effects of the individual's contributions to society. The result was that the rich consistently received light punishments, while the poor suffered much heavier penalties. This form of justice persisted well into the dark ages and the renaissance, only being challenged philosophically in the nineteenth century.

The result of the challenge was the advent of *procedural justice*, wherein the standardization of the process of the administration of justice dictated that all accused individuals were afforded fair and transparent procedures, regardless of physical attributes or economic status. The level of fairness could only be assessed with adequate transparency.

Ultimately, it seems to be the *perception* of justice that is the primary concern of society at large. In the USA, we put a great deal of effort into a system of procedural justice, including the requirements for search warrants, uniform rules of evidence, protections against self-incrimination, yet members of disenfranchised groups (e.g., people of color) are arrested, convicted, and given prison sentences that are multiples (or even orders of magnitude) greater than that of others.

It appears that the *goal* of procedural justice, as noble as it may be, is tainted and ultimately sabotaged by the human tendency toward distributive justice. In the end, afluenza was a viable defense.

Assuming Baxter understood the consequences of his actions, he placed his duty to his family above the interests of others. Many might say that is understandable. Some might even say his prioritization was right and proper. The problem is that he viewed his choice as a duty to his family versus his duty to the company while ignoring all the other stakeholders. Because of that, his decision was profoundly *unjust*—forcing others to pay the price for his inability display the courage required to address the problem at its root cause, exposing the fraud and becoming a whistleblower.

The earlier discussion of principles and codes may sound too theoretical to be relevant to everyday professional life, but in fact, these principles are the basis for many codes of conduct in the professional world. For example, Simms (2019) specifically mapped the mandates of *Ex Corde Ecclesiae* (ECE) to the Code of Ethical Conduct of the American Institute of Certified Public Accountants (2009, see Table 11.1). From ECE, the specific topics are self-awareness, individual values, morality, ethical behavior, continuing growth and learning, impartiality, commitment to the public good, courage, and ethical leadership, cultural diversity, wholeness of the person, and institutional compassion and philanthropy. The full textual mapping can be found in Simms (2019).

Simms (2019) also points out that the basic approach of Cardijn's See-Judge-Act model can be implemented as:

1. Identify the ethical issue;
2. Apply relevant and appropriate principles to analyze the situation and determine the options available to the decision-maker;
3. Take action to address the problem;

Clive Baxter was, by all accounts, a decent person. It seems apparent that he perceived the ethical issues he was facing at Enron. It can be assumed he deliberated on the various options available to him, one of which would have been becoming a whistleblower. The action he took of committing suicide addressed his personal problem but did not address the problem facing other stakeholders. In that sense, his solution failed in the third step because it did not address the *source* of the problem (i.e., Enron's fraudulent reporting), and it left others to suffer the consequences of the problem he did not address. One can speculate on the irony that Baxter may have thought he could avoid or delay a scandal at Enron by ending his own life, when it was his suicide that started the investigation.

Table 11.1 Ex Corde Ecclesiae/AICPA mapping key

Ex Corde Ecclesiae	AICPA/TSBPA	
Topic/paragraph	Part.Topic.Subtopic	Paragraph(s)
Individual values ¶16, 22	0.300.010 Preamble 0.300 Principles of professional conduct	(0.01)
	2.000.020 Ethical conflicts	(0.01)
Morality ¶20, 40	0.300.020 Responsibilities	(0.01)
Ethical behavior ¶13, 18, 23,	0.300.010 Preamble to 0.300 Principles of professional conduct	(0.02) (0.05)
	0.300.070 Scope and nature of services	(0.03)
	2.400.001 Acts discreditable rule	(0.01)
	2.400.005 Application of the conceptual framework for members in business and ethical conflicts	(0.03)
	2.400.010 Discrimination and harassment in employment practices	(0.01)
Continuing personal growth and learning ¶16, 22, 23, 36	0.300.060 Due care	(0.03) (0.04)
Impartiality ¶4, 7	0.300.040 Integrity	(0.01) (0.02) (0.03) (0.05)
	0.300.050 Objectivity and independence	(0.01) (0.02) (0.04)
	0.300.060 Due care	(0.01) (0.02)
	0.300.070 Scope and nature of services	
	0.400 Definitions	(0.21a) (0.21b)
	2.120.010 Offering or accepting gifts or entertainment	(0.04)
Public good ¶7, 12	0.300.010 Preamble to 0.300 Principles of professional conduct	(0.02)
	0.300.030 The public interest	(0.01) (02) (0.03) (0.04) 0.05)
	0.300.070 Scope and nature of services	(0.02)
Courage ¶8, 25, 32	2.170.010 Pressure to breach the rules	(0.02) (0.03)

(continued)

Table 11.1 (continued)

Ex Corde Ecclesiae	AICPA/TSBPA	
Topic/paragraph	Part.Topic.Subtopic	Paragraph(s)
	2.000.010 Conceptual framework for members in business	(0.06c) (0.07)
	2.000.020 Ethical conflicts	(0.03) (0.06)
Ethical leadership ¶9, 22, 24, 32, 33,	0.200.020 Application of the AICPA code	(0.04)
	0.100.010 Principles and rules of conduct	(0.02)
	0.200.020 Application of the AICPA code	(0.04)
The strength of cultural diversity ¶6, 21, 37, 44, 45		
The wholeness of the person ¶5, 21, 23, 34		
Institutional compassion and philanthropy ¶34		

Simms (2019). *Reprinted with permission of the author.*

Conclusion

This essay has presented the suicide of J. Clifford Baxter, formerly of Enron, as a study of the effects of cognitive dissonance as defined by Festinger (1957) and the resulting psychological strain as defined by Zhang et al. (2014). The essay also introduced and explored ways to avoid the trap of *dual-life syndrome.*

The key to avoiding *dual-life syndrome* and the associated cognitive dissonance leading to strain is to accept a single set of values for one's self and demonstrate these fundamental values as an expression of *who you are* as an individual rather than *what you do* in a given situation. The incompatibility between values derived from fundamental principles and the expectations that vary with changing situations can only be resolved through the *application* of values, instead of merely providing platitudes or rationalizations for decisions that are in opposition to the values that define us. In the case of conflict, the individual must change either the situation or his or her internal moral framework. It is ultimately up to the individual to take action that demonstrates a commitment to higher principles. Our personal values are flexible, individualized guides derived from higher, universal principles which are absolute. Ultimately, if your principles are negotiable, you do not have any.

The tragic suicide of Clive Baxter was avoidable, but to him, the alternatives presented by Festinger (1960) of changing either his actions or his values were not possible or unacceptable. He could no longer feel proud of the firm to which he had dedicated so much of his career—the firm that had become identified as a large part of who he felt he *was*. That sense of identification was fundamentally at odds with the person he felt he *should be*. Over time, it created such significant cognitive dissonance that the stress it created ultimately proved to be fatal.

We can control very little in our lives, but we *influence* and *are influenced* by everything and everyone, so we have the responsibility to set the right example and keep changing the world, even in small ways, because the lasting cumulative effect can be profound.

References

Agnew, R. (2006). General strain theory: Current status and directions for further research. In F. T. Cullen, J. P. Wright, & K. Blevins (Eds.), *Taking stock: The status of criminological theory-advances in criminological theory* (pp. 101–123). New Brunswick.

American Institute of Certified Public Accountants. (2009). *Ethics and Independence.* (Accessed 6/30/2021) at http://www.aicpa.org/interestareas/centerforauditquality/resources/caqauditlibrary/pages/ethics%20and%20independence.aspx.

Aristotle (trans. Ross, W.D.). (1999). *Nicomachean ethics.* Hamilton, Ontario, Canada, Batoche Books, available at Ethics.p65 (mcmaster.ca).

Aronson, E. (1997) The theory of cognitive dissonance: The evolution and vicissitudes of an idea. In C. McGarty, & A. Haslam (Eds.), *The message of social psychology: Perspectives on mind and society.* Blackwell Publishing.

Bada, F. (2018). Largest Christian denominations in the world. *World Atlas.* (accessed 6/30/2021 at Largest Christian Denominations in the World – WorldAtlas).

Beauvois, J.-L., & Joule, R.-V. (1982). Dissonance versus self-perception theories: A radical conception of Festinger's theory. *Journal of Social Psychology, 117*(1), 99–113. https://doi.org/10.1080/00224545.1982.9713412

Berenbeim, R. E. (1999). The conference board research report 1243–99–RR. In *Global corporate ethics practices: A developing consensus.*

Bussey, B. (2006). Family transformed: Religion, values, and society in American life. *Journal of Church and State, 48*(3), 706–707.

Cardijn, J. (1982). *La Pensée de Joseph Cardijn, va Libérer mon Peuple!* Vanbraekel Mouscron.

Cooper, J., & Croyle, R. T. (1984). Attitudes and attitude change. *Annual Review of Psychology, 35*, 395–426. https://doi.org/10.1146/annurev.ps.35.020184.002143

Coppola, F., Puzo, M., Ruddy, A. S. *The Godfather* (Motion Picture). Paramount.

Cruver, B. (2002). *Anatomy of greed: The unshredded truth from an enron insider.* Carroll & Graf. ISBN 0786710934.

Durkheim, E. (1951). *Suicide: A study in sociology.* Free Press (Original work published in 1897).

Festinger, L. (1957). *A theory of cognitive dissonance.* Stanford University Press. Festinger, L., & Aronson, E. (1960). *The arousal and reduction of dissonance in social contexts.*

Freeman, R. E., & Reed, D. L. (1983) Stockholders and stakeholders: A new perspective on corporate governance. *California Management Review,3*(25), 88–106. Accessed 7/2/2021 at www.jstor.org/stable/41165018.

Gibney, A. (2005). *Enron: The smartest guys in the room* (Motion picture). Independent.

Greenwald, A. G., & Ronis, D. L. (1978). Twenty years of cognitive dissonance: Case study of the evolution of a theory. *Psychological Review, 85*(1), 53–57. https://doi.org/10.1037/0033-295X.85.1.53

Pope John Paul II. (1993). *On Catholic Universities: Ex Corde Ecclesiae.* Publication No. 399-X, United States Catholic Conference, Washington, D.C. Libreria Editrice Vaticana, Vatican City.

Joule, R. (1986). Twenty five on: Yet another version of cognitive dissonance theory? *European Journal of Social Psychology, 16*(1), 65–78. https://doi.org/10.1002/ejsp.2420160111
Kohlberg, L. (1958). The development of modes of thinking and choices in years 10 to 16. Ph. D. Dissertation, University of Chicago.
Kohlberg, L. (1984). *The psychology of moral development: The nature and validity of moral stages* (Essays on Moral Development, Vol. 2). Harper & Row.
McLean, B., & Elkind, P. (2003). *The smartest guys in the room: The amazing rise and scandalous fall of enron.* Portfolio Trade ISBN: 978-1-59184-053-4
Merriam Webster Unabridged Dictionary. (2021). Accessed 7/3/2021 at www.merriam-webster.com.
Merton, R. K. (1957). *Social theory and social structure.* Free Press.
Miller, D. (2002). *A spiritual audit of corporate America.* Free Press.
OED Online. December 2020. Oxford University Press. http://www.oed.com/viewdictionaryentry/Entry/7179;jsessionid=61494FA30F6628009908C800D2210718. Accessed January 14, 2021.
Roccas, S. (2005). Religion and value systems. *Journal of Social Issues, 61*(4), 747–759.
Sands, J. (2018). Introducing cardinal Cardijn's See–Judge–Act as an interdisciplinary method to move theory into practice. *Religions, 9*(4), 129. https://doi.org/10.3390/rel9040129
Simms, J. (2019). Teaching accounting ethics using Ex Corde Ecclesiae. *Journal of Business Ethics Education, 16*, 191–212.
United States House Energy and Commerce Committee (USHECC). (2002a). *Andersen partner warned on enron in '99: Questioned Partnerships.* (reprinted in the *Financial Post,* 4/3/2002).
United States House Energy and Commerce Committee (USHECC). (2002b). *Andersen under fire over memos: Carl Bass Documents.* (reprinted in the *Financial Post,* 4/4/2002).
Zhang, J. (2005). Conceptualizing a strain theory of suicide (Review). *Chinese Mental Health Journal, 19*(11), 778–782.
Zhang, J., & Lester, D. (2008). Psychological tensions found in suicide notes: A test for the strain theory of suicide. *Archives of Suicide Research, 12*(1), 67–73.
Zhang, J., Dong, N., Delprino, R., & Zhou, L. (2009). Psychological strains found from in-depth interviews with 105 Chinese Rural Youth Suicides. *Archives of Suicide Research, 13*(2), 185–194.
Zhang, J., Lu, J., Zhao, S., Lamis, D., Li, N., Kong, Y., Jia, C., Zhou, L., & Ma, Z. (2014). Developing the Psychological Strain Scales (PSS): Reliability, validity, and preliminary hypothesis tests. *Social Indicators Research, 115*(1), 337–361. Springer. https://www.jstor.org/stable/24720229.

Chapter 12
Workplace Spirituality: Drivers, Challenges, and Way Forward

Shiv K. Tripathi and Ernst von Kimakowitz

Abstract In this chapter, we look at why are we excluding spirituality from the workplace and how we could work toward overcoming this counterproductive exclusion. We know that a vast majority of members of any business organization anywhere in the world have some spiritual or religious anchoring that they claim is important to their professional lives. However, we simultaneously build and operate those very organizations in ways that are excluding spirituality, and in consequence, depriving many members of the organization from something that is of great relevance to their personal well-being. It seems self-evident that it is not in the interest of the organization, as this will adversely affect employee engagement, leading to lower productivity, fewer innovations, or less collaborative aptitudes but also a whole bundle of behaviors which might be unfavorable to organizational performance. The main argument for taking deliberate measures to overcome this predicament is not instrumental but normative in nature. Not only tolerating but embracing people's need for spirituality at the workplace is the right thing to do. It is admitting something that is important to many of us that the corporate world demonstrates respect and appreciation for the intrinsic value of each member of the organization. In this chapter, we propose to elaborate on the above analysis by sharing some reflections on why spirituality is so often excluded from the workplace, and more importantly, what can be done to change that.

Keywords Business and spirituality · Workplace spirituality framework · Humanistic organizations · Ethics in practice

S. K. Tripathi (✉)
Atmiya University, Rajkot, India
e-mail: shiv.tripathi@atmiyauni.ac.in

E. von Kimakowitz
Humanistic Management Center, St. Gallen, Switzerland
e-mail: ernst.von.kimakowitz@humanisticmanagement.org; ernst.vonkimakowitz@unilu.ch

© Jindal Institute of Behavioral Sciences 2022

S. P. Sahni et al. (eds.), *Spirituality and Management*,
https://doi.org/10.1007/978-981-19-1025-8_12

Introduction

Recently, Bob Chapman reflected[1] how his organization responded to the business loss crisis created by global pandemic COVID-19. It was a good example of how businesses can serve to protect or enhance, even during adversities. Despite the great loss of revenue due to the pandemic, the company decided not to lay off its employees. Instead, the company collectively agreed to work for one month with no salary. Through the trust and collective action, together they faced it and came up with a solution that worked. This reminds another example from business history when Henry Ford, founder of Ford Motors, decided to increase the daily wages of his employees to 5$/day which was more than double the average wage rate in automobile industry in the USA at that time. When he was asked later about the rational for this unusual salary hike decision, Ford mentioned "…so that they could buy my cars" (Tripathi, 2021).

In both these examples, we see the "extra mile" approach by the leaders in the organization, which acts as catalyst to drive good. However, an important question emerges regarding what makes the leaders to act with the "extra mile" approach that will drive good? The workplace spirituality helps in strengthening orientation and passion toward good through commitment to continuous improvement in achieving the better and justified performance that will serve the different stakeholders in optimum manner.

While most of the modern organizations, irrespective of the context and nature, have to operate in the fast-changing VUCA (Volatile, Uncertain, Complex, and Ambiguous) business environment, the commitment to workplace spirituality can help significantly in generating effective responses even during the most challenging situations.

The post-pandemic world is all set to see the way businesses will continue to function. This could be due to the combined effect of pandemic as well as the available alternative business models. During the transition toward the new changing situation, the adverse impact of the change can be minimized by application of spirituality in the organizations. This is quite evident that the practice of workplace spirituality would not only help the leaders to understand and effectively respond to the forces in the business environment but will also be effective in developing an environment of collective care within the organizations.

Currently, most of the progressive organizations are realizing that the key to organizational success is in "employee wellbeing", which comprises many dimensions including social, psychological, spiritual, economic, and physical. The spiritual dimension helps in connecting all the other dimensions of spirituality in a holistic way. Spirituality helps in connecting individuals in the organizations at both psychological and social levels. It helps in improving the overall workplace environment

[1] Bob Chapman, Chairperson and CEO of Barry Wehmiller, in conversation with Ernst von Kimakowitz during Leadership Gold opening online event organized by Humanistic Management Network on 22 April 2021.

by emphasizing the commitment toward the "good", which is an important driver of spirituality in the organizations.

Therefore, in this chapter we would explore the different dimensions of workplace spirituality in detail. More specifically, we will answer the following questions:

1. What do we mean by workplace spirituality?
2. What are the drivers of workplace spirituality in any organization?
3. What are the challenges that limit the practice of workplace spirituality in modern organizational context?
4. How can the different challenges be overcome in promoting workplace spirituality?

We understand that performance of the organizations is a combined function of many factors; however, spirituality links these factors in a unique fashion, to produce the optimum performance in any given context. Despite understanding the potential and role of spirituality, the development of workplace spirituality relies mainly on ad hoc approaches, ranging from motivational lectures to workshops and Yoga camps. Some also try to link workplace spirituality with the religious values. It is important to understand here that the workplace spirituality, while drawing significant inputs from the religious values at an individual level, relies more on the collective organizational spirituality. Most of the workplace-linked spiritual values can be traced as common elements across the different religious traditions, as everyone appears to work and pray for good in one's own way, but with common considerations. After all, everyone is a part of a larger humanity with common goals of survival, growth, and achieving excellence.

Understanding Workplace Spirituality in Organizations

Research indicates that the extrinsic individual motivators have a limited life in terms of impact and, therefore, we must plan for a combination of such a motivation system, which will keep people in the organization aligned to the legitimate purpose for which the organization exists. People have both an inner and an outer life. If both are nourished in such a manner that inner life leads to satisfy the outer, it can produce more productive outcomes. By applying spiritual practices at workplace, both the inner and outer life can be balanced (Dandona, 2017). Spirituality can be a source of sustainable motivation; however, we need to understand what spirituality means in the context of workplace.

In the context of workplace, there is no general agreement on a uniform definition of spirituality. Different scholars have understood, analyzed and interpreted the workplace spirituality following certain dimensions they found important. Spiritual workplace can be considered as one enabling the individual's expression of an inner life, as reflected in meaningful work performance in the community (Ashmos & Duchon, 2000). Spirituality at workplace can be considered as a combination of integration with workplace; development of inner life; finding purpose and meaning in work;

and self-transcendence (Sheep, 2004). Workplace spirituality can also be described as "harmony of self with one's work, social and natural environment (Pandey & Gupta, 2008)." Some scholars link workplace spirituality to a state of internal satisfaction linked to transcendence (Giacalone & Jurkiewicz, 2010; Gotsis & Kortezi, 2008).

Based on the common elements in different evolving definitions of workplace spirituality, the following can be considered as some of the major characteristics:

1. Internal and linked to psychological processes of an individual (Internal);
2. Involves a sense of broader purpose (Purpose);
3. Includes an essential component of transcendence (Transcendence); and
4. Leads to satisfaction through integration with the organization and its purpose (Value Alignment).

Figure 12.1 presents these essential characteristics of workplace spirituality. Therefore, we follow this framework as a basis for defining and describing workplace spirituality in the chapter.

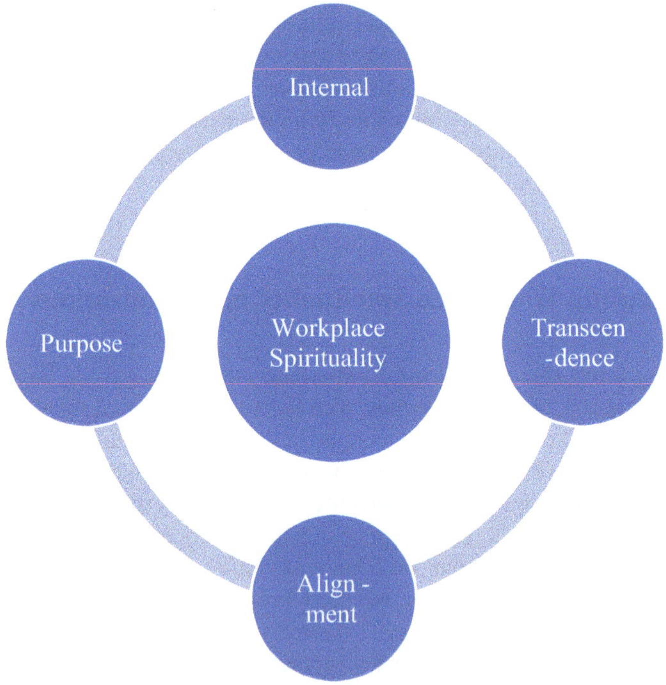

Fig. 12.1 Essential characteristics of workplace spirituality

Factors Driving Workplace Spirituality

There are a good number of studies on different aspects of workplace spirituality and its dimensions. However, it appears that there are significant gaps in terms of studies on what drives workplace spirituality in any given context. Workplace spirituality can be the result of a number of individual- or organization-related factors where one works. Fanggidae (2018) observes:

> Spirituality workplace can be viewed from two levels, namely; level individual, refers to the set of individual values that drive the transcendent experience through work processes…The organizational level refers to a framework of organizational cultural values that encourages the transcendent experience of employees through the process of working,...

Broadly, the two categories of factors, i.e., individual and organizational, can influence the spiritual orientation toward work. Organizations, being an open system, can also experience considerable influence of the different factors in its environment. We also understand that every organization experiences a different set of environmental influences depending on a number of contextual factors. For example, a non-profit organization in healthcare sector may influence completely different kind of spiritual influence than those for profit-seeking hospitality sector enterprise. These contextual factors can also influence significantly the internal environment of the organization. Therefore, in addition to individual- and organization-related factors, there are contextual factors also which can influence the workplace spirituality. Based on the observations and experience in analyzing an open system organization, some of the potential factors influencing workplace spirituality have been summarized in Fig. 12.2.

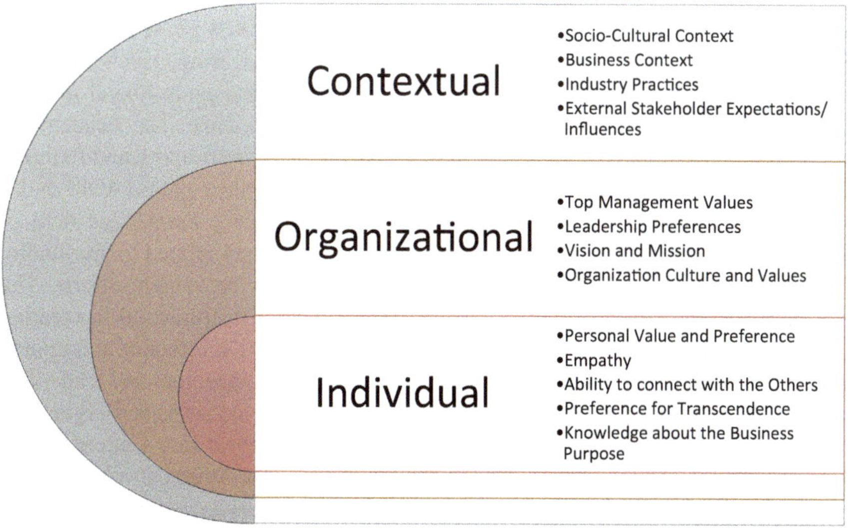

Fig. 12.2 Potential factors influencing workplace spirituality

The factors presented in Fig. 12.2 are quite generic and have been identified on the basis of different organizational analysis framework like the classical PESTEL analysis and Cultural Web (Jhonson & Scholes, 1999, p. 74). Contextual factors, including the cultural context, plays an important role in shaping the behavior of the individuals factors (Hofstede, 1984). Further, this is to be understood that these factors are not mutually exclusive, i.e., some of these factors may also influence in shaping the factors within the same category or other category. For example, the business context and external stakeholder's expectations may quite often interact. The socio-cultural context may also drive the individual values and orientation toward work. For example, in societies and communities with strong religious influences, chances are that the organizational and individual values would also be aligned accordingly. Sometimes, although not generalized, the religious values may significantly influence the spiritual orientation of an individual. However, it may also depend on a number of other related factors like one's personal preferences and experiences, practice of empathetic behavior reflective capacity, or level of mindfulness and life vision. At organizational level, the organizational culture plays an important role in shaping the workplace spirituality. As the culture in itself is a combined effect of a number of other factors, it becomes difficult to describe its formation and impact mechanism.

Workplace spirituality is the result of a number of factors and, therefore, assessing the effect of an individual factor in a given situation may not give precise finding. However, it is recommended that scholars in a specific context may explore the extent of spiritual orientation at the workplace as well as the influencing factors.

Challenges in Realizing Workplace Spirituality

Management is multi-disciplinary by nature. While the initial phase of the evolution of this subject witnessed more inclination toward engineering, psychology, and commerce, later the development in other disciplines like philosophy, liberal arts, and religion attracted the attention of scholars and practitioners alike. The Academy of Management had created a special group on Management, Spirituality and Religion (MSR) to promote scholarly interaction among interested participants (AOM, n.d.).

Despite the scholarly efforts in focused inter-disciplinary knowledge field of "Management and Spirituality," the knowledge and concepts related to spirituality do not appear to be part of mainstream organizational improvement efforts. The role of B-schools and universities, which are considered instrumental in creating and disseminating knowledge, have also not mainstreamed spirituality and related dimensions with focus on application in organizational management and leadership context. As the result, most of the emerging knowledge, debates, and arguments about workplace spirituality are not well organized and appear in a scattered form. Also, looking at a typical curriculum of Master of Business Administration (MBA) in top ranked universities globally, we hardly find any exclusive, dedicated, and core course on workplace spirituality. In some cases, the topic of spirituality is indirectly addressed while touching on other issues like ethics, ethos, morality, values, and humanism. This is quite evident that because of this knowledge development trend, the application of "workplace spirituality" often fails to receive the center stage in discussions on organizational improvement.

When we interacted on the issue of ethics, education, and workplace spirituality with number of senior researchers and faculty members at universities and B-schools across the world, they mostly highlighted that due to "low demand" from organizations as well as potential students, faculty members take interest on these issues only as a matter of personal choice rather as a part of organized institutional or department-level knowledge creation and dissemination efforts. The students are of the opinion that competencies in workplace spirituality do not promise a good job and career, and that their primary motive for studying in a business program is to ensure good job and placement.

Therefore, in any given context, the major challenges in extending workplace spirituality may include one or more of the following:

1. There is lack of student motivation to learn and develop competencies in the space of/context of workplace spirituality.
2. The learning material (like textbooks, references, case studies) in the subject is neither adequate nor well organized as in other business functions like marketing, finance, HR management, and strategy.
3. Organizations do not specify the need for competencies in workplace spirituality while recruiting or promoting executives.
4. The knowledge development and consulting opportunities in this focused area are not very rewarding for the faculty members. Due to this, only a few faculty members make efforts in this direction that too more as a matter of individual effort/ choice.
5. There are not many proven and recorded examples of workplace spirituality showing how it has helped in the performance improvement in the organizations.

Because of these challenging conditions, workplace spirituality has not been in the mainstream of management knowledge and practice in the organizations and/ or B-schools. Perhaps, this is one possible reason behind the unawareness of efforts in the area of workplace spirituality.

The current situation, as often reflected by many of the practitioners and scholars during formal/informal interactions in recent past, presents an indicative scenario of the ecosystem regarding knowledge and practice of workplace spirituality. Further, specific research is suggested to assess the situations as well the related factors in any given context.

A Framework for Promoting Workplace Spirituality

Workplace spirituality (WS) can help not only in improving the organizational performance but also in ensuring the individual well-being simultaneously. We have not tested this through any specific research study. However, based on observation and experience, we recommend that one may explore the possibility of strengthening WS orientation of employees in organizations. The results are likely to positively contribute to the performance and individual well-being.

In order to strengthen the WS orientation at workplace, the given five-step framework (Fig. 12.3) may be followed. However, this is without any recommendation regarding the likely results in terms of performance improvement. While it is strongly believed that the application of WP in organizations will yield better performance results, we recommend assessing and testing its applicability in the given organizational context.

In order to systematically strengthen the WS orientation, the process starts with context assessment and profiling. At this stage, it is important to understand the organizational context, individual employee/leader-related factors as well as the broader socio-cultural context where the organization exists. This is quite important to understand the potential willingness and preparedness to drive WS in the selected context. Once the profile is assessed, the next step is to prepare supporting learning material and evidences, confirming the potential of WS in improving one's contribution toward the organization without any stress or extra efforts. If needed, some "case research" activities may also be undertaken to develop the required material. This phase is the orientation/preparation phase, which also needs to be supported with

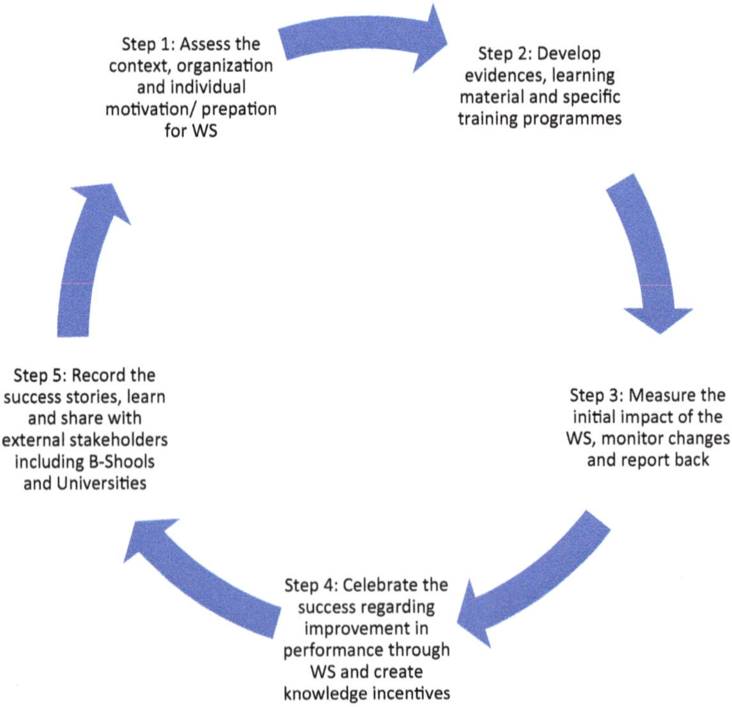

Step 1: Assess the context, organization and individual motivation/ prepation for WS
Step 2: Develop evidences, learning material and specific training programmes
Step 3: Measure the initial impact of the WS, monitor changes and report back
Step 4: Celebrate the success regarding improvement in performance through WS and create knowledge incentives
Step 5: Record the success stories, learn and share with external stakeholders including B-Shools and Universities

Fig. 12.3 Five-step approach for strengthening workplace spirituality

specific training and development interventions for systematic introduction of the WS in the workplace. Different types of activities should be planned for different groups/level of executive learners. Such activities may range from ethical consequence analysis to dilemmas and scenarios dealing with practical wisdom issues in management. Often it is observed that most of the "spirituality" programs are tailored in such a way that these interventions loose connect with the practical work context. While designing plans and programs, the ideal mode do's and don'ts may be avoided and real issues of decision-making and action may be more focused.

While preparing learning material and designing training interventions for integrating WS, it is important to understand the context, organization, and target groups. It is desired that the WS program in the organization should involve participation of all levels of leadership and functional staff, as it requires considerable orientation toward common ground for "empathy" and "dignity of life", irrespective of knowledge, experience, or hierarchy of participating individuals. Further, the feedback from initial training groups can be used for aligning organizational values and vision for future. It is important to understand that the WS is a paradigm of leadership and management rather than an approach for framework. Therefore, mainstreaming of WS would need considerable repeated interventions till it becomes part of the work culture.

The initial phase of WS program requires continuous monitoring and feedback. Once the training and development interventions have been introduced, it is required to monitor the initial impact of the program on the performance and internal work environment, including the employee's feelings about the change. All positive changes and experiences must be celebrated internally with more sustainable incentives, which will continue to motivate the team's commitment toward WS. At this stage, the tangible monetary incentives may not be very effective, and therefore, the knowledge about improvement can be used as an incentive.

Often, the measurements as well as program-based approach to promote WS may appear contradictory to nature of spirituality; however, in the proposed framework we combine the two different "planes" of spirituality and "program management," as in large organization settings it may be essential for optimized efforts.

Finally, based on the changes introduced, positive experiences can be documented and shared with external stakeholders including B-schools and universities. Knowledge sharing about the new experiences and positive changes must be shared with academic and research institutions, as it will help in knowledge development about relatively less popular issues like WS adaptation at workplaces.

The process, once introduced, starts working in a cyclic manner, continuously contributing to improvement through better aligned and WS-oriented employees. The framework is conceptual and generic, which can be customized as per the contextual need. In case of any identified evidence-based need for changes during the implementation, the same may be incorporated and shared for improvement.

Conclusion

The discussion regarding workplace spirituality has gained significance during last few decades. There is no standard agreement on a general definition of WS; however, in most of the academic works, some common characteristics have been found. The chapter identified the essential characteristics of WS, which include its internal nature, transcendence orientation, alignment with organization, and sense of broader purpose. It was found that organizational-, contextual-, and individual-related factors affect the WS in organizations. There are a number of challenges in mainstreaming the WS, as the concept is only less known but also not much tested through research. However, in view of the discussion in the chapter, a five-step generic model is proposed for the customized adaptation of WS in any given context.

References

AOM. (n.d.). Management, Spirituality and Religion Division, Academy of Management (Webpage). Retrieved https://msr.aom.org/home. 30 April 2021.

Ashmos D. P. & Duchon D. (2000). Spirituality at work: A conceptualization and measure. *Journal of Management Inquiry, 9*(2), 134–145 (cited by Dandona, 2017).

Bennett, N., & Lemoine, G. J. (2014). What VUCA really means for you, harvard business review online, Jan-Feb 2014. Retrieved https://hbr.org/2014/01/what-vuca-really-means-for-you. 29 April 2021.

Dandona, A. (2017). Spirituality at workplace. National Conference on Paradigm for Sustainable Business: People, Planet and Profit. Retrieved https://www.researchgate.net/publication/317066061_Spirituality_at_Workplace/citations. 30 April 2021.

Fanggidae, R. E. (2018). Organizational culture and spirituality workplace: Empirical study of influence of organizational culture and spirituality workplace. E3S Web of Conferences. https://doi.org/10.1051/e3sconf/20187311017

Giacalone, R. A., & Jurkiewicz, C. L. (2010), Toward a science of workplace spirituality. In R. A. Giacalone, & C. L. Jurkiewicz (Eds.), *Handbook of Workplace Spirituality and Organizational Performance* (2 ed., p. 360). Armonk, New York, United States of America: M.E. Sharp, Inc. (cited by Dandona, 2017).

Gotsis, G., & Kortezi, Z. (2008), Philosophical foundations of workplace spirituality: A critical approach. *Journal of Business Ethics, 78*(4), 575–600 (cited by Dandona, 2017).

Hofstede, G. H. (1984). Culture's consequences: International differences in work-related values (Abridged edition), Beverly Hills.

Johnson, G., & Scholes, K. (1999). *Exploring corporate strategy* (5th ed). Prentice Hall.

Pandey, A. (2017). Workplace spirituality: Themes, impact and research directions. *South Asian Journal of Human Resources Management, 4*(2), 1–6. SAGE Publications India. https://doi.org/10.1177/232209371773263. Retrieved https://www.researchgate.net/publication/320905289_Workplace_Spirituality_Themes_Impact_and_Research_Directions. 30 April 2021

Pandey, A., & Gupta, R. K. (2008). Spirituality in management: A review of contemporary and traditional thoughts and agenda for research. *Global Business Review, 9*(1), 65–83. Retrieved 12 September 2017, from https://doi.org/10.1177/097215090700900105 (cited by Pandey, 2017).

Sheep, M. L. (2004). Nailing down Gossamer: A valid measure of the person–organization fit of workplace spirituality. *Academy of Management Proceedings, 2004*(1), B1–B6. Retrieved 12 September 2017, from https://doi.org/10.5465/AMBPP.2004.13862520 (cited by Pandey, 2017).

Tripathi, S. K. (2021). Henry Ford's $5 a day wage to bob chapman's 1 month off: Inspiring lessons for shaping humanistic organizations. India CSR online (Posted 28th April 2021). Retrieved https://indiacsr.in/henry-fords-5-a-day-wage-to-bob-chapmans-1-month-off-inspiring-lessons-for-shaping-humanistic-organizations/. 30 April 2021.

Chapter 13
Corporate Management and Spirituality

Sangeeta Pandit

Abstract Philosophers and saints from all over the world have always discussed the dualism in us. We can all dwell in a higher consciousness and live in the normal consciousness. Higher consciousness is the ability to remain detached and be at peace with oneself. It could be described as trying to be spiritual. Normal consciousness is living our lives dictated by emotions, views, and attitudes. Our spiritual self and our worldly self are with us in our journey of life. If we dwell in higher consciousness while pursuing our economic activity and day-to-day mundane tasks, we conquer lust, anger, greed, attachment, pride, and jealousy. Business in today's volatility, uncertainty, complexity, ambiguity (VUCA) environment faces many changes—led by AI, blockchain, IoT, and the like. But basic laws of ethics and commonsense cannot change. For example, everyone in the value chain must be compensated equitably. Good corporate practices enable companies to grow in a sustainable way. A company failure is traumatic to all the stakeholders and has far-reaching impact. To manage the risk of failure, to ensure sustainability and profitability, one of the ways for the companies is to introduce spirituality. This chapter aims to explore what helps companies and their stakeholders to prosper and what does not; to understand the role of spirituality in corporate management; and to study the impact of spirituality on individuals, organizations, and the environment. Secondary data relating to stories of business success and failure are referred to achieve the objectives. Articles, books, and published papers on spirituality and corporate management are sourced. Primary data was obtained through questionnaires and interviews. The chapter concludes by asserting the big role that would be played by spirituality in business. The Fourth Industrial Revolution is ending. It is the dawn of the Fifth Industrial Revolution, Industry 5.0 where spirituality will be a must embed for businesses. Though corporate spirituality makes business sense, intent of spirituality in corporates must be self-actualization.

Keywords Spirituality · Consciousness · Corporate · Management

---

S. Pandit (✉)
Sydenham Institute of Management-SIMSREE, Mumbai, India
e-mail: sangeeta@pdkunte.com

© Jindal Institute of Behavioral Sciences 2022

S. P. Sahni et al. (eds.), *Spirituality and Management*,
https://doi.org/10.1007/978-981-19-1025-8_13

Introduction

1.1 Higher consciousness is the ability to remain detached, to accept joys, and sorrows with equanimity, to be at peace with oneself and in a state of bliss. This higher consciousness state can be achieved by meditation, introspection, constant pursuit of truth and understanding oneself and exploring the self. It could be described as trying to be spiritual. Normal consciousness is succumbing to emotions and being biased. We experience anger, anxiety, grief, joy, attachment, and ego. We oscillate between the two levels and by practice should be more in the higher consciousness. While there are big changes happening in the environment—AI, blockchain, IoT, the importance of triple P (People, Planet, Profit) bottom-line and ESG compliance is gathering importance. Everyone in the value chain must be compensated equitably. Good corporate practices enable companies to grow and be sustainable. Prudent decision making is critical, and for this to happen, one of the ways is that people in managerial positions need to be spiritually inclined, try to be in the higher conscious state. If people at the helm of affairs, the decision-makers are not in such a spiritual state of mind, the company's strategies and goals would be shortsighted and that would in the long run lead to poor performance. If most of the business houses are not enlightened enough, the economy will suffer. Ecology damage, rampant corruption, exploitation and abuse of power will only increase, and all this must be tackled before it is too late.

1.2 Corporate or Company form of organization facilitates economic growth. It is possible in the company model of business to raise capital, make investments and have large-scale level of operations. Companies—small-, medium-sized, or large-, all contribute to the well-being of the economy. Across the world, most of the GDP is contributed by the industrial and service sector. Companies or corporate sectors are much needed for any economy. Factors of production namely land, labor, capital and enterprise come together, and business stories are written. The wheels of trade and commerce are run in a professional manner bringing stability and growth. The limited liability concept helps in raising equity. Equity is comparatively a cheap source though the process of the public offer may be cumbersome and lengthy. Equity capital is permanent capital and dividend, unlike interest, is not a committed cash outflow. A company is a unique form of organization where ownership may be different from management, leading to unbiased working. Over a period, the various stakeholders get more and more dependent on a company. For vendors who supply raw materials and goods, the company is a critical associate. Shareholders, who have invested a portion of their portfolio in the company's shares, depend on the company for achieving their investment goals such as having a good retired life or funding their children's education. Mutual fund managers who have faith in the company have invested common man's money in it. Lenders need to be paid interest on time and be repaid their capital. The company has an onerous responsibility of not disappointing its investors. Employees have structured their life goals and way of life based on their salaries. Lay-offs and downsizing have a snowballing effect, impacting all those dependent on the employee. An ecosystem of distribution outlets is built around a company. Their prosperity is linked to that of the company. Government and society at large are benefitted by the growth and prosperity of a company.

1.3 Corporate governance is governing or managing a company as per a framework of guidelines, standard operating procedures, company policies, and statutes. The concept of corporate governance is much researched, debated, and evolved. The OECD report of 2004-titled "OECD Report of Corporate Governance" discusses issues in relation to people, process, purpose, and performance. People are the employees, customers, suppliers, investors, and lenders. Process is the method of manufacturing or trading or rendering service, extent, and nature of digitization, supply chain logistics, and flow of operations. Purpose is the goal, mission, and vision of the company on a broader perspective and in particular, of each entity involved with the company. If the destination is wrong, the path one chooses is obviously also wrong. Thus, clarity of Purpose is essential. Performance is each person, asset, or process delivering what is expected and not hindering or diluting the purpose of the organization. The reason for most companies that have failed is that of not adhering to corporate governance principles or poor management of the aforesaid 4 Ps of people, process, purpose, and performance.

1.4 The basis of growth, sustainability, and survival of a company is sound management. Management is all about planning, decision making, implementing, and controlling. Management functions are greatly influenced by the culture and leadership environment in the organization. Technology too plays a prominent role. Large companies have enterprise resource planning (ERP) systems and are bound by the software. Standardization, technology, embedded systems and processes contribute to transparency, efficiency, and good corporate practices. However, the most important feature is the personal attitude and value system of the people managing the company. Research has proved that people managing a company, particularly the decision makers, need to be matured and balanced. They need to have a high emotional quotient (Salovey & Myer, 1990). They cannot succumb to negative emotions like greed and fear and must be stoic and far-sighted in looking at issues. Spirituality is one way to enable good governance and prevent business failures. Spirituality in corporate management makes business sense.

1.5 The First Industrial Revolution of 1765 is remembered for the introduction of the steam engine, coal mining, and spinning machines. It brought about industrialization of agrarian economies. The complexion of business radically changed. The Second Industrial Revolution of 1870 saw the discovery of electricity and exploration of fuel sources. We witnessed the advent of cars, airplanes, telegraph, and telephone. With mass production and improved communication, businesses flourished and achieved significant scalability. The Third Industrial Revolution of 1969 saw the growth of nuclear power and electronics. Computers stormed the world. Speed, cost efficiency, and quality improved in business operations. The Fourth Industrial Revolution is said to have commenced around 2011 and is called the digital transformation revolution. Internet, cloud technology, artificial intelligence, and blockchain became part of business. The virtual world and real-world merging have made science fiction stories a reality. Data became the new wealth and decision making improved due to better data and evidence. Despite aggressive use of technology, the importance of human contribution has not, however, lost relevance. People with high emotional quotient, leadership skills, and those adept at human relations are much sought after. Now we are at the cusp of Industry 5.0 or the Fifth Industrial Revolution of Spirituality in Management.

1.6 Company failure can be extremely traumatic to all stakeholders. Companies are supposed to be perpetual. There could be change in ownership, but liquidation or death of a company causes great trauma. To facilitate change in ownership of defaulting companies, The Insolvency and Bankruptcy Code (IBC) was enacted in India in 2016. To mitigate the undesirable consequences of company insolvency and subsequent liquidation, corporate governance is needed that balances interest of all stakeholders. For effective corporate governance, spirituality is needed.

Need for This Study

Laws are constantly amended or enacted due to fraudulent or erroneous corporate practices that have caused grief to people. Yet, business failures continue to happen, whether due to fraud or misgovernance. This research endeavors to find a way to reduce business failures primarily caused by bad management; to understand the impact of adopting spirituality in business; to understand the role of spirituality in corporate success; to assess the impact of Spirituality on the well-being of the employees, investors, and different stakeholders.

Literature Review

Goal Congruence and Agency Issue in Corporate Management

Goals and aspirations of employees/subordinates are often different from those of the bosses/owners of an organization. This is the issue of goal congruence. Shareholders cannot take part actively in the management of their company, it is managed by the Board of Directors and a hierarchy of managers. They become the agents of the shareholders, their decisions cannot always be what shareholders would want, this is the agency issue.

Bouillon et al. (2006) have discussed the benefit of goal congruence and its importance in Management Control Systems. The authors have referred to agency theory (shareholders are principal, and management is agent) and stewardship theory (management serve and care for stakeholders). Alignment of divergent interests is explained. Goals of subordinates, managers, and of the organization are not the same but effective leadership must try to bring them together. Clarity of communication is very necessary; it can bridge the gap between organization goals and those of employees.

Colbert et al. (2008) have described the need of transformational leadership. According to them, leaders must display four basic characteristics of transformational leadership namely, adopting behavior that begets trust; good communication that motivates; creating an environment conducive to change and growth; and understanding the aspirations and needs of people. This could lead to better goal congruence.

Suwaldiman (2004) in his article on goal congruence has emphasized the need for humanitarian approach. Participative management, reward systems, willingness to listen, and climate of transparency to enhance employee commitment and better alignment of employee goals with company's goals.

Cuguero and Rosanas (2012) have explained the complexities in designing management control systems that achieve goal congruence. They have explained the concepts of fairness, justice, subjectivity, objectivity, and goal congruence. Execution must be done in fairness. Systems, whether relating to outcomes, procedures, or communication must be just. Informal management control system can also be implemented to improve goal congruence.

Jensen and Meckling (1976) called a publicly held company as an awesome social invention. People voluntarily invest their money in companies and have no right over it. Investors get disappointed when the management does not use the funds in the desired way. Agency costs are incurred when management (agent) does not manage the affairs of the company in the best interests of the shareholders (principal) to maximize value. Contracts and statutes, controls and monitoring may reduce the agency costs, but they will always exist.

Boshkoska (2015) has described ways to solve the agency problem. There is no one way or perfect answer to the problem. Focusing on internal measures like audit, remuneration, and governance can help. Also, external measures like external audit, laws, and capital markets can facilitate the reduction of agency costs.

Goal congruence can be summarized as difficult to achieve but feasible. With proper strategy, policies, and good leadership, employees in pursuit of their personal goals can also achieve organization's goals.

Agency issue can be tackled by adopting apt policies and procedures and a framework to ensure compliance to them. Also, systems ensure regulatory compliance.

Good Corporate Practices

Heskett et al. (1994) have written a paper on the healthcare sector. Their findings are that what matters is the outcome of a customer purchase and not what was purchased. The outcome must be positive.

Lepner (2017) in his article has discussed performance issues. Often employees' bad performance is not a reflection of their inadequate skill sets. Instead of sending them for training, companies must relook for snags in the processes, resources, and communication channels. He has discussed the mistake of considering repeated information as factual. Often, unnecessary cause and effect relationship is drawn between unconnected events.

Borate (2020) in his article in Mint newspaper has discussed investing in companies based on environmental, social, and governance (ESG) parameters, companies that adhere to corporate governance. Such investments by default become sustainable investments. There are today ESG mutual funds who will not invest in companies that cause pollution, do not follow the labor laws or safety precautions. Globally and in India, such mutual funds are becoming popular. As on October 2020, in India, the ESG index outperformed the Nifty.

Bhal (2015) writes of his experience when he was on an assignment with Boston Consulting Group (BCG). He had to interact with over 500 Sikh truckers. He learnt that in the 1984 riots, many of them lost their homes and trucks. In that dark hour, Tata Motors gifted them a brand-new truck. For these people, this was a ray of hope for better times and gradually, normalcy returned to their lives. These truckers, their family, friends, and future generations will always be loyal to Tata Motors.

It can be concluded that while taking decisions there will always be a conflict as some decisions may not be good for the bottom line. An evolved management will always take prudent decisions that contribute to the long-term survival, growth, and reputation of the company.

Books on Spirituality at Workplace

Lambert III (2011) in Chap. 2 of his book on corporate spirituality has explored its genealogy. He refers to the old Greek word of household from which the three words—economy, ecology, and ecumenical are derived. The household or home was the center of economic activity, and all members shared the same beliefs and traditions. The development today is to make the workplace akin to what a household was in old times. The author has described how the meaning of work itself has changed from the middle ages to the Industrial era. He has described the medieval period, craftsmen labeled as blacksmiths and potters and so on. Even in Biblical times, Jesus is referred to as a carpenter and Peter as a fisherman. This craftsmen classification led to the formation of guilds. Each guild had its own code of conduct and its own patron saint too. Work and spirituality merged. In early Industrialization era, a subcontracting system emerged. But later, workers doing different jobs were brought under one roof. Mechanization and standardization reduced the need for creativity and intellectual contribution. The author has referred to the experiments of Taylor on coal workers in Pennsylvania that made standardization popular. Ford introduced the concept of assembly line. Workers had to do only routine work that did not need much thought. Taylorism and Fordism destroyed individuality and pursuit of spiritual growth. Slums developed near workplaces. Then came the age of welfare capitalism, where industrialists like Pullman and Gastonia built townships with all facilities. Behavioral Sciences started gaining foothold. Human Resource or Personnel departments started in companies. They used industrial psychology to motivate workers and to prevent unrest. Concepts of Corporate Culture and Corporate Conscience emerged.

Fry and Nisiewicz (2012) in Chap. 2 of their treatise about the "*triple bottom line*" and spiritual leadership have discussed the spiritual leadership model. They have discussed the case study of Norman who was a very successful entrepreneur. In his youth, he was a total failure but by turning spiritual and making his company also spiritually inclined, he became successful. The authors have described the need for people to find meaning and purpose of their work, how leadership should be able to motivate, help in making others visualize a better future, build an ethical culture and give the organization a roadmap. Extrinsic motivation is addressing a person's lower end needs like money and reward. It is the intrinsic motivation, which is essential where work becomes the reward.

Research Papers on Spirituality at Workplace

Majeed et al. (2018) have explored the meaning of individual level, group level, and corporate level spirituality in their paper. They have discussed dimensions of workplace spirituality; meaningful work for employees; sense of community; how religion has no place in workplace; role of spirituality in leadership, reducing deviant workplace behavior and organization citizenship. Corporate spirituality could be perceived as that of nurturing the spirit and feelings of workers. It is all about building a work climate that makes people adaptable, assured, and productive. Workplace spirituality reaps dual benefits—the people as well as the companies prosper.

Friedman and Friedman (2014) in their paper have discussed how spirituality or value education must be part of college curriculum. Spirituality is not religion. The spiritual way of life is evoking a lot of interest and people are realizing its power. The financial crisis of 2008, Enron and other scams have reiterated the need of corporate spirituality. Spiritual values include making work meaningful, respect for the creativity of employees, and improving the world. The authors also present case histories of firms that have incorporated spiritual values into the way they conduct business.

Reave (2005) in his paper states that spirituality can give us insight on what can motivate leaders as well as followers. Spiritual values like honesty, integrity, humility form the base for successful leaders. The measurable outcomes should be studied, and certain quantitative bars should be set for the organization to implement spirituality. Motivational tools should be used wisely and not to control employees. Results should be studied with respect to employee satisfaction and their involvement in organization after the implementation of spiritual values in the organization. Instead of imposing spiritual values, it is better to draw on values from the employees. Behavior should be coupled with character.

Fernando and Jackson (2006) in their paper have discussed how the outcome of a decision can be improved after deep introspection. Normally, the response is then the correct way of handling a situation. Implementation of spirituality should be done not only to reap economic benefits but also for the overall development of organization. Religion-based spirituality is practiced by leaders. In difficult times, it helps to connect with a stronger force to be less tensed and troubled. The authors took interviews of 13 leaders of Sri Lanka who admitted being religious and said that praying or connecting to God helps. Such practices do not create divisive culture but help in better decision making. During demanding times, some form of prayer helps to bring solace and hope.

Subramaniam and Natarajan (2013) in their paper, after collecting responses from 70 employees of a bank concluded that employees must be empowered to speak freely. They must be able to achieve work–life balance. They must adopt a spiritual attitude to increase work satisfaction. Leadership should be proactive to usher in spirit of Spirituality at the workplace. Art of living talks about how yoga and meditation could be made a part of bank's training sessions. The leadership should show concern for employees also and not only focus on their material contribution. Spirituality helps to find meaning to the work and the organization's vision. Spirituality can boost morale and reduce stress.

Geh and Tan (2009) in their paper have traced the history of spirituality at the workplace. They have explored the nexus between spirituality and positive outcomes at individual and organization levels. They have described the changes in the work environment and evolution of management thoughts in response to the changes. Their conclusion is that the time has come for introducing spirituality at the workplace. That is the way to move forward.

Application of Spirituality for Success and Self-growth

Dalal (2016), in Chap. 4 of his book, Gita for Professionals, has listed thirteen lessons from Gita, that can be inculcated in our lives for success in career: choice of apt words; habit of sharing; spirit of friendship; ability to sacrifice short-term gains to comply with ethics and goodness; goal setting; creating value addition, discipline; power of forgiveness; harmony in thoughts, words, and actions; attitude of service; being humble; being compassionate and conducting oneself in such a way that does not cause guilt. With stories and examples, he has illustrated how this 13-point-framework can help us be better performers and achieve more. He has described how speech should bring a smile to the other person it should not hurt. Expectations are the cause of a lot of misery and disappointment. We must stop expecting and start sharing and giving. The feeling of brotherhood or sisterhood is necessary. Having a goal or some clarity as to how you want to navigate your life helps. The primary goal must be to be hardworking, professional, competent, and perseverant while earning money could be the secondary goal. One must always ensure contribution; one must add value by one's work. Self-control and self-regulation must be practiced. Mental and physical cleanliness is essential. Forgiveness helps. Thoughts, words, and actions must be congruent.

Tips to Be at a Higher Consciousness

Scott Peck (1978) divides his book—"The Road less Traveled" into four sections, namely discipline, love, growth and religion, and grace. He refers to the art of balancing, the way one needs to develop the much-needed discipline. The lower center of the brain contains the emotion of anger, and the higher center of our brain judges the reason(s) for the anger. We should be able to allow our judgment to control the anger, and then our response system would be flexible to respond as per the situation. We need to understand when to give up. Confrontation should not lead to confusion but enlightenment. He has discussed the scientific tunnel vision—scientists relying only on measurable happenings and ignoring those that are not measurable and rejecting intangibles. Also, what is not known is perhaps not worth studying, which is another fallacy. But gradually with advancement in tools, techniques, statistics, hardware, and software, immeasurable parameters are getting evaluated. In the fourth and last part titled Grace, he has discussed the Alpha (beginning) and Omega (end). We must continuously strive for perfection; we are the beginning and the end.

Scot's book highlights how company failures that traumatized stakeholders financially and emotionally could have been avoided if management had taken decisions when they were in higher consciousness. History is replete with such examples of company failure, Enron, Kingfisher airlines, Lehman Brothers to name a few.

Ways to Manage Oneself and Others

Vaswani (2003) in his book—"A Little Book of Life" writes about anger. He advises to burn anger, before anger burns you. Anger is a fire that burns the qualities that make you a wonderful person. He has referred to Thomas Jefferson's theory—when you are angry, count till ten before speaking and when you are very angry, count till hundred. He has referred to the words of Reinhold Niebuhr: "God grant me the serenity to accept the things I cannot change; the courage to change the things I can;

and the wisdom to know the difference. We must be far-sighted and adapt to changing times."

Budhananda (1998), in his book on character building, has referred to Confucius—"One who is not a true man cannot long stand poverty nor can he stand prosperity for long." Poverty brutalizes, and affluence barbarizes man without enough character. With enough character, our corporate bodies will work like single organisms. Character in good part is conduct. You must become better than yourself. Aim for the absence of anger, excessive elation, unnecessary indignation, avarice, delusion, enmity, and cruelty. Work toward speaking truth, moderation in eating, refraining from exposing others' weak points, freedom from jealousy, sharing one's good things with others, straightforwardness, gentleness, quietude, self-control, and contentment.

Swami Nikhilananda (2001), in his translation of Mahendranath Gupta's work in Bengali about Sri Ramakrishna's teachings has discussed a man's three states of consciousness: waking, dreaming, and deep sleep. One must go beyond the gross, subtle and casual, beyond sattva (light), rajas (motion), and tamas (inertia). One must become one with oneself. Identification of soul with body creates dilemma. One must rid of one's ego by following either the path of reasoning or worship.

The book titled "Message of Gita" (2012) gives Mahatma Gandhi's interpretation of Gita. Mahatma Gandhi has explained how mind must be brought under control. One must observe yama and niyama (rules and discipline of good conduct) with the help of pranayama, asana (proper breathing and yoga). Listening, meditation, analyzing, concentration, and not being obsessed with the results of actions could help a lot.

The book, Karmyogi Swami Vivekanand (2012) reproduces Swami Vivekanand's address given at the Parliament of World Religions at Chicago, USA, on September 11, 1893. Vivekananda spoke on how rivers have different courses and all end in the ocean. Similarly, men may choose different religions, but the goal is the same. A seed uses water, soil, and sunlight and becomes a plant and not water or soil or sunlight. In the same way, each religion can assimilate the spirit of the other yet remain independent. What is important is to help instead of fight; assimilate, not destroy; and work for harmony and peace, not dissension.

Discussion on Variables Identified from the Literature Review

Goal Congruence is when all in a company work in harmony for the achievement of the same goal. In reality, employees and employer have conflicting goals. Team members, managers, and the company have different aims, and hence, attitudes and value systems of the three entities are in conflict. The challenge is to develop strategies and processes so that each one in pursuit of his or her personal goal also works toward the organization's goal.

Agency issue occurs when management, who is the agent, takes decisions, which may not be in the interest of the shareholders, who is the principal. Shareholders are primarily concerned about dividend pay-outs, bonus and rights issues and capital appreciation of their shareholding. Management may not be focused on these issues. This is called agency costs. Such costs can be reduced by internal policies, controls, and by statute.

Good corporate practices include transparency, ethics, preservation of ecology, being fair and compassionate to employees, motivating HR policies, and compliance with all regulatory requirements. Focusing solely on profits, at the expense of corporate governance could be detrimental in the long run. Happy customer experience is essential. The top management must introspect as to the gaps in their interpretation and understanding of internal and external factors, rather than blame employees for bad performance. Image building by just advertising one's good deeds sometimes backfires. Corporate governance is a slow genuine process of giving value to your stakeholders. Long ago, before ESG became an international buzzword and India passed a law recommending 2% of net profits to be used by companies for CSR, the Tata group in India was already investing in building communities. The fact that the Tata group, which entered the industrial sector way back in 1907 is still going strong, is evidence that following ESG guidelines make business sense.

In the olden days, a household was an economic unit by itself. Today, this concept applies to a corporate entity. Everyone involved with the company must work in harmony. Motivation should be such that employees are energized and happy to work. Spirituality in companies must be introduced, not with the objective of economic gains but for the wholesome well-being of all. Spirituality is not a religion, it should not, in any way impose any beliefs or customs or rituals or way of thinking. Each employee must have the self-respect and freedom to adopt his/her thought process that gets aligned to that of the company. The company needs to adopt spirituality, work toward employees achieving self-actualization and not treat them as robots churning profits.

The concept of spirituality can be construed from the holy books. Spirituality at work is good speech, philosophy of sharing, friendship, sacrifice, having purpose, willingness to contribute, to be able to serve, being disciplined, humble, compassionate, having ability to forgive, developing habit of neatness and removing clutter in physical and mental space. Thoughts, words, and actions must work together.

Anger cannot be avoided. It must be managed. We must develop a flexible system to express it as the situation demands. Confrontation too is inevitable. But we must be able to communicate it in such a way that it solves the issue without losing time and causing hurt. We must develop the prudence to know when to stop or else we lose what we have gained. We should be able to accept new thoughts and way of work and not have a tunnel vision. We must strive to reach to our inner self and understand we are the beginning and end of everything.

One must practice acceptance, ability to move forward, and not succumb to anger that destroys. Character building is important. It is only with building of character that organizations work well. One must be able to go beyond base issues and be at peace with oneself. One must learn to control mind. Aim must be harmony and not discord.

Table 13.1 Table of variables

Independent variable	Dependent variable	Moderating variable
Corporate growth and spirituality	Achieving goal congruence	Apt strategies and process or processes?
Value to investors	Reduction of agency costs	Controls and compliance
Well-being of all stakeholders and company's branding	Good corporate practices	Long-term vision and not merely focused on profits
Self-actualization of employees	Corporate spirituality	Not to be confused with religion
Concept of spirituality at workplace	Individuals imbibing good habits, value system, and attitudes	Practice and discipline
Character building	Acceptance, conquering anger, and not having ego	Mind control

Table of variables is constructed to help better collection of primary data (Table 13.1).

Research Methodology

Based on the identified variables and issues that need further study, questionnaire and interview questions were designed.

Questionnaire method was adopted to collect primary data from employees working in middle and lower management positions across seven companies having turnover of more than $700 million. It was a random sample of 300. The questions were asked to understand the expectations of employees from company leadership, their woes, and what keeps them motivated. The respondents had to share their perception of employer's goals, their goals, good practices they appreciated, and issues that they felt need to be solved. 60% of the sample were in the age group of 35 to 55, 20% were above 55 years, and 20% were below 35 years. 20% were females and 80% were males.

Interviews were taken of 50 people in leadership positions at the top level of management handling the helm of affairs. There were 40 males and 10 females. The questions elicited responses of their value system, guiding principles, and their way of creating a positive culture. Conversations with them were to understand their expectations from employees, pain points in managing their company and parameters they considered while taking decisions. The sample of 50 people was fairly represented by all the three sectors of manufacturing, trading, and service.

Interviews were taken of 15 ace equity analysts, 5 were consultants, and 10 working in financial intermediaries. The extent to which they depend on the qualitative factors was probed. They were unstructured interviews and involved repeated conversations to understand the parameters they considered important while doing their analysis.

Excel tools were used to analyze the responses of the questionnaires and interviews.

Findings and Conclusions

The responses of the questionnaire sent to employees can be summarized as below:

5.1 Employees are attracted by high salaries. But it is the qualitative factors which were identified, as stated below, that stem attrition rate and make them loyal to an organization. These factors improve their productivity, encourage creativity, and motivate them to work more than expected.

a. Appreciation: if not appreciated, they feel hurt and are demotivated.
b. Responsibility: Only delegation of work without authority to take decisions is very demeaning and erodes self-esteem.
c. Clarity in Communication: There is no access to top bosses, hierarchy levels are too many. Somehow, a few individuals have direct access and others must access bosses through them. These people, with direct access, are popularly referred in India as *chamchas* or *chelas* (stooges). They could manipulate communication. It is the top bosses who encourage stooges for their positive self-image many a times. A lack of clear communication is extremely frustrating.
d. Inflexibility in Systems: Changes are constantly happening in the external environment. For example, natural disaster may lead to temporary shortage of essentials or rising prices. Train or bus services get disrupted. Any negative news of the company impacts employee standing in society. At a personal level, there may be death or sickness in an employee's home. The company is not sensitive to these changes and employees feel betrayed. Systems must adjust to changes by nimble leadership, taking into consideration delicate sensitivities of staff.
e. Performance Yard Stick: Quantitative measures like profit figures or hours clocked in or number of contracts signed are considered. However, ideas or suggestions by employees are not considered. The same may have been implemented and resulted in improving speed, or quality or efficiency. This discourages "out of box" thinking. Such challenges have to be met fairly and squarely.
f. Outstanding Performers are not Properly Identified: Managements stress on quantitative facts but the above-cited qualitative factors do matter. When all the employees are perceived as one common group, then the outstanding ones, who make a difference to the company's image as well as profits are disappointed and either leave or underperform. Outstanding work needs to be appreciated and rewarded.

g. Compassion and Caring Attitude: The traditional method of controlling people through fear of a scolding that shames, salary cut, demotion, or even dismissal are no longer effective. With the boom in communication, travel opportunities, access to education and information, people are empowered and cannot be subjugated.
h. Perception that Employees' Matter: If company meetings, communication, and discussions have little or no mention of employee contribution or well-being, employees feel let down by the management with whom they have worked so long. Such situations should at best be avoided.

5.2 The responses from people in leadership positions could be summarized as below:

a. There is no generic style of leadership. It must emerge with the changing situation. Leadership style cannot be static, and every situation needs a different approach. (The same is supported by the Blanchard and Hershey's Situational Leadership Theory and Fiedler's Contingency Theory.)
b. Leaders must have the prudence to guide as to which jobs: (i) are best done individually and which should be done by teams; (ii) need to be controlled and which should be given freedom; (iii) need creativity and which should be done in a pre-determined manner; (iv) must have deadline and for ones setting the deadlines would hamper quality.
c. Managers must be focused. The vision and goal must be clear. Their opinion of subordinates should not be influenced by gossip or just out-of-context information.
d. Managers must be stoic and not swayed to take decisions that are not good for the company. Must think long term and not be tempted to attract short-term popularity and media appreciation. Must not succumb to fear and have knee-jerk reactions to crisis. Most of them kept themselves de stressed and tried to be unbiased by engaging in some activity or the other. The activities ranged from playing games to yoga, meditation, and hobbies like dancing, painting, reading, and music.
e. Proactive leadership works better rather than reacting to a happening. Prevention is always better than cure. External and internal dynamics keep changing, so leaders must keep abreast and accordingly take apt decisions.
f. Diversity must be ensured. A good mix of males and females, different age groups, people from different regions, languages and even economic background helps. Issues are looked at from different views which result in creative solutions and leads to better performance and profits.
g. Managers must appreciate when to take a compassionate stand and when to be aggressive. The end result should be that the employee is motivated to work better.
h. Managers have the responsibility to motivate and create a positive culture so that employees can reach their potential and feel a sense of belonging.

5.3 Responses of equity analysts are summarized as below:

a. Careful study of a Company's background and history is a must.
b. Present and future demand for the company's products/services is to be assessed.
c. Financial statement analysis, involving ratio analysis, trends, working out the important measures—Altman Score (formula for predicting bankruptcy), Piotroski F-score (score used to quantify financial strength), cash flow statements, and Valuation of company/shares should be done.
d. Emphasis is exercised on the Notes to Accounts that reveal if a company is ESG compliant, their performance of CSR activities, worker policies, and compliance of labor laws. Composition of Board of Directors and assessing their collective attitude toward Corporate Governance.
e. Risk management policy, disaster management, and Prevention of Sexual Harassment (POSH) guidelines. Also, Whistle-Blowers policy—the person disclosing a major lapse must be protected from the wrath of those in power.
f. Quantitative analysis is done with the help of various tools and techniques driven by software. Human intervention in quantitative analysis is only to the extent of data entry, which is further simplified by various tools available.
g. All the respondents agreed that the skills needed by analysts today is reading beyond the figures, like, (i) to connect the reflection of good governance on performance, (ii) gauging strength of balance sheet due to ethics and long-term vision, (iii) profitability due to employee commitment, and (iv) impact of culture and leadership on financial performance.
h. Analyst's recommendations are used by private equity entities, hedge fund investment managers, asset management companies of mutual funds, wealth managers rendering portfolio management services, and retail investors. They are also referred to by consultants, investment managers, and others. The trend with analysts is to evaluate for long-term survival, growth potential, and value addition to net worth. The analysts explore avoidable company failures, red flags like taking of loans more than the company's ability; capital investments that do not yield adequate cash flows; poor cash management; customers defaulting on payment; vendors offering suboptimal supply quality or credit terms; and the weak reputation of promoters and top management in their compliance standards. Most of these failures stem from weak ethical standards. A company is looked at favorably when they: address investor grievances well; they are efficient in fuel consumption; invest in employees; conduct research activities; dispose of hazardous materials properly; plant trees; and do water conservation. These findings support the set guidelines followed by credit rating agencies and parameters investigated by pension funds before investing in companies. It also describes the features of a well-managed company that can boost the well-being of all stakeholders. It highlights the

importance of good corporate practices that can be followed by adopting spirituality in corporate management.

Conclusion

We are entering the Fifth Industrial Revolution of spirituality in corporate management. Each individual working for the company must strive for self-actualization. Constant introspection and self-discipline will usher in peace and harmony at workplace. It will reduce stress and friction and create a happy atmosphere. Spirituality in the form of caring, helpful, forgiving, and compassionate attitude will be a positive resource for the organization. For this change to happen, enlightened management needs to take steps to help people strive toward self-actualization. It can be done by providing physical space to reflect; training on how to introspect, meditate, understand oneself; and the opportunity to pursue one's hobbies.

A generic model for spirituality in corporate management is presented below:

Model: Spirituality in corporate management

Stakeholders	Receive	Intervention	Spiritual values
a. Promoters	ROI	Share	Generosity
b. Minority shareholders	ROI	Ask questions	Responsibility
c. Independent directors	Information	Code of conduct	Diligence
d. Top management	Freedom	Leadership	Ethics
d. Lenders	Timely receipts	Due diligence	No conflict of interest
e. Vendors	Payments	Offer quality	Honesty
f. Customers	Quality goods	Proactive	Honesty
g. Employees	Fair treatment	Contribute	Discipline
h. Government	Taxes	Infrastructure	No corruption
i. Society	Prosperity	Collaborate	Care for ecology

Spirituality in corporate management is not an accident. It is a sustained continuous process.

a. Promoters must be fair and apportion their gains with everyone in the value chain. As the society supports the growth of the company, promoters of companies must also be philanthropic. They must contribute generously to the society by setting up foundations and donating to charities. This makes business sense as an ecosystem of loyal stakeholders is created, and the promoters achieve a sense of satisfaction and peace.
b. Minority shareholders who are not aware of day-to-day working could get cheated. They must read annual reports (maybe with the help of experts), attend annual general meetings, and ask questions. They must take responsibility for their investment. It is said that God helps only those who help themselves. At

times, for crucial resolutions, they may be unduly influenced, they must remain true to their intent of protecting their investment which will happen with strong corporate governance.

c. Independent directors should be truly independent. They must see that if they dissent on an issue, it should be written down. In India, Schedule IV to the Companies Act 2013 gives a Code of Conduct for Independent Directors, which are accepted values of integrity and working diligently.
d. The top management must develop leadership traits to motivate employees and create a positive culture. They have the responsibility to see that all processes and systems are humane. They must strive to become better individuals and help employees to achieve peace and happiness.
e. Lenders should lend only to credit-worthy companies, and not succumb to any pressure. They must follow established guidelines for lending and recovery.
f. Vendors must supply in quality and at price contracted, not cheat on that.
g. Customers must understand the principle of "Caveat Emptor, Buyer Beware." If there is any issue in quality or service, offer prompt feedback and pursue the issue with the company management in a dignified way. They cannot cheat the company with false or frivolous complaints.
h. Government must do their duty in building good quality infrastructure. They must have and demonstrate zero tolerance toward corruption.
i. Society gains from and gives back to the corporate and both should collaborate to preserve ecology and environment.

Management of a corporate form of organization is very complex with many players involved in it. But it would be an awesome symphony if spirituality is introduced, practiced, and applied.

Corporate vision and thought processes are changing as per changes happening in the environment. Pace of change is very fast, and corporates are relying a lot on technology to help keep up with fast pace of change. The impact of climate change by way of raging forest fires, floods, and tsunami and the unprecedented tragedy of COVID-19 pandemic has made people realize the importance of good corporate management. The same is largely taking prudent decisions that lead to sustainability, long-term survival, and growth of the company. It results in happy stakeholders and all in the value chain. This can happen when management is evolved, committed to ethics and corporate governance. This maturity is reached when spirituality is practiced. Spirituality is trying to be in the higher consciousness. A state of pragmatism, balance, and ability to look at issues from a third part view, without bias and negative emotions. One needs to work toward achieving this state. It could be praying, chanting, yoga, meditation, or any hobby or passion like sports, painting, music, or dancing.

The words of seventeenth-century poet John Hubert (1593–1633) in his poem The Pulley are: "… Let him be rich and weary, that at least, If goodness lead him not, yet weariness May toss him to my breast." Weariness according to the poet Hubert makes one ultimately turn to God. So also, today, corporate world has been scarred by scams, failures, COVID-19 pandemic has added to the woes. Sheer weariness or tiredness is one of the reasons leading to the Fifth Industrial Revolution of Spirituality. The

Fourth Industrial Digital Revolution is ending, and the Fifth Industrial Revolution of Spirituality has commenced making spirituality a necessity in corporate management.

Bibliography

Bhal, A. (2015). Mr. Ratan Tata's trust in—A privilege. *Digital Article* of December 28, 2015. https://www.urbancompany.com/blog/lifestyle/mr-ratan-tatas-trust-in-us-a-privilege/

Borate, N. (2020). ESG investments are fast gaining traction in India. *Mint E-Paper*, November 11, 2020. https://www.livemint.com/money/personal-finance/esg-investments-are-fast-gaining-traction-in-india-11605111323843.html

Boshkoska, M. (2015). The agency problem: Measures for its overcoming. *International Journal of Business and Management, 10*(1), 204–209.

Bouillon, M., Ferrier, G., Stuebs, M., & West, T. D. (2006). The economic benefit of goal congruence and implications for management control systems. *Journal of Accounting and Public Policy, 25*(3), 265–298.

Budhananda, S. (1998). *How to build character* (9th Ed., pp. 16–50). Himalaya Publications.

Colbert, A. E., Kristof-Brown, A. L., Bradley, B. H., & Barrick, M. R. (2008). CEO transformational leadership: The role of goal importance congruence in top management teams. *Academy of Management Journal, 51*(1), 81–96.

Cuguero-Escofet, N., & Rosanas, J. (2012). The just design and use of management control systems as requirements for goal congruence. *IESE Research Papers.* D/949, IESE Business School.

Dalal. (2016). *Gita for professionals* (3rd Ed., pp. 85–102). Bombay Chartered Accountants Society.

Fernando, M., & Jackson, B. (2006). The influence of religion-based workplace spirituality on business leader's decision-making. An inter-faith study. *Journal of Management and Organization, 12*(1).

Friedman, H., & Friedman, L. (2014). Why spirituality belongs in the business curriculum. *SSRN*. https://ssrn.com/abstract=2408224

Fry, L. W., & Nisiewicz, M. S. (2012). *Maximizing the triple bottom line through spiritual leadership.* Stanford University Press.

Gandhi, M. K. (1996). *The Message of the Gita* (6th Ed., pp. 38–41). Navajivan Publishing House.

Geh, E., & Tan, G. (2009). Spirituality at work in a changing world: Managerial and research implications. *Journal of Management, Spirituality & Religion, 6*(4), 287–300.

Heskett, J. L., Jones, T. O., Loveman, G. W., Earl Sasser, W., & Schelesinger, L. A. (1994). Putting the service-profit chain to work. *Harvard Business Review, 72*(2), 164–174.

Jensen, M. C., & Meckling, W. H. (1976). Theory of the firm: Managerial behavior, agency costs and ownership structure. *Journal of Financial Economics, 3*(4), 305–360.

Lambert III, L. (2011). Spirituality, Inc.: Religion in the American workplace. *New York University Press. Business Ethics Quarterly, 21*, 533–537. https://doi.org/10.5840/beq201121330

Lepner, I. (2017). Making HR valuable-evidence-based mindsets. *Digital Magazine E—People Matters*. https://www.peoplematters.in/article/strategic-hr/making-hr-valuable-evidence-based-mindset-16461

Majeed, N., Mustamil, N., & Nazri, M. (2018). Which spirituality at the workplace? Is corporate spirituality the answer. *Arabian Journal of Business and Management Review-Kuwait Chapter, 7*(1), 49–59. https://doi.org/10.12816/0043950

Prabha, G. (2012). *Karmayogi Swami Vivekanand* (1st Ed.). Bharat Vikas Parishad.

Reave, L. (2005). Spiritual values and practices related to leadership effectiveness. *The Leadership Quarterly, 16*, 655–687; *Imagination, Cognition & Personality, 9*(3), 185–211.

Salovy, P., & Mayer, J. (1990). Emotional intelligence. https://doi.org/10.2190/DUGG-P24E-52WK-6CDG

Schwab, K. (2016). The fourth industrial revolution: What it means and how to respond. https://www.weforum.org
Scott Peck, M. (1978). The road less travelled (1st Ed., pp. 64–268). Simon & Schuster Publishers.
Subramaniam, M., & Natarajan, P. (2013). A study of spirituality in a public sector bank in India. *International Journal of advances in Management and Economics, 2*(4), 102–113.
Suwaldiman, S. (2004). Goal congruence: A humanity approach in exercising power and influence to transform individual interest into coordinated activities. *SINERGI, 7*(1), 103–109.
Swami Nikhilananda. (2001). *The gospel of Sri Ramakrishna* (Vol. II, pp. 670–700). Sri Ramkrishna Math.
Vaswani, J. P. (2003). *A little book of life* (1st Ed., pp. 10–45). Sterling Publishers Pvt. Ltd.

Chapter 14
Workplace Spirituality and Psychological Contract in the "New Normal"

Sanjeev P. Sahni and Jeevan Deep Sehgal

Abstract Psychological contract is a construct to understand the employer–employee relationship. Workplace spirituality is a concept undergoing systematic research which contributes to the personal as well as organizational success. The current pandemic since last one and a half years has led to a "new normal" in the organizational perspective. The current chapter seeks to study the two research domains with the objective of exploring the relationship between workplace spirituality and psychological contract and their application in this new normal. Thus, outlining the future agenda for research which integrates workplace spirituality and psychological contract to improve the employee experience in the organizations.

Keywords Psychological contract · Workplace spirituality · Ideological currency · Meaningful work · New normal · COVID-19

Introduction

A President, visiting a space agency, was on the tour of the facility. He drifted from his assigned route, and there he met a Janitor. The janitor was so immersed in his job of mopping the floor that he didn't see the President coming. The President went near him, and asked, "Hello Mr. Janitor, may I know what do you do here?" The janitor looked at the President with calmness, saw him in the eyes, and replied confidently, "I help place man to the moon" (Both-Nwabuwe et al., 2017).

The above anecdote has been shared in various meeting rooms, conference rooms and classrooms by trainers, leaders, and professors. Different people have shared this story at various platforms providing varied lessons. But let us think, how many of us have actually met such people in our day-to-day lives, who are so aligned to the organization in their daily work. Don't we wonder what additional benefits such

S. P. Sahni · J. D. Sehgal (✉)
O. P. Jindal Global University, Sonipat, India
e-mail: jdsehgal@jgu.edu.in

S. P. Sahni
e-mail: drspsahni@jgu.edu.in

© Jindal Institute of Behavioral Sciences 2022
S. P. Sahni et al. (eds.), *Spirituality and Management*,
https://doi.org/10.1007/978-981-19-1025-8_14

people are getting that they are so aligned? Don't we wonder how we can have such employees?

Globally, we are facing a pandemic since early 2020. This has changed not only our personal lives but also the professional ways of working. "New normal" as a term has originated to describe the post-pandemic world. Never in history, the employees were made to work within the boundaries of their homes for so long. Human being—the social animal was never ever asked to maintain social distance from other people. This pandemic has its repercussions on the society as a whole, and it will also have a long-lasting impact on organizational life (Carnevale & Hatak, 2020). For example, it is expected that the concept of work from home (WFH) in the organizations may persist even after the pandemic and organizations will change structurally to accommodate this work practice (Brakman et al., 2021).

This pandemic may also change how the employee perceives the occupational status of their job. Some people working in sectors such as health care may consider an increase in their occupational status as the healthcare sector has got impacted positively, whereas people working in sectors such as hospitality or travel which have been hit hard by the pandemic may get affected negatively with regard to their occupational status. The individual perceptions of meaningful work and calling in the occupations have been influenced by this pandemic (Kramer & Kramer, 2020).

As mentioned in the chapter "Spirituality and Social Activism," "Spiritual emergence can provoke psychological emergencies" (McIntosh & Carmichael, 2019). With the changing focus on workplace spirituality, psychological contract will also get impacted. It is important to study the emerging area of workplace spirituality and psychological contract to understand the future needs of the employees and define the policies and practices to cater to the individual requirements of the employees, so that they feel valued, engaged, become more productive, and remain loyal with the organization for longer duration.

In this article, we will try to explore the topic of workplace spirituality, specifically the meaningful work aspect and understand the relationship between workplace spirituality and psychological contract. We will try to explore how employers can ensure that employees are as aligned and contended as that janitor working in the space agency. We will also explore the importance of workplace spirituality and its relationship with the psychological contract in managing the employees in the "new normal."

Introduction of Workplace Spirituality

Spirituality has various conceptual components. It is complex and not easy to define (Weathers, 2019). It is not exactly same as religion or faith (Barber, 2019; Paul Victor & Treschuk, 2020). Spirituality can be understood as something which provides us motivation and direction (Barber, 2019) and gives life its meaning, purpose, and connection with others (Weathers, 2019). Spirituality is also associated with quality and meaning of life (Paul Victor & Treschuk, 2020). All individuals have spiritual needs, and it is highly personal and an individualized concept (Weathers, 2019).

As organizations are built by group of individuals, it is important to explore how the concept of spirituality is managed in the workplace. Spirituality is about the connection of oneself with himself or herself as well as with the environment around, and with the universe as a whole. Workplace spirituality can be defined as the connection between the employee and the workplace or the organization.

Workplace spirituality has been discussed widely for the last two decades within practitioners as well as academicians (Benefiel et al., 2014; Houghton et al., 2016) Spirituality at workplace as a construct has been the topic of various conferences and intellectual discussions. Still it is difficult to exactly define workplace spirituality accurately (Rathee & Rajain, 2020), and there have been multiple views describing workplace spirituality.

Workplace spirituality is a multi-dimensional construct (Shrestha & Luitel, 2020). Workplace spirituality is directed toward purpose, meaning, and sense of community (Ashmos & Duchon, 2000). Spirituality can be defined in terms of having an inner presence, which is reinforced by interactions and relations among individuals. Duchon and Plowman (2005) have proposed three major dimensions for workplace spirituality, namely "inner life, meaningful work, and belonging to a community." These dimensions have been studied further by various scholars. Duchon and Plowman (2005) hence evolved a more accepted definition of workplace spirituality. The common dimensions are called as meaningful work, sense of community, and alignment with organizational values (Indradevi, 2020). These three primary dimensions have also been noted by various scholars in the course of their specific studies (Houghton et al., 2016).

Meaningful work means being engaged in a work which is felt important by the employee. Sense of community is all about interconnectedness and feeling of belongingness at the workplace. Inner life is the presence of inner strength or spirit, which helps the individual in carrying out their day-to-day activities at work (Mahipalan & Sheena, 2019).

The development of interest of organizations in spirituality is not only regarded as a trend, but as a movement (Fourie, 2014). According to Mahipalan and Sheena (2019), employees perceive workplace to be meaningful when they are able to bring their heart and soul, i.e., their complete self at work, and hence, it is important to focus on workplace spirituality.

In their study to integrate workplace spirituality with the organizational literature, Pawar (2009) posits that workplace spirituality may have two interpretations—employee's experience of spirituality at the workplace and an organization's facilitation of employee experience of spirituality at workplace. So we can infer that what the employee experiences and interprets of workplace spirituality may naturally differ from what the organization facilitates as workplace spirituality. Hence, it is important to understand what the employee beliefs are about such obligations related to workplace spirituality.

In simple terms, we can state that the connection between the employee and the organization defines workplace spirituality. While we talk about the relationship between the employee and the organization, there are some other constructs which define this connection as well. The psychological contract is one such construct which is used to study the employer–employee relationship. The detailed association between the workplace spirituality and the psychological contract will be further discussed in this chapter.

This brings us to the concept of psychological contract, which is about the individual's beliefs about the mutual obligations.

Introduction of Psychological Contract

Psychological contract is a construct to understand the relationship between the employer and the employee. It is defined as "an **individual's** belief regarding the terms and conditions of a reciprocal exchange agreement between that focal person and the other party" (Rousseau, 1989). These beliefs can originate from various sources which can be internal, also called experiences of the employee, or external, which include the employment contract and the employment situations (Hansen, 2019). According to recent studies, the psychological contract is a mental model and a system of beliefs, which represents an individual's perceptions of the obligation of others as well as his or her own self. The obligations are defined as the duties or responsibilities one feels bound to perform (Hansen, 2019).

The psychological contract is not a written document, rather it is implicit and versatile (Knapp et al., 2020). The psychological contract influences how the employee interprets the various actions of the employer.

Rousseau has defined four types of psychological contracts (Rousseau, 2000). The first is relational psychological contract, which is based upon trust and loyalty. These are long term in nature. Transactional psychological contract is of a short term and has focus on the economic exchange. Third type of psychological contract is the balanced psychological contract which is based upon the dynamic and open-ended employment arrangements, which lead to the financial success of the organization and provide career development opportunities to the employees. The last and the fourth type of psychological contract defined according to Rousseau is the transitional psychological contract, which comprises of elements of mistrust, uncertainty, and erosion due to the change and transition of employee.

Ideological currency as a concept was introduced by Thomson and Bunderson, in their study in 2003, and they also conceptualized another type of psychological contract which they named as ideological psychological contract (Thompson & Bunderson, 2003). Ideological psychological contract describes perceived obligations related to mission, values, and principles of an organization (Vantilborgh & Bidee, 2012).

The reason for which people go to work and why the work is being done in the way which it is being done is changing. According to the latest research in the field of psychological contract, it is important to study the changing nature of work and its implication on the formation of the psychological contract (Griep et al., 2019).

An individual is more likely to develop psychological contract with the other party, when there is a larger degree of perceived dependency or trust (Knapp et al., 2020). Hence, it is important for the organizations to focus on workplace spirituality and trust which can improve psychological contract and the overall employee engagement of the employees.

This chapter attempts to establish the relationship between workplace spirituality, specifically the meaningful work aspect, and the ideological psychological contract. The chapter will explore the relationship between psychological contract and workplace spirituality and also highlights the future direction in the area of workplace spirituality and psychological contract.

What is Workplace Spirituality?

In 1994, a new philosophy of organization design was proposed by Mitroff et al. (1994). They introduced world service or spiritual center as one of the emerging functions where the focus of the organizations should be to use the resources to develop a healthier society and world. They stated that there is a very thin line between spirituality and the morality of organizations. According to them, spirituality is an act of recognition that there is a connection between one's daily job duties and the larger issues of humanity.

In their study, Mitroff and Denton posit that no organization can survive long without the element of spirituality. Also, they defined spirituality in one word as "interconnectedness" (Mitroff & Denton, 1999).

Diversity of the workforce leads to multiple views of workplace spirituality, and it is important to understand the meaning of these. These multiple views may have their own benefits for the organization (Krishnakumar & Neck, 2002).

While recruiting, the human resource professionals interview employees and assess the intellect, the behavioral competencies, and the skills of the employees. We can say that these three are the equivalent of head, heart, and hands which employees bring to the organizations. But no one assesses the spirituality aspect, which can and does make a difference. Currently, the main focus of research is on the spiritual domain of an individual, in order that the quality of life can be enhanced (Mahipalan & Sheena, 2019). Also, workplace spirituality can facilitate in providing meaning to the work and the employee would feel that his or her job has a bigger purpose in consonance with their beliefs. This can be attributed to the example stated in the introduction, where the Janitor understood the bigger purpose of his job.

Dimensions of Workplace Spirituality

Spirituality is an abstract and subjective concept with various assumptions (Paul Victor & Treschuk, 2020). Different early studies provided various dimensions to measure the workplace spirituality. Compassion, right livelihood, selfless service, meditative work, and the problem of pluralism were given as themes to understand the relationship of managers with spirituality (McCormick, 1994). In 1999, another study defined eight different dimensions of spirituality, namely, charity (a sense of giving or service), community (a sense of connection or relationship), compassion, forgiveness (and peace), hope, learning opportunities, meaning (purpose), and morality (a sensitivity to right and wrong) (Mahoney & Graci, 1999).

Krishnakumar and Neck (2002) proposed a spiritual freedom model of implementation of workplace spirituality where managers encourage employees to follow their own individual spiritual path and align these paths or beliefs to the organizational goals. They also studied the intrinsic origin view and existentialist perspective of spirituality. Intrinsic origin view argues that spirituality as a concept or principle originates from the inside of the individual, whereas existentialist view of spirituality is related to the concept of searching for meaning in what one is doing at workplace.

Various studies have provided different dimensions of workplace spirituality. In their study to develop the scale for measuring workplace spirituality, Pradhan et al. (2017) defined four dimensions of workplace spirituality, namely spiritual orientation, compassion, meaningful work, and alignment of values. After numerous studies, number of scholars have agreed to the three dimensions provided originally by Ashmos and Duchon in 2000 (Houghton et al., 2016).

These three dimensions include "inner life," "meaningful work," and "sense of community and connectedness." The inner life aspect is within the definition of intrinsic—origin view (Houghton et al., 2016) which is mainly how spiritual a person actually is.

There are various factors which influence how individuals interpret the meaning and meaningfulness of their work; it can be values, motivation, and beliefs of the individuals (Rosso et al., 2010). Nowadays, workplace supports the individual's personal spiritual development (Neal, 2018).

Sense of community and connectedness occurs when individuals see themselves as an integral part of the community. (Duchon & Plowman, 2005).

Employee beliefs and opinions about the organization's support to the cause may depend on whether the opportunities for involvement are available to the employees (Bingham et al., 2013). According to a study, when an employee is able to participate and provide personal support to the organizational legitimate cause, employee commitment becomes actionable, which means employees make evaluations based on not only the cause, but also their own behavioral support. Practitioners, as well as academicians, seem increasingly interested in employee–employer relationships based on commitment to socially responsible causes.

Early studies of Mitroff and Denton (1999) provide few pointers toward the meaningful work. Employees find work meaningful when they believe that he or she has full ability to realize his or her full potential as a person, the work is interesting and they feel privileged to be associated with a good and ethical organization.

In their study, Hisam and Sanyal (2021) found meaningful work to have the most significant and positive relationship with organizational commitment. Sense of community and intention to stay also had a strong relationship (Thakur et al., 2017).

More importantly during the pandemic, it has been observed that employees working in organizations such as consumer product companies or healthcare companies found it as an inspiration and see their work as contributing to the society. Employees prefer to contribute to their organization when they learn that their talent is making an impact on the larger goals (Volini et al., 2020).

During the last one year, we have seen three kinds of employees: first who have lost their jobs, second who were advised to work from home, and the third who were still working from their workplace and were rather working very hard. These included health workers, journalists, people working in essential services, and other frontline workers. When the risk was so high, what made these people work more? It was the purpose or the larger goal or the meaningful work, which made them going. According to a report of Mckinsey (Dhingra et al., 2021), 70% of the employees say that they define their purpose through work. Hence, it becomes important for organizations to provide meaningful work to their employees.

Since the last two decades, researchers have studied the varied dimensions of the workplace spirituality. Though different researchers have discussed varied dimensions, majorly researchers have agreed on the three dimensions provided by Ashmos and Duchon (2000). Workplace spirituality is an evolving concept, especially since the pandemic individuals have started to focus more on the purpose and meaningful work they are carrying in their day-to-day jobs. Hence, it is important for employers to understand and focus on the meaningful work aspect.

Benefits and Importance of Workplace Spirituality

There are different and important benefits of the workplace spirituality as discussed by the various studies. Workplace spirituality not only impacts the organizational performance in terms of improved retention and commitment of employees, but also leads to the financial success of the organization (Krishnakumar & Neck, 2002).

Organizations have realized that employees are not satisfied with only materialistic things or monetary benefits, rather they want more to satisfy themselves (Indradevi, 2020). Workplace spirituality needs to be integrated into the organizational culture and organizational policies and necessary procedures need to be refined to reflect the same. Workplace spirituality is gradually being recognized as a feasible solution to various challenges faced by human resource professionals (Indradevi, 2020).

Workplace spirituality has been conceptualized as a predictor of employee engagement, with specific reference to meaningful work (Rathee & Sharma, 2019). In another study conducted, workplace spirituality has shown a positive correlation with employee engagement (Singh & Chopra, 2018). Workplace spirituality also has an impact on innovative work behavior (Ranasinghe & Samarasinghe, 2019) and job satisfaction (Zaidi et al., 2019). In yet another study conducted, it was found that without institutionalizing the workplace spirituality, it is difficult to obtain employee commitment, job satisfaction, and work–life balance, all of which are important aspects of employee well-being (Garg, 2017). Workplace spirituality has been found to be a strong predictor of employee commitment (Jena & Pradhan, 2018).

Workplace spirituality is not only a concept which helps in retention of the employees but also helps in reducing the negative work attitude among the employees (Ashfaq et al., 2020a).

Workplace spirituality has a significant positive effect on intrinsic motivation. Studies undertaken show that when the intrinsic motivation is high, workplace spirituality has a significant impact on the innovative work behavior (Ranasinghe & Samarasinghe, 2019). Research shows that the meaningful work dimension of workplace spirituality specifically has been found to impact the innovative work behavior positively (Saxena, 2019). Innovative work behavior is not only the generation of ideas but also implementation and realization of these ideas.

Empirical support was found in various studies where workplace spirituality has shown a significant positive relationship with the various organizational outcomes, for example job performance (Bharadwaj & Jamal, 2020; Do 2018).

Workplace spirituality has been studied to be positively related with employee performance in India (Bharadwaj & Jamal, 2020). Workplace spirituality is responsible for creating a new organizational culture where employees are content and thus achieve more. Also with workplace spirituality, employee motivation and experience of job satisfaction are enhanced (Fourie, 2014). Workplace spirituality has been found to have significant and negative correlation with turnover intention (Anvari et al., 2017).

It has been empirically proved that workplace spirituality has a positive association with all forms of well-being, namely emotional well-being, psychological well-being, social well-being, and spiritual well-being (Pawar, 2016).

The workplace spirituality helps employers as well as employees. It helps employers to improve the organization's earnings and performance. At the employee level, workplace spirituality helps in giving them a sense of identity, provides them with capacity to care and tolerate, and also nurture innovation and creativity (Bhatia & Arora, 2017) for the benefit of the organization.

With many people being convinced of the notion that work can be meaningful and fulfilling, workplace spirituality is becoming a grassroots movement (Schutte, 2016).

The workplace is becoming more dynamic and demanding, and the work pressure is mounting and exposing employees to various psychological problems (Pandey, 2017). In the current scenario, the pandemic has put heavy pressure on mental health. Today, it is required that the employers focus on employee well-being as a central and strategic business priority to manage the worries created by various issues such as remote working, job fears and ongoing health concerns (Walker, 2021). Focusing on workplace spirituality can not only help in managing the employee well-being or providing them meaningful work, but it will also help in maintaining the psychological contract of the employee, so that the employees remain engaged and be more productive.

Implementation of workplace spirituality can be viewed either from organization-centered perspective or from individual-centered perspective (Krishnakumar & Neck, 2002). Organization-centered perspective assumes that organization consists of individuals only, and hence, to understand and implement the workplace spirituality, organizations need to make an attempt to understand the views of their employees and the organizations need to acknowledge that employees not only bring their competencies and skills to the organization (Sparrow & Knight, 2006), but they bring their whole self, including their beliefs and their unique spiritual values which impact the workplace spirituality. The implementation of individual-centered perspective leads to the meaningful work which an employee does on day-to-day basis. During the last two decades, various studies have suggested that organization-level spirituality may play a greater role in encouraging key outcomes than individual-level spirituality (Houghton et al., 2016).

Workplace spirituality experienced at individual level is determined based on the attitudes or behaviors demonstrated by fellow colleagues (Shrestha & Luitel, 2020). According to Indradevi (2020), eliminating fear among employees and knowing each employee individually are few of the initiatives which can help in nurturing workplace spirituality. It has been stated that it is important to empirically test the significance of workplace spirituality on employee engagement (Rathee & Sharma, 2019).

When the employee is completely aligned with the organization, employee brings his or her complete self to the work and contributes more toward the organization. In the process, the organization becomes more spiritual. The more spiritual the organization is, the better the environment it provides to employees to work and contribute. This cycle continues. Hence, it is important to understand how to connect employees with the organization in a better manner. In order to understand the employees, their expectations, and their value, we would like to introduce the concept of psychological contract. The construct of psychological contract helps in understanding the employer–employee relationship.

What is Psychological Contract?

The concept of psychological contract was originally conceptualized by Argys in 1960s. Though it was only after three decades, the researchers started studying the concept in detail.

Psychological contract can be assessed using three different approaches, namely content, features, or characteristics and evaluation (Rousseau & Tijoriwala, 1998). The content of the psychological contract can be made of different obligations of the employer such as job content, career development, and organizational policies. Employees join the organization with a perceived notion about their obligations and the employer's obligations (Montes et al., 2015). The various characteristics of the psychological contract measure the nature of the contract (Muresano, 2017). The psychological contract can be studied based on the tangibility, scope, stability, time frame, exchange symmetry, and contract level (Rousseau & Tijoriwala, 1998). The third approach of studying the psychological contract is the evaluation (Rousseau & Tijoriwala, 1998). The perceived obligations in the psychological contract may impact the feelings of the employee. The employee evaluates the content, and if they feel that the obligations are fulfilled, they may feel contented else they may have feeling of breach or even feel violated which is the extreme affected reaction that follows the breach (Conway & Briner, 2009).

Psychological contract is a tool to understand the employer-employee relationship. Through better understanding of the psychological contract, we can work toward understanding as well as improving the relationship between the employer and the employee.

Rousseau defined four types of psychological contract (Rousseau, 2000). Later, in their study, (Thompson & Bunderson, 2003) defined one more type of psychological contract called ideological psychological contract which is the shared mutual agreements between employees and their organization that is built on a set of shared values, objectives, mission, and/or purpose the organization is believed to strive for. These relationships are built on reciprocal exchange of ideological currency where both the employee and their organization are committed to support the cause in subjectively equal forms.

Though on one hand, the employees are working hard at the expense of their families, hobbies, and even health, on the other hand, the employees are also striving to find meaning in their work relationships (Dixon-Fowler et al., 2019). Even in such contradictory situations, employees keep on working devotedly. Literature on ideology infused or ideological psychological contract may provide some explanation to this phenomenon.

Ideological Psychological Contract

When employee's expectations are not grounded solely in personal entitlements but also derive from a belief that by contributing to the organization, they are contributing to a valued cause, we say that the ideological currency has been infused (Thompson & Bunderson, 2003). Ideological currency can be defined as credible commitments to pursue a valued cause (not limited to self-interest) that are implicitly exchanged at the nexus of the individual/organizational relationship as a term of employment. In simple terms, ideological psychological contracts develop when the organization cares about a cause, which an employee also subscribes to (Dixon-Fowler et al., 2019).

Jones and Griep (2018) state that the way ideological psychological contracts (iPCs) are developed and navigated by employees is unique from relational and transactional psychological contracts. The mutual agreements that create the iPC are highly related to work context of the employee and the value which an employee places on aspects of their personal and organizational ideology. As a result, breach of ideological contract as perceived by one employee may not necessarily be perceived as breach by another employee. Hence, the ideological psychological contracts seem to have a better fit with the concept of workplace spirituality.

When the employee's own ethical beliefs are in contradiction to the apparent ethical climate of the organization, the employee's personal values may overpower

(Grobler & Nicolaides, 2014). Where there is a good psychological contract, there is transparency, mutual appreciation, and understanding between employer and employees, and an organization is likely to be more effective.

Even organizations have realized the benefits of exchanging the ideological currency with the employees. Sometimes this is also done by the organizations to exploit the employees using the emotional appeal (Dixon-Fowler et al., 2019). When the relationship between the employee and the employer is based on this ideological currency rather than mere economic reasons or socio-emotional exchanges, employee starts acting as an ambassador of the organization, as it provides an opportunity for the employee to lay credible claim to the values that the company seeks to represent and also justify why the employee works hard in the organization.

The ideological obligations in the psychological contract are unique in nature (Vantilborgh et al., 2014). The ideological psychological contract and the meaningful work can be a "double-edged" sword (Jones & Griep, 2018). The employee may work harder when there is iPC breach, though this increase can be limited and eventually lead to the burnout and stress for the employee.

Though there has been ample research regarding the relational and transactional contracts, there is not the required good understanding of the ideological psychological contracts (Kappelides & Jones, 2018). Hence, we propose and emphasize the importance to study the relationship of ideological currency, ideological psychological contracts, and workplace spirituality.

Dynamic Model of Psychological Contract

Amidst the many discussions about the dynamic nature of the psychological contract, a new phase-based model of psychological contract has been proposed (Rousseau et al., 2018). The four phases, namely creation, maintenance, renegotiation, and repair, have been defined in the new model. According to the researchers, these phases cover the complete employment lifecycle and hence provide clarity on the construct of psychological contract. According to this model, psychological contract is dynamic in nature and evolves over time. The new definition provided by Rousseau et al. (2016) states that the obligations need not be reciprocal in nature while defining psychological contract. Though they have agreed with the perceptual nature of this contract, according to the new model, psychological contract has been defined as a construct at the individual level. It is important to understand that this new model emphasizes the dynamic nature of the psychological contract.

Benefits and Importance of Psychological Contract

Though psychological contract is a construct which is almost three decades old, still there is lot of research happening on this construct recently. The researchers have understood the importance of the psychological contract and its impact on the various organizational and employee-related characteristics and constructs. This section will be reviewing few of the studies highlighting the relationship between the psychological contract and the various other constructs and will highlight the importance of studying the psychological contract.

Empirical studies have proven that relational psychological contracts affect employee engagement (Agarwal & Gupta, 2016).

Psychological contract breach has been negatively related to organization citizenship behavior (Coyle-shapiro et al., 2017), job satisfaction (Rehman et al., 2019), and turnover intentions (Moquin et al., 2019).

Interestingly, psychological contract breach is positively related to the idea generation and idea implementation (Niesen et al., 2017).

The literature of psychological contract has consistently talked about the changing nature of psychological contract (Rousseau et al., 2018). Change is an accepted aspect of the psychological contract (Persson & Wasieleski, 2015).

The dynamic nature of the psychological contract posits that psychological contract needs to be maintained and can be repaired as well. The authors of this article emphasize the need of workplace spirituality to maintain and repair psychological contract, specifically the ideological component of psychological contract.

During the last one year, the expectations of employees have changed from their employers. According to a report of Randstad, COVID Impact—Employee Pulse Survey 2020, 29% of the employees expect support from the employer to maintain their mental health. According to another survey done by Deloitte (Volini et al., 2020) to understand the pandemic's impact on working women, 48% of women employees expect their organizations to provide more flexible working options. The various survey results indicate the revision in the psychological contract of employees due to the pandemic, and it is very important for us to address these new legitimate and practical expectations.

Association Between Workplace Spirituality and Psychological Contract

In a critique written in 2014 to understand psychological contract and spirituality, it has been discussed by Grobler and Nicolaides (2014), that the relationship between the two is dynamic, fluid, and bidirectional. It is important to understand the changing ideologies and values of the employees (Kappelides & Jones, 2018) which may impact the employee–employer relationship.

A unique concept of Second Adulthood had been studied by Moore and Moore in 2012, and it was found that there are people who want to remain employed in meaningful jobs well into their sixties and beyond. Employees prefer the organizations with viewpoints, where each employee is seen as an invaluable rare resource with unlimited potential (Moore & Moore, 2012). Hence, organizations are focusing on long-term relational psychological contract with a focus on spiritual needs of the employees.

Social exchange relationships are developed when employers take care of their employees (Kappelides & Jones, 2018). Due to dynamic nature of psychological contract, it is important to study how workplace spirituality may impact the psychological contract.

It is important for managers to understand the different views of spirituality of its employees and to encourage it within the organization. This helps in building a holistic spirituality at workplace.

In this section, we discuss the relationship between workplace spirituality and psychological contract.

As we have already stated that there are multiple views of workplace spirituality. Though there are no second views about the importance of spirituality in today's modern workplace, employers are still struggling to understand the concept and encourage it.

The section tries to establish the relationship between workplace spirituality and psychological contract, specifically the ideological currency. Also, we will be able to understand the various ideological currencies of the employees. The accumulation of these ideological currencies will help us in building spirituality at workplace, where the employees feel interconnected with their workplace and where they find meaningful work.

There are a few employees, who prefer to align with their own principles and spiritual values, irrespective of its impact on their status at workplace or a long-term impact on their career.

It has been observed that workplace spirituality and psychological contract have a positive impact on turnover intentions of employees (Ashfaq et al., 2020b). It has been studied that when employees feel that organization is fulfilling their psychological contract, they reciprocate and it leads to retention of the employees (Ashfaq et al., 2020b). In another study, workplace spirituality has been studied to significantly moderate the link between psychological contract breach and employee workplace behaviors (Jan & Wali, 2019).

Hence, we can say that to improve the retention of employees and their workplace behavior, and it is important to focus on the redeeming features of workplace spirituality and psychological contract.

In a study, it was observed that when teachers experience meaningful work, they have a sense of calling which can impact the work attitude (Willemse & Deacon, 2015).

While an organization cannot decide to hire employees that perceive a calling toward a particular type of work, they can play an important role in improving the employees' affective occupational commitment by ensuring that the work being provided and allocated to the employees is meaningful to them (Sawhney et al., 2019).

There have been few empirical studies which prove that there is a significant relationship between workplace spirituality and psychological contract (Ashfaq et al., 2020b). Workplace spirituality is proven to moderate the relationship between psychological contract breach and employee workplace behavior. In a study conducted by Jan and Wali in Pakistan, it was observed that with workplace spirituality, the negative impact of psychological contract breach on organizational citizenship behavior (OCB) is less significant in the magnitude of negativity (Jan & Wali, 2019).

In a research conducted in Turkey, a positive and meaningful relationship was empirically proven between the organizational spirituality and transactional contract dimension of the psychological contract (Demet et al., 2017).

In a study done in Australia, the researchers found that spirituality was a critical part of the relational psychological contract of the employees (Lakisa et al., 2020).

Commitment to a cause which is distinct from the organizational sponsorship may act as an antecedent to the commitment of employee to an organization sponsored cause (Bingham et al., 2013). This extends our understanding that the pre-employment beliefs of the employee impact the employer–employee relations which has a significant bearing on workplace spirituality.

In another study conducted in Istanbul, the researchers have found that spirituality has a significant influence on the psychological contract of the members of a faith-based organization (Handayani et al., 2020).

Though there are meager empirical studies where the workplace spirituality and psychological contract have been studied, it has been established by various studies that there is a fit between the two constructs. Hence, we propose that there is a need to study workplace spirituality and psychological contract and their impact on the employee engagement.

Conclusion and Future Directions

Introduction of psychological contract in the literature of workplace spirituality provides useful contribution to understand the meaningful work and workplace spirituality from the lens of psychological contract with ideological currency in specific. This chapter explored the concept of psychological contract and relationship of ideological currency and workplace spirituality. This chapter discussed the importance of workplace spirituality and how it impacts the psychological contract of the employees. Though the literature has provided various ways to build and sustain workplace spirituality, this chapter provided a reason to focus on the relationship of workplace spirituality and psychological contract to build a workplace, where employees feel that there is a fair environment. The focus should be to build an organization where employees are not only aligned to the principles of the organization but also become advocates for the organization. By focusing on workplace spirituality and ideological currency, the organizations will ensure that the employees will find purpose and get retained accordingly. In this way, we can work toward having employees who may work as a janitor but with a purpose to put the man on the moon as mentioned earlier which implies the devoted commitment of the employee to the organizations' cause.

Workplace spirituality at work brings out the best of employees (Rathee & Rajain, 2019). It has been stated that with spirituality in the workplace, chances of psychological contract breach will be minimized (Grobler & Nicolaides, 2014). Hence, it is important to study this supplementary or subjective fit and relationship between workplace spirituality and psychological contract.

This chapter will be helpful for the human resource (HR) professionals who want to improve the employee experience, as they will be able to understand the relationship between psychological contract and the workplace spirituality. The HR professionals need to work on improving the workplace spirituality to enhance the psychological contract which further impacts on the employee engagement and employee experience.

Pandemic will strengthen the current trend toward the automation and robotization of work (Brakman et al., 2021). The various societal changes are introducing new facets of psychological contract which are building on the concerns such as work–life balance (Montes et al., 2015). Empirical research has proven that when employees understand that they are contributing in reducing the human sufferings, they become more productive and satisfied (Kendall, 2019).

Employees actually become attached to their organization because of the prospect of it addressing their goals (Kim et al., 2018). Relationship between psychological contract and workplace spirituality is reciprocal. The calling of the work leads to meaningful work, and this meaningful work can also be called as predictor of calling. The authors have observed that there are very few empirical studies with focus on the relationship between workplace spirituality and the psychological contract. Hence, there is a need to further research in this area and the relationship between workplace spirituality and psychological contract.

This chapter argues the importance of ideological currency of the psychological contract and the importance of workplace spirituality. Focusing on workplace spirituality and psychological contract can help us in cultivating employees who are as aligned to the values and purpose of the organization as the janitor in the space agency. Also, with the new normal of the work, with changing priorities of the employees, the focus on understanding workplace spirituality in general and the meaningful aspect in specific will ensure a positive impact on psychological contract of the employees and they will be more productive and satisfactorily engaged in the workplace.

This chapter addresses the importance for integrating the workplace spirituality with the psychological contract which is a construct of organization development and important for the management to understand the employer–employee relationship. Improving the workplace spirituality helps in managing the psychological contract better and will further improve the retention of employees in the organization. Understanding of this relationship between the workplace spirituality and the psychological contract will help in building a sustainable model of employer–employee relationship which may lead to the engaged and productive employees. Especially in the context of new normal, which has forced the employees to reflect on the purpose of their lives (Dhingra et al., 2021), it is important to improve the workplace spirituality to have a positive impact on the psychological contract.

Taking this perspective in future, researchers should further study and elucidate the psychological aspect of workplace spirituality and relationship of employee beliefs with spirituality at workplace.

References

Agarwal U. A., & Gupta, R. K. (2016). Examining the nature and effects of psychological contract: Case study of an Indian organization. *Wiley Online Library, 49*(5), 630–631.

Anvari, R., Barzaki, A. S., Amiri, L., Irum, S., & Shapourabadi, S. (2017). The mediating effect of organizational citizenship behavior on the relationship between workplace spirituality and intention to leave. *Intangible Capital, 13*(3), 615–639.

Ashfaq, M., Mustapha, I., & Irum, S. (2020a). The impact of workplace spirituality on turnover intentions in Malaysian banking sector. *European Journal of Molecular and Clinical Medicine,* 7(3), 197–219.

Ashfaq, M., Yunus, F. M., Gillani, S. A., Zaidi, H. R., & Irum, S. (2020b). increasing challenge of turnover intention in banking sector of pakistan. *European Journal of Molecular and Clinical Medicine, 7*(3), 101–115.

Ashmos, D. P., & Duchon, D. (2000). Spirituality at work. *Journal of Management Inquiry, 9*(2), 134–145.

Barber, C. (2019). Working within a spiritual framework. *British Journal of Nursing, 28*(4), 229.

Benefiel, M., Fry, L. W., & Geigle, D. (2014). Spirituality and religion in the workplace: History, theory, and research. *Psychology of Religion and Spirituality, 6*(3), 175–187.

Bharadwaj, S., & Jamal, M. T. (2020). In search of spiritual workplaces: An empirical evidence of workplace spirituality and employee performance in the Indian I.T. industry. *International Journal of Scientific and Technology Research, 9*(3), 1116–1124.

Bhatia, S., & Arora, E. (2017). Workplace spirituality: An employer-employee perspective. *International Journal of Innovative Research & Development, 6*(1), 106–111.

Bingham, J. B., Mitchell, B. W., Bishop, D. G., & Allen, N. J. (2013). Working for a higher purpose: A theoretical framework for commitment to organization-sponsored causes. *Human Resource Management Review, 23*(2), 174–189.

Both-Nwabuwe, J. M. C., Dijkstra, M. T. M., & Beersma, B. (2017). Sweeping the floor or putting a man on the moon: How to define and measure meaningful work. *Frontiers in Psychology, 8*(SEP), 1–14.

Brakman, S., Garretsen, H., & van Witteloostuijn, A. (2021). Robots do not get the coronavirus: The COVID-19 pandemic and the international division of labor. *Journal of International Business Studies.*

Carnevale, J. B., … & Hatak, I. (2020). Employee adjustment and well-being in the era of COVID-19: Implications for human resource management. *Human Resource Development International,* 665–670 (May).

Conway, N., & Briner, R. B. (2009). Fifty years of psychological contract research: What do we know and what are the main challenges? *International Review of Industrial and Organizational Psychology,* 24, 71–131.

Coyle-shapiro, J. A.-M., Diehl, M.-R., & Chang, C. (2017). *The Employee—Organization Relationship and Organizational Citizenship Behavior in The Oxford Handbook of Organizational Citizenship Behavior.* Oxford, UK: Oxford University Press.

Demet, C., Enver, A., & Mehmet, A. (2017). The influence of perceived organizational spirituality on the psychological contract. *The European Proceedings of Social & Behavioural Sciences* (December 2017).

Dhingra, N., Samo, A., Schaninger, B., & Schrimper, M. (2021). *Help Your Employees Find Purpose—Or Watch Them Leave.* McKinsey.Com. Retrieved July 31, 2021, from https://www.

mckinsey.com/business-functions/organization/our-insights/help-your-employees-find-purpose-or-watch-them-leave.

Dixon-Fowler, H., O'Leary-Kelly, A., Johnson, J., & Waite, M. (2019). Sustainability and ideology-infused psychological contracts: An organizational- and employee-level perspective. *Human Resource Management Review, 30*(3),100690.

Do, T. T. (2018). How spirituality, climate and compensation affect job performance. *Social Responsibility Journal.*

Duchon, D., & Plowman, D. A. (2005). Nurturing the spirit at work: Impact on work unit performance. *Leadership Quarterly, 16*(5), 807–833.

Fourie, M. (2014). Spirituality in the workplace: An introductory overview. *In Die Skriflig/In Luce Verbi, 48*(1), 1–8.

Garg, N. (2017). Workplace spirituality and employee well-being: An empirical exploration. *Journal of Human Values, 23*(2), 129–147.

Griep, Y., Cooper, C., Robinson, S., Rousseau, D. M., Hansen, S. D., Tomprou, M., ... & Linde, B. J. (2019). *Psychological Contracts: Back to the Future.* Edward Elgar Publishing.

Grobler, A., & Nicolaides, A. (2014). A critique of the psychological contract and spirituality in the South African workplace viewed in the light of utilitarianism and deontology. *African Journal of Hospitality, Tourism and Leisure, 3*(1).

Handayani, E., Kurnianto, H., Tjahjono, & Darmawan, A. (2020). Uniqueness of psychological contract in a faith-based organization (FBO). *International Journal of Research in Business and Social Science, 9*(6), 58–64.

Hansen, S. D. (2019). Psychological contracts: Time for some conceptual clarity. In *Handbook of Research on the Psychological Contract at Work.* Edward Elgar Publishing.

Hisam, M. W., & Sanyal, S. (2021). Impact of workplace spirituality on organizational commitment—A study in an emerging economy. *Turkish Journal of Computer and Mathematics Education, 06*(02), 37–48.

Houghton, J. D., Neck, C. P., & Krishnakumar, S. (2016). The what, why, and how of spirituality in the workplace revisited: A 14-year update and extension. *Journal of Management, Spirituality and Religion, 13*(3), 177–205.

Indradevi, R. (2020). Workplace spirituality: Successful mantra for modern organization. *Journal of Critical Reviews, 7*(6), 437–440.

Jan, S. A., ... & Wali, R. (2019). Dynamic linkages between psychological contract breach and employees' workplace behaviors in power sector of Pakistan. *International Transaction Journal of Engineering, Management, & Applied Sciences & Technologies, 11*(03), 1–12.

Jena, L. K., & Pradhan, S. (2018). Workplace spirituality and employee commitment: The role of emotional intelligence and organisational citizenship behaviour in Indian organisations. *Journal of Enterprise Information Management, 31*(3), 380–404.

Jones, S. K., & Griep, Y. (2018). 'I can only work so hard before i burn out.' A time sensitive conceptual integration of ideological psychological contract breach, work effort, and burnout. *Frontiers in Psychology, 9*, 1–14 (Feb).

Kappelides, P., & Jones, S. K. (2018). *Ideological Components of Psychological Contracts: Future Directions for Volunteer and Employment Research.* Elgaronline.Com.

Kendall, M. (2019). Workplace spirituality and the motivational impact of meaningful work: An experimental study. *Journal of Organizational Psychology, 2019*(1), 74–92.

Kim, S. S., Shin, D., Vough, H. C., Hewlin, P. F., & Vandenberghe, C. (2018). How do callings relate to job performance? The role of organizational commitment and ideological contract fulfillment. *Human Relations, 71*(10), 1319–1347.

Knapp, J. R., Diehl, M. R., & Dougan, W. (2020). Towards a social-cognitive theory of multiple psychological contracts. *European Journal of Work and Organizational Psychology, 29*(2), 200–214.

Kramer, A., & Kramer, K. Z. (2020). The potential impact of the Covid-19 pandemic on occupational status, work from home, and occupational mobility. *Journal of Vocational Behavior* (January).

Krishnakumar, S., & Neck, C. P. (2002). The 'what', 'why' and 'how' of spirituality in the workplace. *Journal of Managerial Psychology, 17*(3), 153–164.

Lakisa, D., Taylor, T., & Adair, D. (2020). Managing psychological contracts: Employer-employee expectations and non-athlete Pasifika professionals in the National Rugby League (NRL). *Journal of Global Sport Management*, 1–22.

Mahipalan, M., & Sheena, S. (2019). Workplace spirituality, psychological well-being and mediating role of subjective stress: A case of secondary school teachers in India. *International Journal of Ethics and Systems, 35*(4), 725–739.

Mahoney, M. J., & Graci, G. M. (1999). The meanings and correlates of spirituality: Suggestions from an exploratory survey of experts. *Death Studies, 23*(6), 521–528.

McCormick, D. W. (1994). Spirituality and management. *Journal of Managerial Psychology, 9*(6), 5–8.

McIntosh, A., & Carmichael, M. (2019). Spirituality and social activism. In *The Routledge International Handbook of Spirituality in Society and the Professions* (pp. 302–312).

Mitroff, I. I., Mason, R. O., & Pearson, C. (1994). Radical surgery: What will tomorrow's organizations look like? *Academy of Management Perspectives, 8*(2), 11–21.

Mitroff, I., & Denton, E. (1999). A study of spirituality in the workplace. *Sloan Management Review, 40*(4), 83–92.

Montes, S. D., Rousseau, D. M., & Tomprou, M. (2015). Psychological contract theory. *Wiley Encyclopedia of Management* (2013), 1–5.

Moore, T. W., & Moore, H. L. (2012). The effect of spirituality on the psychological contract: Towards the relational. *Journal of Organizational Psychology, 12*(1), 32–42.

Moquin, R., Riemenschneider, C. K., & Wakefield, R. L. (2019). Psychological contract and turnover intention in the information technology profession. *Information Systems Management, 36*(2), 111–125.

Muresano, D. (2017). Theoretical approach of the measure of the psychological contract of employees. *The Annals of the University of Oradea. Economic Sciences* Tom XXVI 2(2), 405–409.

Neal, J. (2018). *Overview of Workplace Spirituality Research* (Vols. 1–2).

Niesen, W., Van Hootegem, A., Elst, T. V., Battistelli, A., & De Witte, H. (2017). Job insecurity and innovative work behaviour: A psychological contract perspective. *Psychologica Belgica, 57*(4), 174–189.

Pandey, A. (2017). Workplace spirituality: Themes, impact and research directions. *South Asian Journal of Human Resources Management, 4*(2), 212–217.

Paul Victor, C. G., & Treschuk, J. V. (2020). Critical literature review on the definition clarity of the concept of faith, religion, and spirituality. *Journal of Holistic Nursing, 38*(1), 107–113.

Pawar, B. S. (2009). Some of the recent organizational behavior concepts as precursors to workplace spirituality. *Journal of Business Ethics, 88*(2), 245–261.

Pawar, B. S. (2016). Employee relations: The international journal article information. *Employee Relations, 43*(5), 1–43.

Persson, S., & Wasieleski, D. (2015). The seasons of the psychological contract: Overcoming the silent transformations of the employer-employee relationship. *Human Resource Management Review, 25*(4), 368–383.

Pradhan, R. K., Jena, L. K., & Soto, C. M. (2017). Workplace spirituality in Indian organisations: Construction of reliable and valid measurement scale. *Business: Theory and Practice, 18*, 43–53.

Ranasinghe, V. R., & Samarasinghe, S. M. (2019). The effect of workplace spirituality on innovative work behavior. *International Business Research, 12*(12), 29.

Rathee, R., & Rajain, P. (2019). An empirical assessment of workplace spirituality and its outcomes. *Journal of Organisation & Human Behaviour, 8*(1), 1–9.

Rathee, R., & Rajain, P. (2020). Workplace spirituality: A comparative study of various models. *Article Jindal Journal of Business Research, 9*(1), 27–40.

Rathee, R., & Sharma, V. (2019). Workplace spirituality as a predictor of employee engagement. *Asian Journal of Management, 8*(2), 284.

Rehman, S., Ali, S., Hussain, M. S., & Kamboh, A. Z. (2019). The role of physiological contract breach on employee reactions: Moderating role of organizational trust. *Pakistan Journal of Humanities and Social Sciences, 7*(2), 233–244.

Rosso, B. D., Dekas, K. H., & Wrzesniewski, A. (2010). On the meaning of work: A theoretical integration and review. *Research in Organizational Behavior, 30*(C), 91–127.

Rousseau, D. M. (1989). Psychological and implied contracts in organizations. *Employee Responsibilities and Rights Journal, 2*(2), 121–139.

Rousseau, D. M. (2000). *Psychological Contract Inventory Technical Report, 53*(9), 1689–1699.

Rousseau, D. M., Hansen, S. D., & Tomprou, M. (2016). A dynamic phase model of psychological contract processes hi I am writing a book on evidence-based management view project religious identity in the workplace view project. *Article in Journal of Organizational Behavior, 39*(9), 1081–1098.

Rousseau, D. M., Hansen, S. D., & Tomprou, M. (2018). A dynamic phase model of psychological contract processes. *Journal of Organizational Behavior, 39*(9), 1081–1098.

Rousseau, D. M., & Tijoriwala, S. A. (1998). Assessing psychological contracts: Issues, alternatives and measures. *Journal of Organizational Behavior, 19*(Suppl.), 679–695.

Sawhney, G., Britt, T. W., & Wilson, C. (2019). *Perceiving a Calling as a Predictor of Future Work Attitudes: The Moderating Role of Meaningful Work.*

Saxena, A. (2019). Workplace spirituality and employee well-being: An opportunity for innovative behaviour at work. *Research Journal of Humanities and Social Sciences, 10*(2), 623.

Schutte, P. J. W. (2016). Workplace spirituality: A tool or a trend? *HTS Teologiese Studies/Theological Studies, 72*(4), 1–5.

Shrestha, A. K., & Luitel, B. C. (2020). *Conceptualization of Workplace Spirituality in an Eastern Context.*

Singh, J., & Chopra, V. G. (2018). Workplace spirituality, grit and work engagement. *Asia-Pacific Journal of Management Research and Innovation, 14*(1–2), 50–59.

Sparrow, T., & Knight, A. (2009). Applied EI: The importance of attitudes in developing emotional intelligence. John Wiley & Sons.

Thakur, K., Singh, J., & Kaur, P. (2017). A study of spirituality at work and organisational commitment of university teachers. *Pertanika Journal of Social Sciences and Humanities, 25*(4), 1501–1514.

Thompson, J. A., & Bunderson, J. S. (2003). Violations of principle? Ideological currency in the phycological contract. *Academy of Management Review, 28*(4), 571–586.

Vantilborgh, T., & Bidee, J. (2012). Effects of ideological and relational psychological contract breach and fulfilment on volunteers' work effort. *European Journal of Work and Organizational Psychology, Taylor & Francis, 23*(2), 217–230.

Vantilborgh, T., Bidee, J., Pepermans, R., Willems, J., Huybrechts, G., & Jegers, M. (2014). Effects of ideological and relational psychological contract breach and fulfilment on volunteers' work effort. *European Journal of Work and Organizational Psychology, 23*(2), 217–230.

Volini, E., Schwartz, J., Denny, B., Mallon, D., Van Durme, Y., Hauptmann, M., Yan, R., & Poynton, S. (2020). *Deloitte 2020 Global Human Capital Trends Special Report: Returning to Work in the Future of Work* (1–16).

Walker, V. (2021). Why a wellbeing recovery will be needed post pandemic. *Occupational Health & Wellbeing, 73*(1), 11.

Weathers, E. (2019). What is spirituality. *Spirituality in Healthcare: Perspectives for Innovative Practice*, 1–22.

Willemse, M., & Deacon, E. (2015). Experiencing a sense of calling: The influence of meaningful work on teachers' work attitudes. *SA Journal of Industrial Psychology, 41*(1).

Zaidi, H., Ghayas, M. M., & Durrani, T. I. K. (2019). Impact of work place spirituality on job satisfaction. *RADS Journal of Business Management, 1*(1), 49–57

Chapter 15
Spirituality and Quality-of-Life: a Conceptual Approach to Adaptability and Workplace Subjective Wellbeing

Harry G. Nejad and Fara G. Nejad

Abstract This chapter considers the effects of spirituality as well as meaning and purpose on the quality-of-life and more specifically in the workplace subjective well-being, under the umbrella of the adaptability construct. Facing life challenges and changes may often be overwhelming and stressful. People learn that to deal with challenges and changes, they must become adaptable. This means that they must either have or develop the ability, purpose, and means to regulate their personal (mental, emotional, and behavioral) resources to achieve subjective well-being. Meaning and purpose are claimed to be a psychological well-being factor that often plays a regulatory role which can be described as the motivational propeller aiming for gratifying future endeavors and plans. Spirituality commonly is described as one's ensuing life with meaning and purpose, and it is a notion, concept, and enlightenment that consequently leads to self-transcendence. It can rightfully be deduced that spirituality and meaning and purpose are cognate constructs. Emerging research on workplace spirituality has shown that workers, who find meaning in their work, function effectively and attain greater satisfaction in their work–life, which may also generate higher profitability for enterprises. The following analysis will demonstrate the relationship among meaning and purpose, spirituality, and adaptability and then the significant outcomes of those factors on workplace well-being. Accordingly, it will be conferring the role of workers' spiritual beliefs at work for business organizations and society as a whole.

Keywords Adaptability · Meaning and purpose · Spirituality · Workplace · Quality-of-life · Welfare and well-being

---

H. G. Nejad (✉)
Ph.D., MACP, BASc, REBT, CCPA, Yorkville University, Graduate Faculty of Counselling Psychology - and - O. P. Jindal Global University, JSPC, Sonipat, India

F. G. Nejad
Athabasca University, Athabasca, Canada

© Jindal Institute of Behavioral Sciences 2022

S. P. Sahni et al. (eds.), *Spirituality and Management*,
https://doi.org/10.1007/978-981-19-1025-8_15

Introduction

> Try not to resist the changes that come your way. Instead, let life live through you. And do not worry that your life is turning upside down. How do you know that the side you are used to is better than the one to come?
>
> Rumi *(1207–1273)*

It is the change that we fear the most, and yet, it is the change that makes us stronger, agile, buoyant, resilient, and the survivors we ought to be. Our lives undergo profound changes on every front, as does the world around us, and consequently, our lives are personified and affected by chronic variability, novelty, and ambiguity. Life variabilities, changes, and challenges as major transitional milestones would include (but are not limited to) events such as start going to school, leaving home, beginning a new career, changing jobs, adapting to new colleagues and coworkers, getting married, child rearing/caregiving, and retiring. In addition, marginal unplanned daily life events typically include the varying quality of responsibilities and circumstances during the day in the workplace, which can, in theory, disrupt habits and familiar patterns of scheduled work–life that workers need to adjust and adapt to.

How we approach and manage life challenges has played a pivotal role in theorizing and reasoning endeavors of scholars and philosophers such as Rumi (Jalāl ad-Dīn Muhammad Rūmī [Persian: انالومیموردمحمنیدلالاج] (1207–1273), the Buddha (Siddhārtha Gautama (563 to 483 B.C.), and many others.

Frankl (1984) quotes Nietzsche: "He who has a *why* to live for can bear with almost any *how*" to demonstrate that life with a purpose is worth suffering. In his famous book, "Man's Search for Meaning," he expressed that people without reason and purpose in their life would descend in despair and agony and fail to acquire true self-actualization (1984). He asserts that spiritual free will and ascend (that cannot be influenced or taken away by others) make life meaningful, spiritual, and purposeful. Further, Frankl believed that there are three ways in which one can achieve meaning in life (including work–life): carrying out a selfless act of being involved in meaningful and purposeful work; experiencing or expressing passion for something or someone [meaningful and significant]; and moving through suffering, despair, and failure in life with acceptance (1984). Finally, he emphasized that only a small number of people are truly capable of reaching such a level of self-actualization. The majority of people often lose their belief and spirituality while letting themselves be lost in psychological and physical decay and despair.

Informed by the above discussion, it would be prudent to presume that personal life and work–life may be intertwined in today's world and are synonymous with each other. Therefore, people are burdened with ample degrees and levels of challenges and changes in their personal and work lives.

Statistically speaking, workers and employees spend as much as one-third of their daily life (and one-half of their lifetime) at their workplace, which makes up a considerable part of their lives encompassed by all its joy and despair, ups and downs, success and failures, and overall stress. Individuals learn at an early age that they need to become adaptable if they have to survive these ups and downs, the changing, challenging, and uncertain life situations and circumstances they are faced with. One way to rise above the difficulties in life is to become self-actualized. It may be encapsulated in adaptability, meaning and purpose, and spirituality. Adaptability is people's capacity to positively and effectively regulate their personal resources (cognition, emotion, and action) in the interest of dealing with and managing life's difficult, demanding circumstances and conditions (Nejad, 2014). Further, spirituality commonly is understood as a quest to discover and realize life's meaning and purpose, which is a notion and enlightenment that guides a person toward self-transcendence (Garcia-Zamor, 2003). Likewise, meaning and purpose is argued to be the motivational aspiration in people's lives where meaning is the outcome and cause of owning and achieving that self-defined purpose. Consequently, spirituality and meaning and purpose essentially have more likenesses than disparities. The developing and recent studies concerning the role of spirituality in the workplace have demonstrated that employees who discover meaning in their vocation and trade would have better performance and attain higher job satisfaction in their work and work environment (Foster & Wall, 2019). Recent research has postulated that spirituality is an overarching concept that includes meaning and purpose, and often, religiosity. Habitually, religious people tend to have some degree of spirituality in their belief system. However, not every person with meaning and purpose in their life is necessarily spiritual or religious. Yet, spiritual people are presumed to have found meaning and purpose in their lives (Steger et al., 2012), even if an impermanent one.

Collectively, it is hypothesized that spirituality in the workplace would play a significant role in workers' sense of belonging, engagement, job satisfaction, performance, self-esteem, self-efficacy, resiliency, buoyancy, defense mechanism, and subjective well-being (Fachrunnisa et al., 2014; Milliman et al., 2003; Saks, 2011). Furthermore, it is also postulated that adaptability, along with personality, the belief about ability (the incremental theory of ability), gender, age, and socioeconomic status play a significant role in shaping and understanding meaning and purpose (including spirituality). Furthermore, recent research has also shown that spirituality and adaptability have a bidirectional relationship (Milliman et al., 2003). Even in a workplace environment, it can be utilized to improve workers' performance and productivity that may translate into larger profitability.

The following sections will unravel the bidirectional relationship between spirituality and adaptability by understanding those factors and other relevant concepts, including meaning, purpose, subjective well-being pertinent to the workplace, and workplace performance. Later the discussion on how this is relevant to business practices in the twenty-first century, followed by the implications for intervention and summary sections, will be presented.

Adaptability

Adaptability is described by the American Psychological Association (APA) as "the capacity to make appropriate responses to challenging or changing situations;

the ability to modify or adjust one's behavior in meeting diverse circumstances or different people" (American Psychological Association, 2021). Therefore, consistent with the description mentioned above, a new adaptability measurement instrument was developed to evaluate people's ability to aptly regulate and adjust psychological and behavioral capacity in reaction to the novel, challenging, difficult conditions, and ambiguous life situations were constructed and confirmed (Martin, 2012; Martin et al., 2012; Nejad, 2014).

The following section builds on these recent studies and provides evidence that while adaptability stock is influenced by personality and implicit theory factors within individuals, yet it significantly predicts the degrees and qualities of satisfaction with life and self-esteem (also known as happiness), and meaning and purpose (which may well be under the umbrella of spirituality). Furthermore, the emergent study evinces that meaning in life (i.e., meaning and purpose) is a catalyst among the following constructs:

- Well-being and religion (Krok, 2014; Zika & Chamberlain, 1992);
- Subjective well-being and innate religious nature (Ardelt, 2003);
- Life satisfaction and spirituality (religiousness) (Steger & Frazier, 2005).

Consistent with the studies mentioned above, it is posited that meaning and purpose, and adaptability are closely associated, which would have a relevant impact on workplace enjoyment and functioning (Krok, 2015).

Nejad (2014) unfolded the adaptability concept to examine its more appropriate elements explicitly, cognitive, emotive, behavioral regulations experiencing change, uncertainty, variability, and novelty throughout life. Cognitive regulation signifies modifications in the way we think and how we deal with change and uncertainties. Behavioral regulation denotes adjustments in the quality, level, degree of behavior, and actions to manage novel and varying circumstances (Heckhausen, 1999; Heckhausen & Schulz, 1995; Nejad, 2014; Schulz & Heckhausen, 1996; Tomasik et al., 2010). It is critical to emphasize that job performance is defined as equivalent to behavior. In this context, what individuals do can be monitored and measured in terms of each person's skill or contribution level (Campbell et al., 1993; Pulakos et al., 2000). Emotional regulation is judged in terms of the emotional adjustment that has the propensity to modulate in response to macro and microenvironmental challenges and uncertainties (Gross, 1998; Nejad, 2014; Pekrun, 2012; Pekrun & Stephens, 2009).

Martin and colleagues developed the adaptability scale based on this multilateral perspective of the hypothesized adaptability construct (Martin et al., 2012). The scale encompassed variables, which fulfilled the following three principles: (i) appropriate thinking, behavioral or emotional modification in an attempt to deal with (ii) ambiguity, difficulty, and novelty that leads to (iii) a positive goal and objective result. Based on a sample of 2731 high school students, exploratory and confirmatory factor analysis (EFA and CFA) identified adaptability as a higher-order factor subsumed by a reliable first-order cognitive–behavioral factor and a reliable first-order affective factor—but for operational purposes, a single global adaptability factor was also deemed appropriate (Martin et al., 2012; Nejad, 2014). The study showed that incremental beliefs of ability, buoyancy, agreeableness, extraversion, conscientiousness, and openness are positively associated with adaptability. On the other hand, adaptability is negatively associated with neuroticism and entity beliefs.

Furthermore, achievement, enjoyment of school (or workplace), meaning and purpose, and life satisfaction (including job satisfaction) are positively associated with adaptability (Martin et al., 2012; Nejad, 2014). The adaptability research was conducted within the high school setting and with students. However, as it will be discussed in the upcoming sections, it is appropriate to replace "students" with "workers" and "school" with "workplace" in this workplace-related analysis because the adaptability capacity, primarily, is an innate stock that can be improved, developed, and primed through learning new strategies and techniques (Nejad, 2014).

Adaptation Paradigms

Theories and studies applicable to subjective psychological well-being have also examined the way individuals adjust to desirable and undesirable events and circumstances in life. One of the leading works in this domain is the adaptation model of well-being (Diener et al., 2006). The adaptation theory is established on an instinctive conditioning conjecture that an entity responds to change from its present acclimatization and modification levels and abilities (Diener et al., 2006). Diener and associates (2006) have sketched out several modifications to the theory that include the notion that people differ in the particular approaches they employ to make adjustments. In the adaptability analysis, this is explored utilizing disparities in the thinking, behavioral, and emotional modification managing ambiguity and change.

Moreover, they also pointed out that people perceive adaptation based on their personal inclination toward adaptation and the microenvironment in which they grow up. The above assertion suggests the need to investigate dispositional predictors (personality, incremental theory, and implicit theory) of adaptability. Finally, it is contended in this work that the modifications made by Diener and colleagues are in line with the hypotheses the authors of the current chapter made about adaptability, workers, workplace spirituality, and well-being.

Adaptability and Human Development

The more current applications of Buss and Cantor (1989) work in the educational framework investigated an adaptability growth model in terms of (a) people's temperaments or characteristics inclination effect and (b) the approaches they utilize to deal with their environmental impositions that impact (c) their well-being in such circumstances. This outlook on human performance recognizes approaches that guide the connection between temperament and different responses (Kyl-Heku & Buss, 1996). It further focuses on how personalities can be progressively communicated to unravel challenges by responding to various triggers and situations to attain favorable outcomes (Cantor, 1990; Rossier et al., 2017).

Martin et al. (2012) researched the various theories and conceptual models of temperaments and disposition. They were understood as implicit beliefs about intelligence and personality. They also described the individual's approach to adaptability and well-being as academic (such as connectedness and disconnectedness) and non-academics (such as satisfaction with life, self-esteem, meaning and purpose in life, and emotional instability such as neuroticism, excessive worrying, and tension) factors. The researchers incorporated individual background factors such as prior achievement and socio-demographic factors to account for personal as well as microenvironmental factors. Furthermore, the investigators incorporated self-regulation and buoyancy factors in conjunction with adaptability to examine its uniqueness from these seemingly equivalent concepts and factors.

The theoretical models are introduced in various figures in Martin and colleagues' published work (2012). Accordingly, as shown in their research, personality and the implicit theories predict adaptability; buoyancy and self-regulation are located alongside adaptability as cognate-correlates to control; adaptability (and buoyancy and self-regulation) predicts academic (under the workplace framework, this would be denoted as the workplace) and non-academic (non-work-related) well-being, as do personality and the implicit theories; and socio-demographic and achievement covariates are included in the model. Moreover, Hall and Chandler (2005) affirmed that people (workers) with a high and advanced level of adaptability would have the faculty and competency to participate proficiently, proactively, and effectively in activities that require establishing goals, conjuring efforts, and attaining psychological and work-related success (O'connell et al., 2007). Therefore, it is concluded that the ability to establish goals, conjuring efforts to carry out and achieve those goals, and attain psychological (self-actualization and happiness) and work-related success are the aims (purpose) of workers at work.

Taken together, the human developmental model reaffirms that the ability to be adaptable and possess the capacity to utilize adaptability resources is to plan ahead and/or fight against immediate complications. To fight the complications that life throws at us is not only a survival instrument or instinct but also a means for achieving excellence and an actualized self. The type of excellence and actualization lends itself (partly or entirely) to feeling happy, content, and satisfied with life.

Well-being Modules

Relevant to youth, it is suggested that academic and psychological well-being encompasses adaptive and maladaptive aspects of academic as well as non-academic welfare. Similarly, relevant to workers, the emerging studies propose that workplace subjective mental health progresses toward effective job satisfaction and productivity (Pulakos et al., 2000; Tariq et al., 2011; Van Dam et al., 2010) which includes adaptive and maladaptive aspects of the work and non-work-related well-being.

Martin and colleagues hypothesized that students low in adaptability (and hence less capable of negotiating uncertainty and challenges) might anticipate low efficacy, and a greater probability of poor performance may thus be more predisposed to maneuver defensively (e.g., self-handicap) or give up trying (disengage) all together (2001). Similarly, negative well-being in the workplace can be described as work-related stress, anxiety, absenteeism, substandard performance, disengagement, and even burnout (Coetzee & Harry, 2014). On the other hand, positive academic well-being factors consist of positive intentions, class participation, and enjoyment of school (Covington, 1992; Martin et al., 2001). Equally, constructive work environment well-being research validates that a higher degree of adaptability results in adaptive workplace well-being which in turn presents itself as higher productivity, higher attendance, and more positive and healthier relationship with superiors and employers (Collie & Martin, 2016; Pulakos et al., 2000; Tariq et al., 2011; Van Dam et al., 2010) and overall harmony.

A study by Sony and Mekoth (2016) regarding the effects of adaptability and emotional intelligence on job performance and job satisfaction asserted that adaptability plays a key factor (similar to job satisfaction) in organizational outcomes. They argued that since an adaptable employee (as an asset for the organization and customers) is prepared to adjust their psychological resources to meet the needs and demands of the workplace, customers, and themselves, which ultimately benefits all parties involved (Cullen et al., 2013, 2014; Chebat & Kollias, 2000; Ahearne et al., 2005; Nesbit & Lam, 2014; Pulakos et al., 2000; Clark, 2000; Keillor et al., 2011). Consequently, it seems reasonable to discern and believe that organizations would want workers who can adjust and apply their adaptability resources through the use of the personal sense of meaning and purpose, and the organizational collective creed to achieve the psychological well-being and job satisfaction that would benefit all.

En masse, subjective well-being in the workplace may well be conjectured as a motivator toward excellence. However, to achieve excellence and perform to the best of one's ability, one must be adaptable and willing to adjust and manage his or her personal resources to become resilient, buoyant, and flexible. Furthermore, people also need to use a catalyst and mediator to promote and stimulate the functioning and fine-tuning of their adaptability capacity. It is surmised that spirituality can assist individuals with their adaptability resource inspiration, management, and modifications.

Positive Non-work-related Well-being

Observing through a life span conjecture lens, the ability to control is achieved by positively modifying thinking and behavior and participating in different and select paths that set the groundwork for an improved inventory of meaning and purpose capacity (Wrosch & Scheier, 2003). Additionally, the enhanced ability to control, moderate, and adjust thinking and behavioral and emotional capitals are likely linked to the subjective sense of welfare and well-being components such as self-respect, self-approval, self-worth, and life satisfaction (2003). For example, the successful modification should result in goal attainment and fewer failure experiences, leading to a higher sense of self-esteem and perceived self-worth (Wrosch et al., 2003). Research has also linked life satisfaction with broadened[1] cognitive capacity and resources (Fredrickson, 2001). This broadening of capacity is aligned with the adaptability concept. The adaptability measurement work found that adaptability significantly correlated with people's sense of meaning and purpose ($r = 0.55$) and life satisfaction ($r = 0.62$) (Martin et al., 2012).

Meaning and Purpose: A Constructive Welfare and Well-being Concept

Frankl (1984) claimed that anguish and agony without reason (purpose) bear despair; henceforth, a person lacking reasoning (meaning and purpose) would succumb to hopelessness and fail to realize his or her true potentials and inner achievement. He contended such a spiritual autonomy and ascend, that cannot be crumpled or seized by others, would promote spiritual, meaningful, and purposeful life. He also proposed that there are three ways that one can realize and achieve meaning in life—through love, work, and suffering (1984). Similarly, he emphasized that merely a handful of people can reach such great spiritual heights and most people lose their belief and spiritual holds throughout their lives, letting themselves decline and become subject to psychological and physical decay and despair.

Life span control research contends that failure to adopt alternative approaches to unattainable goals and maladaptive self-regulation is associated with psychological distress and poor mental health outcomes (Wrosch et al., 2003). In the present chapter, poor mental health is viewed in the form of emotional instability. Emotional instability refers to individuals' moodiness, worry, emotional confusion, and tendency to be unsettled and upset (Marsh, 2007). As a result of the merging trajectories among life span theory with adaptability, meaning and purpose, and spirituality, a distinct and compelling pathway emerges. A pathway that leads to the inauguration and effects of spirituality as an inspiration and a propelling force toward purposeful and satisfying life that is fused with happiness, contentment, success, and ultimately to an actualized life.

Workplace Subjective Well-being

Positive workplace subjective well-being factors are shown to be job satisfaction, a higher sense of belonging, improved performance, and positive intentions (Wills, 2007). These factors have been validated in previous research (Harter et al., 2002),

[1] Fredrickson's broaden-and-build theory of positive emotions argues that positive feelings have a significant and extensive effect on individuals thinking and behavior range. This theory intends to define a model that describes the process behind positive feelings and their effects on our psychological and physical being and how they are significant to our well-being.

and it is argued to be the motivators for workers in their workplace that provide them with the means, purpose, and satisfaction they need to remain loyal, encouraged, and happy (Sageer, 2012). Negative workplace subjective well-being factors, on the other hand, are stress, anxiety, disengagement, absenteeism, low or weak performance, and burnouts (Coetzee & Harry, 2014).

Collectively, the dispositional, general belief about ability, socio-demographics, personality, and adaptability capacity factors predict subjective well-being. Adaptability capacity plays a significant role in this process by predicting its meaning and purpose positively and significantly. It, however, requires a regulatory agent to stimulate, maintain, and/or develop its resources. Thus, it is argued that spirituality and/or psychological interventions are perhaps valuable instruments of change and the development of adaptability.

Non-workplace Welfare and Well-being

Positive non-workplace welfare and well-being factors include the sense of self-esteem, sense of meaning and purpose, satisfaction with life, and negative non-workplace well-being which manifests itself as emotional instability such as stress (Wrosch & Scheier, 2003). That said, the authors also appreciate the fact that non-workplace well-being, in reality, shares a close association with workplace well-being, and together they affect workers' performance and sense of belonging (Winter-Collins & Mcdaniel, 2000) which ultimately benefits everyone who is involved.

Meaning and Purpose

Meaning and purpose, which often is inspired by spirituality, offers individuals a sense of direction, hope, vigor, drive, and focus on a decided target. It gives us a reason to endure and push through suffering, difficult times, and situations. It provides us with the direction and stamina to move forward toward bettering ourselves, thus becoming the better version of ourselves. It helps us become worthy of reaching the holistic and actualized self, which is the source of happiness and eternal love (Leider, 2008).

It is proposed and confirmed here that the correlation among life span theory, adaptability, and presage factors (covariates, dispositional and characteristic, and cognate), meaning and purpose, and spirituality may significantly predict subjective well-being factors. Meaning and purpose is theorized to be an overarching factor that may include religiosity. Although it can stand on its own, it is often a part of the larger construct of spirituality. Meaning and purpose provides people with the reason to live and act in a certain way; it may make suffering purposeful and disbands despair. Consequently, it is recommended that while workers must seek and follow a workplace condition that gives them a positive meaningful and purposeful path, employers and businesses must also search for ways to create and maintain a holistic and wholesome environment. A workplace environment that responds to the needs of the employees becomes more satisfying and motivating which, as a byproduct, might result in higher profits for the business (Steger, 2016).

Spirituality

Spirituality is theorized to be the driving cause behind people's will to achieve a state of affairs that transcends their physical and basic needs, a state of mind (and being) that is over and above the self. Spirituality provides a *why* for every *how* (e.g., why am I here? And how to live a better life?) and is an overarching concept that nurtures a human's purpose in life (Holmberg et al., 2021). A person who acquires spirituality finds his/her meaning and purpose in life. However, a person who finds meaning and purpose in life does not need to acquire spirituality. Spirituality has habitually been exploited and utilized interchangeably with religiosity and sporadically with meaning and purpose (Van Niekerk, 2018; Zinnbauer et al., 1997). It is argued that spirituality is not similar in meaning nor semantics to religiosity or meaning and purpose. Religion has been defined as "a social institution in which a group of people participates rather than an individual search for meaning" (Steiger & Lipson, 1985, p. 212). Accordingly, religion is primarily about an organized system within a group of people in societies that practice certain rituals, beliefs, and traditions (Dyson et al., 1997). However, this does not refute the fact that religion may play a distinctive role in spiritual beliefs for some people. In fact, in some cases, it may provide a platform for spirituality and its manifestation for some people (1997). Furthermore, Hay (1989) proposes that spiritual well-being results in the enhancement of one's inner resources (e.g., the adaptability resources) that would lead to growth in personal as well as professional advancements.

Meaning and purpose is the pursuit of finding meaning in life that is materialized through the pivotal relationship with self, others, and God (or the supreme power), which contributes to finding such purpose (Dyson et al., 1997). Howden (1992) asserts that meaning and purpose in life is a vital feature in spirituality which includes a quest for relationships, a significant person, objects, beliefs, or situations that provide a sense of worth and motivation to live for.

In comparison, religion has commonly been described in behavioral terms, comprised of partaking in culturally based rituals and practices (Johnstone et al., 2008). In contrast, spirituality has been characterized in emotional, experiential, and cognitive terms, which often relates to feelings or experiences of reverence, marvel, congruence, serenity, peace, or connectedness with the universe or higher power (2008). Taken together, the results of various studies suggest that religion and spirituality are distinct yet cognate constructs (2008). Subsequently, founded on the preceding discussion, it is shown that spirituality is an overarching construct that may include meaning and purpose as well as religiosity, depending upon circumstances and the individuals. It is also demonstrated that adaptability mediates life satisfaction, enjoyment of work, job satisfaction, sense of esteem, and meaning and purpose (Nejad, 2014).

Workplace performance and connectedness studies have shown that a worker's strong spiritual belief about a higher power who watches over him/her, who also watches his/her actions, and is aware of his/her thoughts, tries to become an even better person (which includes a better worker) so he/she can become worthy of the divine union (Robert et al., 2006; Walt & Klerk, 2014). It is through such dynamics that workers find the purpose of their existence within their organization and hence form meaning in the work they perform, which in due course leads to a higher level of connectedness, work engagement, job satisfaction, and healthier subjective well-being at work and workplace. Therefore, it seems important that organizations and managers provide an environment for spirituality within their organizations and among their employees to nurture work ethics, effective performance, and positive workplace subjective well-being. That being said, employers need to invest in personal development and after-work training programs that aim at employees' spirituality that aligns with ethics (Lama, 2001), self-fulfillment, personal growth, and self-actualization. This should not be a reason for discrimination; instead, it is a way for businesses and organizations to invest in their employees' personal development combined with professional development that would benefit both parties. Spirituality emphasizes the value of truthfulness and thoughtfulness, tolerance for practices, beliefs, and appreciation for the insights of other religious communities (Seybold & Hill, 2001), arriving at inner peace, purifying egocentrism, promoting altruism, and becoming the best version of self.

Spirituality and Subjective Well-being

The notion of well-being (also referred to as subjective well-being) looks at the assessments of how individuals experience their lives (clearly in a workplace analysis, this notion would look at the workplace life) which includes both negative and positive experiences (Wills, 2007). Individuals can and do judge and measure their subjective well-being as cognitive and/or affective responses (emotionally and/or cognitively) to either as a whole (also referred to as the top-down attitude) or domain-specific (also referred to as the bottom-up attempt) throughout their life (2007). Wills (2007), in his research, introduced and tested a proposed new domain (satisfaction with spirituality and religiosity) to account for the role of spirituality contributing to satisfaction with life, which is a more comprehensive global scale. He concluded that spirituality (and, to some extent, religiosity) significantly predicts satisfaction with the life domain. Cohen (2002) also contends that there is a significant association between spirituality and happiness in Christian nations. Spiritual experiences correlate positively with people's sense of meaning and purpose in life (Kas et al., 1991; Wills, 2007). Wills (2007) further adds that spiritual believers contend that a person is a segment and feature of a superior whole, which shapes and affects how a person acts. Therefore, spiritual well-being becomes a lifelong pursuit of connecting and unifying with the divine whole. This implies and necessitates a process of bonding with self, people, nature, environment, and ultimately the divine or the sacred (Van Dierendonck & Mohan, 2006; Wills, 2007). To bond with the divine, one needs to reach out and become the best version of him/herself. Then, it is logical and natural to imply that spirituality significantly predicts subjective well-being, which provides the drive and motivation to become the best version of oneself. Furthermore, it was conveyed that to become the best in what one can be is to survive; to survive is to be the fittest; to be the fittest, one must be adaptable; and to be adaptable, one needs to recognize her or his adaptability resources to whether utilize them or, if necessary, improve them to overcome the life challenges (Nejad, 2014).

Founded on the preceding discussion, it is shown that spirituality is an overarching construct that includes meaning and purpose as well as religiosity depending upon circumstances and individuals. Furthermore, it is also shown that adaptability mediates life satisfaction, enjoyment of work, job satisfaction, sense of esteem, and meaning and purpose (Nejad, 2014). Therefore, it is suggested that workers who pursue and attain happiness and satisfaction in their work–life tend to perform more effectively and efficiently. Spirituality provides the drive and will to accomplish this pursuit more effectively.

Well-being and Workplace Performance

Workers' performance is affected by strain or boredom when demands in the workplace exceed or fall below the personal resources (also referred to as the adaptability factors or resources) and worker's expectations (Harter et al., 2002). Workers' positive emotions and thoughts lead to a positive appraisal of the workplace, resulting in higher job satisfaction, higher life satisfaction, and better, more efficient performance (2002). The scopes of health and quality-of-life are interdependent and tightly woven (WHOQL Group, 1998), and through this irrefutable relationship among adaptability, quality-of-life or life satisfaction, spirituality, and health, it is plausible to presume that these are complementary and exceedingly dominant factors in people's lives. It is equally permissible to postulate that the workers' well-being is tightly entwined with their sense of belonging, job satisfaction, self-worth, and a sense of purpose in the workplace. Their participation and positive contribution increase overall workplace well-being, which further translates into emotionally healthy workers and higher performances that might yield more significant profits for businesses.

Discussion

As postulated, research shows that people's temperament and belief about their intelligence (the implicit theory) notably predicted adaptability (over and above the influences of past achievements and socio-demographics) (Martin et al., 2012).

Furthermore, as conjectured, adaptability predicted academic (also workplace) and non-academic (non-work-related) idiosyncratic welfare and well-being. Noticeably, adaptability also demonstrated and described the deviation in well-being over and above the influences of past achievement, socio-demographics, temperament, belief about intelligence, and other related factors (self-regulation and buoyancy). It was also highlighted in the preceding discussions that adaptability factors (cognitive, emotional, and behavioral) positively predicted Wrosch and Scheier's positive self-esteem, meaning and purpose (which often is a facet of spirituality), and negatively emotional instability (also known as neuroticism) (2003). Furthermore, it was shown that spirituality, while is informed by adaptability resources, also presents itself as a regulatory means for the emerging and evolving adaptability capacities (Southwick et al., 2011). Adaptability is significantly mediated by the relationship between personality, incremental beliefs, and subjective well-being (see Fig. 2). It is also revealed that spirituality is an overarching construct that includes meaning and purpose as well as religiosity depending upon the circumstances and the individuals. Likewise, since adaptability mediates life satisfaction, enjoyment of school (work), job satisfaction, sense of self-esteem, and meaning and purpose (Nejad, 2014); it is suggested that workers who pursue happiness and satisfaction in their work–life tend to perform more effectively. Justifiably so, spirituality provides the drive and the will to accomplish subjective well-being more successfully.

Adaptability, Meaning and Purpose, Spirituality, and Well-being

Adaptable workers are more determined in their imminent goals and objectives (constructive adaptive intention). They develop a stronger ability to meet the demands of the fast-paced and challenging nature of their work (contribution at work and resiliency), enjoy greater job-related subjective well-being (job contentment), and are reluctant to behave reactionary and defensively (self-handicapping) or disengage (Collie, & Martin, 2016; Martin et al., 2012; Pulakos et al., 2000; Tariq, Anwar, & Aslam, 2011; Van Dam, et al., 2010). Regarding non-work-related well-being and welfare, the authors turned into life span and adaptation contexts to claim that adaptability should significantly predict idiosyncratic sense of welfare and well-being (Diener et al., 2006), purposefulness and spirituality (Wrosch, et al., 2003), and predicted mental anxiety negatively (Wrosch, et al., 2003).

In line with suppositions made by the researchers, adaptability distinctively predicted the idiosyncratic welfare and well-being constructs (namely spirituality and meaning and purpose) in the projected path. Studies indicate the relationships between religious coping and psychological well-being are facilitated by spirituality and finding meaning in life (Krok, 2015). Moreover, the relationship between temperament and well-being in addition to incremental beliefs and well-being is significantly facilitated by adaptability. This facilitating capacity also detailed the salient deviation over and above the other related academic constructs of self-regulation and buoyancy. Therefore, peoples' intellectual, emotional, and behavioral modifications to disruption, uncertainty, and challenges in life contribute to their well-being, over and above the adversity-related features of buoyancy and the regulatory features of self-regulation.

Consequently, as it was highlighted in the earlier discussions, adaptability factors (cognitive, emotional, and behavioral) positively predicted life satisfaction, self-esteem, meaning and purpose (a component of spirituality), and negatively predicted emotional instability (also known as neuroticism) (Wrosch et al., 2003, Wrosch, Scheier, Miller, et al., 2003). Further, it was shown that spirituality, while informed by adaptability resources, also presents itself as a regulatory means for emerging and evolving adaptability capacities (Southwick et al., 2011).

En masse, it is plausible to presume that the existing relationship among adaptability, quality-of-life or life satisfaction, spirituality, and health are complementary factors and are exceedingly dominant in people's lives. It is equally acceptable to suggest that the workers' well-being is tightly entwined with their sense of belonging, job satisfaction, self-worth, and higher and a healthier sense of purpose in a workplace. Well-being at the workplace considering the mentioned parameters will lead to healthier workers and better performance that might generate higher profits for businesses.

Implications for Intervention

The authors suggest that adaptability aims at cultivating or sustaining individuals' ability to deal with change and novelty, "on the front foot" strategy, and on an ongoing basis, utilizing spirituality as the medium of facilitating, improving, and regulating such ability. Adopting this framework, adaptability intervention might comprise the following steps:

- The individual is taught how to realistically and effectively recognize change and novelty that might require adaptability and spiritual interventions.
- People are taught how to make appropriate adjustments to behavior, cognition, and emotion.
- These adjustments assist the individuals to deal with change and challenges in life (and at work).
- Individuals are encouraged to recognize the value of these regulations and then refine and improve them.
- These continuous refinement and implementation of behavioral, cognitive, and emotive modification sustain the individual's ability to deal with ongoing change, variability, novelty, and uncertainty in life.

- The recognition of the complementary role that spirituality and adaptability play in the development, sustainment, and improvement of people's subjective well-being, including workplace well-being.
- The recognition of the role that well-being plays in today's business world and how it can improve performance and profitability.

Additionally, the adaptability interventions need to take into account another factor in helping people, that is, the contributions of a meaningful and purposeful life and—relevant to that context—the contributions of spirituality. There is significant and vast research on cognitive-behavioral and emotional treatment and counseling indicating that people can adjust thinking, behavior, and feelings to more productively and efficiently function in work and academic environment (Craven et al., 1991; Hattie, 2009; McInerney et al., 1997; O'Mara et al., 2006). These well-aimed treatments and counseling sessions may be a basis for generating the form of modifications and regulations necessary to efficiently respond to uncertainty, challenges, and difficulties, particularly in the age of COVID-19 and afterward.

Summary

Human life is in constant transition and change, and to survive, we must adapt and adjust our thoughts, emotions, and behavior. Therefore, we need a mechanism to equip us in this endeavor. It is suggested that adaptability might be that mechanism. Adaptability denotes the proper adjustment in thinking, behavior, and emotion against the novel, challenging, and difficult life conditions. Based on previous research on establishing the psychometric features of the Adaptability Scalethey need to be mentioned and discussed in the paper, the current chapter succinctly discussed the personality and the implicit theories factors of adaptability and how adaptability predicted vocational idiosyncratic welfare and well-being, and non-work-related well-being. It also showed that spirituality could be the driving force behind the improved performance, job satisfaction, employee/worker engagement, and workplace subjective well-being. Results support experimental and theoretical applications for scholars and mental health specialists pursuing to learn more about responses to the challenges and variabilities that are realities of the world for the workforce, particularly in the age of COVID-19 and afterward. The present work allows managers and business leaders to comprehend better their employees and how to inspire them to accomplish more beneficial outcomes and profits.

References

Ahearne, M., Mathieu, J., & Rapp, A. (2005). To empower or not to empower your sales force? An empirical examination of the influence of leadership empowerment behavior on customer satisfaction and performance. *Journal of Applied Psychology, 90*(5), 945.

American Psychological Association. (2021, April 15). https://dictionary.apa.org/adaptability.
Ardelt, M. (2003). Empirical assessment of a three-dimensional wisdom scale. *Research on Aging, 25*(3), 275–324. https://doi.org/10.1177/0164027503025003004
Buss, D. W., & Cantor, N. (1989). *Personality psychology: Recent trends and emerging directions.* Springer.
Campbell, J. P., McCloy, R. A., Oppler, S. H., & Sager, C. E. (1993). A theory of performance. In N. Schmitt & W. C. Borman (Eds.), *Personnel selection in organizations* (pp. 35–70). Jossey-Bass.
Cantor, N. (1990). From thought to behavior: 'Having' and 'doing' in the study of personality and cognition. *American Psychologist, 45*, 735–750.
Chebat, J. C., & Kollias, P. (2000). The impact of empowerment on customer contact employees' roles in service organizations. *Journal of Service Research, 3*(1), 66–81.
Clark, B. H. (2000). Managerial perceptions of marketing performance: efficiency, adaptability, effectiveness, and satisfaction. *Journal of Strategic marketing, 8*(1), 3–25.
Coetzee, M., & Harry, N. (2014). Emotional intelligence as a predictor of employees' career adaptability. *Journal of Vocational Behavior, 84*(1), 90–97. https://doi.org/10.1016/j.jvb.2013.09.001
Cohen, A. B. (2002). The importance of spirituality in well-being for Jews and Christians. *Journal of Happiness Studies, 3*(3), 287–310. https://doi.org/10.1023/a:1020656823365
Collie, R. J., & Martin, A. J. (2016). Adaptability: An important capacity for effective teachers. *Educational Sciences: Practice and Theory, 38*(1), 27–39. https://doi.org/10.7459/ept/38.1.03
Covington, M. V. (1992). *Making the grade: A self-worth perspective on motivation and school reform.* Cambridge University Press.
Craven, R. G., Marsh, H. W., & Debus, R. L. (1991). Effects of internally focused feedback and attributional feedback on the enhancement of academic self-concept. *Journal of Educational Psychology, 83*, 17–26.
Cullen, K. L., Edwards, B. D., Casper, W. C., & Gue, K. R. (2013). Employees' adaptability and perceptions of change-related uncertainty: Implications for perceived organizational support, job satisfaction, and performance. *Journal of Business Psychology 29*,1–12.
Cullen, K. L., Edwards, B. D., Casper, W. C., & Gue, K. R. (2014). Employees' adaptability and perceptions of change-related uncertainty: Implications for perceived organizational support, job satisfaction, and performance. *Journal of Business Psychology, 29*(2), 269–280.
Lama, D. (2001). *Ethics for the new millennium.* Riverhead Books.
Diener, E., Lucas, R., & Scollon, C. N. (2006). Beyond the hedonic treadmill: Revising the adaptation theory of well-being. *American Psychologist, 61*, 305–314.
Dyson, J., Cobb, M., & Forman, D. (1997). The meaning of spirituality: A literature review. *Journal of Advanced Nursing, 26*(6), 1183–1188. https://doi.org/10.1111/j.13652648.1997.tb00811.x
Fachrunnisa, O., Adhiatma, A., & Mutamimah, M. (2014). The role of workplace spirituality and employee engagement to enhance job satisfaction and performance. *International Journal of Organizational Innovation, 7*(1), 15–35.
Frankl, V. E. 1. (1984). *Man's search for meaning.* Washing Square Press.
Fredrickson, B. L. (2001). The role of positive emotions in positive psychology. *American Psychologist, 56*, 218–226.
Foster, S., & Wall, T. (2019). Organizational initiatives for spiritual well-being. In *Encyclopedia of the UN sustainable development goals good health and well-being* (pp. 527–539).https://doi.org/10.1007/978-3-319-95681-7_94
Galek, K., Flannelly, K. J., Ellison, C. G., Silton, N. R., & Jankowski, K. R. B. (2015). Religion, meaning and purpose, and mental health. *Psychology of Religion and Spirituality, 7*(1), 1–12. https://doi.org/10.1037/a0037887
Garcia-Zamor, J. (2003). Workplace spirituality and organizational performance. *Public Administration Review, 63*(3), 355–363. https://doi.org/10.1111/1540-6210.00295
Gross, J. J. (1998). The emerging field of emotion regulation: An integrative review. *Review of General Psychology, 2*, 271–299.

Hall, D. T., & Chandler, D. E. (2005). Psychological success: When the career is a calling. *Journal of Organizational Behavior, 26*(2), 155–176. https://doi.org/10.1002/job.301

Harter, Schmidt, & Keyes, (2002). Well-being in the workplace and its relationship to business outcomes: A review of the gallup studies. In C. L. Keyes & J. Haidt (Eds.), *Flourishing: The positive person and the good life* (pp. 205–224). American Psychological Association.

Hattie, J. (2009). *Visible learning: A synthesis of over 800 meta-analyses relating to achievement*. Routledge.

Hay, M. W. (1989). Principles in building spiritual assessment tools. *American Journal of Hospice Care, 6*(5), 25–31. https://doi.org/10.1177/104990918900600514

Heckhausen, J. (1999). *Developmental regulation in adulthood: Age-normative and socio-structural constraints as adaptive challenges*. Cambridge University Press.

Heckhausen, J., & Schulz, R. (1995). A lifespan theory of control. *Psychological Review, is It Adaptive, 102*, 284–304.

Holmberg, Å., Jensen, P., & Vetere, A. (2021). Spirituality—A forgotten dimension? Developing spiritual literacy in family therapy practice. *Journal of Family Therapy, 43*(1), 78–95. https://doi.org/10.1111/1467-6427.12298

Howden, J. W. (1992). *Development and psychometric characteristics of the spirituality assessment scale*. Texas Woman's University, UMI Dissertation Services. (Unpublished doctoral dissertation), Ann Arbor.

Johnstone, B., Yoon, D. P., Franklin, K. L., Schopp, L., & Hinkebein, J. (2008). Re-conceptualizing the factor structure of the brief multidimensional measure of religiousness/spirituality. *Journal of Religion and Health, 48*(2), 146–163. https://doi.org/10.1007/s10943-008-9179-9

Kas, J. D., Friedman, R., Lescrman, J., Zuttermeister, P. C., & Benson, H. (1991). Health Outcomes and a new index of spiritual experience. *Journal for Scientific Study of Religion, 30*, 203–211.

Keillor, B. D., Pettijohn, C. E., & d'Amico, M. (2011). The relationship between attitudes toward technology, adaptability, and customer orientation among professional salespeople. *Journal of Applied Business Research, 17*(4), 31–40.

Krok, D. (2014). The mediating role of coping in the relationships between religiousness and mental health. *Archives of Psychiatry and Psychotherapy, 16*(2), 5–13. https://doi.org/10.12740/APP/26313

Krok, D. (2015). The role of meaning in life within the relations of religious coping and psychological well-being. *Journal of Religion and Health, 54*(6), 2292–2308. https://doi.org/10.1007/s10943-014-9983-3

Kyl-Heku, L. M., & Buss, D. M. (1996). Tactics as unit of analyses in personality psychology: An illustration using tactics of hierarchy negotiation. *Personality and Individual Differences, 21*, 497–519.

Leider, R. (2008). *The power of purpose: Creating meaning in your life and work*. Read How You Want.

Marsh, H. W. (2007). *Self-concept theory, measurement and research into practice: The role of self-concept in educational psychology*. British Psychological Society.

Martin, A. J. (2012). Adaptability and learning. In N. M. Seel (Ed.). *Encyclopedia of the sciences of learning*. Springer.

Martin, A. J., Marsh, H. W., & Debus, R. L. (2001). Self-handicapping and defensive pessimism: Exploring a model of predictors and outcomes from a self-protection perspective. *Journal of Educational Psychology, 93*, 87–102.

Martin, A. J., Nejad, H., Colmar, S., & Liem, G. A. D. (2012). Adaptability: Conceptual and empirical perspectives on responses to change, novelty, and uncertainty. *Australian Journal of Guidance and Counselling, 22*, 58–81.

McInerney, V., McInerney, D. M., & Marsh, H. W. (1997). Effects of metacognitive strategy training within a cooperative group learning context on computer achievement and anxiety: An aptitude-treatment interaction study. *Journal of Educational Psychology, 89*, 686–695.

Milliman, J., Czaplewski, A. J., & Ferguson, J. (2003). Workplace spirituality and employee work attitudes. *Journal of Organizational Change Management, 16*(4), 426–447. https://doi.org/10.1108/09534810310484172

Nejad, H. (2014). *Adaptability in youth: components, predictors, and consequences.* [Doctoral dissertation, the University of Sydney, Australia].

Nesbit, P. L., & Lam, E. (2014). Cultural adaptability and organizational change: A case study of a social service organization in Hong Kong. *Contemporary Management Research, 10*(4).

O'connell, D. J., Mcneely, E., & Hall, D. T. (2007). Unpacking personal adaptability at work. *Journal of Leadership and Organizational Studies, 14*(3), 248–259. https://doi.org/10.1177/1071791907311005

O'Mara, A. J., Marsh, H. W., Craven, R. G., & Debus, R. (2006). Do self-concept interventions make a difference? A synergistic blend of construct validation and meta-analysis. *Educational Psychologist, 41*, 181–206.

Pekrun, R. (2012). Emotion regulation. In N. Seel (Ed.), *Encyclopedia of the sciences of learning.* Springer.

Pekrun, R., & Stephens, E. J. (2009). Goals, emotions, and emotion regulation: Perspectives of the control-value theory of achievement emotions. *Human Development, 52*, 357–365.

Pulakos, E. D., Arad, S., Donovan, M. A., & Plamondon, K. E. (2000). Adaptability in the workplace: Development of a taxonomy of adaptive performance. *Journal of Applied Psychology, 85*(4), 612–624. https://doi.org/10.1037/0021-9010.85.4.612

Robert, T. E., Young, J. S., & Kelly, V. A. (2006). Relationships between adult workers' spiritual well-being and job satisfaction: A preliminary study. *Counseling and Values, 50*(3), 165–175. https://doi.org/10.1002/j.2161-007x.2006.tb00053.x

Rossier, J., Ginevra, M. C., Bollmann, G., & Nota, L. (2017). The importance of career adaptability, career resilience, and employability in designing a successful life. *Psychology of Career Adaptability, Employability and Resilience*, 65–82.https://doi.org/10.1007/978-3-319-66954-0_5

Sageer, A. (2012). Identification of variables affecting employee satisfaction and their impact on the organization. *IOSR Journal of Business and Management, 5*(1), 32–39. https://doi.org/10.9790/487x-0513239

Saks, A. M. (2011). Workplace spirituality and employee engagement. *Journal of Management, Spirituality and Religion, 8*(4), 317–340. https://doi.org/10.1080/14766086.2011.630170

Schulz, R., & Heckhausen, J. (1996). A life span model of successful aging. *American Psychologist, 51*, 702–714.

Seybold, K. S., & Hill, P. C. (2001). The role of religion and spirituality in mental and physical health. *Current Directions in Psychological Science, 10*(1), 21–24. https://doi.org/10.1111/1467-8721.00106

Sony, M., & Mekoth, N. (2016). The relationship between emotional intelligence, frontline employee adaptability, job satisfaction, and job performance. *Journal of Retailing and Consumer Services, 30*, 20–32. https://doi.org/10.1016/j.jretconser.2015.12.003

Southwick, S. M., Litz, B. T., & Charney, D. S. (2011). *Resilience and mental health: Challenges across the lifespan.* Cambridge University Press.

Steger, M. F. (2016). Creating meaning and purpose at work. In *The Wiley blackwell handbook of the psychology of positivity and strengths-based approaches at work* (pp. 60–81).https://doi.org/10.1002/9781118977620.ch5.

Steger, M. F., Dik, B. J., & Duffy, R. D. (2012). Measuring meaningful work. *Journal of Career Assessment, 20*(3), 322–337. https://doi.org/10.1177/1069072711436160

Steger, M. F., & Frazier, P. (2005). Meaning in Life: One link in the chain from religiousness to well-being. *Journal of Counseling Psychology, 52*(4), 574–582. https://doi.org/10.1037/0022-0167.52.4.574

Steiger, N. J., & Lipson, J. G. (1985). *Self-care nursing: Theory and practice.* Brady Communications.

Tariq, M. R., Anwar, M. S., Aslam, M. (2011). Impact of employee adaptability to change towards organizational competitive advantage. *Global Journal Of Management and Business Research, 11*(7).

Tomasik, M. J., Silbereisen, R. K., & Heckhausen, J. (2010). Is it adaptive to disengage from demands of social change? Adjustment to developmental barriers in opportunity-deprived regions. *Motivation and Emotion, 34*, 384–398.

Van Dam, K., Schipper, M., & Runhaar, P. (2010). Developing a competency-based framework for teachers' entrepreneurial behaviour. *Teaching and Teacher Education, 26*(4), 965–971.

Van Dierendonck, D., & Mohan, K. (2006). Some thoughts on spirituality and eudaimonic well-being. *Mental Health, Religion and Culture, 9*(3), 227–238.

Van Niekerk, B. (2018). Religion and spirituality: What are the fundamental differences? *HTS Teologiese Studies/Theological Studies, 74*(3). https://doi.org/10.4102/hts.v74i3.4933.

Vanden Bos, G. R. (2007) (Ed). *American psychological association dictionary of psychology*. American Psychological Association.

Walt, F. V., & Klerk, J. J. (2014). Workplace spirituality and job satisfaction. *International Review of Psychiatry, 26*(3), 379–389. https://doi.org/10.3109/09540261.2014.908826

WHOQL Group. (1998). The World health organization quality of life assessment (WHOQL): Development and general psychometric properties. *Social Science and Medicine, 46*, 1569–1585.

Wills, E. (2007). Spirituality and subjective well-being: Evidences for a new domain in the personal well-being index. *Journal of Happiness Studies, 10*(1), 49–69. https://doi.org/10.1007/s10902-007-9061-6

Winter-Collins, A., & Mcdaniel, A. M. (2000). Sense of belonging and new graduate job satisfaction. *Journal for Nurses in Staff Development (JNSD), 16*(3), 103–111. https://doi.org/10.1097/00124645-200005000-00002.

Wrosch, C., & Scheier, M. F. (2003). Personality and quality of life: The importance of optimism and goal adjustment. *Quality of Life Research, 12*, 59–72.

Wrosch, C., Scheier, M. F., Miller, G. E., Schulz, R., & Carver, C. S. (2003). Adaptive self-regulation of unattainable goals: Goal disengagement, goal reengagement, and subjective well-being. *Personality and Social Psychology Bulletin, 29*, 1494–1508.

Zika, S., & Chamberlain, K. (1992). On the relation between meaning in life and psychological well-being. *British Journal of Psychology, 83*(1), 133–145. https://doi.org/10.1111/j.2044-8295.1992.tb02429.x

Zinnbauer, B. J., Pargament, K. I., Cole, B., Rye, M. S., Butter, E. M., Belavich, T. G., …, Kadar, J. L. (1997). Religion and spirituality: Unfuzzying the fuzzy. *Journal for the Scientific Study of Religion, 36*(4), 549.https://doi.org/10.2307/1387689.

Chapter 16
Spiritually Empowered Leadership through Historical Reflection

Umesh Mukhi

Abstract The theme of leadership continues to attract scholarly attention within the history and management literature. Leadership training courses and management gurus today equally emphasize the importance of IQ and EQ as an essential factor for developing leaders. Yet there is space for scholars to discuss the tacit factors of leadership traits with respect to spirituality and how it influences the leader's decision and its outlook. In this chapter, I argue that it is important to reflect on lives of historical leaders to distill the link between spirituality and leadership. Abraham Lincoln, Dr. Martin Luther King Jr., Mahatma Gandhi, and Gautama Buddha are some exemplary leaders with their actions and thoughts having spiritual roots. They admired achievements but they were also compassionate. Furthermore, these leaders were also integrated in the social system in which they were exercising core functions of leadership in politics, social, and civic sphere that eventually impacted society and the world. Spiritually inspired leadership thus looks inward to build a strong base for inspiration for the individual self. This chapter would thus discuss the importance of spiritually bounded leadership and how managers can pursue it.

Keywords Spirituality · Leadership · Spiritual intelligence · Historical reflection · Sustainable leadership · Learning spaces

Introduction

> I used to think that top environmental problems were biodiversity loss, ecosystem collapse and climate change. I thought that thirty years of good science could address these problems. I was wrong. The top environmental problems are selfishness, greed and apathy, and to deal with these we need a cultural and spiritual transformation. And we scientists don't know how to do that.

Gus Speth

U. Mukhi (✉)
Fundação Getulio Vargas's Sao Paulo School of Business Administration, (FGV EAESP), São Paulo, Brazil
e-mail: umesh.mukhi@fgv.br

© Jindal Institute of Behavioral Sciences 2022

S. P. Sahni et al. (eds.), *Spirituality and Management*,
https://doi.org/10.1007/978-981-19-1025-8_16

(Environmental advisor to Presidents Carter and Clinton, founder of the Natural Resources Defense Council and World Resources Institute, administrator of the U.N. Development Program, dean of the Yale School of Forestry and Environmental Studies, now a professor at Vermont Law School, in conversation with host Steve Curwood, NRDC cofounder, February 13th 2015.)

The study of leadership has received much attention in the recent years. To such an extent that business schools, training organizations, and professional coaches churn out programs promising their clients to become better leaders. Indeed, it must be acknowledged that research in leadership has led to development of various tools to identify deficits and challenge of the leaders. On the positive side, the democratization of knowledge has created a wide pool of knowledge, which could help all the levels of management to develop leadership and development potential in their organization. On the contrary, we do witness that undergoing a leadership training program does not guarantees that a person will become an effective leader. This has become more evident and obvious especially when we look back in the last decade post financial crises about how the global economy has evolved under varied social, political, and environmental scenario in developing and developed nations. While the progress made in Paris Agreement gave us the hope for tackling global warming, extreme rise in inequality, refugee crises rise in racial and social tensions also divided the society. Interestingly, these events were not exclusively limited to the Global South but also to the Global North. Such circumstances present opportunities and challenges for leaders in social, public, and private sector organizations to reflect on past and present to set the trends for future.

Vulnerability to such challenges thus forces us to reflect on what could be effective leadership interventions and mechanisms to help leaders in their sector or situation-specific challenges. For example, to deal with stress in corporate world in recent years, there has been growing interest in studying practices such as Yoga, mindfulness which finds its roots in Indian and Buddhist teachings. For Climate Change, we see Pope Francis's encyclical on ecology in Christianity. Laudato Si emphasizes Christians to tackle this challenge with moral responsibility. In Islam, we observe how Islamic finance tends to incline toward socially responsible and conscious investments. History shows us that religion, thus, has been an integral part of guiding human decision making as well as plays crucial role in setting the societal values. It is also important to highlight the difference of spiritually elevated religious decision making which seeks to build harmony compared to extremist religious beliefs which may bring in divisive elements. History thus brings in the positive and negative contrasts of the critical incidents thereby provoking the sense of making of spiritual essence of religion and the role it plays in developing leadership potential for the just cause. I thus propose that history could help us in developing such interventions, where more specifically we can learn from the lives of the leaders who have been recognized globally for their contribution in various spheres.

In this Chapter, I will provide the brief sketches of the lives of four leaders, namely Gautama Buddha, Abraham Lincoln, Mahatma Gandhi, and Dr. Martin Luther King Jr. First, I will briefly highlight how each one of them went through the churning process of developing a subtle view of Religion, to which I refer as Spirituality. By developing strong spiritual base, these leaders were able to develop their personal and professional competencies required to act in the times of crises Second, I will compare the learnings which could be key takeaways for the leadership. Third, I propose guiding framework, which could help leaders to undertake their own journey so that they could curate and map their path of leadership potential. Finally, I conclude that leaders can have lasting impact in professional and personal sphere. In doing so, they must understand the value of spirituality and true religion through history and develop an innate sense to develop the transforming potential for their leadership journey.

Learning from Spiritually Empowered Leaders

In this section, I will briefly give the overarching view about the lives of the selected leaders in the chronological order. I have specifically selected the four leaders namely Gautama Buddha, Abraham Lincoln, Mahatma Gandhi, and Dr. Martin Luther King Jr. The reason for choosing these leaders stems from the real-world scenario which is grappling with various societal issues. These are racist discourses, diversity, anti-global movements and increasing awareness about mental health and meditation techniques. For example, the Black Lives Matter Movement in USA serves as a critical incident to revisit the lives of the leaders who have fought for equality. Consequently, the increasing awareness of spirituality and well-being leads us to revisit lives of leaders who were able to establish spirituality as a principal foundation for achieving their goals. Lastly, our business courses overwhelmingly deal with business leaders, thereby creating the gap where spiritual leadership can still serve as an excellent case for their significant contribution.

Siddhartha Gautama ([1]563 BCE—483 BCE)

Siddhartha Gautama was born in the Shakya Clan. His father was King and thus was the chief of the clan and therefore Buddha belonged to the royal family. Legends refer that Buddha's future about becoming the enlightened one was prophesied by the priest who was called upon by the King to predict the future of the newly born prince. The King, however, had other aspirations and therefore restricted the life of Buddha within the palace. As a result, Buddha lived the life of luxury and was trained in all the traditional arts and sciences to acquire the throne. From this, we could infer that Buddha was living in a bubble, which would eventually burst, thereby sparking the quest of spiritual journey. Eventually, this moment came when he saw the real world and witnessed the transitional nature of human life, i.e., sickness,

---

[1] https://www.notablebiographies.com/Br-Ca/Buddha.html, Also note that dates of birth and death of Buddha are not definitive and may vary in different sources.

Table 16.1 Eightfold path

Ethical conduct	Mental discipline	Wisdom
Right action Right livelihood Right bond	Right effort Right mindfulness Right concentration	Right view/Understanding Right intention

old age, and death. This moment triggered the spiritual quest, which led him to leave the luxurious life in search of spiritual realization. In his journey, Buddha met many religious scholar, and went to extreme of spiritual and physical practices. He eventually attained enlightenment in 528 BC Bodh Gaya under the tree. From here, we see Buddha's life takes another turn. He became a teacher, a spiritual master whose sole purpose was to disseminate the spiritual path, which could help people to achieve the same state achieved by Buddha.

One may question, what has Buddha got to do with leadership and where do we see his impact. We see it clearly from how Buddha navigated through the maze and myriads of knowledge and yet decided to be firm to achieve the spiritual wisdom. Clearly if we were to see from economic or self-interest perspective, if Buddha wanted, he could have led a luxurious life. Yet we see that there was a force inside him, which compelled him to embrace the uncertainty. One may even imagine what would be the logic of leaving his kingdom without knowing the path even in the geographical or philosophical sense. His leadership journey was stimulated by the outward turbulence, yet it was his inner seeking, which gave him persistence to continue the hard path to enlightenment. Buddha's[2] Dhamma emphasize about the importance of mind in developing leadership potential.

> Whatever an aggressor might do to an aggressor, or an enemy to an enemy a mind that is badly directed can do far worse than that to him. Mother and father might not do for him, or other relatives, much good as a mind that is well-directed can do for him.

Through his grit and grasp over mind he was able to attain the Nirvana (enlightenment) but he did not stop even after achieving this goal. He took on the collective task by engaging in creating a fellowship of followers. The fellowship known as "Sangha," were the ones to practice Buddhism and spread the values for a greater impact on the society. Thus, leaders can learn from the Buddha's Noble Eightfold Path, which could be classified in three sections as shown below in Table 16.1:

The eightfold path lays out the basic principles of ethical conduct for everyone and has guided civilizations to pursue the path of harmony. To illustrate this, I would highlight King Ashoka's example on how he renounced the violence and took to Buddhism. It is one of such concrete example where one sees direct relationship on how Buddha's preaching influenced the state affairs. Furthermore, many other regions officially adopted Buddhism, which highlights increasing importance of how spirituality plays a crucial role in governing state. Similarly, organizations and individuals can inspire from such principles to create the purpose-oriented charter for their conduct.

[2] Dhamma verses of Buddha from the chapter about the mind sourced from Sutta central.

Finally, one may also recall that Buddha's influence still persists in the modern world, Buddha's philosophy of "The Noble Eightfold Path" has inspired many people in East and West to take up to Buddhism. Scientific research on meditation, importance of meditation in corporate world, and people seeking harmony in life have drawn inspiration from Buddhism and have benefitted many seekers.

Abraham Lincoln (1809–1865)

Abraham Lincoln, the 16th president of the USA has been the inspiration for scholars, historians, and even Presidents. Lincoln by far is known to show exemplary leadership during the American Civil War and for his efforts to restore the union through Emancipation Proclamation to end racial inequality. When Lincoln assumed the Presidency, the Civil War presented one of the greatest crises faced by USA economically, politically, morally, and legally which could destabilize the union. The President, however, was also leading another battle on the personal front as he lost his son William Willie in 1962 due to typhoid. The President and his wife could never recover from this profound loss, yet even more challenging was to deal with the state affairs and toll of death during the Civil War. Often during such times, although the President became vulnerable emotionally, and physically, he could not escape his responsibilities. He came to realize that he was left with no choice and had to rely on his inner strength and resilience to lead in challenging times. The President never really expressed his religious views but spiritually one may see his reflection on how he intended to uproot slavery, which was the root cause of Civil War.

It must be emphasized that while it makes moral and ethical sense in our present times to see that each human being needs to be treated with dignity, the American society during that time was still shackled in the bond of slavery. Within USA during that period, the Civil War was waged between the Northern US, which was anti-slavery, and the South (Confederacy) being proslavery. Owing to the loss of certain battles, the President was also subject to severe criticism from the politicians, press, and civil society. As Koehn (2017) highlights in her book Forged in Crises, there were times where President could not bear the loss of life, he often felt miserable and criticized himself of why he was put in such a tight situation. In light of these events, we may ponder how the President managed to lead such a controversial issue, which ripped the society apart. What we know from his life is that he was a self-learned and self-trained individual and that he read a lot. Thus, we could only imply that the series of events in the society coupled with his thirst of knowledge led him to develop the broader and yet universal view of human suffering. Furthermore, excerpts from the President's correspondence give us the insight of his thinking about how he gradually came to see the greater cause of Civil War. As the war became more intense, he witnessed what was controllable and what was uncontrollable and amidst these forces, he evolved spiritually. For the purpose of the illustration, I will highlight certain excerpts of Presidents Correspondence, which highlights this gradual development of spiritual worldview.

> [3]That I am not a member of any Christian Church, is true; but I have never denied the truth of the Scriptures; and I have never spoken with intentional disrespect of religion in general, or of any denomination of Christians in particular. (Lincoln, 1846)
>
> [4]I think that if anything can be proved by natural theology, it is that slavery is morally wrong. God gave man a mouth to receive bread, hands to feed it, and his hand has a right to carry bread to his mouth without controversy. (Lincoln, 1860)
>
> [5]I claim not to have controlled events but confess plainly that events have controlled me. Now, at the end of three years struggle the nation's condition is not what either party, or any man devised, or expected. God alone can claim it. Whither it is tending seems plain. If God now wills the removal of a great wrong, and wills also that we of the North as well as you of the South, shall pay fairly for our complicity in that wrong, impartial history will find therein new cause to attest and revere the justice and goodness of God. (Lincoln, 1864)

The excerpts (as above) of President Lincoln provide us a glimpse of how he saw the divine or rather metaphysical representation of events happening in the society. Through his knowledge and interpretation of Bible, he was able to contrast the picture of those following religion in the strict sense and not adhering to the basic human principle of equality versus those adhering to basic human principles that automatically leads to living life as per Bible. Thus, we may also infer that based on his intrinsic faith, the President was also able to make courageous decisions such as issuing the Emancipation Proclamation in 1862. Until then, the focus of the war was to preserve the union. However, as he realized that slavery was the root cause of war, the emancipation of slaves fighting for the rebels was extremely necessary to end the war and eventually prepare the country for abolishing the slavery. We thus see an exemplary act of using the presidential powers to achieve the goal of racial equality.

Mohandas Karamchand Gandhi (1869–1948)

The world knows Gandhi because of Satyagraha, a unique weapon to combat social injustice. It is important to shed light on what created the spiritual and material basis for this weapon to come into action. Gandhi's quest for spirituality was not kindled till he had set foot in foreign land. During his stay in England, he was approached by the Olcott Brothers about the meaning of certain Sanskrit words from the sacred scripture of Bhagavad Gita. But, Gandhi felt ashamed, as he was not able to interpret Sanskrit and could not give a proper translation. Nevertheless, this first encounter with "Bhagavad Gita" made a deep impression on his mind for his lifetime. In his autobiography, he comments:

> The verses in the second chapter If one Ponders on objects of the sense, there springs Attraction; from attraction grows desire, Desire flames to fierce passion, passion breeds

[3] The excerpt from the President's Lincoln's response to Handbill Replying to Charges of Infidelity on July 31, 1846.

[4] The excerpt from Speech at Speech at Hartford, Connecticut on March 5, 1860.

[5] The excerpt from Letter to Albert G. Hodges on April 4, 1864.

> Recklessness; then the memory all betrayed Lets noble purpose go, and saps the mind, Till purpose, mind, and man are all undone. made a deep impression on my mind, and they still ring in my ears. The book struck me as one of priceless worth. The impression has ever since been growing on me with the result that I regard it today as the book par excellence for the knowledge of Truth. It has afforded me invaluable help in my moments of gloom. (Gandhi, 1927, p 82)

The feeling of shame coupled with lack of knowledge stimulated Gandhi to take the challenge to learn about major religious books like Bible and the Qur'an. As portrayed in his autobiography, he took on to avid reading of various religions thereby trying to find the commonality in their preaching.

> But the New Testament produced a different impression, especially the Sermon on the Mount which went straight to my heart. I compared it with the Gita. The verses, 'But I say unto you, that ye resist not evil: but whosoever shall smite thee on thy right cheek, turn to him the other also. And if any man take away thy coat let him have thy cloke too,' delighted me beyond measure and put me in mind of Shamal Bhatt's 'For a bowl of water, give a goodly meal' etc. My young mind tried to unify the teaching of the Gita, The Light of Asia and the Sermon on the Mount. That renunciation was the highest form of religion appealed to me greatly. (Gandhi, 1927 p83)

It is important to recall that Gandhi derived the inspiration for his social movement from this spiritual base. It permeated in every sphere of his life thereby creating an image of a leader who walks the talk. This became possible because Gandhi firmly believed on applying the spiritual practices on himself to experiment and learn from it. In his struggle, Gandhi underwent physical, emotional, and political hardships from the colonial oppressors. From where did he find the courage to stay in minimum clothing, engage in freedom struggle, fast, and manage the expectations of fellow activists? The inspiration for undergoing this goes back to some of the eternal principles of Indian scriptures, spirituality and Yoga as enunciated by Gita. Giving up self in the service of God without expecting results, standing for the truth and developing compassion for fellow human beings were the principles which he was trying to implement through his life. Finally, it is not surprising that Gandhi has cited numerous times about the how he was helped in extreme situations, which he attributed some divine connection. We also witness that Gandhi tried to break away from the shackles of myopic worldview to develop a universal approach by studying other religions. In doing so, he had developed unique leadership competencies to bridge different segments of the society from all religions. We could thus say that he developed spirituality in subtle way which would propel not only his material goal but rather find the commonness in his personal and professional objective.

Dr. Martin Luther King Jr. (1929–1968)

Dr. King won the Nobel Prize for his activism and is known for his speech "I have a Dream." He became one of the foremost names in the history of USA to promote racial justice. There was no dearth of knowledge of scriptures and religion for him, as he was the Church Pastor. It is interesting to draw the linkage between the efforts of President Lincoln and Dr. King, Lincoln via 13th amendment by abolishing slavery had created a platform via constitutional means to promote racial equality yet the conscience of American society was not ready to heal. Dr. King witnessed segregation, a common practice that led to racial tensions thereby stimulating series of protests during the time. It is during this time that he emerged as visionary leader providing voice to the marginalized but also envisioning the equitable and harmonious future between the black and whites. In 1957, he was elected as the President of the Southern Christian Leadership Conference (SCLC), which immediately gave him a nationwide platform to organize the protests against discrimination. While King banked upon his Christian ideals to develop a firm moral character, he still sought out new tools, which could be deployed to further the cause he was fighting for. In essence, King also saw that the real message of Christ was neither fully practiced nor implemented by American White because of their discriminatory practices. Building on the purest principles and the message of Christ, he created the confluence of East and West where he looks upon Gandhi as an eternal resource to guide his struggle via the means of non-violence. In 1959, he visited India to understand the Gandhian philosophy of Satyagraha and came back to USA with a deeper commitment toward the struggle for his fellow African-Americans. In principle, Dr. King had to travel across the continent to expand his horizon; he took on not only the outward journey but also inward journey to expand and rethink his ideals so that he could create the confluence of his faith in God as per his Christian ideals with Gandhi's Satyagraha.

> [6]Since being in India, I am more convinced than ever before that the method of nonviolent resistance is the most potent weapon available to oppressed people in their struggle for justice and human dignity. In a world since Mahatma Gandhi embodied in his life certain universal principles that are inherent in the moral structure of the universe, and these principles are as inescapable as the law of gravitation. (King, 1959)

Like Gandhi, Dr. King also faced regular death threats, pressure from the community and police brutality. He was arrested nearly twenty times and assaulted at least four times. One such instance of death threat came via phone call just few days before the bus boycott.

> Nigger, we are tired of you and your mess now. And if you aren't out of this town in three days, we're going to blow your brains out and blow up your house." Shaken, King went to the kitchen to pray. "I could hear an inner voice saying to me, 'Martin Luther, stand up for righteousness. Stand up for justice. Stand up for truth. And lo I will be with you, even until the end of the world.' (as cited in White, 1988)

The above anecdote highlights that how in the existential crises' leaders like King, though a Pastor, still had to testify to restore faith in the divinity. Without this faith, he would have not pursued protests. As leaders and managers, we often tend to look at the superficial level the impact of such historical and phenomenal protests, which change the course of history. Yet if we look at the life of Dr. King, we could see the subtler side from where he drew inspiration, faith, and security during the insecure times.

---

[6] Excerpt of Dr. King's taped recording at All India Radio, 1959.

Practical Application and Toward the Guiding Framework of Spiritually Empowered Leadership

Although brief description of these leaders is not sufficient, yet it gives us an overall perspective about their journey and impact. In this section, I highlight key insights by developing a guiding framework of spiritually empowered leadership followed by a tabular comparison of the lives of leaders. In doing so, the idea is to develop key take away for the managerial implications with some comparative insights. Furthermore, some key characteristics observed in the lives of these leaders are highlighted, and lastly, how I was able to put this into practice in the leadership training course is shared and discussed. Instead of proposing a leadership model, the effort here is to provide a guiding framework for managers who are trying to resolve complex issues but yet are not able to seek or find inspiration from the existing sources.

The table below shows how the leaders discussed above faced crisis, which eventually created an everlasting impact on them to undertake spiritual inquiry. Table 16.2 below shows how as a result of critical incident, they were able to or rather forced to come out of comfort zone. In doing so, they were able to develop their own distinct strategies and techniques to enhance their spiritual insights, which would eventually help them to pursue their goals.

In Fig. 16.1, the process of leadership is highlighted through a guiding framework. It showcases how the quest of leadership is instigated by the crises, which may lead a

Table 16.2 Comparing leadership challenges

Leader	Critical incident	Resultant	Outcome	Societal impact
Buddha	Leaving the bubble of palatial life	Leaving the comfort zone for inquiry about purpose of existence	Engaging with spiritual scholars, finding the balanced Buddhist path	Establishment of Buddhism
Gandhi	Inquiry about Gita translation	Stimulated thirst for reading all the scriptures	Developed Satya Graha as a tool for civil disobedience	Crucial part in India's freedom struggle
Abraham Lincoln	American civil war	Seeking solace in higher power, rethinking significance of controllable/uncontrollable incidents	Working on emancipation proclamation and constitutional amendment to abolish slavery	Keeping the USA united amidst and post crises
Dr. King	Facing the death threats	Fear forced to seek security and faith in higher power	Adoption of Gandhian approach for racial activism	Equal rights for black communities in USA

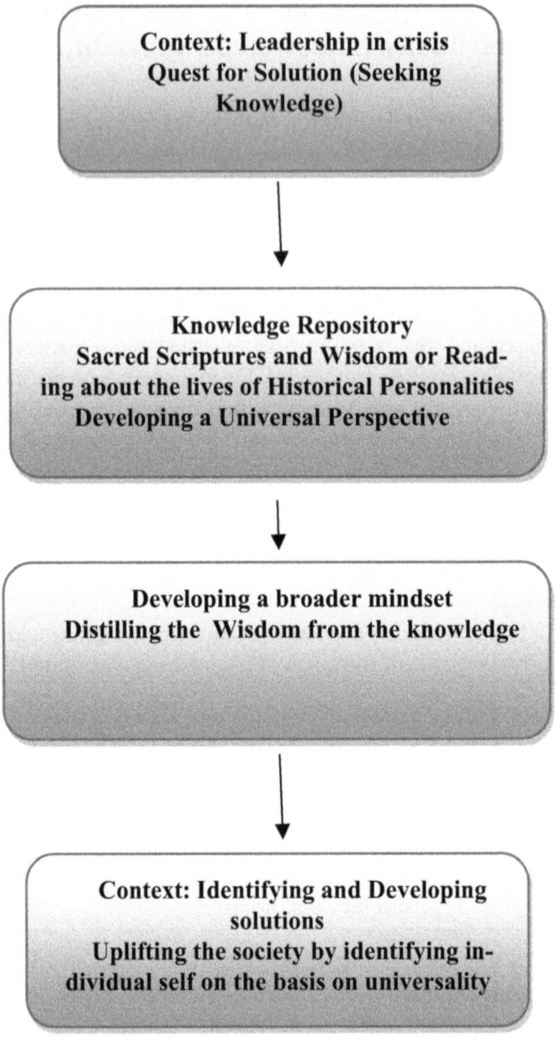

Fig. 16.1 Guiding framework for spiritually inspired leadership

manager in the complex domain of problem solving. Hypothetically, if the manager is not able to find the solution or is grappling with the issue consistently, he or she is thus encouraged to undertake the spiritual journey for seeking the knowledge in order to broaden the mindset. Scriptures do play an essential role in developing a holistic perspective. Alternatively, if scriptures are complex to interpret, the managers are encouraged to read the lives of historical personalities discussed above.

It should also be noticed that along with scriptures, the leaders should seek intellectual and other didactical and interactive means of knowledge development. That is to say that these leaders do not become hermits, rather they do exercise their core professions. By developing higher conscience and interacting with outside world, they can develop a broader perspective. In doing so, they have both micro and macro level perspective of challenges they face. Lastly, they also undertake the practical and experimental approach in which they start deploying their leadership tools with concrete mechanisms for example Buddha's Eightfold Path, or Gandhi's Satyagraha.

The guiding framework could thus serve as a decision-making tool for the leaders or managers who are trying to achieve micro or macrogoals which. Rather than imposing a specific model of leadership, the guiding framework encourages the manager to carve its own personalized path of leadership in order to develop effective leadership traits. Thus, it encourages leaders to:

1. Not to imitate the leadership style of peers;
2. Develop introspection and knowledge seeking and inspiration from the history and spirituality;
3. Develop its own leadership style by identifying its strengths and weakness;
4. Developing the humane and compassionate relationship with the peers.

Individual Level: Developing Spiritual Intelligence (SQ or SI)

Recent research on developing Spiritual Quotient (SQ) as a construct is growing within the psychological literature and coaches thereby indicate that the concept is gaining importance. Zohar defines SQ as

> SQ, or spiritual intelligence, underpins IQ and EQ. Spiritual intelligence is an ability to access higher meanings, values, abiding purposes, and unconscious aspects of the self and to embed these meanings, values, and purposes in living richer and more creative lives. Signs of high SQ include an ability to think out of the box, humility, and an access to energies that come from something beyond the ego, beyond just me, and my day-to-day concerns. (Zohar as cited in Systems Thinker)

It could also be inferred that the leaders described above were able to undertake the journey to enhance their spiritual intelligence. Fragments of SQ in their lives could be witnessed where these leaders were able to reconcile with their faith, undertake an inner journey, keep their ego aside, and be open to new ideas. The ability for critical incidents to spark the SQ is both an **inside out and outside in process**. It is developed in constant churning with individual sense to make not only inner sphere of higher level of consciousness but also at external sphere interactions with external society.

Organizational Level: Experimentation and Walking the Talk

We also witness that these leaders were able to put into practice what they believed; this is clearly visible from Gandhi's attire to Buddha's way of living. It helped them to build credibility among the peers, which was extremely important to develop the collective action. Hence, it is witnessed that these leaders were able to develop and mobilize their organization based on their values. By reducing the discrepancy between individual beliefs and organizational identity, they were able to create a unique organization with clear goals and purpose. Aligning individual values with the organizational values catalyzes the power of collective work and encourages peers to work and contribute to the organizational objectives.

Societal Level: Engaging in Broader Dialogue

It is also witnessed that these leaders were able to engage in a larger dialogue with different stakeholders. Historical accounts show for example, how Buddha interacted with various stakeholders from Kings to common men. President Lincoln was often seen interacting with soldiers and visiting hospitals. Similarly, Lincoln, Gandhi, and Dr. King's life highlight dialogue and interaction with stakeholders who may not be directly related to them. By breaking the hierarchy and disciplinary boundaries, they were able to expand their sphere of influence. In return, this also helped them to develop broader worldview of stakeholder's expectations. Leaders and organizations have tendency to stay away from CSR or investment efforts in which they do not see any links. Broader dialogue with the society can therefore help organizations to break away from their prejudices to explore new models of thinking to undertake new initiatives.

Teaching Leadership through Historical Reflection in Business Schools

The COVID-19 resulted in the development of new and complex problems such as schools are going online, work from home and issues related to mental health, volatility in stock markets, governments acting under public pressure, and many more social, environmental and economic issues. Leaders and organizations can deal with such situations effectively if they are trained to deal with the volatile and complex environment. In such scenarios, pressure and uncertainty dictate the ambience and tests if the managers and the management of the organizations are ready to deal with decision making.

I believe it is in such scenario the concepts from history and spirituality can offer some tips for managers as in how they can equip themselves so that they could navigate through this crisis. Based on my personal experience of teaching two experimental electives for executive program, I highlight how the faculty can use autobiographies as a pedagogical tool to develop reflective processes for spiritually conscious Leadership.

The elective of "Sustainable Leadership" was offered as part of Master's Program for Executives at Foundation Getulio Vargas Sao Paulo School of Business Administration (FGV EAESP) in the first semester of 2020. The course took the approach of how leadership can be learnt by adopting historical and biographical approach of leaders who managed to have deep impact on society. The course adopted the analysis of the lives of President Abraham Lincoln and Nelson Mandela during which participants read the biography and autobiography of the leaders. During the course, the participants engaged in individual and group reflection about various topics, which are crucial for developing leadership competencies such as emotional intelligence, teamwork, empathy, and decisiveness. They further complemented their learning experiences via various didactical means such as analyzing letters and speeches (e.g., Gandhi's letter to Hitler, President Lincoln's letters, Mandela's speeches). Analyzing these archives helped them to understand how leaders shaped their thoughts. As a next step, the participants were also asked to practice speech delivery and writing letter on important topics to sharpen communications skills. Lastly, participants were also encouraged to write an article about their learning, which could be shared with fellow executives. This led to creation of an article about key lessons of leadership, which was written by the students. Some of them even ended up being published in mainstream newspapers and on the official webpage of South African Consulate. The quotes below highlight the student feedback about their learning experiences from the course.

> The discipline promotes a vision of differentiated leadership, outside the theoretical standard of leadership classes. Promotes relevant discussions and contextualized experiences. Student A
>
> A different and light view on the theme of leadership. We have looked at everything so aggressively these days that the way we see critical examples of the past in a different way has gradually provoked me more and more. Student B
>
> There is a possibility for FGV to sponsor some initiative so that this initiative does not end after the completion of the course. I say this, because leadership is not a topic that is talked about everywhere. There could be a channel to maintain it, and the people with these reflections can exercise and collaborate with the reflections to spread the message to as many people as possible. And this right approach of the people of FGV will help people to become market leaders. Student C

I have observed that while we continue to emphasize the need for teaching responsible leadership in mainstream management, our pedagogical content often embraces traditionalist teaching approach usually limited to orthodox analytical trappings of business education. Leadership, as a subject per se, needs to be refined and imparted in a holistic way which may require educators to redesign the curriculum that instigates self-introspection, spiritual enquiry, creativity, problem solving and team work along with exposure to real-world issues. Thus, in the present context where online teaching can lead to digital fatigue, curriculum and programs should be perceived as "learning spaces" in which students go through reflective process on their own by reading historical insights. We may be able to stimulate emotional, intellectual, and spiritual experience for them so that they become capable to face uncertain and complex challenges.

Conclusion

Through this chapter, I have tried to present the idea that by studying about the lives of these leaders we can develop reflections to develop spiritually empowered leadership. A stark contrast could be observed specifically with respect to religion, where extremism and rigid views have created stereotypes. As a result, there is a tendency to go toward atheism to keep distance from discussing religion. Gandhi's life is a good example, rather than sticking to one view he studied all, including atheism before he came to his own conclusion about his spiritual connect. Thus, spiritually empowered leadership does not necessarily means adopting the religious perspective; rather it seeks the understanding from history and its scriptures and tries to build a universal approach. Spiritually empowered leadership discards extremist approach and embraces universal harmony. In fact, the lives of these leaders show that they engaged in spiritual enquiry by being curious, reading about religious texts, contemplating, discussing, and experimenting. In doing so, they were able to develop a subtle sense of universal approach, which helped them to develop leadership qualities such as confidence, compassion, decisiveness, equality, harmony, and non-violence.

Leaders or managers confront some or the other issue on a daily basis. Similarly, organizations led by them also confront various challenges. Spiritually empowered leadership thus can provide a useful tool for reflection and reorganization of personal and organizational values. Leadership often gets trapped into the web of limited set of recommendations or a magic formula, which can resolve all the challenges. Rather, history shows that spiritually empowered leadership values curation and development of leadership path by valuing various sets of competencies such has developing resilience, intuition, interpersonal abilities, ability to bridge metaphysical, and religious beliefs which can provide guiding compass for generations to come.

References

Dhamma Verses, weblink https://suttacentral.net/dhp33-43/en/anandajoti. Accessed on 31/12/2021

Gandhi, M. (1927). *Autobiography: The story of my experiments with truth.* Navajivan Trust. https://thesystemsthinker.com/spiritual-intelligence-a-new-paradigm-for-collaborative-action/. Accessed on 31/12/2021

King. (1959). *Martin Luther King Recording Found In India*, NPR Weblink https://www.npr.org/templates/story/story.php?storyId=99480326. Accessed on 31/12/2021

Koehn, N. (2017). *Forged in crisis: The power of courageous leadership in turbulent times*. Simon and Schuster.

Lincoln, A. (1846). President's Lincoln's response to handbill replying to charges of infidelity on July 31, 1846, weblink http://www.abrahamlincolnonline.org/lincoln/speeches/handbill.htm. Accessed at 31/12/2021

Lincoln, A. (1860). *Collected works of Abraham Lincoln. Volume 4. Speech at Hartford, Connecticut.* The Abraham Lincoln Association. Weblink https://quod.lib.umich.edu/l/lincoln/lincoln4/1:2.1?rgn=div2;view=fulltext. Accessed on 31/12/2021

Lincoln, A. (1864). *Collected works of Abraham Lincoln. Volume 7. Collected works of Abraham Lincoln. Volume 7.* The Abraham Lincoln Association. Weblink https://quod.lib.umich.edu/l/

lincoln/lincoln7/1:617.1?rgn=div2;singlegenre=All;sort=occur;subview=detail;type=boolean;view=fulltext;q1=I+claim+not+to+have+controlled+events%2C+but+confess+plainly+that+events+have+controlled+me. Accessed on 31/12/2021

White, J. E. (1988). *Martin Luther King*. Times weblink http://content.time.com/time/magazine/article/0,9171,988163-2,00.html. Accessed on 31/12/2021

Zohar, D. *Spiritual intelligence: A new paradigm for collaborative action,* weblink accessed on https://thesystemsthinker.com/spiritual-intelligence-a-new-paradigm-for-collaborative-action/. Accessed on 31/12/2021

Chapter 17
Prophetic Leadership and Spiritual Maturing

H. W. Sneller

Abstract Researchers have not explored the dimension of prophetic in understanding the notion of prophetic leadership extensively. This chapter attempts to present the concept of prophetic leadership. The work of the twentieth-century philosophers, Ludwig Klages and Hermann Friedmann, helps in the understanding of the conceptual implications of the chapter. The first section of the chapter examines the two characteristics of leadership, namely plurality and morality. Different forms of leadership ideals need to be reflected upon while considering the diversity of human cultures and societies with a particular attention to bring the moral code of leadership to consciousness through careful identification and sensitivity. In the third section of the chapter, an indispensable characteristic of leaders, which is vision, is discussed. Vision as an essential notion of leadership can help with the identification of the transient orientation of moral constructs in leaders. The fourth section of the chapter addresses the ambiguity in the term "vision" mostly with the notion of both "conviction" and "apparition" in it. Taking into account the concept of "maturation" is immensely important when reflecting on leadership. Reinterpreting leadership by focusing on the spiritual dimensions will help to link the lost moral connotation today in our understanding of leaders and leadership.

Keywords Prophecy · Spirituality · Mysticism

Introduction

Among the various conceptions of leadership, forms of leadership worth considering include *prophetic* dimensions. The word "prophetic", while at first sight takes us back to the pre-Modern era, yet it needs not be interpreted as obsolete. What matters in the first place is that the concept's anthropological implications are elucidated and made sufficiently acceptable. As far as (1) the notions of "leadership" and "vision" can justifiably be held as mutually implicative, and (2) the origin

H. W. Sneller (✉)
Alternative Approaches and Global Concerns, Leiden, Netherlands

© Jindal Institute of Behavioral Sciences 2022
S. Sahni et al. (eds.), *Spirituality and Management*,
https://doi.org/10.1007/978-981-19-1025-8_17

of the phenomenon "vision" is all too often unjustly taken for granted, I argue that reconsidering the latter in light of the former makes sense.

My hypothesis is that prophetic leadership cannot leave the subject position of the alleged "leader" unscathed. To further underpin it, I will examine the notion of "maturing." As I believe that this notion can only be helpful if the locus of its application (i.e., the subject) is reconsidered in tandem, I suggest that considering speaking of *spiritual* maturing becomes relevant and necessary. This will prevent the mere optimization of a *distorted* anthropology interrupts a more extensive fathoming of human nature.

For my argument, I partly rely on a fruitful distinction made by the twentieth-century philosophers Ludwig Klages (1872–1956) and Hermann Friedmann (1873–1957), between an *optic* and a *haptic* approach, that is, a worldview, which departs from the sense of seeing, and a worldview, which departs from the sense of *touching*. While the latter has become predominant in the Western philosophical tradition, the former is held more promising. What I have just called a "distortive" anthropology comes down to a view of the human being, which refuses to take consciousness as layered and vision as unfathomable. It reduces human nature to an object for scientific research and vision to an epiphenomenon. Such a reductive account cannot fail to distort conceptions of leadership.

Leadership

When scrutinized, the concept of "leadership" contains two characteristics: plurality and morality. Let me begin with the first characteristic, plurality.

Plurality

It is known that there is a plurality of *views* on leadership. It is only likely, therefore, that there will also be a plurality of *forms* of factual leadership. Obviously, the latter need not necessarily comply with the former. A lot of leaders do not actually stay faithful to their views on leadership once they are in a leader's position. One can think of so many idealistic politicians who end up abusing their power for mere self-interest (e.g., Robert Mugabe, Jacques Chirac, Juan Carlos). In that case, the incompatibility of views and practices may be internal and due to character weakness.

In addition, there may also be external grounds for this incompatibility: the so-called reality principle that thwarts ideals and confuses idealists exercising their responsibilities. Some would rather prefer to talk about "pragmatism."

But the plurality of *forms* of leadership need not just reflect practical impediments (internal or external), thwarting eminent views and ideals, and prompting disparity in their modes of realization. It can equally reflect the plurality of these views and ideals themselves. As opposed to what obdurate Platonists might think, there can be more than one form of ideal leadership. If one seriously takes the diversity of human cultures and societies (both historically and synchronically), let alone the different *fields* where leadership applies (international and national, State and companies, Church and organizations, etc.), how to avoid accounting for different forms of leadership ideals? "Democratic" states may need other forms of leadership than indigenous tribes, and not-for-profit organizations than profit-seeking companies. Moreover, in proportion to the development, or even spiritual maturing processes, of societies (cf post-war Germany, Rwanda after the genocide, post-colonial India, etc.), always-new forms of leadership seem requisite. None of them is bad in itself. Aristotle has already emphasized in his *Politics* the need for a variety of forms of government, depending on the nature of culture, people, and their living conditions.[1] Those who think that this view underestimates the "democratic" potential of many non-Western nations are partly wrong. They may instead overestimate the democratic nature of their own *forms* of democracy and unjustifiably appropriate the predicate of "democratic" for their particular interpretations. Intrinsically, the concept of "leadership" brings with it its own division and pluralization. Leadership entails a conceptual reference to those who are *led*, and since the latter are neither uniform nor unalterable by nature, its multiformity must be accepted. Platonic States exist only in our imagination or not even there, at times. Rational abstractions thrive on the ongoing repression of particularities, and one cannot be sure whether those particularities have been eliminated sufficiently. Even if there were an unalterable uniform human nature, the essence of leadership is such that it cannot bypass the immediate plurality and multifariousness of human behavior. Unless one condemns this plurality and multifariousness as evil and something-to-be-suppressed by leaders (but that would be a ridiculous take), the plurality of subjects and citizens inescapably requires a plurality of leadership ideals.

Morality

There is a second aspect, which the concept of "leadership" implies, beyond intrinsic plurality. I am referring here to morality. "Leadership," if this term is to be applicable at all, presupposes *good* leadership. *Bad* leadership is no leadership; the combination of word in itself is self-defeating. A leader who leads people *toward* destruction does not truly *lead*. It requires a little conceptual or linguistic sensitivity to identify the moral implications of the term. True, these implications have often been made invisible due to vulgarization of the term "leadership". Such vulgarization ???is consequent upon the blind acceptance of the legitimacy of a State,

[1] Cf *Politics* IV, 1 (1288b22ff). Aristotle points at the need to always consider the *conditions* (τἀὑποκείμενα) under which state forms must be realized.

company, or organization. Instead, the moral core of the term "leadership," *provided* it is carefully unearthed and brought to consciousness, might well be capable of denying legitimacy to the powers. That it can be done in the case of the Third Reich is clearly evident: The Führer ("Leader") brutally misled his followers. But it could deny legitimacy to leaders of profit-seeking companies is less obvious (unless if one is Marxist and rejects the market economy altogether). Granted, hardly anyone (except hardcore anarchists) would question that the States of India, Israel, or China, or organizations such as the UN or Amnesty International are in need of leaders and leadership; but it becomes more difficult when for example the American National Rifle Association, the Goa mafia in India, or IS are concerned—organizations which pursue a more or less criminal goal. The latter seem to have a leadership structure, but do they really *need* a leader? How to conceive such a "leader"? Doesn't the immoral *interests* of these organizations highlight the irrepressible *moral* resilience of the terms "leader" and "leadership"? Aren't their alleged "leaders" better qualified as "robber chiefs"?

Following different moral premises (e.g., Marxist or anarchist), one may doubt the adequacy of my illustrations given above. But what I want to assert is that the concept of "leadership" entails a *justifiable* goal or purpose. The gradual change of such a goal over time negatively affects the *need* for a leader while gradually transforming the factual "leader" into a *gang* leader or a mere chief. Some examples where a leader was not required are the disintegration of Austro-Hungarian and the Ottoman Empire, the Soviet-Union, the Warsaw Pact, etc. But then how could NATO do so? Or could Exxon Mobil? Or could Eveready Industries India Ltd. (EIIL), formerly known as Union Carbide India Limited, for that matter? One would like to know about assessing Apple in this respect, or Google or Amazon.

It would be preposterous to suggest that profit seeking and maximization of gain are illicit in themselves. The leadership question becomes urgent only when the *mode* of profit seeking (e.g., when it brings environmental pollution or inhuman labor conditions) or the *nature* of the business (e.g., arm trade) is arguably immoral. Depending on the *context*, one could even claim that pursuing seemingly neutral businesses have imperceptibly subtle immoral goals; for example, stock market speculating companies, societies where education and healthcare are increasingly being forced to economize, or social housing companies whose investment policy entails taking huge financial risks.

"Leadership," therefore, should always be somehow relatable to a moral goal. They should be conceived as a *means* toward that goal. A moral goal is a goal, which can be defended through using moral grounds; implying the grounds, which are respected, promote or invigorate humanity. How *factually* pursued goals relate to *moral* goals will always remain subject to debate. It is clear that *modes* of pursuing goals, or the *context* in which they are pursued, can gradually alter the moral quality of human actions, even if the moral nature of these goals themselves is beyond question. Extreme examples (the chemical industry IG Farben being involved in the production of poisonous gas for extermination purposes during the Third Reich) will elucidate what could be wrong with more customary—and therefore, more ambiguous—practices (clothing manufacturing companies increasingly relying on outsourced child labor; law firms handling the legal affairs of tax evaders or polluting industries; civil servants serving the bureaucratic system rather than citizens, etc.). Emphasizing this, I consider "more customary" here as "more ambiguous," as it would be simple to pretend no place for debate here. Debate begins when the *modes* of goal pursuit make the goal gradually invisible (clothing industries exploiting laborers of poor countries), or when the allegedly *neutral* goal becomes questionable due to recontextualization (a nation's legal system after a military coup).

Vision

I will further discuss an indispensable characteristic of leaders: vision. According to me, "vision" is an acceptable substitute for what was once seen as the "metaphysical" dimension of leadership, or what, in today's term, is called its "spiritual" dimension. Prophecy highlights this. But it also highlights what might be a basic flaw of a trend in Western thinking: to favor tactility over vision..

If leadership is concomitant both with a plurality of forms and a moral focus—to the point of depriving egocentric agency of this epithet, it could be rightfully asked whether leaders are in need of a deeper form of awareness or not. The plurality of forms of leadership only underlines the difficulty of *identifying* moral goals for companies or organizations, especially in times of rapid change and development. Moral goals of the past might be seen as immoral goals for the present, and in the future too. Values such as "equity," "human flourishing," or "justice" apply by virtue of their infinite malleability. It makes their identification with a descriptive content an almost impossible and onerous task.

Here, I would like to resort to "prophecy" as a category, which, despite its obsolete reminiscences, could help reconsider leadership by virtue of its spiritual–metaphysical resources. Leo Strauss, political philosopher of the twentieth century, indirectly inspired by Carl Schmitt, rediscovered medieval Jewish and Islamic prophetology as a relevant political category. Strauss' reading of hitherto obscure thinkers such as al-Farabi or Maimonides, and Schmitt's of the even more obscure Donoso Cortés, prepared for a reappreciation of a political elite.[2] In times of secularism, Schmitt and Strauss managed to link politics and metaphysics—albeit in

[2] Cf. Leo Strauss (1935). *Philosophie und Gesetz*. In Leo Strauss (1997). *Gesammelte Schriften*. Bd. 2 *Philosophie und Gesetz. Frühe Schriften*. Stuttgart/Weimar: J. B. Metzler; Carl Schmitt (1996, 1922). *Politische Theologie. Vier Kapitel zur Lehre von der Souveränität*. Berlin: Duncker & Humblot, Ch. IV; and Schmitt (1929). Der unbekannte Donoso Cortés. In Carl Schmitt (1994, 1940). *Positionen und Begriffe im Kampf mit Weimar—Genf —Versailles 1923–1939*. Berlin: Duncker & Humblot, pp. 131–137.

different ways.[3] In terms of my article, where I propose to re-instill "spirituality" in our thinking about politics, organization, and management, I argue that "prophecy" could shed a new light on the notion of "vision," as an indispensable ingredient of leadership. A politician who does "not show leadership" is often someone who, allegedly, "lacks vision." On the other hand, the stronger the vision someone has, the more convincing will be this visionary person's outlook as a future leader. Note that I am exploiting the ambiguities of the word "vision" here, which oscillate between two extremes: "conviction," on the one hand, and "apparition," on the other. If I do not want to pinpoint them here by selecting one single meaning, it is precisely for reasons, which will become clear hereafter.[4] The essential advantage of the notion of "vision," especially while discussing leadership, is that it can better cope with the transience of moral constructs while preserving their urge: Its ocular orientation makes it less prone to identification.

As mentioned earlier, the stronger a moral value is identified with a descriptive content, the more it is likely to succumb to private interest and lose its moral focus. This is a famous Kantian insight. Unfortunately, his rigor brought Kant to reject the moral decisiveness of "values" altogether. So he threw away the baby with the bathwater by formalizing ethics completely. He grounded ethics on a purely *non*-descriptive moral commandment (the categorical imperative), thereby factually paralyzing the moral agent—this is at least the critique expressed by Hegelians and neo-Aristotelians. While I cherish the astuteness of Kant's ethics, I believe that Kant is still indebted to a basic presupposition. This presupposition characterizes not only Kantian thinking but also the Western tradition at large. Several early *twentieth*-century thinkers have insisted on the tacitly assumed primacy in the Western tradition of *tangibility* and *tactility*. The primacy of the tactile sense, they argue, which privileges touching over seeing, ends up in the world of *concrete things* or *objects* with which we have become too familiar. It ultimately leads to fixation, objectification, and reification of Being. The term "reality" (*realitas rerum*) implicitly betrays this assumption. These thinkers suggest that an alternative focus on vision, visibility, or contemplation would lead to an altogether different account ("view") of Being.

The German philosopher Ludwig Klages, for example, repeatedly refers to the assets of Chinese thinking in this respect, with its overall insistence on *vision*.[5] The Japanese philosopher Yasuo Yuasa supports this view. He points out that the focus

[3] Inspired by Strauss, several contemporary philosophers continued to draw from classical Jewish sources to nourish modern political thinking. Cf Michael Walzer, Menachem Lorberbaum and Noam J. Zohar and their book series *The Jewish Political Tradition* (New Haven/London: Yale University Press, 2000ff).

[4] For my view of concepts as ambiguities, I am inspired by Deleuze and Guattari's *Qu'est-ce que la philosophie?* Paris: Minuit, 1991, Ch. 1 (Qu-est-ce qu'un concept?). Also see P. K. Feyerabend (1996). *Ambiguità e armonia*. Roma: Laterza, id., *Against Method*[3], 1993; quoted in Hein van Dongen (1999). *Geen gemene maat*. Budel: Damon, p. 65.

[5] L. Klages (1981, 1929–1932). *Der Geist als Widersacher der Seele*. Bonn: Bouvier Verlag, pp. 339ff; 358f.

on vision, combined with the particularity of the Chinese language and its pictographic writing system, warrants a closer bond with immediate experience. Yuasa asserts that the Indo-German tendency to create unambiguous *nouns* lacks this bond and is at the risk of being led astray (*mis*-led, sic!) by its own grammar.[6] Another extremely interesting German philosopher Hermann Friedmann makes an explicit distinction between a *haptic* and an *optic* approach. He tries to show the existential gains that can be made by shifting our general emphasis from the former to the latter. "Rigid links rooting in the essence of a haptic world," Friedmann writes, "still captivate our contemporary psychology, logic and metaphysics within this world. Only persistent impregnation, completion and experiencing [*einbeharrlichesDurchdringen, Ergänzen und Erleben*] of our optic-morphological concepts and ideas can lead to a fully consistent theory and practice of the form".[7] I am not elaborating the subsequent psycho-philosophical developments issuing from the proposal to re-shift the focus on *vision*, for example in Gestalt thinking, or in C. G. Jung's theory of archetypes. At least these developments show that a reassessment of *vision*, even beyond the narrow *empiricist* confines to which a 'haptic' approach would immediately reduce it (thereby making it harmless), can be existentially rewarding.[8] If it is existentially rewarding, it will simultaneously be morally, and even *ontologically* rewarding. It goes to the extent that one is ready to situate moral at the heart of *Being* rather than relegate it to its "subjectivist" fringes (in which case visions would not survive outside of the sheer subject, and lose their social relevance).

By this brief account of vision, I do not suggest that a sharp distinction between vision (*optic*, *ocularity*) and tactility (*haptic*) can, or even should, always be made —this would even be a "haptic" claim. Nor do I want to imply that my account suffices to convince skeptics. I only want to contend that "vision" can be an unfathomable form of awareness and that it thrives on receiving rather than on capturing or delineating. When approaching Being, following the beckons of vision unfailingly asks for a revision (sic!) of our (often reductive) anthropologies; the latter are largely based on haptic approaches and cannot do justice to the spiritual–metaphysical depths of consciousness. Exploring the potentials of these depths for (a reflection on) leadership is the aim of my essay.[9]

A leader, I would argue, is someone with a vision. This does not mean, however, that a leader has in mind a blueprint of the future. That would imply an identification of a value with descriptive content. Purported leaders like Hitler, Pol Pot, or Stalin relied on such a blueprint. They identified goodness with what they had in

---

[6] Yuasa Yasuo (2008). *Overcoming Modernity. Synchronicity and Image-Thinking*. Albany: SUNY Press, Ch. 2.

[7] Friedmann, Hermann (1930/1925). *Die Welt der Formen. System eines morphologischen Idealismus*. München: C. H. Beck'sche Verlagsbuchhandlung, p. 61; mytrans.

[8] For an example, cf Paul W. Pruyser (1983). *The Play of the Imagination. Toward a Psycho analysis of Culture*. New York: International Universities Press.

[9] For a more in-depth study, see Rico Sneller (2020). *Perspectives on Synchronicity, Inspiration, and the Soul*. Newcastle: Cambridge Scholars.

their minds. Their policy led to unspeakable horror. In terms of the thinkers just mentioned, they relapsed into "tactility". According to Ludwig Klages, the association of vision and tactility was already Plato's original sin. Plato, the father of Western philosophy, conceived of *ideas* (literally: "views") in terms of concrete *entities*, which can be "touched" and "delineated" by the mind.[10] Instead, prophetic vision abandons itself to images, which prevent the visionary leader from identifying them. Martin Luther King's *I have a dream* is paradigmatic for visionary leadership, whereas Hitler's visions are its caricature.

Let us take a brief look at both. King's and Hitler's visions, for all their radicality, could serve as extreme foci that could help assess contemporary forms of leadership.

Martin Luther King's famous speech is well known. Let us reread part of it:

> I have a dream that one day this nation will rise up and live out the true meaning of its creed: 'We hold these truths to be self-evident: that all men are created equal.' I have a dream that one day on the red hills of Georgia the sons of former slaves and the sons of former slave owners will be able to sit down together at a table of brotherhood. I have a dream that one day even the state of Mississippi, a state sweltering with the heat of injustice and sweltering with the heat of oppression, will be transformed into an oasis of freedom and justice. I have a dream that my four little children will one day live in a nation where they will not be judged by the colour of their skin but by the content of their character. I have a dream today.[11]

King's dream is prophetic as far as it regards the future ("one day") and the present ("today") simultaneously. It starts with reminding the audience of a "self-evident" norm, the true meaning of which is *still* to be witnessed ("one day this nation will rise up and live out the true meaning of its creed"). Meanwhile, this future revelation is *already* accessed in a dream ("I have a dream that one day…"). Present and future are entwined, and the *meaning* or *intent* of the norm is yet to be revealed. The content of the dream is the meaning of the norm. And yet, its descriptive content should not be overestimated ("the sons of former slaves and the sons of former slave owners will be able to sit down together at a table of brotherhood", "will be transformed into an oasis of freedom and justice", "will one day live in a nation where they will not be judged by the colour of their skin but by the content of their character"). One could perhaps say that the past ("*former* slaves", "*former* slave owners") and the vividly sketched present ("the *red hills* of Georgia", "Mississippi, a state *sweltering* with the heat of injustice and *sweltering* with the heat of oppression") are surpassed ("over-looked") by a future whose sole "visibility" regards peace, hospitality, and togetherness. King's vision entails a dream, which while probably being ignited by the present non-violent crowds ("I have a dream *today*"), faintly *sees* reparation of past suffering and injustice. At this point I am inclined to say that visions are always provisional and preliminary. They are liable to reviewing and expanding, if but the "self-evidence" of "humans having

[10] Cf Klages, op. cit., Ch. 33.

[11] https://www.npr.org/2010/01/18/122701268/i-have-a-dream-speech-in-its-entirety?t=1600166735583, retrieved at 15 September 2020.

been born equal" is respected as their foundation. It is noteworthy that "evidence" contains a reference to "*seeing*" (*videre*). However, this "*seeing*" does not come down to a superficial use of a physiological function but is temporary. If a truth is evident, it enables us to look at the future.[12]

Hitler's "visionary" leadership, I think, can be seen as opposite but more precisely as the *caricature* of King's. As a possible testimony, I will quote part of a discussion Hitler had in Weimar around 1931 or 1932 with Otto Wagener, a former major general. The latter had been close to Hitler for several years before he fell in disgrace. In the immediate aftermath, Wagener wrote down his memoirs, which were published posthumously.

> Actually," Wagener quotes Hitler, "I'm now and then aware [*Ich ertappemichsogarselbstbisweilendarauf*] that it is not *I* who is speaking, but that something speaks through me. [...] Now and then ideas, concepts, views occur to me that I have read nowhere, heard nowhere, and never before thought, nor can I justify them by logic, and they do not even seem to me capable of being logically justified.[13]

When asked if Hitler believes whether his intuitions come from a transcendent region, or are they just worldly, mediated by a human voice, he answers,

> In general, at such moments I have a sensation like an inner vibration, as if I were being touched by an invisible charge [*wiewenn ich von einemunsichtbarenKontaktberührtwürde*]. Whenever I have seized the impulse [*Habe ich den Moment erfasst*], what I said or did as a result of that feeling always turned out to be correct. Whenever I have let it go, almost invariably it turned out later that it would have been right to follow the inner voice.[14]

At the end of the exchange, Hitler explicitly mentions his mission.

> Suddenly a bright light glowed in Hitler's eyes, and staring into space, he continued: "I, too, may be predestined to march before the rest of you with the torch of perception. Behind me, you must carry out the work. *I* must follow my inspiration and my task. But *you*, behind me, can see and recognise things as they are. The torch only occasionally casts its flickering flame on the path before me. But those of you who come behind me march in its light. That is why we belong together, the rest of you and I! I, the one who leads through the dark, and you who, seeing, are meant to complete the task [*Ich, der durch das Dunkel Führende, und Ihr, die Ihrsehendvollendensollt!*].[15]

---

[12] The "prophetic" nature of King's speech becomes explicit in the following quotation from *Isaiah* 40, 4–5: "I have a dream that one day every valley shall be exalted, every hill and mountain shall be made low, the rough places will be made plain, and the crooked places will be made straight, and the glory of the Lord shall be revealed, and all flesh shall see it together." "I have a dream that one day" is King's addition to the Biblical verses.

[13] The German original adds a sentence which remarkably lacks in the translation: "Aber siestellensichspäterdannmeistensdochalsrichtigheraus": "they still turn out to be right at a later moment". H. A. Turner Jr, Ed. (1978). *Hitler aus nächster Nähe. Aufzeichnungen eines Vertrauten 1929–1932*. Frankfurt: Ullstein, p. 269; trans. Ruth Hein (1985). *Hitler—Memoirs of a Confidant*. New Haven: Yale University Press, p. 150. Also see Bernhard Horstmann (2004). *Hitler in Pasewalk. Die Hypnose und ihre Folgen*. Düsseldorf: Droste Verlag, p. 122.

[14] Turner, 1978, p. 270, trans., p. 151; Horstmann, 2004, p. 123.

[15] Turner, 1978, p. 272; trans., p. 153.

Whereas King can connect his dream to the American Declaration of Independence ("We hold these truths to be self-evident: that all men are created equal"), Hitler's "ideas, concepts, views" are groundless and apparently even unjustifiable ("they do not even seem to me capable of being logically justified").[16] Instead, they are supported by an inner touch ("In general, at such moments I have a sensation like an inner vibration, as if I were being touched [*berührt*] by an invisible charge [*unsichtbarenKontakt*]."). They do not brighten the future ("The torch only occasionally casts its flickering flame on the path before me") but rather the past or the present ("*you*, behind me, can see and recognize things as they are", "those of you who come behind me march in its light"). Clearly, Hitler's views are blinded by the dark through which he walks. So I feel that either Hitler was a blinded visionary, or with no vision at all, despite appearances.

These two extreme leadership positions, Martin Luther King's and Adolf Hitler's, make up for the two *paradigmatic foci* between which actual leadership moves. Leadership, I claimed, is a moral job, it should be relatable to a moral goal, the essence of which is better accessed in vision than in a tactile encounter. The fact that Martin Luther King's dream speech has become so famous and is referred to so often by subsequent leaders speaks volume. It implies that its core message is recognized and even acknowledged, perhaps *by virtue of* its prophetic character. Even if these leaders lack King's charisma, their recognition of the dream gives them a share in the prophetic vision. However, the constantly changing world and human living conditions make it crucial that the images used are not isolated from their immediate context. King's "red hills of Georgia" and "Mississippi" should be replaceable by always-new contexts of leadership. Even King's vision of a prospective "brotherhood" is the need of the hour complemented along with "sisterhood" or just "friendship". And who knows the future might demand people to find a term for the peaceful companionship between humans and animals.

Maturing

I have already insisted on the ambiguity of the term "vision". It can mean both "conviction" and "apparition." The difference between these two extremes is that the former means to tend toward pure subjectivity, whereas the latter pretends to imply objectivity. Drawing on this ambiguity, I further stated that the notion of "vision" can better cope with the transience of moral constructs: In virtue of its optic-ocular orientation, it hardly identifies. The consequence was that leaders who *cling* to their vision are at risk of losing it altogether.

I would like to set a final step and highlight a vital implication of the ambiguity, which I have already mentioned. The term "vision" essentially conceals the extent

[16] Interesting in this respect is Carl Schmitt's comment on Hitler's dealing with the threatening SA insurgence.

to which the subject of vision is involved in what is seen. This non-vagueness should not be eliminated in favor of a purely "objective" vision a leader should follow. Instead, the ambiguity of the term "vision" points at the insoluble link between subject and object of the alleged vision. The visionary person is thoroughly affected by the vision in the structure of their subjectivity. It is as if the malleability of the envisioned vision is reflected by an *equally* malleable visionary subject. This means that visionary leaders might continuously feel disturbed and bewildered. However, we should realize that this disturbance or bewilderment solely regards a standardized, stabilized personality, or character structure. Beyond these, a deeper form of consciousness might hide, which surfaces in tandem with the vision, and which is stable and imperturbable.[17] I interpret this dialectic dialogue between disturbance and inner stability, issuing from vision, as a process of "maturing." I define maturing as the "realization of spiritual growth in conformity to the vision." Visions elicit a maturing process.

In the Western philosophical tradition, full-fledged maturing usually plays no explicit role. It could be argued that Spinoza, who defines *thinking* as participation at the divine attribute of infinite thinking, indirectly accounts for it. The subsequent Enlightenment tradition—and Hegel in its wake—has reduced the process of maturing to a mere *intellectual* process, which can principally come to a close. It was C.G. Jung (year??) who, drawing on nineteenth century Romantic philosophy, attributed a central role to maturing as a more embracing or even all-comprehensive process. Psychological maturation processes, Jung said, may reproduce the outer world as an extension of the mind.[18] External events will start reflecting, or corresponding to, what is going on inside, entailing for example synchronicity experiences. This confirms my earlier analysis of "vision" as a term, which ambiguously combines subject and object.

I believe that the concept of "maturation" is immensely important and should be taken into account when reflecting on leadership. It allows one to criticize a person who is in a leadership position, and whose words or actions are rationally irrefutable and yet unsatisfactory. For it cannot be excluded that a very immature soul proffers a highly acerb, sophisticated argument. "Darwin," a Joseph Joachim says in his conversation with the composer Johannes Brahms, "was a great man; he made one of the most momentous discoveries in all human history, but only along materialistic lines. Spiritually, he was very backward in his own evolution". And he

[17] Cf Arjuna in the *Bhagavad-gita*: "Then, bewildered and astonished [*vismaya-āviṣṭaḥ*], his hair standing on end [*hrstaroma*], Dhanañjaya [= Arjuna] bowed his head to offer obeisance and with folded hands began to pray to the Supreme Lord." (XI, 14–16), or the prophet Daniel in the Biblical book of *Daniel*: "I, Daniel, was troubled in spirit [אֶתְכְּרִיַּת רוּחִי/ètkeriyatruhi], and the visions that passed through my mind [חֶזְוֵי רֵאשִׁי/*hezwērēshi*: 'the visions of my head'] disturbed me [יְבַהֲלֻנַּנִי/*yevahelunnani*]. (*Daniel* 7, 15) In both cases, or so it seems, an *outward* disturbance is suggested.

[18] Ferenczi remarks that precipitate maturation may ensue trauma. Cf. Sándor Ferenczi (1933). Sprachverwirrung zwischen den Erwachsenen und dem Kind. In Sándor Ferenczi, *Schriften zur Psychoanalyse II*, p. 311.

continues that, "the fundamental error of these leading Victorian scientists of today, is that they believe only that which is revealed to the five senses; that which can be measured, weighed or proved by chemical analysis. Now scientific analysis ignores completely the true relation of the world to mankind; there are many higher spiritual values such as beauty, love, intuition, harmony, order, inspiration, laws, wonderful messages of the flowers, and music, which defy scientific analysis; and yet they are no less real than the palpable phenomena to which these scientists attach such importance. In fact, they are more because these higher values are eternal, whereas those gross material things are fleeting and transitory. [...] The immature materialistic doctrine—that the marvelous law and order prevailing in the universe—is the result of a 'fortuitous concord of atoms,' is, to my way of thinking, a far greater draft on the credulity than the crudest anthropomorphic conception of Divinity."[19]

It can be said that development does *not necessarily* imply maturity (cf the radicalization of freedom fighters such as Robert Mugabe or Winnie Mandela), though it *could* do so. On the other hand, it would be too easy to claim a neutral spectator position for oneself when assessing maturity in others. However, "good" leaders tend to stimulate "the best" in their subjects by holding up a mirror for them which shows how they *could* be. Likewise, they tend to defy the vehement defense mechanisms in those who resist maturing to such an extent that they run a higher risk of being killed or eliminated (cf the murders of Ghandi, Martin Luther King, Olof Palme, etc.).

Let me quote in conclusion two authors, the Romanian thinker Emil Cioran and the Austrian–American psychoanalyst Otto Rank, who equally interpret maturing as a dialectic of inner bewilderment or struggle, on one hand, while inner peace or self-confidence, on the other.

"When you no longer believe in yourself," Cioran writes in his essay 'De l'inconvénient d'être né,' "you stop producing or struggling, you even stop raising questions or answering them, whereas it is the contrary which should have occurred, since it is precisely at this moment that, being free of all bonds, you are likely to grasp the truth, discern what is real and what is not. But once your belief in your own role, or your own lot, has dried up". He continues, "(Y)ou become incurious about everything else, even the 'truth,' though you are closer to it than ever before."[20] In line with Cioran's quote, one would say that maturing is similar

---

[19] Abell, Arthur M. (2016, 1955). *Talks with Great Composers*, ebook. The 19th-century spiritualist philosopher Carl du Prel writes that "Wer der Volksmetaphysik entwächst, ohne doch für die höhere Metaphysik reif zu sein, wird sich seine Weltanschauung unter einseitiger Berücksichtigung der Naturwissenschaften bilden, das heisst dem Materialismus verfallen." Karl du Prel (2012, 1890). *Das Kreuz am Ferner. Ein hypnotisch-spiritistischer Roman.* Austria: Verlag vergriffenerBücher, p. 175. And in his novel *Glasperlenspiel* Hermann Hesse warns that science and art must be protected against the intrusion (*Zudrang*) of "the young men who have nothing but talent" (the *Nurbegabten*) who falsify (*verfälscht*) the whole meaning of pedagogy and service, and betray the Spirit (*Verrat am Geist*). Hermann Hesse (1979, 1943). *Das Glasperlenspiel.* Frankfurt: Suhrkamp; trans. Richard and Clara Winston (2002). *The Glass Bead Game.*

[20] E. M. Cioran (1995). *Œuvres.* Paris: Gallimard, p. 1395; trans. Richard Howard (2011). *The Trouble with Being Born.* New York: Seaver Books.

to waging an inner battle, inspired by an invincible self-confidence, to seize what is right and real. It comes down to slow ripening of revelatory potencies due to gradually acquired insight and experience over a lifetime. Leadership capabilities, so I would add, increase in proportion to the ripening of these potencies.

Otto Rank, famous for his notion of birth anxiety, argues that maturing is the equivalent to dealing with a human *Grundkonflikt* ("basic conflict") throughout a process of inner growth: "the overcoming of previous supporting egos and ideologies from which the individual has to free himself according to the measure and speed of his own growth [*nachAusmaß seines Wachstumsprozesses*]". This is extremely difficult since "the victory is always, at bottom and in some form, won over a part of one's own ego".[21]

Both Cioran and Rank insist on the inner struggle as part and parcel of maturing, and therefore of leadership qualities. "Struggling," I believe, is a helpful notion, which contributes to a better understanding of the inner dialectic of bewilderment and inner stability. Maturity represents the outcome of a preceding inner struggle elicited by vision. Ideal leaders are those who have experienced a maturing process along with inner struggles and impediments. It makes sense to equate vision with the capability of enhanced seeing. "Leaders" without vision can be said to be blind. Their *alleged* "struggle," then, might rather have been a struggle to *prevent* an inchoate *seeing*.[22]

---

[21] Otto Rank (2000, 1932). *Kunst und Künstler. Studien zur Genese und Entwicklung des Schaffensdranges*. Giessen: Psychosozial-Verlag, p. 318; trans. Charles Francis Atkinson (1975). *Art and Artist. Creative Urge and Personality Development*. New York: Agathon Press, p. 375.

[22] Interestingly, the verb *to see* (*sehen*) plays a larger role in Hitler's *Mein Kampf* (*My Struggle*) than *to hear* (*hören*), starting with his first *seeing* of historical truth due to his history teacher ("Geschichte 'lernen' heisst die Kräfte suchen und finden, die als Ursachen zu jenen Wirkungen führen, die wir dann als geschichtliche Ereignisse vor unseren Augen sehen."), over his first meeting with a Jew in Vienna ("Ich beobachtete den Mann verstohlen und vorsichtig, allein je länger ich in dieses fremde Gesicht starrte und forschend Zug um Zug prüfte, um so mehrwandelte sich in meinem Gehirn die erste Frage zu einer anderen Fassung: Ist dies auch ein Deutscher?") to his final breakdown at the Flemish battlefields ("Schon einige Stunden später waren die Augen in glühende Kohlenverwandelt, es war finster um mich geworden.") This is how Hitler describes his final 'recovery' at the Pasewalk field hospital: "Der bohrende Schmerz in den Augenhöhlen liess nach; es gelang mir langsam, meine Umgebung in groben Umrissenwieder unterscheiden zu lernen. Ich durfte Hoffnung hegen, wenigstens so weit wieder sehend zu werden, um später irgend einem Berufe nachgehen zu können. Freilich, dass ich jemals wieder würdezeichnen können, durfte ich nicht mehr hoffen. So befand ich michimmerhin auf dem Wege der Besserung, als das Ungeheuerlichegeschah." For a further discussion of Hitler's 'possession,' see my *Perspectives on Synchronicity, Inspiration, and the Soul*. Newcastle: Cambridge Scholars, 2020, p. 176ff.

Conclusion

In this article, I have argued for a prophetic conception of leadership. Rather than mystifying the latter, I intended to show that the notion of prophetic "vision," by virtue of its inherent ambiguity, is helpful to re-interpret leadership. Vision, as I have already stated, enables to account both for a plurality of forms of leadership and the trans-subjective mind-set, which should be connected with leadership. As opposed to tactility-based approaches, which tend to define and identify, vision prevents grasp, and always opens new perspectives. My background assumption was that leadership is a moral category. Without a moral focus, a leader deteriorates to a robber chief.[23]

It is tragic that the notions of "leader" or "leadership" have increasingly lost their immediate moral connotation today. This confuses so many leadership courses and training sessions, which reduce ideal leadership to the possession of *skills,* which can be learned. Without denying that skills matter (in fact, I have been negligent in discussing them in this article), I believe that disregarding the spiritual dimensions of leadership are far more detrimental to the modern world. The overall secularization of the modern world and its institutions (governments, universities, NGOs, etc.), for all its achievements, has prompted the illusion that leaders can be made. Continuing to follow this illusion will only hasten the next global crisis.

[23] For an interesting recent article on leadership and spirituality, see Jeroen A. van Lawick van Pabst (2019). Personal Leadership as a Spiritual Way in Today's World. Exploring Christian Spirituality's Contribution to Today's Personal Leadership through Works of de Certeau and Ciszek. In *Studies in Spirituality* 29, pp. 237–256, https://doi.org/10.2143/SIS.29.0.3286945.

Chapter 18
How to Become an Effective Leader

Kamlesh Patel

Abstract An effective leader is defined by those human qualities of the heart that have been revered throughout human history, and which develop as a result of a practical approach to inner development. This has been the hallmark of Yoga in India since ancient times, and during the last 100 years it has seen a significant revival, most recently in the schools of management. This chapter explores the qualities that define an effective leader, the reasons we struggle to inculcate them, the role of meditative practices in developing the needed qualities, and the science behind why they work. The effect of meditation on the various functions of the mind—consciousness, thinking, intellect, and ego—is discussed as well as the importance of having a spiritual teacher and the impact of yogic Transmission. This chapter provides the necessary practical approach to move from a theoretical model of spirituality in management to the real application of spirituality in management. No amount of learning can make a person wiser. It is our presencing, or level of awareness, that brings wisdom and that needs to be nurtured in order to become an effective leader.

Keywords Conscious leadership · Heartful leadership · Role of meditation · Science of meditation · Yogic Transmission · Spirituality in management · Presencing · Wisdom in management · Universal values · Emotional intelligence · Social intelligence · Inner excellence · Default Mode Network · Heartfulness · Compassion

What Qualities Define an Effective Leader?

I think most of us would list qualities like vision and purpose, poise, courage, compassion and generosity, integrity and sincerity, good communication skills, the ability to listen and remain open-minded, self-awareness and self-improvement, resilience, clarity of thinking and decision making, wisdom, humility, the ability to know when

K. Patel (✉)
Heartfulness Guide, Heartfulness Institute, Kanha Shanti Vanam, Hyderabad, India
e-mail: kamlesh@srcm.org

President, Shri Ram Chandra Mission, Shahjahanpur, India

© Jindal Institute of Behavioral Sciences 2022

S. P. Sahni et al. (eds.), *Spirituality and Management*,
https://doi.org/10.1007/978-981-19-1025-8_18

to act and when to press the pause button, and the willingness to make a difference in the lives of others. The list can be much longer—this is just a start. These are qualities that develop with a spiritual focus on life, which we can also call inner awakening (Patel, 2019b). In this article, I hope to shed light on how such an inner awakening leads to outer behavioral transformation, and how that in turn, leads to the development of leadership skills and being a role model. It all starts from within!

In the worldly sense, it means striving to live a noble life, to live by universal values with a sense of goodness, to do the right thing for those we meet, and to contribute positively to the world we live in. There is nothing new in this—wise people have said the same since time immemorial. In modern management vocabulary, it is known as cultivating or nurturing emotional and social intelligence.

But it is not enough to know all this. What matters is the ability to live it; to integrate those qualities into our thoughts, feelings, behavior, and sphere of influence in day-to-day life, including our workplaces. It all sounds so simple, and yet so few of us actually succeed in attaining such an awakened level of leadership. Those who do so are put on a pedestal because they are rare. Actually, if it were really so easy then most of the world's great literature on philosophy, spirituality, and ethics would never have been written, nor would the different religions of the world have arisen.

Still today, we find ourselves harking back to the dialogues between the sage Ashtavakra and King Janaka from the time of the Ramayana in the Ashravakra Gita (Patel, 2019c), the discourses of the ancient Greeks and Egyptians on consciousness and ethics in governance, e.g., The Republic by Plato, Lao Tzu's Tao Te Ching on the principles of leadership, especially on the battlefield, and the Bhagavad Gita. We discover that great leaders of consequence strive to excel in their inner nature, and that is as true today in our modern secular societies, where science is the main paradigm, as it has been for those leaders who have bowed before the higher authority of God. The same human qualities are valued in a leader, whether we approach life from a scientific or from a spiritual perspective. And we can unearth the same qualities in ourselves if we put our hearts into doing so. This ability to become the best possible versions of ourselves takes focus, hard work, a set of practices, and a teacher who can support us to keep progressing along the path of continuous self-improvement known as the spiritual path. Our degree of presencing, our level of awareness, which results from this inner approach, brings the wisdom we need to become an effective leader. No one can teach us to become the best leaders, just as no one can teach us to become the best musician or engineer.

There is a humorous story about this (Patel, 2016). Once there was a master thief who lived in ancient Persia. He was famous across the country, but he was getting old, and his son decided it was time to take over the family business. So, he asked his father to teach him how to be the best thief. The old man smiled and said, "Yes! Let's scope out a certain house in town, and tonight we will go there together to steal the richest haul of gold and jewels in town." The boy was exhilarated by the opportunity, and the two of them went to scope the house and make their plans.

Around midnight, father and son went together to do the job, and after breaking into the house, they went to the basement where there was a large metal chest. The father watched as the boy quietly picked the lock, and then he asked the boy to climb into the chest and hand him out all the treasures. Once the boy was inside, the father quickly closed the lid, locked the chest, and left the house making a terrible din of "Thief! Thief!" The boy was dumfounded, but also now had to be completely alert and ready for action. First, the people in the household woke up, and then the whole neighborhood woke up, and very soon they were all in the basement ready to catch the thief. The owner opened the chest, but the boy thought fast, and while meowing like a cat he sprang out of the chest and escaped, using the darkness as cover, to the frustration of the townsfolk. He ran and ran, with the whole entourage chasing him, until he came to the outskirts of town. He came upon a well, and again thought fast. He threw a big rock down the well and then hid in the bushes nearby, watching the townsfolk stop and discuss, and eventually agree that he had jumped into the well. So after some time they gave up the chase and all went back to bed.

Once things calmed down, the boy returned home to find his father waiting up for him. He was furious and yelled at his father, "How could you do that to me! I could have been killed!".

The father replied, "Yes, but you weren't. You showed the ingenuity and bravery to escape and survive. You have shown me that, indeed, you will make a very good thief. Congratulations! I am now ready to retire."

This may be an extreme example, but it highlights the need for inner skills and qualities that cannot be taught in any profession. It is even more true for an effective leader.

Why Do We so Often Fail to Be Effective Leaders?

To become effective leaders, we first need to become effective human beings. Today, scientists have unearthed a few reasons why we find it so difficult to improve our behavior patterns and become good role models. Programs formed in our subconscious minds in the past determine our thought patterns, emotional responses, and habitual behavior. We are not able to easily master or change these patterns because our minds are automatically governed by a build-up of our past reactions (Lipton, 2008). Also, we don't do much to regulate our minds during our waking hours. Hence, our wishes and desires, fears, and habits, pull us in all directions like autumn leaves blown about in the wind. Research by Killingsworth and Gilbert (2010) shows that most people's minds are wandering roughly 47% of the time, thinking about things other than what is happening in the present moment. They also discovered that this mind wandering generally makes people unhappy. The mind is scattered into many different channels, and it is weakened as a result. Also, most of these thoughts are negative in nature (Hanson, 2013). This active state of mind wandering, self-referencing, and negative thinking has been called the Default Mode Network (Raichle, 2015). Just imagine, for most people it is the default, the norm!

Yogic scientists have long understood why this happens and how to fix it. In fact, the purpose of a yogic practice is to remove all the activity of inner turbulence in the mind in order to reach a state of absolute stillness, peace, and oneness. This is done through a fourfold practical approach:

1. Bringing our attention inward to a deeper level of consciousness that is not scattered and buffeted by external stimuli, taking us to the center of our being through the heart. Here we find peace and stillness. This is done through meditation.
2. Removing the layers of accumulated impressions or samskaras that determine what we respond to in the Default Mode Network, and even more complex patterns, and letting go of the associated tendencies and behaviors. This is done through a daily mental cleaning practice.
3. Learning to connect with the center of our being to find inner inspiration, wisdom, and stillness at any time of the day or night. This is done through the practice of prayer, especially at bedtime.
4. Benefiting from the support of a teacher who will support us along the path of stepwise inner change, so as to have a better chance of success.

These practices help us to center ourselves in an integrated state of balance and poise, leading to the development of qualities like contentment, calmness, compassion, courage, and clarity of mind.

How Does Meditation Help?

Meditation is the daily practice that accomplishes the first of the four skills listed above—we practice going to the center of our being. The first step prior to diving deeper is to regulate the mind, to bring it from scattered outward activity to a single channel of inner focus. As a result, the mind of someone who has been meditating daily for some time is focused and well regulated. Studies have shown that the Default Mode Network is less active during and after meditation, offering a greater ability to refrain from brooding and worrying about things (e.g., Brewer et al., 2011). So, unless and until we regulate our minds properly through meditation, we will struggle to improve ourselves. In fact, through a heart-based meditation practice supported by yogic Transmission, we can change the Default Mode Network itself.

Understanding Our Make up: The Three Bodies

Let us backtrack a bit and introduce the concept of the three bodies (Chandra, 2018; Patel, 2017, 2019a).

The first is our physical body, and the nature of this body is action, the movement of the sense organs, and perception. While we can improve the body according to how we live our lives, we cannot change its fundamental structure. For example, we can become fitter, but we cannot become one foot taller or develop extra limbs.

Physical evolution happens over longer periods than one lifetime, so we don't expect our physical bodies to truly evolve.

The second is our energy field or mental body, also known as the astral body, the subtle body, the vibrational body, and the mind. Think of it as the field of the heart and mind. It has the characteristics of thinking, feeling, and understanding. This is the realm of thoughts, feelings and emotions, intuition, inspiration, ego, intellect, wisdom, courage, and love. Its field of action is consciousness. There are both movement and rest in it. It can either be turbulent and complex, like a roaring ocean during a storm, or, at the other end of the spectrum, it can be like a still pond where even a feather landing on the surface creates a ripple.

The third is our spiritual body, also known as the causal body (the cause of our existence) or the soul. The causal body is the center of our existence. Peace, joy, and rest are its qualities, and it contains everything in seed form. The soul is pure and unchangeable so its evolution is not something we can work on directly. It evolves as a natural outcome of the fourfold inner practices mentioned above.

The body where transformation happens is the middle body, the subtle body. This is where we can become better versions of ourselves. Our transformation is a result of the evolution and purification of our subtle body. This is even true of physical well-being: without the mind's intention to eat well, sleep well, and exercise well, and the heart's willpower and courage to bring about these lifestyle changes, we cannot inculcate healthy habits into our lifestyle.

Our subtle body improves incrementally as we remove the layers of complexities and impurities, which purifies our thoughts and emotions. Through the second practice of Cleaning, all our mental and emotional functions become light and clear and our consciousness matures. Thus, we are able to remove all the negative and unwanted subconscious patterns and also cultivate more effective habits.

Understanding the Subtle Body

The subtle body is made up of a number of different functions, including the senses, the flows of energy through the human system, and four very important elements that we work with for continuous improvement (Patel, 2017). They are consciousness (*chit*), thinking and feeling (*manas*), intellect and wisdom (*buddhi*), and ego (*ahankara*), which form our identity. They exist together to make up what we know as the mind, and we call them the four main subtle bodies or elements of the subtle body. Three of these subtle bodies—*manas*, *buddhi* and *ahankara*—are refined and transformed through meditative practices, and the result is pure and expanded consciousness.

We can focus on each of them. What happens to our thinking and feeling function (*manas*) when we do these daily practices? We learn to simplify our thinking process from many channels to one channel, so that effortless concentration develops naturally. This is the first step. Then, as we dive into the heart, thinking deepens into feeling. In fact, the habit of feeling evolves from thinking. Our waking consciousness is then elevated considerably, as we tap into the intuitive capacities of the heart, thus bypassing the slower rational thinking modalities of the cortex of the brain.

Brewer (2017) has demonstrated that focus is easier through feeling and meta-attention, compared to having scattered thoughts at the surface level of the mind. Research has shown that the heart responds much faster than the brain to both external and internal cues (Childre & Martin, 2000; Wulliemier, 2019). It is not that we stop thinking, but our potential increases as our consciousness expands and elevates to include the spectrum of the feeling level of existence. We are able to stay in the present moment, which has been called "flow—the psychology of optimal experience" by Csíkszentmihályi (1990). For example, someone who is able to work in this state of flow is the basketball player Michael Jordan. When Phil Jackson took over as coach at the Chicago Bulls, he made sure that all the team members meditated regularly. As a result, their individual skills and team skills improved amazingly. A player of Jordan's innate capacity was then able to regularly be in the flow.

The Broader Impact of Meditation on Performance During the Day

A by-product of good meditation is the ability to absorb and expand that meditative condition so that it keeps being enhanced throughout the rest of the day. This capacity to remain constantly connected with the inner state is known as constant remembrance. With constant remembrance, we are able to master thoughts, emotions, and behavioral tendencies to an even greater degree. When we are in this "flow", the canvas of our consciousness cannot be spoilt; it remains fresh and impervious to all the stimuli and impressions that might otherwise create turbulence.

As a result of this self-mastery, consciousness can expand along its spectrum into both the subconscious and superconscious realms, opening up our human potential (Patel, 2017). What was earlier buried in the subconscious comes into conscious awareness, and what was earlier beyond our grasp in the superconscious becomes accessible. In other words, we go deeper and deeper into the vastness of the heart from our starting point at the surface. This also takes us to successively higher and higher dimensions of insight and wisdom.

To understand this better, imagine that the heart–mind field is on a spectrum of consciousness that spans the subconscious, conscious and superconscious states. Swami Vivekananda once explained it as, "Consciousness is a mere film between two oceans, the subconscious and the superconscious" (Vivekananda, 1947). You can also imagine the subconscious like the ocean, consciousness like the surface of the land, and superconscious like the sky expanding infinitely into the universe.

The Role of the Intellect in Leadership

The intellect (*buddhi*) is also one of the main elements of the subtle body that we use every day in a leadership role. In this process of diving deeper in a daily meditation practice, the intellect becomes progressively more heart-based. It expands from the limited mental ability to solve problems to encompass wisdom and sagacity. The role of the intellect is associated with the first of the yogic sadhanas or practices, known as *Viveka*. *Viveka* is the ability to discern or discriminate—to make wise choices and understand their consequences. Obviously, this capacity of *Viveka* is necessary for any leader to succeed. *Buddhi* becomes progressively more refined and precise with heart-based meditation. Intuition and inspiration develop, and *buddhi* becomes like a fine-tuned sensitive antenna, able to pick up the deeper signals within the heart. Usually, we assume a wise person to be someone who makes the best choices, but that is not the end of it—that sort of wisdom is just a stage along the way. As we proceed further, we move into a different dimension all together where choice is no longer required, because the wisdom of the heart is always pure and correct. That absolute state of the intellect is the outcome of a spiritual practice (Patel, 2017).

There is a very big difference between an intellectual person and a wise person. Here comes the role of the third of the four practices mentioned above as a very dynamic method to help us to move from mere intellect to wisdom. This is the practice of prayer. The Heartfulness approach to prayer takes us through the heart to our original center, our highest Self. With this connection, and the resulting vacuum-like state that unfolds in the heart, all our ego-based defenses drop. This prayer is a daily practice that curbs both ego and desire, both of which inhibit self-transformation (Patel & Pollock, 2018). We learn to evaluate our actions, let go of our mistakes, and decide how to change our behavior so as not to repeat those mistakes. This is the wisdom of remaining flexible and open to continuous improvement. When you compare this to the lower level of consciousness of making the same mistakes day after day, feeling frustrated at being unable to change, the impact on leadership is obvious. We become wiser when we allow our consciousness to follow the flexible path of evolution. When we live with this attitude every moment, wisdom flourishes.

Wisdom means to use all our faculties at their best. This translates into having the maximum output with the minimum input; minimum action leads to the maximum results (Patel, 2019a). It means we work smarter rather than necessarily harder. And we can only expect to have such good results with a meditative mind that impacts our daily life.

Maintaining the Purity of the Subtle Body

For self-transformation to be a continuous process, the subtle body must be regularly purified, just as we clean our physical bodies daily. Otherwise, it becomes like a muddy lake, where the bottom of the lake is not visible due to the presence of turbulent water. Similarly, when there is no clarity in a turbulent mind, confusion and lack of vision follow. Hence, the second of the four practices listed above, the Heartfulness Cleaning, becomes vital for us to become the best version of ourselves.

How do impressions form (Patel, 2019a)? Imagine for a moment what it feels like when your consciousness is completely pure and still, like a crystal-clear pool of water. When a thought, an emotion or an experience enters that peaceful state it creates a ripple, which may either die down or create more turbulence, just as a disturbance does in water. If the ripples are not removed, knots of energy form, known as impressions. As the impressions deepen and harden, they become samskaras. Samskaras are the root cause of our subconscious programs. They create our habits, based on our fears and our desires. When repeated again and again, they are like drops of rainwater becoming a stream, which eventually becomes a river.

Unless we remove these samskaras, we stay trapped in our patterns and cannot easily break free, no matter how much we may want to change. To discover how to clean the impressions from your mind, you may experience the practice of Heartfulness Cleaning for yourself. For more information on these practices, please read the book, *Simple Heartfulness Practices*, https://heartfulness.org/en/simple-heartfulness-practices/.

The Role of the Ego in Leadership

The next element of the subtle body is the ego or *ahankara*. An unruly ego is something that plagues leaders in all fields of endeavor, whether due to the arrogance and superiority that develop with power over others, or to feelings of inferiority and inadequacy that accompany a high-profile role. Both are damaging expressions of ego that keep us from being the best versions of ourselves. This is because ego plays a vital role in whether or not our consciousness can expand along its spectrum. "The ego is often seen as the bad guy, but it is an essential element of the subtle body for our evolution (Patel, 2019a)." It is fundamental to our identity, our motivation, our willpower, and our ability to act and think. My first spiritual Guide, Ram Chandra of Shahjahanpur (2014) writes:

> 'We possess mind, senses and faculties, which work incessantly in their own ways. We do not bother to understand and take into account whether they go in the right course or the wrong. This is the main difficulty in almost every case, for which we usually blame the mind or the ego.
>
> 'In my opinion, the mind and the ego are the only two things in man, the best and the most useful. In fact, ego refers to the real Being, and mind searches it out. Really, we have to learn the proper utilization of everything in man. There must not be misuse of anything. That is humanity in the true sense, which is our human duty.'

Ego is the active function of the mind that gives us our ability to do and think, and we need it in every aspect of daily life, including the intention to better ourselves. Ego provides our identity. It is the activating motivating force within us. Used wisely it serves us well, like any other resource, but when misused it creates havoc. When the ego is selfish, it becomes arrogant and self-important, or self-pitying and victim-like. In contrast, when we constantly refine the ego, we improve very rapidly (Patel, 2019a).

What does it mean to refine the ego? It is a gradual progression from egotism to humility, flexibility, and love. All wise leaders throughout human history have valued this transition so highly that humility is seen as important whether it is directed toward a child, a poor person, or a stranger.

When humility is not present in a person's character, the ego is "like a black hole. It can have a very strong gravitational pull upon consciousness, preventing consciousness from expanding (Patel, 2019a)." Instead, the subtle body becomes tethered and much more rigid. The result is self-obsession and a limited worldview. Just as the Earth's gravitational pull does not allow us to fall into infinite space, likewise our ego can hold consciousness to its core. We see this in a very narcissistic person, whose consciousness contracts in on itself and reverts to that stone-like state associated with a tamasic personality. In contrast, by becoming more and more humble, consciousness may expand infinitely.

Ego manifests itself in so many ways. For example, a flautist performing in a concert may receive a standing ovation from the audience, but even if she is happy with her performance, will she be happy if she is not surpassing her previous performances each time? In this case, the ego helps her to perform better and better and continue to strive for excellence. In contrast, if the same flautist thinks that no one can play the flute better than her, it is a restricting manifestation of ego. Ego becomes our best friend when we use it for continuous improvement in all fields of action in our lives.

How Does Thinking Evolve Through Meditation?

The fourth and final element of the subtle body is *manas*, which is the function of contemplation, thinking and feeling, and meditation is the greatest help with refining this aspect of the mind (Patel, 2019a). Think about what we do when we prepare to meditate every day: After we settle in our meditation space and our preferred sitting position, we relax and turn our attention inward away from the sensory stimuli of the outside world. The next step is to bring the mind to the heart, allowing it to gradually let go of its normal activity of many and varied thoughts and settle on just one thought. But that is just the precursor to meditation, known as in Yoga. That thought is like a doorway opening inward, and it will usually leave at some point so that the object of meditation can be felt directly through personal experience in the heart.

If you were to continue thinking that one thought throughout the meditation, you would develop a headache and your awareness would not be able to soar. That initial focus on one thought is only a springboard to take you deeper, so that you are able to dissolve into the experience of the presence of Divinity (Patel, 2019a). When you feel the divine presence, slowly you disappear in the vastness of the center of your own being, and you reach a level where feeling too disappears. In this state, the ego is refined to its original state, and you are swimming in universal consciousness.

So, as *manas* evolves through meditation, first the level of feeling flourishes. Then we reach a state where we are happy to exist without the need to experience feelings. But then something pushes us beyond that also, and we enter a state in which we want to become something more—a state of becoming better and better versions of ourselves. Finally, we also transcend the need to become something and reach a state where we merge into absolute existence, where we are one with the unmanifested universal consciousness (Patel, 2019a).

Making Use of an Elevated Consciousness in Leadership

As intellect, thinking, and ego are refined, consciousness becomes lighter, clearer and simpler, like the still pond with minimal ripples (Patel, 2019a). It is now free to expand and evolve. It is important to remember that this will only happen by doing these meditative practices, not just by reading about them.

Also, we need to support the evolution of the subtle body in an integrated, balanced way. For example, what happens when a child is taught at school by rote learning without developing other mental skills like problem solving, decision making, introspection, and feeling? The memory faculty of manas becomes highly developed at the expense of other aspects of thinking, intellect and ego. Similarly, what happens when a meditator focuses all their attention on observing and letting go of thoughts without judgment, as happens in some secular systems of meditation today? They become very skilled at this mental process, which is the first step of *Pratyahara* in Yoga (Patel, 2018), but this happens at the expense of the development of deeper levels of consciousness. There is an imbalance of the mental faculties, and once again consciousness cannot evolve. So, it is important to find a practice that allows consciousness to expand along the full spectrum described by Swami Vivekananda as is already explained in this article.

How is This Elevated Consciousness Helpful?

Imagine for a moment that after your morning meditation practice you have a particularly expanded and elevated state of mind. Insights and wisdom are flowing in. You feel light and free, as if you are functioning along a much greater range of the spectrum of consciousness. Then you go to work and face the everyday problems and challenges. Many of these challenges involve your relationships with other people—your colleagues, employees, clients, or partners. So, if your inner transformation is to impact your leadership skills, it is not enough just to retain that condition for yourself. You will need to radiate your inner sense of calm and joy to others, willfully and consciously, with the confidence that wherever you go it will spread its fragrance. You will then be externalizing your inner state and sharing it with others.

It is this capacity that will result in heartful leadership. Wise decision making will happen effortlessly, empathy and resilience will be natural, and virtues and noble qualities we so wish to manifest in our behavior as leaders will radiate out of us. It all starts with meditation.

So, every day, try to meditate before starting your daily activities. And after you finish meditating, very lightly and subtly suggest that, "The condition within me is also outside me. Everything around me is absorbed in a similar state. When I look at people, talk to them, listen to them, and even when I am silent, let that condition spread everywhere." Let your elevated consciousness expand wherever it can go.

Do We Need Help to Achieve All This?

The fourth of the four practical approaches mentioned earlier is to seek out a teacher who will support you along the path of stepwise inner change, so as to ensure a higher chance of success. Many people ask questions like, "Is this really necessary?", "Can't I follow this process on my own?", and "After all, the techniques have been given freely, and I prefer to do this in my own time without someone else having to see all my faults and weaknesses."

There is nothing stopping you from trying it on your own. Please go ahead. But a good teacher or guide is a boon in any field of learning, because they help us to improve much faster than we could possibly do on our own. We know this from personal experience. The guidance and support of someone who has already mastered a field is supremely helpful. That's why we have teachers and subject matter experts who act as coaches in different areas of our personal and professional life. Isn't it why we go to school?

Those who excel in their chosen profession or skill expect to keep learning to stay ahead of the game. For example, the best athletes and sports stars have coaches; peer review in cutting-edge academic research is an accepted part of the process; and the best musicians in the world enjoy playing with each other, so as to keep improving their skills. Anyone who is really good at what they do will welcome guidance and feedback. "That is the evolutionary approach to learning and life. And the further we go in any field, the more important it is to have guidance to continue to move forward. This is even more important in the spiritual field, where we are constantly venturing into new, unexplored areas, so the guide is an important person in the life of a spiritual seeker (Patel, 2019a)."

It is also interesting to note "something called coherence, where the teacher and the student resonate with one another, and a heart-to-heart osmosis happens in which skills and knowledge are transferred effortlessly. In fact, scientists are now realizing that much more is transferred and transmitted heart to heart than they'd previously thought, just as happens between a mother and her children (Patel, 2019a)."

The problem is always whom to trust as a guide on this inner journey. Unfortunately, there are many guides in the "spiritual marketplace" these days. People are right to be cautious until they find someone they trust. Many also have a very wrong notion about the role of a guide. They think that he or she is someone to worship, or someone who will wave a magic wand and solve all their problems. Reasons may differ, but lack of awareness of the true role of a spiritual guide is found in both the East and the West (Patel, 2019a).

It is therefore, important to evaluate the person before accepting them as your spiritual guide. Rather than mental gymnastics and knowledge, only direct experience matters in this field. An orator who impresses outwardly with eloquence and showmanship may be at the lowest level of inner attainment, because knowledge of books is not a measure of wisdom. Even parrots can quote the Vedas! In fact, if you really wish to find a guide of the highest capacity, look for the humblest person, who has no interest in greatness and who dwells in a state of total innocence.

Actually, the best way is to let your heart guide you. A genuine guide will travel with you on your inner journey, and for this they must already know the path. How will you know when you have found the right person? It is the million-dollar question, and yet the answer is very simple. Ask yourself: Does the sun need to do anything for you to recognize its grandeur? When it shines, do you need to be told to feel warm? In the same way, when a capable guide appears, your heart will naturally feel the impulse. It feels the divine current. Simply listen to your heart and follow its direction.

Once you find a guide for your inner journey of self-improvement, how will use make the most of their support? Just as the top athletes in the world rely on their coaches to continue to guide them, the top leaders in the world also maintain a healthy attitude of growth and self-improvement by accepting a guide with utter humility and an attitude of open-mindedness. No one is perfect, and leadership is not about knowing everything. To illustrate this point, there is a wonderful story about the famous psychotherapist, Carl Jung. Somebody once asked him why his colleagues all considered him to be the most successful therapist at the time. His answer was so revealing. To paraphrase, Jung said something like: I am also evolving and growing all the time. My patients know this about me—I don't try to hide it from them. Because I am imperfect and always trying to do better, it gives them permission to be imperfect and try to do better. In this day and age, effective leadership does not require a hierarchical, imposing approach. Rather, it requires an inclusive, team-based approach that values the skills and talents of every team member. To develop this attitude, the help of a spiritual guide is invaluable.

The Role of Transmission

In fact, it is the capacity to transmit the essence of God that is the true test of a spiritual guide. Some people say that Transmission automatically happens in the company of a saint, but that is only the automatic radiation of the saint's fine vibrations to those who are near them (Chandra, 2014). Actually, vibrations radiate from everyone, so if you are with an evil person your thoughts will flow in their direction for some time. This effect of radiation is temporary and disappears the moment you move away. The singing of sacred music in chorus is another situation where people claim that Transmission flows, but it is the result of the vibrations produced by the sound of the singing. Again, it is not permanently transformative.

Transmission is a yogic attainment of a very high order, by which a guide is able to infuse the essence of Divinity into others and remove whatever is blocking their spiritual progress (Chandra, 2020). The guide can do this when seekers are with them or even when they are far away, as Transmission is not bound by time and space. So, the answer to the question, "Who should you select as a guide?" is not complicated: Select one with the capacity to transmit from the highest level. If you select one with lesser capacity, you will be restricted accordingly.

Are Spiritual Practices Enough to Become an Effective Leader?

The various spiritual practices mentioned in this chapter create the right inner environment for transformation, but on their own they cannot make us good leaders. That is why in every tradition there have also been codes of conduct, like the Ten Commandments of Judaism and Christianity, the *Yamas* and *Niyamas* of Yoga, the Eightfold Path of the Buddha, and the Ten Maxims of Heartfulness. Inner transformation is essential, but it is useless unless we also mold our outer behavior and personality. Even the most capable spiritual guide cannot wave a magic wand and bring this about, no matter how hard they try.

It is our responsibility to mold our living to such a high order that we inspire others and evoke the same qualities in them. It requires the coming together of all aspects of our spiritual practice and lifestyle. It requires the awareness, refinement, and moderation required for transformation. A true leader leads by example, and there is no shortcut to becoming such a leader. It means creating a way of life that evokes love wherever we go.

In fact, the real proof of our inner transformation is in our outer behavior and lifestyle, which are reflected in our day-to-day dealings and duties. They are known as *vyavahara* in Yoga. Our way of living includes how we interact with each other, how we communicate, how we respond in a particular environment, how we dress, our body language, the way we judge or value others, and so on. The way we conduct ourselves says everything about our lifestyle. For example, do we create envy or jealousy in others through our actions? It means simplifying life so as not to hurt others.

When we are able to fulfill our duties, our *vyavahara* (Patel, 2020), we automatically create a resonance with others. When we fail in our duties, others will not respect us. What happens, for example, when you are too busy to spend proper time mentoring and supporting new colleagues? Eventually, those colleagues will lose respect for you. We need to make sure that others are not hurt by our way of living—that they are not hurt because of the way we speak, because we ignore them, by the fact that we don't smile, or because we are always reminding them subtly of our own authority. We have to be very simple, acting with a sense of reverence and respect for others. This requires a great degree of emotional maturity.

So, ask yourself: "What is my duty in this moment in my relationships, at work, at home, with friends, and toward the larger society? What is my duty toward the environment in which I find myself? What is my contribution here?".

Is your conscience happy with your behavior? Analyze yourself. If you yell at an employee, or judge them unfairly, how does it make you feel? Most of us do have a conscience, but do we really listen? Is it awakened enough to affect our actions? It will help to develop sensitivity. Each time our inner voice prompts us to do something worthwhile, we need to listen to it, otherwise we lose the capacity to evolve. This requires a commitment to listen to our conscience about the day-to-day mundane things. If we have to be reminded of our duty again and again, our consciousness will not have the space to expand, and it might be too late by the time our conscience bites. It is when we have not done our duty that the reminder comes.

The qualities that are valued in today's leaders are vastly different from those that were valued thirty years ago in the business world. We find a shift away from hierarchical power and control toward emotional intelligence and compassion. This correlates with the findings of research done in the fields of neuroscience and quantum physics demonstrating that we are connected to everything in the universe through consciousness (e.g., Bohm, 1980; Csíkszentmihályi, 1990). Nature is innately intelligent, and that intelligence manifests in conscious form in human beings, so we have an additional responsibility to take care of each other. And we know that we have the means to do this by consciously improving upon our inner nature.

Conscious leadership starts from within, by refining ourselves, and then permeates outward so that we are moderating our impulses and transforming our behavior. Only then will we inspire others. All of us have the potential to lead in whatever stage or position we are in. To be a leader means to live a life that inspires others, whether in the family, at school, in the community, in the workplace, or in the world at large.

The day-to-day practical application of this is in every moment. It applies to every facet of our existence. And small steps bring about big changes. As a start, try the following: Pay attention to your speech, to what you say and how you say it. Bring your heart into coherence with your whole being before you speak, by bringing your attention to your heart. If it helps, breathe in and out five times from your heart. Smile from your heart when you speak. Choose your words correctly. Keep your tone balanced, calm, soothing, and compassionate. Speak truthfully yet without hurting others. Help them to feel comfortable. When your speech is calm, your emotions will be calm, your body will be calm, and your thoughts will be calm. When you practice this consistently with awareness, it will transform your life, and be the first step to becoming an effective leader.

Conclusion

Since the advent of management as an academic discipline, the biggest challenge for management schools has been to equip students, faculty, and professionals alike with the human qualities that make for wise and effective leadership. But this is nothing new: From the times of Raja Janaka and the Egyptian Pharaohs to the modern day, it has been the challenge for leaders everywhere. The very nature of the leadership role exposes leaders to power and responsibility, and the need to wield this power wisely for the good of all. How are we addressing this in our halls of management? Certainly, the approaches that have been taken during the last century are not sustainable, and new tools are needed in our educational programs if we are to bring this much-needed ethical dimension to the discipline of management.

In this chapter, I have endeavored to introduce a practical approach to the problem, by introducing a set of simple practices that will equip faculty and students with the skills to make wise choices and shoulder responsibilities without succumbing to stress and emotional reactivity. These practices also foster open-mindedness, emotional intelligence, clarity of thinking, and humility, which are essential qualities of an effective leader.

Theoretical models of spirituality in management are all well and good, but without a daily practical application those models will never yield results. In fact, the practical approach has been the foundation of the Indian tradition since time immemorial, where leaders have always consulted with sages and rishis for guidance. It is perhaps more important than ever today, as we face issues that threaten the survival of the human species, such as climate change, and the need for sustainable approaches to business, government, education, and social services have become paramount. It is not enough to laud the achievements of the greatest leaders from the past and present. We also need to become like them ourselves, otherwise we miss the point of the relevance of spirituality in management. Only by learning to manage ourselves will we be able to manage others, and for this purpose the approach of Yoga as described by Lord Krishna in the Bhagavad Gita, "*Yogah Karmasu Kaushalam,*" has stood the test of time. That is why I urge you all to take up meditative practices to refine the mind and open the heart.

References

Bohm, D. (1980). *Wholeness and the Implicate Order*. Routledge.

Brewer, J., Worhunsky, P. D., Gray, J. R., Tang, Y., Weber, J., & Kober, H. (2011). Meditation experience is associated with differences in default mode network activity and connectivity. *Proceedings of the National Academy of Sciences of the United States of America, 108*(50), 20254–20259

Brewer, J. (2017). A simple way to break a bad habit. *Mindful* (Vol. 11). www.mindful.org

Chandra, R., (Babuji). (2014). *Complete Works of Ram Chandra* (Vol. 4). Shri Ram Chandra Mission.

Chandra, R., (Babuji). (2020). *Reality at Dawn*. Shri Ram Chandra Mission.

Chandra, R., (Lalaji). (2018). *Truth Eternal*. Shri Ram Chandra Mission.

Childre, D., & Martin, H. (2000). *The Hearthmath Solution.* HarperOne. www.heartmath.org
Csíkszentmihályi, H. (1990). *Flow: The Psychology of Optimal Experience.* HarperCollins.
Hanson, R. (2013). *Hardwiring Happiness: The new brain science of contentment, calm and confidence.* Harmony Books
Killingsworth, M., & Gilbert, D. T. (2010). A wandering mind is an unhappy mind. *Science, 330*(6006), 932. https://doi.org/10.1126/science.1192439
Lipton, B. H. (2008). *The Biology of Belief: Unleashing the power of consciousness, matter and miracles.* Hay House.
Patel, K. D. (2016). https://www.sahajmarg.org/newsletter/sahajsandesh/2016.68
Patel, K. D. (2017). The evolution of consciousness. *Heartfulness* (Vol. 2, 12). Sahaj Marg Spirituality Foundation. https://www.heartfulnessmagazine.com/editions/december-2017/
Patel, K. D. (2018). Pratyahara: Refining the attention, aligning the senses inwards. *Heartfulness* (Vol. 3, 12, pp. 42–50). Sahaj Marg Spirituality Foundation. https://www.heartfulnessmagazine.com/pratyahara/
Patel, K. D. (2019a). *Designing Destiny: Heartfulness Practices to Find Your Purpose and Fulfil Your Potential.* Hay House.
Patel, K. D. (2019b). *Travels and conversations with Daaji*, 31 July 2019. https://www.daaji.org/travels-conversations-daaji-31-july-2019/
Patel, K. D. (2019c). Yogic psychology, Part 9—Viskhepas: Avirati and Bhrantidarsana. *Heartfulness* (Vol. 4, 9). Sahaj Marg Spirituality Foundation. https://www.heartfulnessmagazine.com/yogic-psychology-4/
Patel, K. D. (2020). A user's guide to living: Love in action. *Heartfulness* (Vol. 5, 10). Sahaj Marg Spirituality Foundation. https://www.heartfulnessmagazine.com/a-users-guide-to-living-part-10/
Patel, K. D., & Pollock, J. (2018). *The Heartfulness Way: Heart-based Meditations for Spiritual Transformation.* Westland.
Raichle, M. E. (2015). The brain's default mode network. *Annual Review of Neuroscience, 38*, 433–447. https://doi.org/10.1146/annurev-neuro-071013-014030
Vivekananda, S. (1947). Sayings and Utterances (#40). *Complete Works of Swami Vivekananda* (Vol. 8). Advaita Ashrama.
Wulliemier, F. (2019). Become faster than your emotions. *Heartfulness* (Vol. 4, 3, pp. 15–17). Sahaj Marg Spirituality Foundation.www.heartfulnessmagazine.com

Ingram Content Group UK Ltd.
Milton Keynes UK
UKHW020634220523
422136UK00003B/6

9 789811 910272